INNOVATIVE
EXPERIENCES IN
ACCESS TO FINANCE

INNOVATIVE EXPERIENCES IN ACCESS TO FINANCE

Market-Friendly Roles for the Visible Hand?

Augusto de la Torre, Juan Carlos Gozzi, and
Sergio L. Schmukler

 **WORLD BANK GROUP**

Latin American Development Forum Series

This series was created in 2003 to promote debate, disseminate information and analysis, and convey the excitement and complexity of the most topical issues in economic and social development in Latin America and the Caribbean. It is sponsored by the Inter-American Development Bank, the United Nations Economic Commission for Latin America and the Caribbean, and the World Bank, and represents the highest quality in each institution's research and activity output. Titles in the series have been selected for their relevance to the academic community, policy makers, researchers, and interested readers, and have been subjected to rigorous anonymous peer review prior to publication.

Advisory Committee Members

Alicia Bárcena Ibarra, Executive Secretary, Economic Commission for Latin America and the Caribbean, United Nations

Inés Bustillo, Director, Washington Office, Economic Commission for Latin America and the Caribbean, United Nations

Augusto de la Torre, Chief Economist, Latin America and the Caribbean Region, World Bank

Daniel Lederman, Deputy Chief Economist, Latin America and the Caribbean Region, World Bank

Santiago Levy, Vice President for Sectors and Knowledge, Inter-American Development Bank

Roberto Rigobon, Professor of Applied Economics, MIT Sloan School of Management

José Juan Ruiz, Chief Economist and Manager of the Research Department, Inter-American Development Bank

Ernesto Talvi, Director, Brookings Global-CERES Economic and Social Policy in Latin America Initiative

Andrés Velasco, Cieplan, Chile

Titles in the Latin American Development Forum Series

Stop the Violence in Latin America: A Look at Prevention from Cradle to Adulthood (2017) by Laura Chioda

Beyond Commodities: The Growth Challenge of Latin America and the Caribbean (2016) by Jorge Thompson Araujo, Ekaterina Vostroknutova, Markus Brueckner, Mateo Clavijo, and Konstantin M. Wacker

Left Behind: Chronic Poverty in Latin America and the Caribbean (2016) by Renos Vakis, Jamele Rigolini, and Leonardo Lucchetti

Cashing in on Education: Women, Childcare, and Prosperity in Latin America and the Caribbean (2016) by Mercedes Mateo Diaz and Lourdes Rodriguez-Chamussy

Work and Family: Latin American and Caribbean Women in Search of a New Balance (2016) by Laura Chioda

Great Teachers: How to Raise Student Learning in Latin America and the Caribbean (2014) by Barbara Bruns and Javier Luque

Entrepreneurship in Latin America: A Step Up the Social Ladder? (2013) by Eduardo Lora and Francesca Castellani, editors

Emerging Issues in Financial Development: Lessons from Latin America (2013) by Tatiana Didier and Sergio L. Schmukler, editors

New Century, Old Disparities: Gaps in Ethnic and Gender Earnings in Latin America and the Caribbean (2012) by Hugo Ñopo

Does What You Export Matter? In Search of Empirical Guidance for Industrial Policies (2012) by Daniel Lederman and William F. Maloney

From Right to Reality: Incentives, Labor Markets, and the Challenge of Achieving Universal Social Protection in Latin America and the Caribbean (2012) by Helena Ribe, David Robalino, and Ian Walker

Breeding Latin American Tigers: Operational Principles for Rehabilitating Industrial Policies (2011) by Robert Devlin and Graciela Moguillansky

New Policies for Mandatory Defined Contribution Pensions: Industrial Organization Models and Investment Products (2010) by Gregorio Impavido, Esperanza Lasagabaster, and Manuel García-Huitrón

The Quality of Life in Latin American Cities: Markets and Perception (2010) by Eduardo Lora, Andrew Powell, Bernard M. S. van Praag, and Pablo Sanguinetti, editors

Discrimination in Latin America: An Economic Perspective (2010) by Hugo Ñopo, Alberto Chong, and Andrea Moro, editors

The Promise of Early Childhood Development in Latin America and the Caribbean (2010) by Emiliana Vegas and Lucrecia Santibáñez

Job Creation in Latin America and the Caribbean: Trends and Policy Challenges (2009) by Carmen Pagés, Gaëlle Pierre, and Stefano Scarpetta

China's and India's Challenge to Latin America: Opportunity or Threat? (2009) by Daniel Lederman, Marcelo Olarreaga, and Guillermo E. Perry, editors

Does the Investment Climate Matter? Microeconomic Foundations of Growth in Latin America (2009) by Pablo Fajnzylber, Jose Luis Guasch, and J. Humberto López, editors

Measuring Inequality of Opportunities in Latin America and the Caribbean (2009) by Ricardo de Paes Barros, Francisco H. G. Ferreira, José R. Molinas Vega, and Jaime Saavedra Chanduvi

The Impact of Private Sector Participation in Infrastructure: Lights, Shadows, and the Road Ahead (2008) by Luis Andres, Jose Luis Guasch, Thomas Haven, and Vivien Foster

Remittances and Development: Lessons from Latin America (2008) by Pablo Fajnzylber and J. Humberto López, editors

Fiscal Policy, Stabilization, and Growth: Prudence or Abstinence? (2007) by Guillermo Perry, Luis Servén, and Rodrigo Suescún, editors

Raising Student Learning in Latin America: Challenges for the 21st Century (2007) by Emiliana Vegas and Jenny Petrow

Investor Protection and Corporate Governance: Firm-level Evidence across Latin America (2007) by Alberto Chong and Florencio López-de-Silanes, editors

Natural Resources: Neither Curse nor Destiny (2007) by Daniel Lederman and William F. Maloney, editors

The State of State Reform in Latin America (2006) by Eduardo Lora, editor

Emerging Capital Markets and Globalization: The Latin American Experience (2006) by Augusto de la Torre and Sergio L. Schmukler

Beyond Survival: Protecting Households from Health Shocks in Latin America (2006) by Cristian C. Baeza and Truman G. Packard

Beyond Reforms: Structural Dynamics and Macroeconomic Vulnerability (2005) by José Antonio Ocampo, editor

Privatization in Latin America: Myths and Reality (2005) by Alberto Chong and Florencio López-de-Silanes, editors

Keeping the Promise of Social Security in Latin America (2004) by Indermit S. Gill, Truman G. Packard, and Juan Yermo

Lessons from NAFTA: For Latin America and the Caribbean (2004) by Daniel Lederman, William F. Maloney, and Luis Servén

The Limits of Stabilization: Infrastructure, Public Deficits, and Growth in Latin America (2003) by William Easterly and Luis Servén, editors

Globalization and Development: A Latin American and Caribbean Perspective (2003) by José Antonio Ocampo and Juan Martin, editors

Is Geography Destiny? Lessons from Latin America (2003) by John Luke Gallup, Alejandro Gaviria, and Eduardo Lora

Contents

Chapter 8: Microfinance: BancoEstado's Experience in Chile   221

Chapter 9: Concluding Thoughts and Open Questions on the Role of the State in Fostering Finance   253

Boxes

Figures

Tables

Foreword

Improving access to finance is one of the key challenges for financial and economic development. The state's role in promoting this process—beyond establishing the enabling environment, improving competition policy, and strengthening regulations and supervision—has been a source of debate for decades. Inevitably, the extent of direct interventions by the state depends on initial conditions.

This book tackles these difficult issues by reviewing and analyzing the experience of Latin America, where the state has traditionally played a central role. It offers examples of innovative public-private partnerships in Brazil, Chile, and Mexico that illustrate the important role for the state in overcoming coordination failures, first-mover disincentives, and obstacles to risk-sharing and distribution. They demonstrate how the state can play a useful catalytic function in kick-starting financial products and services.

Case studies of innovations such as these will be useful to policy makers not only in Latin America but also around the globe. The World Bank has committed itself to the goal of universal access to basic financial accounts by 2020, but data from the Global Findex project show that there is still a long way to go. Likewise, data collected by the World Bank on firms' use of finance show glaring disparities between high- and low-income countries, as well as between large and small firms in low-income countries. Achieving the World Bank's twin goals of ending extreme poverty and boosting shared prosperity will require narrowing the gap on both of these metrics.

The case studies also serve to advance the debate on financial development. The authors propose a new view of financial development that they call *pro-market activism*, which attempts to identify conditions for market-friendly state interventions. While many questions remain about how effectively such a policy approach can promote development, this book will surely provide readers with plenty of food for thought.

Asli Demirgüç-Kunt
Director, Development Research Group
World Bank

Acknowledgments

This book is part of a regional study conducted by the Office of the Chief Economist for Latin America and the Caribbean (LAC) of the World Bank. We would like to thank all of the people who helped us to obtain information about the documented case studies, in particular, Remigio Alvarez Prieto, Miguel Benavente, Alessandro Bozzo, Carlos Budar, Alexander Galetovic, Javier Gavito, Timoteo Harris, Miguel Hernández, Francisco Meré, and Jaime Pizarro. We would also like to thank Miriam Bruhn for work on earlier versions of the material in chapter 7. For excellent research assistance, we would like to thank Facundo Abraham, José Azar, Francisco Ceballos, Leonor Coutinho, Sebastián Cubella, Lucas Núñez, and Matías Vieyra.

For very useful comments and suggestions, we are grateful to Aquiles Almansi, Stijn Claessens, Carlos Cuevas, Asli Demirgüç-Kunt, José de Gregorio, Pablo Guidotti, Patrick Honohan, Graciela Kamnisky, Eduardo Levy Yeyati, Giovanni Majnoni, Maria Soledad Martínez Pería, Martin Naranjo, José Antonio Ocampo, Guillermo Perry, Liliana Rojas Suárez, Luis Servén, Joseph Stiglitz, Marilou Uy, and Jacob Yaron. In addition, we received very helpful feedback from participants at several presentations held at the Central Bank of Argentina's Annual Conference and "Access to Financial Services" workshop (Buenos Aires); the Central Bank of Colombia's conference, "Access to Financial Services" (Bogotá); the Foro Iberoamericano de Sistemas de Garantía y Financiamiento para la Micro y PYME (Santiago); the Global Development Network (Washington, DC); Columbia University Initiative for Policy Dialogue, Financial Markets Reform Task Force (University of Manchester, Manchester); the Inter-American Development Bank conference, "Public Banks in Latin America" (Washington, DC); the World Bank conference, "Access to Finance" (Washington, DC); the World Bank course, "Financial Sector Issues and Analysis Workshop" (Washington, DC); the World Bank Africa Region (Washington, DC); and the World Bank Latin America and the Caribbean Region (Washington, DC).

About the Authors

Augusto de la Torre has been adjunct professor at Columbia University's School of International and Public Affairs (SIPA) since March 2017. He previously worked for the World Bank from 1997 to the end of 2016, serving as chief economist for Latin America and the Caribbean during the last 10 of those years. Other positions held while at the Bank were senior adviser in the Financial Systems Department and senior financial sector adviser, both in the Latin America and the Caribbean Region. From 1993 to 1997, de la Torre was the head of the Central Bank of Ecuador, and in November 1996 he was chosen by *Euromoney* magazine as the year's Best Latin Central Banker. From 1986 to 1992 he worked at the International Monetary Fund (IMF), where, among other positions, he was the IMF's resident representative in the República Bolivariana de Venezuela (1991–92). De la Torre has published extensively on a broad range of macroeconomic and financial development topics. He is a member of the Carnegie Network of Economic Reformers. He earned his M.A. and Ph.D. degrees in economics at the University of Notre Dame and holds a bachelor's degree in philosophy from the Catholic University of Ecuador.

Juan Carlos Gozzi is an assistant professor in the Economics Department at the University of Warwick. His research area is international finance and financial markets and institutions. In particular, his research focuses on financial globalization, financial crises, bank financing to small and medium enterprises, and the transmission of financial shocks. From 2011 to 2013, he worked as an economist in the International Finance Division at the Board of Governors of the Federal Reserve. He has also worked at the World Bank, McKinsey & Company, and Standard and Poor's. He earned his M.A. and Ph.D. degrees in economics at Brown University and holds a bachelor's degree in economics from CEMA University of Argentina.

Sergio L. Schmukler is the lead economist in the World Bank's Development Research Group. His research area is international finance and international financial markets and institutions. In particular, he works on emerging market finance, financial globalization, financial crises and contagion, financial development, and institutional investor behavior. He received his Ph.D. in economics from the University of California, Berkeley, in 1997, when he joined the World Bank's Young Economist and Young Professionals programs. He has also served as treasurer of the Latin America and Caribbean Economic Association (since 2004), and as associate editor of the *Journal of Development Economics* (2001–04). He taught in the Department of Economics at the University of Maryland (1999–2003), and worked in the International Monetary Fund's Research Department (2004–05). He has also worked at the U.S. Federal Reserve Board, the Inter-American Development Bank's Research Department, and the Argentine Central Bank, and he has visited the Dutch Central Bank and the Hong Kong Institute for Monetary Research of the Hong Kong Monetary Authority, among other places.

Abbreviations

ABS	asset-backed security
ATM	automated teller machine
BCBS	Basel Committee on Banking Supervision
BEME	BancoEstado Microempresas
CEF	Caixa Econômica Federal
CGAP	Consultative Group to Assist the Poor
CGFS	Committee on the Global Financial System
CLO	collateralized loan obligation
CMO	collateralized mortgage obligation
ECB	European Central Bank
FHLMC	Federal Home Loan Mortgage Corporation
FIRA	Fideicomisos Instituidos en Relación con la Agricultura
FIRST	Financial Sector Reform and Strengthening
FNG	Fondo Nacional de Garantías
FNMA	Federal National Mortgage Association
FOGAPE	Fondos de Garantías para Pequeños Empresarios
GDP	gross domestic product
GNMA	Government National Mortgage Association
IDLO	International Development Law Organization
IFC	International Finance Corporation
IIED	International Institute for Environment and Development
IMF	International Monetary Fund
IOSCO	International Organization of Securities Commissions
LIBOR	London Interbank Offered Rate
MBS	mortgage-backed security
MGA	mutual guarantee association
NAFIN	Nacional Financiera
NAFTA	North American Free Trade Agreement

OECD	Organisation for Economic Co-operation and Development
POS	point of sale
RIETI	Research Institute of Economy, Trade and Industry
ROSCA	rotating savings and credit association
SBA	Small Business Administration
SBIF	Superintendencia de Bancos e Instituciones Financieras
SHF	Sociedad Hipotecaria Federal
SIFMA	Securities Industry and Financial Markets Association
SMEs	small and medium enterprises
UPU	Universal Postal Union
WTO	World Trade Organization

CHAPTER 1

Introduction

Overview

Well-functioning financial systems play a key role in supporting economic development. Financial markets and institutions emerge to mitigate frictions—such as information asymmetries and transaction costs—that prevent capital from seamlessly flowing from those with available funds to those with profitable investment opportunities.[1] By ameliorating these frictions, financial systems can have a significant effect on the mobilization and allocation of resources.

Consistent with this argument, a large and by now well-established body of empirical research shows that well-functioning financial markets and institutions help to channel resources to their most productive uses, boosting economic growth, improving opportunities, and reducing poverty and income inequality.[2] By and large, research in this area has traditionally relied on financial sector depth (measured as the ratio of financial assets, such as bank credit, to gross domestic product, GDP) as the main indicator of financial development.[3] The implicit assumption that depth is a good proxy for financial development may be justifiable when it comes to empirical research, given nontrivial data constraints.[4] But the intricate web of institutional and market interactions at the heart of financial development can hardly be reduced to a single dimension. It is financial development in all of its dimensions—not just depth—that lubricates and boosts the process of economic development. It is not surprising, therefore, that the academic and policy discussion has widened to consider other dimensions of finance. These include stability, diversity, and—the focus of this book—access to finance.

Interest by both researchers and policy makers in the issue of access to financial services has mushroomed since the early 2000s. A growing body of academic literature has analyzed the extent and determinants of access to finance, and the topic has moved up in the policy agenda. In recent years, about 50 countries have adopted explicit policies to foster the penetration of financial services (World Bank 2014), and the G-20 (Group of Twenty) has made financial inclusion a key issue in its development agenda. In 2013, the World Bank postulated the goal of universal access to basic financial accounts by 2020 as an important milestone toward financial inclusion (World Bank 2013b).[5]

Several factors have contributed to the increasing interest in access to finance. First, theoretical arguments suggest that one of the channels through which financial development fosters economic growth is by facilitating the entry of new firms. Most prominent in this regard is the Schumpeterian argument, compellingly restated by Rajan and Zingales (2003), that financial development causes growth because it fuels the process of "creative destruction"—and that it does so by moving resources to efficient uses and, in particular, to the hands of efficient newcomers. What is relevant in this perspective is the access dimension of financial development—through broader access to finance, talented newcomers can compete with established incumbents. In other words, financial development can stimulate the process of creative destruction—and thus the growth process—by expanding economic opportunities and leveling the playing field.

Second, interest in access to finance also stems from the fact that modern development theories suggest that lack of access to credit may not only impede growth but may also generate persistent income inequalities.[6] In the presence of market frictions, such as information asymmetries and transaction costs, access to credit will depend on both the expected profitability of investment projects and the availability of collateral, connections, and credit histories. As a result, low-income households and new firms, lacking accumulated wealth and connections, may not be able to obtain external financing. This lack of access to credit may prevent these households and entrepreneurs from investing in human capital accumulation or starting their own businesses. This not only affects growth, because profitable investment projects will not receive funding, but also might generate persistent income inequalities and poverty traps.

A third reason for the increasing interest in the study of access is the sheer lack of access to and use of financial services in developing countries. Whereas in most developed countries the use of bank accounts to save and make payments is almost universal, in developing countries account use is much lower, despite significant improvements in recent years. For instance, data from the World Bank's Global Financial Inclusion (Global Findex) Database show that more than 90 percent of adults in high-income countries had an account at a financial institution in 2014, compared to about 29 and 51 percent of adults in Sub-Saharan Africa and Latin America, respectively. Similarly, large cross-country differences have been observed in the use of formal credit services, with the fraction of adults who borrowed from a financial institution averaging less than 9 percent in low- and middle-income countries in 2014, compared to more than 17 percent in high-income countries. Differences in access to finance across countries are also illustrated by studies showing that firms in developing countries, especially SMEs (small and medium enterprises), display a low use of formal credit and must therefore rely mostly on internal funds to finance their activities. For instance, firm-level surveys conducted by the World Bank in over 140 countries show that only 26 percent of small firms in low- and middle-income countries had a line of credit or a loan from a financial institution in 2013, compared to 42 percent of small firms in high-income countries.

Despite the increasing awareness of the importance of access to finance among both researchers and policy makers, there are still some major gaps in our understanding of the main drivers of access (or lack thereof), as well as about the impact of different policies in this area.

With the goal of providing new insights and contributing to the policy debate, this book analyzes some innovative experiences with broadening access to finance in Latin America.[7] These programs seem to be driven by an emerging new view on the role of the state in financial development, which recognizes a limited role for the state in financial markets but contends that there might be room for restricted interventions in collaboration with the private sector to overcome barriers to access to finance. We analyze several initiatives in Latin America that illustrate this view and, in light of these experiences, discuss some open policy questions about the role of the state in broadening access to finance.

The book is organized as follows. In this introductory chapter, we discuss why access to finance matters, presenting some evidence on the extent of access to financial services in developing countries and briefly reviewing theoretical and empirical research on the impact of access on growth and inequality. In addition, this chapter discusses the role of the state in broadening and deepening access, analyzing the two contrasting views that have traditionally dominated the debate in this regard and their policy prescriptions. It also describes the emerging third view mentioned above, which seems to be behind the experiences described in this book.

Chapter 2 presents a conceptual framework for studying problems of access to finance and their underlying causes, which we use throughout the book to analyze the different experiences. It also discusses how the institutional environment affects access to finance. Although this framework explains how the different initiatives work and where their value added may lie, it is not required for understanding the discussion in the rest of the book. Readers who are less interested in theoretical issues can skip this chapter without much loss of continuity.

Chapter 3 discusses the role of the state in broadening access, expanding the discussion from this introductory chapter.

Chapters 4 through 8 describe the different initiatives to broaden access to finance in Latin America that are the focus of this book. In particular, chapter 4 discusses the use of structured finance transactions to facilitate access to credit, describing two transactions brokered by FIRA (Fideicomisos Instituidos en Relación con la Agricultura), a Mexican development finance institution, to provide financing to the agricultural sector.

Chapter 5 describes the experience of Nacional Financiera, a Mexican development bank that created an online market for factoring services to facilitate access by SMEs to working capital financing.

Chapter 6 analyzes the use of partnerships between financial institutions and commercial entities for the distribution of financial services, focusing on the case of correspondent banking in Brazil.

Chapter 7 discusses the use of credit guarantee schemes to increase access to finance, analyzing the case of FOGAPE (Fondos de Garantías para Pequeños Empresarios), a credit guarantee fund created by the Chilean government to provide partial guarantees for loans to microenterprises and small firms.

Chapter 8 analyzes the role of the public sector in fostering microfinance activities, describing the experience of BancoEstado, a Chilean state-owned bank that established a large-scale microfinance program.

Chapter 9 concludes by discussing some open policy questions about the roles of the public and private sectors in broadening access to finance in light of these experiences.

Two important clarifications are worth making here at the outset regarding the scope of this book. First, among the wide set of products covered under the "financial services" label—including savings, payments, insurance, and credit— we focus our analysis mostly on credit services. We believe that, regarding issues of access, these services are particularly challenging from an analytical point of view and from policy makers' perspective because the provision of credit entails many complexities that may lead providers to exclude very diverse groups of borrowers.[8]

Second, we do not attempt to make a comprehensive assessment of the different initiatives described throughout the book or to claim that, balancing benefits and costs, they have been successful. Rather, we use these experiences to illustrate the emerging new view on the role of the state in financial development mentioned above and to explain how this view has been translated into specific policy initiatives in practice. An analysis of these experiences might provide a better understanding of whether there is room for the types of interventions favored by this view and might also highlight potential problems in their design and implementation. We believe that the analysis of these experiences raises a number of important policy questions that deserve further study.

The rest of this chapter is organized as follows. The next section presents some data on the extent of access to and use of financial services around the world. Then, "Why Access to Finance Matters" provides a short review of the theoretical models and empirical evidence on the impact of access to finance on growth and inequality. "The Role of the State in Broadening Access" describes the different views on the role of the state in financial markets. The final section briefly concludes.

Access to Financial Services around the World

Although indicators of the depth of banking systems and capital markets exist for a large cross section of countries and relatively long time series, comparable cross-country data on the extent of access to and use of financial services are not as readily available.[9] Until recently, there was little systematic information on how extensive the use of financial services is across countries and who the users of these services are.

Since the early 2000s, in line with the increased interest in access to finance, a large number of studies have attempted to overcome these data limitations and quantify the use of financial services by households and firms around the world. Earlier studies focused on analyzing the use of financial services and its determinants in particular countries or regions.[10] This approach, despite yielding useful insights, did not provide consistent measures of the use of financial services that could be easily compared across countries and over time. Several studies have attempted to overcome this limitation by collecting consistent data on the use of financial services for a large cross section of countries.

These cross-country studies have followed two alternative approaches. One set of studies has relied on aggregate density indicators, such as the number of deposit accounts and loans scaled by population, to measure the use of financial services.[11] These data are usually compiled by surveying financial service providers and/or regulators. Although available for a large number of countries, this information is not without its limitations. Aggregate figures may be only rough proxies for the extent of the use of financial services. For instance, the total number of deposit accounts in a country may differ significantly from the number of actual users because individuals may have more than one account. Also, most countries do not distinguish between corporate and individual deposit accounts.[12] Moreover, these data do not provide details on the characteristics of the households and firms that hold deposit accounts and/or receive loans, and therefore cannot be used to analyze how the use of financial services differs according to individual characteristics, such as gender or income level.

An alternative approach to measuring the extent of access to and use of financial services is relying on data from household and firm surveys. Household surveys that measure the use of financial services became available only in the early 2000s, and initially covered a relatively small subset of countries.[13] Moreover, surveys differed in terms of question wording and data collection methods, making comparisons across surveys and countries quite difficult.[14] These data limitations have now been overcome with the release of the Global Findex, built by the World Bank in cooperation with the Bill & Melinda Gates Foundation and Gallup, Inc. This database includes information—from surveys conducted in 2011 and 2014 of over 150,000 individuals—on how adults in almost 150 economies around the world save, borrow, make payments, and manage risks. On the firm side, the World Bank's Enterprise Surveys, conducted since the 1990s, provide detailed information on the financing patterns and financial constraints faced by over 130,000 firms around the world.

Before turning to a brief overview of the different measures, it is important to highlight that what we can observe in practice and collect data on the actual use of financial services. Firms and households may not be using these services, even when available, because they do not need them. For instance, firms may have enough funds to finance their investments and therefore not need to borrow. Such a lack of demand for financial services is not directly observable. Therefore, researchers must rely on indicators of the actual use of these services. We return to this issue in chapter 2.

Use of Savings and Payments Services

The use of savings and payment services presents wide variations both within and across countries. Household surveys show that, whereas in most developed countries the use of bank accounts to save and make payments is almost universal, in developing countries observed use is much lower. According to data from Global Findex, over 90 percent of adults in high-income countries had an account with a financial institution in 2014, compared to only 22 percent in low-income countries. Among developing regions, East Asia has the highest account penetration rates (with the fraction of adults having an account with a financial institution reaching 69 percent), followed by Eastern Europe (51 percent) and Latin America (51 percent) (figure 1.1, panel a). There are also significant differences across countries within a given region. For instance, as shown in panel b of figure 1.1, in Brazil more than 68 percent of adults have an account with a financial institution, whereas in Peru this figure is less than 29 percent.

In addition to the low observed use of accounts with a financial institution in developing countries, the data suggest that in most of these countries, accounts are restricted to higher-income households. For instance, Demirgüç-Kunt and Klapper (2013) show that in developing economies, on average, the top 20 percent of adults in terms of income are more than twice as likely as the poorest 20 percent to have a bank account. In developed countries, in contrast, the difference in account use between the top 20 percent and the bottom 20 percent is only about 5 percentage points. In many developing countries, minimum account balances and account charges are extremely high when compared to per capita income, restricting access to bank accounts to high-income households. For instance, data from the World Bank (2008) show that in 17 countries

FIGURE 1.1 Household use of savings and payment services around the world

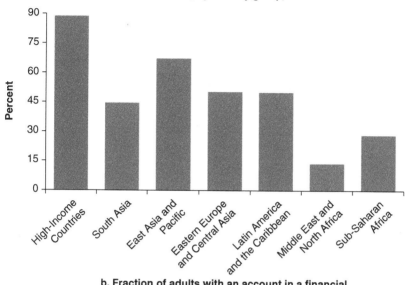

a. Fraction of adults with an account in a financial institution, by country group, 2014

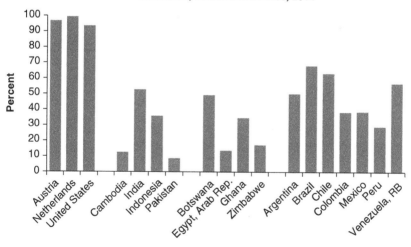

b. Fraction of adults with an account in a financial institution, selected countries, 2014

Source: World Bank Global Findex Database.
Note: Panel a shows cross-country averages of adults (age 15 or older) with an account at a formal financial institution; data cover 156 countries. Panel b shows the same information for selected countries only.

(out of 54 developing countries with data available), the annual cost of maintaining a bank account exceeds 2 percent of GDP per capita, making financial services unaffordable for large fractions of the population.

Use of Credit Services

The use of formal credit services also presents large differences across countries. Household surveys show that individuals in developed countries are more likely to borrow from formal sources, whereas those in developing countries tend to rely more on informal sources, such as family, friends, and informal lenders. Data from Global Findex show that the fraction of adults who borrowed from a financial institution reached 17.3 percent in high-income countries in 2014, compared to 12 and 6 percent in Eastern Europe and the Middle East, respectively (figure 1.2, panel a). These figures may actually underestimate differences between developed and developing countries in the use of formal credit services because the extensive access to credit cards in developed countries may reduce the need for short-term loans from financial institutions (World Bank 2014; Demirgüç-Kunt et al. 2015). In high-income countries almost half of adults reported owning a credit card in 2014 (figure 1.2, panel b). In contrast, despite significant growth in credit card penetration in recent years, only 11 percent of adults in middle-income countries—and only 1 percent in low-income countries—reported having a credit card.

The data also suggest that in many developing countries, bank lending focuses mostly on high-income borrowers. Data from CGAP (2009) show that in 18 developing countries (out of 51 countries with data available), the average loan amount is equivalent to more than five times annual GDP per capita. In many developing countries, minimum loan amounts and loan fees are very high when compared to per capita income, restricting access to bank credit to high-income households. According to data from the World Bank (2008), in 16 countries (out of 53 developing countries with data available) the minimum amount of consumer loans exceeds annual per capita income. These high costs are present in Latin American countries (de la Torre, Ize, and Schmukler 2012; Martinez Peria 2014).

Cross-country firm surveys also show that access to external financing varies widely across countries and is highly correlated with firm size. According to data from the World Bank Enterprise Surveys covering more than 74,000 firms in over 120 developing countries, 49 percent of large firms in these countries have a line of credit or a loan from a financial institution, compared to 40 percent of medium-sized firms and only 26 percent of small firms.[15] As panel a of figure 1.3 shows, significant regional variations exist in firm use of formal credit. For example, the fraction of large firms with a credit line or a loan from a financial institution varies from 68 percent in Latin America to 43 percent in the Middle East and North Africa and 40 percent in Sub-Saharan Africa. Similarly, whereas only 17 percent of

FIGURE 1.2 Household use of credit services around the world

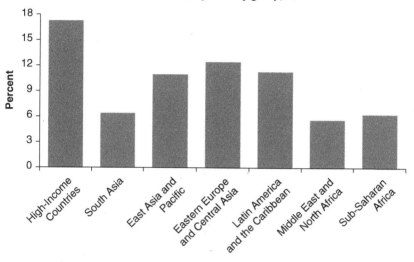

a. Fraction of adults who borrowed from a formal financial institution, by country group, 2014

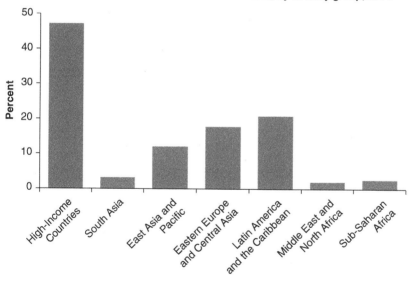

b. Fraction of adults who have a credit card, by country group, 2014

Source: World Bank Global Findex Database.
Note: The figure shows cross-country averages of the fraction of adults (age 15 or above) who borrowed from a formal financial institution (panel a) or report owning a credit card (panel b) for different country groups; data cover 156 countries.

FIGURE 1.3 Firms' use of credit services around the world

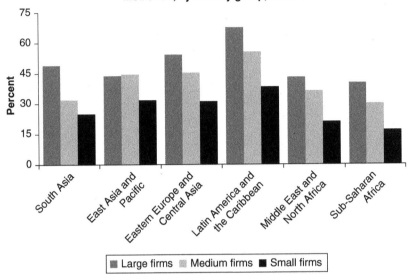

a. Fraction of firms that have a loan or a credit line from a financial institution, by country group, 2006–14

Legend: ▨ Large firms ▧ Medium firms ■ Small firms

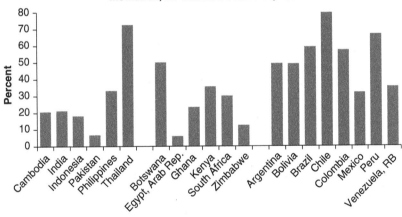

b. Fraction of firms that have a loan or a credit line from a financial institution, for selected countries, 2006–14

Source: World Bank Enterprise Surveys.
Note: Panel a shows the cross-country average of the fraction of firms that have a credit line or a loan from a financial institution, according to firm size, for different regions. Panel b shows the fraction of firms that have a credit line or a loan from a financial institution for selected countries. The data cover more than 74,000 firms in 124 developing countries. Small firms are those with fewer than 20 employees, medium firms are those that have between 20 and 99 employees, and large firms are those with 100 or more employees. Data come from firm surveys conducted between 2006 and 2014. When several surveys were available for the same country, data from the latest survey were considered.

small firms in Sub-Saharan Africa have credit from a financial institution, this figure reaches 32 percent in Eastern Europe and 38 percent in Latin America. Within regions, there are also large differences across countries (figure 1.3, panel b). For instance, the fraction of firms with a credit line or a loan from a financial institution reached almost 80 percent in Chile in 2014, compared to only 32 percent in Mexico. Moreover, the low observed used of bank credit by small firms is usually not compensated for by other sources of external financing, such as capital markets or trade credit; as a result, smaller firms need to rely more on internal funds to finance their activities (Beck, Demirgüç-Kunt, and Maksimovic 2008; Kuntchev et al. 2014). In recent years, banks in Latin America have started to focus more on SMEs, and other financing sources have also started to develop (de la Torre, Martinez Peria, and Schmukler 2010).

Why Access to Finance Matters

Finance and Growth and Inequality: Theory

Modern development theories emphasize the role that a lack of access to finance plays in generating persistent income inequality and impeding growth. According to these theories, exclusion from financial markets can inhibit human and physical capital accumulation and affect occupational choices. In a world with frictionless and complete financial markets, access to credit to finance education, training, or business projects would depend only on individual talent and initiative. However, in the presence of market frictions, such as information asymmetries and transaction costs, this might not be the case. For instance, theories that stress the role of human capital in the development process argue that financial market imperfections may create barriers to obtaining financing for education. As a result, schooling decisions will be determined by parental wealth and not just ability. Smart, poor kids will get too little education because their parents do not have enough resources and cannot borrow to pay for their schooling, despite the high returns of this potential investment. This can lead to a suboptimal allocation of resources and can generate persistent income inequalities across generations.

Other theories stress the role of financial markets in affecting occupational choices and, in particular, who can become an entrepreneur.[16] With perfect capital markets, those with the most entrepreneurial talent and profitable investment projects would get external financing. However, in the presence of asymmetric information and contract enforcement costs, financial intermediaries could demand collateral to ameliorate agency problems. As a result, access to credit for business endeavors will depend not only on entrepreneurial ability but also on the availability of collateral. Society's resources will not be channeled to those with the best business opportunities but rather will flow disproportionately to those with accumulated assets. The initial wealth distribution will affect who can get financing.

Hence, financial imperfections will not only affect growth, because profitable investment projects will not receive funding, but might also generate persistent income inequalities and poverty traps.

Theories of financial intermediation also highlight the role of access to finance in promoting growth. Financial intermediaries and markets arise to deal with market frictions, such as information asymmetries and transaction costs, and, by ameliorating these frictions, can have a significant effect on the mobilization and allocation of resources. Some arguments stress the role of financial intermediaries in increasing financial depth by making more financial resources available. For instance, financial institutions can reduce the costs associated with collecting savings from disparate investors, thereby exploiting economies of scale, overcoming investment indivisibilities, and increasing the volume of lending.

Financial intermediaries can also reduce the costs of acquiring and processing information. Without intermediaries, each investor would face the large (and mostly fixed) costs of evaluating business conditions, firms, managers, and so forth to allocate their savings. Financial intermediaries undertake the task of researching investment opportunities and then sell this information to investors or profit from it by charging an (explicit or implicit) intermediation fee.[17] By economizing on information acquisition costs, these intermediaries improve the assessment of investment opportunities, with positive ramifications on resource allocation and growth. Financial intermediaries may also boost the rate of technological innovation by helping identify entrepreneurs that are more likely to successfully carry out profitable projects and launch new products.[18]

This view lies at the core of the Schumpeterian argument, compellingly restated by Rajan and Zingales (2003), that financial development causes growth because it fuels the process of "creative destruction" by moving resources to the hands of efficient newcomers. What matters from this perspective is not the overall volume of credit in the economy but rather the access dimension of financial development, that is, whether all firms (both incumbents and new entrants) with profitable investment projects are able to obtain external financing.

Finance and Growth and Inequality: Empirical Evidence

Since the beginning of the 1990s, a growing and by now well-established body of empirical work (including broad cross-country and panel studies, time series analyses, individual country case studies, and firm- and industry-level analyses) has provided evidence supporting the view that financial development is not just correlated with economic growth but is actually also one of its drivers. Cross-country studies tend to find that financial depth predicts future economic growth, physical capital accumulation, and improvements in economic efficiency, even after controlling for initial income levels, education, and policy indicators.[19] Several papers have extended the analysis by using country-level panel data, exploiting both the time series and cross-country variations in the data.[20] These studies find that both stock markets and banking systems have a positive impact on capital accumulation, economic growth, and productivity. This evidence is confirmed by time series analyses and country case studies, which tend to find that the evolution of financial systems over time is positively related to a country's growth pace.[21] Alternatively, some researchers have employed both industry- and firm-level data across a broad cross section of countries to resolve causality issues and to document in greater detail the mechanisms, if any, through which finance can affect economic growth. For instance, Rajan and Zingales (1998) show that, in countries with well-developed financial systems, industries that rely relatively more on external financing because of technological reasons grow faster (compared to industries that do not rely so heavily on external capital). Similarly, Demirgüç-Kunt and Maksimovic (1998) show that firms in countries with deeper financial systems tend to grow faster than they would be able to do if their financing were restricted to internal funds and short-term debt.[22]

In recent years, the empirical literature has extended the analysis beyond the finance–growth nexus to study the impact of financial development on other relevant variables, such as income distribution and poverty. The empirical evidence suggests that financial development is associated with lower poverty rates and reduced income inequality. For instance, Beck, Demirgüç-Kunt, and Levine (2007) find that, in countries with more developed financial systems, the income of the poorest 20 percent of the population grows faster than average GDP per capita and income inequality falls at a higher rate.[23] Within-country studies of policy changes in India (Burgess and Pande 2005) and the United States (Beck, Levine, and Levkov 2010) also provide evidence that the geographic expansion of bank branches is associated with lower income inequality and poverty rates. Bruhn and Love (2014) find that increased credit availability for lower-income households in Mexico is associated with reductions in poverty rates, particularly because it has a positive effect on the creation and sustainability of informal businesses.

The empirical literature provides evidence consistent with the idea that one way in which financial development contributes to economic growth is by facilitating the entry of new firms. For instance, Rajan and Zingales (1998) find that financial development affects industry growth mostly by increasing the number of firms, rather than by leading to an expansion of existing firms. Klapper, Laeven, and Rajan (2006) analyze the determinants of firm entry across countries and find that entry in more financially dependent industries is higher in countries with more developed financial systems. Consistent with the argument that finance contributes to firm creation, Black and Strahan (2004) and Kerr and Nanda (2009) find that the elimination of restrictions on the geographic expansion of bank branches within U.S. states, which improved the functioning of state banking systems, leads to a significant increase in the number of start-ups and new incorporations. Cross-country evidence also shows that financial development disproportionately benefits smaller firms (Beck, Demirgüç-Kunt, and Maksimovic 2005; Beck et al. 2006; Beck, Demirgüç-Kunt, and Martinez Peria 2007).

Evidence of the impact of access to finance at the household level is more limited. Some researchers have analyzed self-employment and entrepreneurship decisions, finding that, consistent with the theoretical arguments discussed above, wealth and liquidity constraints affect occupational choices and, in particular, who becomes an entrepreneur.[24] The microfinance literature has also analyzed the effects of access to finance on low-income households. Although further research in this area is necessary, evidence from randomized evaluations suggests that, contrary to the claims of most microfinance proponents, microloans tend to have little effect on poverty reduction or income. However, these loans do help households manage risks and deal with income shocks.[25]

The Role of the State in Broadening Access

Given the major potential benefits of the access-enhancing financial development described above, a relevant question, especially in countries with underdeveloped financial systems, is whether state intervention to foster financial development and broaden access is warranted and, if so, what form this intervention should take. Although most economists would agree that the state can play a significant role in fostering financial development, the specific nature of state intervention in financial markets to broaden access to finance has been a matter of much debate. Opinions on this issue tend to be polarized in two highly contrasting but well-established views: the *interventionist* and the *laissez-faire* views.

The interventionist view argues that broadening access to finance requires active, direct state involvement in mobilizing and allocating financial resources, because private markets fail to expand access, or to guarantee access, to all. In contrast, the laissez-faire view contends that governments can do more harm than good by intervening directly in the allocation of financial resources, and argues that government efforts should instead focus on improving the enabling environment, which helps reduce agency problems and transaction costs and mitigate problems of access. We now turn to a brief overview of these two different views.

The Interventionist View

The interventionist view dates back to the 1950s and dominated financial development policy thinking at least until the middle to late 1970s. This view regards problems of access to finance as resulting from widespread market failures that cannot be overcome in underdeveloped economies by leaving market forces alone.[26] The key contention is that expanding access to finance beyond the narrow circle of privileged borrowers—mainly, large firms and well-off households—requires the active intervention of the state. This view emphasizes the state's role in addressing market failures and calls for direct state involvement in mobilizing and allocating financial resources, with the state becoming a substitute for (rather than a complement to) private intermediaries and markets.

The interventionist view is closely related to the prevailing development thinking during the 1950s and 1960s, which emphasized the need for state intervention to spur capital accumulation and technological progress.[27] Consistent with this view, the growth strategies of most developing countries during this period focused on accelerating capital accumulation and technological adoption through direct state intervention. The role of the state was to take the "commanding heights" of the economy and allocate resources to those areas believed to be most conducive to long-term growth. This led to import substitution policies, state ownership of firms, subsidization of infant industries, central planning, and a wide range of state interventions and price controls.

The interventionist view resulted in a pervasive state influence on the allocation of credit in many countries—not only directly, through lending by state-owned banks, but also indirectly, through regulations such as directed credit requirements and interest rate controls.[28] State ownership of financial institutions was expected to help overcome market failures in financial markets, enhancing savings mobilization, mobilizing funds toward projects with high social returns, and making financial services affordable to larger parts of the population. Through directed lending requirements, which mandated private banks to allocate a certain share of their funds to specific sectors, governments expected to channel funds to borrowers that otherwise may not receive enough financing because of information asymmetries or the failure of private intermediaries to internalize the positive externalities of lending to them. Interest rate controls were expected to result in lower costs of financing and greater access to credit.

The experience with these policies in most developing countries has not been very successful. Cross-country evidence and country-specific studies suggest that state ownership of financial institutions tends to have a negative (or, at best, neutral) impact on financial development and banking sector outreach.[29] Incentive and governance problems in state-owned institutions led in many cases to such recurrent problems as wasteful administrative expenditures, overstaffing, capture by powerful special interests, political manipulation of lending, and plain corruption.[30] All these factors resulted in poor loan origination and even poorer loan collection, which, coupled with interest rate subsidies and high administrative expenses, typically led to large financial losses and the need for recurrent recapitalizations. Moreover, the evidence suggests that extensive state intervention in the operation of financial markets has significant costs in terms of economic efficiency and growth, and tends to stifle, rather than promote, financial development.[31]

The Laissez-Faire View

Mostly as a reaction to the perceived failure of direct state intervention in the allocation of financial resources, a second, entirely opposite view has gained ground over time: the laissez-faire view. According to this view, market failures in the financial sector are not as extensive as assumed by proponents of the interventionist view, and private parties by themselves, given well-defined property rights and good contractual institutions, may be able to address most of these problems. Additionally, the costs of government failures are likely to exceed those of market failures, rendering direct interventions ineffective at best, and in many cases counterproductive. Therefore, this view recommends that governments exit from bank ownership and lift restrictions on the allocation of credit and the determination of interest rates. Instead, the argument goes, government efforts should be deployed toward improving the enabling environment for financial contracting.

The laissez-faire view is consistent with the general shift of thinking about the role of the state in the development process during recent decades. The experiences of most developing countries in the 1970s and 1980s showed that widespread state intervention in the economy—through trade restrictions, state ownership of firms, financial repression, price controls, and foreign exchange rationing—resulted in a large waste of resources and impeded, rather than promoted, economic growth.[32] This led economists and policy makers to conclude that constraining the role of the state in the economy and eliminating the distortions associated with protectionism, subsidies, and public ownership are essential to fostering growth. Much of this vision was reflected in the so-called Washington Consensus and guided most reform programs during the 1990s.[33]

This laissez-faire view led to the liberalization of financial systems and the privatization of state-owned banks in many countries during the 1990s. Countries eliminated or downscaled directed lending programs, deregulated interest rates, lifted restrictions on foreign borrowing, and dismantled controls on foreign exchange and capital transactions.[34] Several countries also embarked on large-scale bank privatization programs.[35] The laissez-faire view also resulted in a barrage of reforms aimed at creating the proper institutions and infrastructure for financial markets to flourish, including reforms of bankruptcy laws, improvements in the legal protection of minority shareholder and creditor rights, the establishment of credit bureaus and collateral registries, and improvements in the basic infrastructure for securities market operations, such as clearance and settlement systems and trading platforms.[36]

Despite the intense reform effort, in many developing countries the observed outcomes in terms of financial development and access to finance have failed to match the (high) initial expectations of reform.[37] Although financial systems in many countries have deepened over the past decades, in most cases there has been little convergence toward the indexes of financial development observed in more developed countries. Several developing countries experienced strong growth in deposit volumes over the 1990s, but this growth failed to translate into an increase of similar magnitude in credit for the private sector, with corporate financing in particular lagging behind (Hanson 2003; de la Torre, Ize, and Schmukler 2012). Similarly, although domestic securities markets in many emerging economies have expanded in recent decades, their performance has been disappointing in terms of broadening access to finance for many corporations (Didier, Levine, and Schmukler 2015). The general perception of a lack of results from the reform process has led to reform fatigue and increasing pressures for governments to take a more active role.

The global financial crisis brought to the forefront the discussion on the role of the state in the financial sector. The crisis highlighted many of the fault lines of the laissez-faire view—including the belief that financial markets self-regulate—giving greater credence to the idea that an active state involvement in the financial sector can be beneficial. In addition, direct state intervention in the financial sector expanded significantly following the crisis, as governments around the world took over troubled financial institutions and pursued a variety of strategies to step up financing to the private sector, including increased lending by state-owned banks and the expansion or creation of credit guarantee schemes targeting sectors perceived to be underserved by private financial intermediaries.[38] Although the crisis reignited the debate on the need for direct state intervention in financial markets, it is fair to say that the laissez-faire view still seems to be the predominant view on the role of the state in financial development, at least among those in the economics profession (World Bank 2013a, 2015).

Although the arguments of the laissez-faire view are quite compelling and have attained widespread support, the associated policy prescription is not free of problems. Improving the enabling environment is easier said than done. Even if we knew exactly what needed to be done, and in what sequence, there is no denying that the actual reform implementation would face glitches and would likely be affected by the two-steps-forward-one-step-back phenomenon. But the reality is that we do not know exactly all that needs to be done; there is no ex ante formula for achieving access-enhancing financial development. Financial development is not amenable to a one-size-fits-all or "template" approach, not least because of its evolutionary, path-dependent nature. A good enabling environment is in effect the historical result of a complicated and rather delicate combination of mutually reinforcing institutional innovations and market dynamics, which cannot be transplanted at will from one country to another. Hence, financial reforms that are partial, inadequately complemented, or wrongly sequenced could lead to dysfunctional yet self-reinforcing institutional hybrids, which might be subsequently hard to dislodge.

The Pro-Market Activism View

If one thinks in terms of nonconflicting long- and short-run policy objectives, it is possible to rationalize some recent experiences of state intervention, like the ones described in this book, into a third, middle-ground view, which we denominate *pro-market activism.* In a sense, this view is closer to the laissez-faire view, to the extent that it recognizes a limited role for the state in financial markets and acknowledges that improving institutional efficiency is the best way to achieve high-quality financial development in the long run. However, it does not exclude the possibility that some direct state interventions to broaden access may be warranted. Although the laissez-faire view rightfully emphasizes that the public sector in most cases has little or no advantage relative to private financial intermediaries in directly allocating and pricing credit, it tends to understate the role of collective action problems (uninternalized externalities, coordination failures, or free-rider problems) and risk-sharing limitations, which might prevent the private sector from broadening access to financial services in a healthy and sustainable manner. The pro-market activism view contends instead that there is a role for the state in helping private financiers overcome collective action frictions and possibly also risk-spreading limitations to address the underlying causes of access problems. The appropriate role of the state, according to this view, is to complement private financiers, rather than replace them, by focusing on areas where the state may have some relative advantages.

The main message of pro-market activism is that there is a role for the visible hand of the state in promoting access in the short run, while the fruits of ongoing institutional reform are still unripe. However, the state must be highly selective in its interventions, always trying to ensure that it promotes the development of deep domestic financial markets and fosters the growth of the financial sector by working with it, rather than replacing it. Careful analyses need to precede any intervention. Interventions need to be directed at addressing the underlying causes of problems of access, not at increasing the use of financial services per se, and can be justified only if they can do this in a cost-effective manner.

To a large extent, the evolution of policy thinking about the role of the state in broadening access to finance in recent decades mirrors the evolution of development policy thinking more broadly. From this perspective, the pro-market activism view can be seen as part of an emerging view on development policies, based on the experience of recent decades. While still far from providing completely coherent, fully articulated thinking, this view tends to argue that, although a good enabling environment is a necessary condition for sustainable long-term growth, it may not be enough to initiate the development process, and that selective state interventions to address specific market failures and help jump-start economic growth may be required.[39] This view is more nuanced than previous development policy views in its take on the role of the state in the development process. It recognizes that, although the market is the basic mechanism for resource allocation, the state can play a significant role in addressing coordination failures and knowledge spillovers that may constrain the birth and expansion of new (higher-productivity) sectors.

This emerging view calls for policy diversity, selective and modest reforms, and experimentation. In fact, its salient characteristic is perhaps the recognition of the need to avoid one-size-fits-all strategies and to follow a more targeted approach, taking into account country specificities.[40] The lack of clear guidelines regarding what works in igniting growth calls for more nuanced policy prescriptions and an experimentalist approach to development policies, based on relatively narrow targeted policy interventions that create room for a process of trial and error to identify what works and what does not in a particular institutional setting. Although a more nuanced approach to development policies may be warranted, it is worth pointing out that this view runs the risk of degenerating into an "anything-goes" approach. A major challenge for this view is translating its recommendations into specific operational guidelines for devising development policies, without degenerating into a rigid blueprint.

Conclusions

This book analyzes some innovative experiences in broadening access to finance in Latin America. These initiatives seem to be driven by an emerging view on the role of the state in financial development, which we denominate pro-market activism. This view seems to be in the middle ground between the two highly contrasting views that have traditionally dominated the debate regarding the nature of state intervention in financial markets. It recognizes a limited role for the state in financial markets but contends that there might be room for well-designed, restricted interventions in collaboration with the private sector to address problems of access to finance.

For all its potential appeal, the emerging pro-market activism view raises many questions. Are there actually cases where state intervention does not displace or crowd out private financial market activity but rather encourages it? Can direct interventions indeed be designed to ensure that they foster access in a sustainable manner and to minimize distortions and avoid the government failures that have accompanied many previous attempts at intervention? If a given state intervention is efficient—in the sense that it leads to greater, mutually beneficial financial contracting without any (explicit or hidden) subsidies—why do private financial intermediaries not take the initiative? Is direct state intervention actually necessary in this case, or, given the right incentives, would these private financial intermediaries step forward?

Although it is very difficult to provide definitive answers to these questions, we try to address them by analyzing how pro-market activism has worked in a number of cases in Latin America. Our analysis provides a framework for studying the types of interventions linked to this view in a more systematic manner, and for thinking about state interventions in financial markets in general. Studying these initiatives can help us understand to what extent actual experiences have conformed to the stylized description of this view presented above. These experiences may also highlight potential problems in the design and implementation of pro-market interventions. We believe that this analysis can provide a better understanding of whether the pro-market activism view can actually constitute a viable alternative to broaden access to finance in developing countries. Moreover, even if one believes that direct state intervention is not warranted, the experiences described in this book and our conceptual analysis yield valuable insights. First, the experiences we describe illustrate some of the activities that might help to expand access to finance, regardless of whether the private sector or the public sector takes the lead. Second, even if one disagrees with these policies, in many developed and developing countries the state continues to play a significant role in credit allocation through direct interventions in financial markets, and this role has expanded since the global financial crisis. Given this significant role, understanding the forms that direct state interventions in financial markets can take—along with their motivations, design, and potential impact—remains important.

Notes

1. A large theoretical literature shows that market frictions create incentives for the emergence of financial intermediaries. See Levine (1997, 2005) and Freixas and Rochet (2008) for reviews of this literature.

2. The literature on the real effects of financial development is vast. Reviews of this literature can be found in a variety of forms that can suit all sorts of different tastes. A comprehensive review is given by Levine (2005). Rajan and Zingales (2003) and Levine (2014) provide shorter reviews in less technical language. Beck (2009) presents an overview of the empirical methodologies used to analyze the real effects of finance, and Beck (2013) discusses new directions for research in this area. See also World Bank (2013a).

3. More recent research has pointed to significant nonlinearities in the relationship between financial depth and economic growth and has also highlighted the limitations of simple measures of financial depth. For instance, empirical evidence suggests that the effect of financial depth on growth is strongest among middle-income countries and decreases as countries become richer (Rioja and Valev 2004a, 2004b; Aghion, Howitt, and Mayer-Foulkes 2005; Reshef and Phillipon 2013). Arcand, Berkes, and Panizza (2012) and Law and Singh (2014) find that financial depth has a positive effect on growth only up to a certain threshold; beyond this threshold, a larger financial system is associated with lower economic growth. Beck et al. (2012) find that the growth effect of financial deepening is driven by business lending rather than by household credit. Beck, Degryse, and Kneer (2014) show that only the expansion of intermediation activities by the financial sector,

rather than overall financial depth, is associated with higher growth and lower volatility in the long run. See Beck (2014) for an overview of this empirical evidence.

4. Čihák et al. (2013) analyze cross-country indicators encompassing different dimensions of financial development (depth, access, efficiency, and stability) and find that the correlation among the different dimensions is not very high, underscoring the fact that each dimension captures a unique facet of financial development. Moreover, they also find that none of the different dimensions is clearly superior to the others in explaining long-term growth or poverty reduction.

5. In 2015, the World Bank Group and its public and private sector partners issued numeric commitments to help promote financial inclusion and achieve Universal Financial Access by 2020, defined as all adults worldwide having access to transaction accounts to store money and send and receive payments. The World Bank Group committed to enabling 1 billion people to gain access to a transaction account through targeted interventions.

6. See, for example, Banerjee and Newman (1993), Galor and Zeira (1993), and Aghion and Bolton (1997). Demirgüç-Kunt and Levine (2008) and Karlan and Morduch (2010) present reviews of this literature.

7. In companion pieces, we document the extent of financial development and access to finance in Latin America and the Caribbean (de la Torre, Ize, and Schmukler 2012; Didier and Schmukler 2014).

8. Beck and de la Torre (2007) analyze conceptual issues in access to payment and savings services. See also Committee on Payments and Market Infrastructure and World Bank (2016) for a discussion of policies to increase access to payment services.

9. Čihák et al. (2013) construct an extensive data set of financial system characteristics for 205 economies starting in 1960 (Global Financial Development Database). See also Beck, Demirgüç-Kunt, and Levine (2000, 2010) for earlier efforts to construct databases of financial sector depth for a large cross-section of countries over a relatively long time period.

10. These studies include, among many others, Kumar (2005) for Brazil; World Bank (2003a) for Colombia; Basu and Srivastava (2005) for India; Atieno (1999) for Kenya; Diagne and Zeller (2001) for Malawi; World Bank (2003b) and Caskey, Ruíz Durán, and Solo (2006) for Mexico; and Satta (2002) and Beegle, Dehejia, and Gatti (2006) for Tanzania.

11. Christen, Rosenberg, and Jayadeva (2004) collect data on the number of accounts held in institutions that focus on providing financial services to low-income households—such as microfinance institutions, postal savings banks, financial cooperatives, rural banks, and development banks—for a large cross-section of countries. Peachey and Roe (2006) augment these data with figures for additional savings banks. Beck, Demirgüç-Kunt, and Martinez Peria (2007) collect aggregate data on the use of financial services from commercial banks for 57 countries. These data were subsequently updated and augmented by World Bank (2008), CGAP (2009), and Kendall, Mylenko, and Ponce (2010). Most of this provider-side information has now been collected by the International Monetary Fund as part of the Financial Access Survey (http://fas.imf.org).

12. Despite these potential limitations, aggregate indicators tend to be closely correlated with measures of financial depth and with the proportion of households that use financial services estimated from household surveys (Beck, Demirgüç-Kunt, and Martinez Peria 2007; Honohan 2008).

13. Household surveys that compile data on the use of financial services are surveyed by Peachey and Roe (2004) and Claessens (2006). Also, Beck, Demirgüç-Kunt, and Honohan (2008) review household surveys from seven developing countries, and Honohan and King (2009) analyze surveys from 11 African countries and Pakistan.

14. See Barr, Kumar, and Litan (2007) for more discussion of these issues.

15. The World Bank Enterprise Surveys define small firms as those with fewer than 20 employees, medium firms as those that have between 20 and 99 employees, and large firms as those with 100 or more employees.

16. See, for example, Banerjee and Newman (1993) and Aghion and Bolton (1997).

17. Boyd and Prescott (1986), Allen (1990), and Greenwood and Jovanovic (1990) present theoretical models in which financial intermediaries arise to generate information on firms and sell it to investors.

18. See, for example, King and Levine (1993a), Blackburn and Hung (1998), Galetovic (1996), and Acemoglu, Aghion, and Zilibotti (2006).

19. This literature was initiated by Goldsmith (1969). Also see King and Levine (1993b), Levine and Zervos (1998), and Levine, Loayza, and Beck (2000).

20. See, for example, Levine, Loayza, and Beck (2000), Rousseau and Wachtel (2000), and Beck and Levine (2004).

21. See Rousseau and Wachtel (1998), Xu (2000), and Arestis, Demetriades, and Luintel (2001) for time series analyses. Wright (2002) presents a detailed study of how the financial system in the United States created conditions for economic growth after 1780. Haber (1991, 1997) compares industrial and capital market development in Brazil, Mexico, and the United States between 1830 and 1930. See also Cameron (1967) and McKinnon (1973) for historical case studies.

22. Also see Wurgler (2000), Claessens and Laeven (2003), Love (2003), and Beck, Demirgüç-Kunt, and Maksimovic (2005).

23. Li, Squire, and Zou (1998) and Clarke, Xu, and Zou (2006) find that financial development is associated with lower levels of income inequality. Most of the studies that show a link between financial market development and poverty reduction do not identify whether this is caused by an expansion in the breadth of access, or simply by an increase in income levels that favors lower-income sectors. Calibrating a general equilibrium model for the Thai economy, Gine and Townsend (2004) find that most of the effect of financial development on income inequality comes from indirect labor market effects through higher employment and wages. Similarly, Beck, Levine, and Levkov (2010) find that the elimination of restrictions on bank branch expansion across U.S. states led to a reduction in income inequality by increasing the demand for lower-skilled works. In the case of Mexico, Bruhn and Love (2014) find that increased credit availability for lower-income households led to a reduction in poverty rates by increasing informal business creation and helping existing informal business owners continue their operations.

24. See, for example, Evans and Jovanovic (1989), Holtz-Eakin, Joulfaian, and Rosen (1994), Blanchflower and Oswald (1998), Paulson and Townsend (2004), Blanchflower and Shadforth (2007), and Demirgüç-Kunt, Klapper, and Panos (2011).

25. See Armendáriz de Aghion and Morduch (2005), Karlan and Morduch (2010), and Rosenberg (2010) for discussions of the empirical challenges in identifying the effects of microcredit programs, as well as overviews of earlier empirical evidence. Several recent studies have used randomized experiments to try to identify the causal effect of microcredit, finding evidence that microloans have little or no effect on income and poverty but help households to cope with income shocks and to better manage risks. This suggests that microcredit may have a positive effect, but this is not coming through poverty reduction, as microcredit proponents claim. See Attanasio et al. (2015) and Banerjee, Karlan, and Zinman (2015) for reviews of these studies. We discuss some of these issues in more detail in chapter 8.

  Starting in the early 1990s, many microcredit institutions expanded the range of financial products they offered, moving away from "microcredit," which focused almost exclusively on lending, and toward "microfinance," which encompasses a wide range of financial services, including credit, savings, payment and transfer services, and insurance. Randomized evaluations of microsavings tend to find relatively large positive impacts on welfare from improvements in access to and usage of formal savings. See Karlan, Ratan, and Zinman (2014) for a review of these studies.

26. Gerschenkron (1962) was one of the first researchers to argue that the private sector alone is not able to overcome problems of access to finance in a weak institutional environment.

27. See, for example, Rosenstein-Rodan (1943), Hirschman (1958), Gerschenkron (1962), and Rostow (1962).

28. See Fry (1988) and World Bank (1989) for reviews of these policies and numerous examples.

29. See, for example, Barth, Caprio, and Levine (2001, 2004), Caprio and Honohan (2001), Caprio and Martinez Peria (2002), La Porta, Lopez-de-Silanes, and Shleifer (2002), IDB (2005), Beck, Demirgüç-Kunt, and Martinez Peria (2007), and World Bank (2013a).

30. Sapienza (2004), Dinç (2005), Khwaja and Mian (2005), Micco, Panizza, and Yañez (2007), Cole (2009), Carvalho (2014), and Lazzarini et al. (2015) present evidence of political manipulation of lending by state-owned financial institutions.

31. These policies were initially challenged by Goldsmith (1969), and later by McKinnon (1973) and Shaw (1973), who coined the term "financial repression" to describe them. Empirical studies tend to find a negative relation between financial repression and economic growth (Lanyi and Saracoglu 1983; World Bank 1989; Roubini and Sala-i-Martin 1992; Easterly 1993).

32. Confidence in the ability of governments to foster economic development diminished dramatically, as growing evidence showed that government failure was widespread in developing countries, and in many cases outweighed market failure (see, for example, Krueger and Tuncer 1982; World Bank 1983; Srinivasan 1985; and Krueger 1990). The theoretical literature also started to focus on the causes of government failure,

such as rent seeking and capture by special interests (Buchanan 1962; Tullock 1967; Stigler 1971; Krueger 1974).

33. The term "Washington Consensus" was coined by Williamson (1990). See Birdsall, de la Torre, and Valencia Caicedo (2011) for an analysis of reforms implemented in Latin America following the Washington Consensus. World Bank (2005) reviews the reforms implemented in developing countries during the 1990s and discusses the resulting policy lessons.

34. See Williamson and Mahar (1998) for an overview of the financial liberalization process around the world. Also, a large literature discusses the costs and benefits of capital account liberalization (see Kose et al. 2009; Henry 2007; and Rodrik and Subramanian 2009 for reviews of this literature).

35. Megginson (2005) reviews the empirical literature on bank privatization.

36. Reports from the World Bank's Doing Business project present detailed accounts of reforms to collateral laws and procedures around the world. Djankov, McLiesh, and Shleifer (2007) analyze the effects of the establishment of credit bureaus on financial development; de la Torre and Schmukler (2004) and de la Torre, Ize, and Schmukler (2012) analyze the evolution of securities markets and related reforms in recent decades, with a focus on Latin America.

37. See de la Torre and Schmukler (2004), World Bank (2005), and de la Torre, Ize, and Schmukler (2012) for discussions of this issue.

38. See World Bank (2013a) for an overview of the policy responses to the global financial crisis.

39. Different renditions of this view, which tend to differ on how significant market failures are considered to be and the extent and nature of state interventions required to overcome them, have been presented by Rodrik (2002, 2006, 2009); Hausman and Rodrik (2003, 2006); World Bank (2005); Stiglitz (2008); Lin (2012); Lin, Monga, and Stiglitz (2014); and IDB (2015), among many others.

40. This view regarding the lack of clear policy guidelines to ignite growth and the need for pragmatism and context-specific policies is perhaps best represented by the Commission on Growth and Development (2008) report. Similar views have been expressed by a wide spectrum of economists (see, for example, Easterly 2001; Lindauer and Pritchett 2002; Harberger 2003; Barcelona Development Agenda 2004; World Bank 2005; Rodrik 2006, 2014; and Solow 2007).

References

Acemoglu, Daron, Philippe Aghion, and Fabrizio Zilibotti. 2006. "Distance to Frontier, Selection, and Economic Growth." *Journal of the European Economic Association* 4 (1): 37–74.

Aghion, Philippe, and Patrick Bolton. 1997. "A Theory of Trickle-Down Growth and Development." *Review of Economic Studies* 64 (2): 151–72.

Aghion, Philippe, Peter Howitt, and David Mayer-Foulkes. 2005. "The Effect of Financial Development on Convergence: Theory and Evidence." *Quarterly Journal of Economics* 120 (1): 173–222.

Allen, Franklin. 1990. "The Market for Information and the Origin of Financial Intermediation." *Journal of Financial Intermediation* 1 (1): 3–30.

Arcand, Jean-Louis, Enrico Berkes, and Ugo Panizza. 2012. "Too Much Finance?" IMF Working Paper 12/161, International Monetary Fund, Washington, DC.

Arestis, Philip, Panicos O. Demetriades, and Kul B. Luintel. 2001. "Financial Development and Economic Growth: The Role of Stock Markets." *Journal of Money, Credit and Banking* 33 (1): 16–41.

Armendáriz de Aghion, Beatriz and Jonathan Morduch. 2005. *The Economics of Microfinance, First Edition.* Cambridge, MA: MIT Press.

Atieno, Rosemary. 1999. "Access to Credit by Women in Agribusiness Trade: Empirical Evidence on the Use of Formal and Informal Credit Sources in Rural Kenya." Institute for Development Studies, University of Kenya.

Attanasio, O., B. Augsburg, R. De Haas, E. Fitzsimons, and H. Harmgart. 2015. "The Impacts of Microfinance: Evidence from Joint-Liability in Mongolia." *American Economic Journal: Applied Economics* 7 (1): 90–122.

Banerjee, Abhijit V., Dean Karlan, and Jonathan Zinman. 2015. "Six Randomized Evaluations of Microcredit: Introduction and Further Steps." *American Economic Journal: Applied Economics* 7 (1): 1–21.

Banerjee, Abhijit V., and Andrew F. Newman. 1993. "Occupational Choice and the Process of Development." *Journal of Political Economy* 101 (2): 274–98.

Barcelona Development Agenda. 2004. "Consensus Document Resulting from Forum Barcelona 2004," Barcelona, September 24–25.

Barr, Michael S., Anjali Kumar, and Robert E. Litan, eds. 2007. *Building Inclusive Financial Systems: A Framework for Financial Access.* Washington, DC: Brookings Institution Press.

Barth, James R., Gerard Caprio, and Ross Levine. 2001. "Banking Systems around the Globe: Do Regulation and Ownership Affect Performance and Stability?" In *Prudential Regulation and Supervision: Why Is It Important and What Are the Issues?* edited by Frederic S. Mishkin, chapter 2. Cambridge, MA: National Bureau of Economic Research.

———. 2004. "Bank Regulation and Supervision: What Works Best?" *Journal of Financial Intermediation* 13 (2): 205–48.

Basu, Priya, and Pradeep Srivastava. 2005. "Scaling-Up Access to Finance for India's Rural Poor." Policy Research Working Paper 3646, World Bank, Washington, DC.

Beck, Thorsten. 2009. "The Econometrics of Finance and Growth." In *Palgrave Handbook of Econometrics, Vol. 2: Applied Econometrics*, edited by T. Mills and K. Patterson, 1180–1209. London: Palgrave McMillan UK.

———. 2013. "Finance, Fragility and Growth: The Role of Government, Maxwell Fry Lecture of Global Finance 2012." *International Journal of Accounting, Banking and Finance* 5: 49–77.

———. 2014. "Finance, Growth, and Stability: Lessons from the Crisis." *Journal of Financial Stability* 10: 1–6.

Beck, Thorsten, Berrak Büyükkarabacak, Felix Rioja, and Neven Valev. 2012. "Who Gets the Credit? And Does It Matter? Household vs. Firm Lending across Countries." *B.E. Journal of Macroeconomics* 12 (1).

Beck, Thorsten, Hans Degryse, and Christiane Kneer. 2014. "Is More Finance Better? Disentangling Intermediation and Size Effects of Financial Systems." *Journal of Financial Stability* 10: 50–64.

Beck, Thorsten, and Augusto de la Torre. 2007. "The Basic Analytics of Access to Financial Services." *Financial Markets, Institutions And Instruments* 16 (2): 79–116.

Beck, Thorsten, Asli Demirgüç-Kunt, and Patrick Honohan. 2008. *Finance for All? Policies and Pitfalls in Expanding Access.* Washington, DC: World Bank.

Beck, Thorsten, Asli Demirgüç-Kunt, Luc Laeven, and Vojislav Maksimovic. 2006. "The Determinants of Financing Obstacles." *Journal of International Money and Finance* 25 (6): 932–52.

Beck, Thorsten, Asli Demirgüç-Kunt, and Ross Levine. 2000. "A New Database on the Structure and Development of the Financial Sector." *World Bank Economic Review* 14 (3): 597–605.

———. 2007. "Finance, Inequality and the Poor." *Journal of Economic Growth* 12 (1): 27–49.

———. 2010. "Financial Institutions and Markets across Countries and over Time." *World Bank Economic Review* 24 (1): 77–92.

Beck, Thorsten, Asli Demirgüç-Kunt, and Vojislav Maksimovic. 2005. "Financial and Legal Constraints to Growth: Does Firm Size Matter?" *Journal of Finance* 60 (1): 137–77.

———. 2008. "Financing Patterns Around the World: Are Small Firms Different?" *Journal of Financial Economics* 89 (3): 467–87.

Beck, Thorsten, Asli Demirgüç-Kunt, and Maria Soledad Martinez Peria. 2007. "Reaching Out: Access to and Use of Banking Services across Countries." *Journal of Financial Economics* 85 (1): 234–66.

Beck, Thorsten, and Ross Levine. 2004. "Stock Markets, Banks, and Growth: Panel Evidence." *Journal of Banking and Finance* 28 (3): 423–42.

Beck, Thorsten, Ross Levine, and Alexey Levkov. 2010. "Big Bad Banks? The Winners and Losers from Bank Deregulation in the United States." *Journal of Finance* 65 (5): 1637–67.

Becker, Gary S., and Nigel Tomes. 1979. "An Equilibrium Theory of the Distribution of Income and Intergenerational Mobility." *Journal of Political Economy* 87 (6): 1153–89.

Becker, Gary S., and Nigel Tomes. 1986. "Human Capital and the Rise and Fall of Families." *Journal of Labor Economics* 4 (3): S1–39.

Beegle, Kathleen, Rajeev H. Dehejia, and Roberta Gatti. 2006. "Child Labor and Agricultural Shocks." *Journal of Development Economics* 81 (1): 80–96.

Birdsall, Nancy, Augusto de la Torre, and Felipe Valencia Caicedo. 2011. "The Washington Consensus: Assessing a Damaged Brand." In *The Oxford Handbook of Latin American Economics,* edited by José Antonio Ocampo and Jaime Ros. New York: Oxford University Press.

Black, Sandra E., and Philip E. Strahan. 2004. "Business Formation and the Deregulation of the Banking Industry." In *Public Policy and the Economics of Entrepreneurship,* edited by Douglas Holtz-Eakin, and Harvey S. Rosen. Cambridge, MA: MIT Press.

Blackburn, Keith, and Victor T. Y. Hung. 1998. "A Theory of Growth, Financial Development and Trade." *Economica* 65 (257): 107–24.

Blanchflower, David G., and Andrew J. Oswald. 1998. "What Makes an Entrepreneur?" *Journal of Labor Economics* 16 (1): 26–60.

Blanchflower, David G., and Chris Shadforth. 2007. "Entrepreneurship in the UK." *Foundations and Trends in Entrepreneurship* 3 (4): 257–364.

Boyd, John H., and Edward C. Prescott. 1986. "Financial Intermediary-Coalitions." *Journal of Economic Theory* 38 (2): 211–32.

Bruhn, Miriam, and Inessa Love. 2014. "The Real Impact of Improved Access to Finance: Evidence from Mexico." *Journal of Finance* 69 (3): 1347–76.

Buchanan, James M. 1962. "Politics, Policy, and the Pigovian Margins." *Economica* 29: 17–28.

Burgess, Robin, and Rohini Pande. 2005. "Can Rural Banks Reduce Poverty? Evidence from the Indian Social Banking Experiment." *American Economic Review* 95: 780–95.

Cameron, Rondo E. 1967. "Some Lessons of History for Developing Nations." *American Economic Review* 57: 312–24.

Caprio, Gerard, and Patrick Honohan. 2001. *Finance for Growth: Policy Choices in a Volatile World.* New York: Oxford University Press for the World Bank.

Caprio, Gerard, and Maria Soledad Martínez Pería. 2002. "Avoiding Disaster: Policies to Reduce the Risk of Banking Crisis." In *Monetary Policy and Exchange Rate Regimes: Options for the Middle East*, edited by E. Cardoso and A. Galal. Cairo: Egyptian Center for Economic Studies.

Caskey, John. P., Clemente Ruíz Durán, and Tova M. Solo. 2006. "The Urban Unbanked in Mexico and the United States." Policy Research Working Paper 3835, World Bank, Washington, DC.

Carvalho, Daniel. 2014. "The Real Effects of Government Owned Banks: Evidence from an Emerging Market." *Journal of Finance* 69 (2): 577–609.

Christen, Robert P., Richard Rosenberg, and Veena Jayadeva. 2004. *Financial Institutions with a Double Bottom Line: Implications for the Future of Microfinance.* Washington, DC: Consultative Group to Assist the Poor.

Čihák, Martin, Aslı Demirgüç-Kunt, Erik Feyen, and Ross Levine. 2013. "Financial Development in 205 Countries, 1960 to 2010." *Journal of Financial Perspectives* 1 (2): 1–19.

CGAP (Consultative Group to Assist the Poor). 2009. *Financial Access 2009: Measuring Access to Financial Services around the World.* Washington, DC: CGAP.

Claessens, Stijn. 2006. "Access to Financial Services: A Review of the Issues and Public Policy Objectives." *World Bank Research Observer* 21 (2): 208–40.

Claessens, Stijn, and Luc Laeven. 2003. "Financial Development, Property Rights, and Growth." *Journal of Finance* 58 (6): 2401–36.

Clarke, George R. G., Lixin Colin Xu, and Heng-fu Zou. 2006. "Finance and Income Inequality: What Do the Data Tell Us?" *Southern Economic Journal* 72 (3): 578–96.

Cole, Shawn A. 2009. "Fixing Market Failures or Fixing Elections? Elections, Banks, and Agricultural Lending in India." *American Economic Journal Applied Economics* 1 (1): 219–50.

Commission on Growth and Development. 2008. *The Growth Report: Strategies for Sustained Growth and Inclusive Development.* Washington, DC: World Bank.

Committee on Payments and Market Infrastructure and World Bank. 2016. *Payment Aspects of Financial Inclusion.* Washington, DC: World Bank.

de la Torre, Augusto, Alain Ize, Sergio L. Schmukler. 2012. *Financial Development in Latin America and the Caribbean: The Road Ahead.* Washington, DC: World Bank.

de la Torre, Augusto, Maria Soledad Martinez Peria, and Sergio L. Schmukler. 2010. "Bank Involvement with SMEs: Beyond Relationship Lending." *Journal of Banking and Finance* 34 (9): 2280–93.

de la Torre, Augusto, and Sergio L. Schmukler. 2004. "Coping with Risks through Mismatches: Domestic and International Financial Contracts for Emerging Economies." *International Finance* 7 (3): 349–90.

Demirgüç-Kunt, Asli, and Leora F. Klapper. 2013. "Measuring Financial Inclusion: Explaining Variation in Use of Financial Services across Countries and within Countries." *Brookings Papers on Economic Activity*, Spring.

Demirgüç-Kunt, Asli, Leora F. Klapper, and Georgios A. Panos. 2011. "Entrepreneurship in Post-Conflict Transition: The Role of Informality and Access to Finance." *Economics of Transition* 19 (1): 27–78.

Demirgüç-Kunt, Asli, Leora F. Klapper, Dorothe Singer, and Peter Van Oudheusden. 2015. "The Global Findex Database 2014: Measuring Financial Inclusion Around the World." Policy Research Working Paper 7255, World Bank, Washington, DC.

Demirgüç-Kunt, Asli, and Ross Levine. 2008. "Finance and Economic Opportunity." Policy Research Working Paper 4468, World Bank, Washington, DC.

Demirgüç-Kunt, Asli, and Vojislav Maksimovic. 1998. "Law, Finance, and Firm Growth." *Journal of Finance* 53 (6): 2107–37.

Diagne, Aliou, and Manfred Zeller. 2001. *Access to Credit and Its Impact on Welfare in Malawi*. Research Report 116. Washington, DC: International Food Policy Research Institute.

Didier, Tatiana, and Sergio L. Schmukler. 2014. *Emerging Issues in Financial Development*. Washington, DC: World Bank.

Didier, Tatiana, Ross Levine, and Sergio L. Schmukler. 2015. "Capital Market Financing, Firm Growth, and Firm Size Distribution." Policy Research Working Paper 7353, World Bank, Washington, DC.

Dinç, I. Serdar. 2005. "Politicians and Banks: Political Influences on Government-Owned Banks in Emerging Markets." *Journal of Financial Economics* 77 (2): 453–79.

Djankov, Simeon, Caralee McLiesh, and Andrei Shleifer. 2007. "Private Credit in 129 Countries." *Journal of Financial Economics* 84 (2): 299–329.

Easterly, William. 1993. "How Much Do Distortions Affect Growth?" *Journal of Monetary Economics* 32: 187–212.

———. 2001. "The Lost Decade: Developing Countries' Stagnation in Spite of Policy Reform 1980–1990." *Journal of Economic Growth* 6: 135–57.

Evans, David S., and Boyan Jovanovic. 1989. "An Estimated Model of Entrepreneurial Choice under Liquidity Constraints." *Journal of Political Economy* 97 (4): 808–27.

Freixas, Xavier, and Jean-Charles Rochet. 2008. *Microeconomics of Banking*. Cambridge, MA: MIT Press.

Fry, Maxwell J. 1988. *Money, Interest, and Banking in Economic Development*. Johns Hopkins Studies in Development. Baltimore: Johns Hopkins University Press.

Galetovic, Alexander. 1996. "Specialization, Intermediation, and Growth." *Journal of Monetary Economics* 38 (3): 549–59.

Galor, Oded, and Daniel Tsiddon. 1997. "Technological Progress, Mobility, and Economic Growth." *American Economic Review* 87 (3): 363–82.

Galor, Oded, and Joseph Zeira. 1993. "Income Distribution and Macroeconomics." *Review of Economic Studies* 60 (1): 35–52.

Gerschenkron, Alexander. 1962. *Economic Backwardness in Historical Perspective: A Book of Essays*. Cambridge, MA: Harvard University Press.

Gine, Xavier, and Robert M. Townsend. 2004. "Evaluation of Financial Liberalization: A General Equilibrium Model with Constrained Occupation Choice." *Journal of Development Economics* 74 (2): 269–307.

Goldsmith, Raymond W. 1969. *Financial Structure and Development*. New Haven, CT: Yale University Press.

Greenwood, Jeremy, and Boyan Jovanovic. 1990. "Financial Development, Growth, and the Distribution of Income." *Journal of Political Economy* 98 (5): 1076–107.

Haber, Stephen H. 1991. "Industrial Concentration and the Capital Markets: A Comparative Study of Brazil, Mexico, and the United States, 1830–1930." *Journal of Economic History* 51 (3): 559–80.

———. 1997. *How Latin America Fell Behind: Essays on the Economic Histories of Brazil and Mexico, 1800–1914.* Stanford, CA: Stanford University Press.

Hanson, James A. 2003. "Banking in Developing Countries in the 1990s." Policy Research Working Paper 3168, World Bank, Washington, DC.

Harberger, Arnold C. 2003. "Foreword." In *Latin American Macroeconomic Reforms: The Second Stage*, edited by José Antonio González, Vittorio Corbo, Anne O. Krueger, and Aaron Tornell. Chicago: University of Chicago Press.

Hausmann, Ricardo, and Dani Rodrik. 2003. "Economic Development as Self-Discovery." *Journal of Development Economics* 72 (2): 603–33.

———. 2006. "Doomed to Choose: Industrial Policy as Predicament." Discussion Paper, Harvard University, Cambridge, MA.

Henry, Peter Blair. 2007. "Capital Account Liberalization: Theory, Evidence, and Speculation." *Journal of Economic Literature* 45 (4): 887–935.

Hirschman, Albert O. 1958. *The Strategy of Economic Development.* New Haven, CT: Yale University Press.

Holtz-Eakin, Douglas, David Joulfaian, and Harvey S. Rosen. 1994. "Entrepreneurial Decisions and Liquidity Constraints." *RAND Journal of Economics* 25 (2): 334–47.

Honohan, Patrick. 2008. "Cross-Country Variation in Household Access to Financial Services." *Journal of Banking and Finance* 32 (11): 2493–500.

Honohan, Patrick, and Michael King. 2009. "Cause and Effect of Financial Access: Cross-Country Evidence from the Finscope Surveys." World Bank Conference on Measurement, Promotion, and Impact of Access to Financial Services, Washington, DC, March.

IDB (Inter-American Development Bank). 2005. *Economic and Social Progress Report (IPES) 2005: Unlocking Credit—The Quest for Deep and Stable Bank Lending.* Washington, DC: IDB.

———. 2015. *Rethinking Productive Development, Sound Policies, and Institutions for Economic Transformation.* Washington, DC: IDB.

Karlan, Dean, and Jonathan Morduch. 2010. "Access to Finance." In *Handbook of Development Economics*, edited by Dani Rodrik and Mark Rosenzweig, 4703–84. Amsterdam: Elsevier.

Karlan, Dean, Aishwarya Lakshmi Ratan, and Johnathan Zinman. 2014. "Savings by and for the Poor: A Research Review and Agenda." *Review of Income and Wealth* 60 (1): 36–78.

Kendall, Jake, Nataliya Mylenko, and Alejandro Ponce. 2010. "Measuring Financial Access Around the World." Policy Research Working Paper 5253, World Bank, Washington, DC.

Kerr, William R., and Ramana Nanda. 2009. "Democratizing Entry: Banking Deregulations, Financing Constraints, and Entrepreneurship." *Journal of Financial Economics* 94 (1): 124–49.

Khwaja, Asim Ijaz, and Atif Mian. 2005. "Do Lenders Favor Politically Connected Firms? Rent Provision in an Emerging Financial Market." *Quarterly Journal of Economics* 120 (4): 1371–411.

King, Robert G., and Ross Levine. 1993a. "Finance and Growth: Schumpeter Might Be Right." *Quarterly Journal of Economics* 108 (3): 717–37.

———. 1993b. "Finance, Entrepreneurship, and Growth: Theory and Evidence." *Journal of Monetary Economics* 32 (3): 513–42.

Klapper, Leora, Luc Laeven, and Raghuram Rajan. 2006. "Entry Regulation as a Barrier to Entrepreneurship." *Journal of Financial Economics* 82 (3): 591–629.

Kose, M. Ayhan, Eswar Prasad, Kenneth Rogoff, and Shang-Jin Wei. 2009. "Financial Globalization: A Reappraisal." *IMF Staff Papers* 56 (1): 8–62.

Krueger, Anne O. 1974. "The Political Economy of the Rent-Seeking Society." *American Economic Review* 64 (3): 291–303.

———. 1990. "Government Failures in Development." *Journal of Economic Perspectives* 4 (3): 9–23.

Krueger, Anne O., and Baran Tuncer. 1982. "An Empirical Test of the Infant Industry Argument." *American Economic Review* 72 (5): 1142–52.

Kumar, Anjali. 2005. *Access to Financial Services in Brazil: A Study.* Washington, DC: World Bank.

Kuntchev, Veselin, Rita Ramalho, Jorge Rodríguez-Meza, and Judy S. Yang. 2014. "What Have We Learned from the Enterprise Surveys Regarding Access to Credit by SMEs?" Policy Research Working Paper 6670, World Bank, Washington, DC.

Lanyi, Anthony, and Rsudu Saracoglu. 1983. "The Importance of Interest Rates in Developing Economies." *Finance and Development* 20: 20–23.

La Porta, Rafael, Florencio Lopez-de-Silanes, and Andrei Shleifer. 2002. "Government Ownership of Banks." *Journal of Finance* 57 (1): 265–301.

Law, Siong Hook, and Nirvikar Singh. 2014. "Does Too Much Finance Harm Economic Growth?" *Journal of Banking and Finance* 41: 36–44.

Lazzarini, Sergio, Aldo Musacchio, Rodrigo Bandeira de Mello, and Rosilene Marcon. 2015. "What Do State-Owned Development Banks Do? Evidence from BNDES, 2002–2009." *World Development* 66: 237–53.

Levine, Ross. 1997. "Financial Development and Economic Growth: Views and Agenda." *Journal of Economic Literature* 35 (2): 688–726.

———. 2005. "Finance and Growth: Theory and Evidence." In *Handbook of Economic Growth*, edited by Philippe Aghion and Steven N. Durlauf, 865–934. Amsterdam: Elsevier.

———. 2014. "In Defense of Wall Street: The Social Productivity of the Financial System." In *The Role of Central Banks in Financial Stability: How Has It Changed?* edited by Douglas Evanoff, Cornelia Holthausen, George Kaufman, and Manfred Kremer. World Scientific Studies in International Economics. Singapore: World Scientific Publishing.

Levine, Ross, Norman Loayza, and Thorsten Beck. 2000. "Financial Intermediation and Growth: Causality and Causes." *Journal of Monetary Economics* 46 (1): 31–77.

Levine, Ross, and Sara Zervos. 1998. "Stock Markets, Banks, and Economic Growth." *American Economic Review* 88 (3): 537–58.

Li, Hongyi, Lyn Squire, and Heng-fu Zou. 1998. "Explaining International and Intertemporal Variations in Income Inequality." *Economic Journal* 108 (446): 26–43.

Lin, Justin Yifu. 2012. *New Structural Economics: A Framework for Rethinking Development and Policy.* Washington, DC: World Bank.

Lin, Justin Yifu, Celestin Monga, and Joseph E. Stiglitz. 2015. "Introduction: The Rejuvenation of Industrial Policy." In *The Industrial Policy Revolution I: The Role of Government Beyond Ideology*, edited by Joseph E. Stiglitz and Justin Yifu Lin. New York: Palgrave Macmillan.

Lindauer, David L., and Lant Pritchett. 2002. "What's the Big Idea? The Third Generation of Policies for Economic Growth." *Journal of LACEA Economia* 3 (1): 1–28.

Loury, Glenn C. 1981. "Is Equal Opportunity Enough?" *American Economic Review* 71 (2): 122–26.

Love, Inessa. 2003. "Financial Development and Financing Constraints: International Evidence from the Structural Investment Model." *Review of Financial Studies* 16 (3): 765–91.

Martinez Peria, Maria Soledad. 2014. "Financial Inclusion in Latin America and the Caribbean." In *Emerging Issues in Financial Development*, edited by Tatiana Didier and Sergio L. Schmukler. Washington, DC: World Bank.

McKinnon, Ronald I. 1973. *Money and Capital in Economic Development*. Washington, DC: Brookings Institution Press.

Megginson, William L. 2005. "The Economics of Bank Privatization." *Journal of Banking and Finance* 29 (8): 1931–80.

Micco, Alejandro, Ugo Panizza, and Monica Yañez. 2007. "Bank Ownership and Performance. Does Politics Matter?" *Journal of Banking and Finance* 31 (1): 219–41.

Paulson, Anna L., and Robert Townsend. 2004. "Entrepreneurship and Financial Constraints in Thailand." *Journal of Corporate Finance* 10 (2): 229–62.

Peachey, Steven, and Alan Roe. 2004. *Access to Finance*. Brussels: World Savings Banks Institute.

———. 2006. *Access to Finance: What Does It Mean and How Do Savings Banks Foster Access?* Brussels: World Savings Banks Institute.

Rajan, Raghuram G., and Luigi Zingales. 1998. "Financial Dependence and Growth." *American Economic Review* 88 (3): 559–86.

———. 2003. *Saving Capitalism from the Capitalists*. New York: Crown Business Division of Random House.

Reshef, Ariell, and Thomas Philippon. 2013. "An International Look at the Growth of Modern Finance." *Journal of Economic Perspectives* 27 (2): 73–96.

Rioja, Felix, and Neven Valev. 2004a. "Does One Size Fit All? A Reexamination of the Finance and Growth Relationship." *Journal of Development Economics* 74 (2): 429–44.

———. 2004b. "Finance and the Sources of Growth at Various Stages of Economic Development." *Economic Inquiry* 42 (1): 127–40.

Rodrik, Dani. 2002. "After Neo-Liberalism, What?" *Economic Times*, November 19.

———. 2006. "Goodbye Washington Consensus, Hello Washington Confusion? A Review of the World Bank's Economic Growth in the 1990s: Learning from a Decade of Reform." *Journal of Economic Literature* 44 (4): 973–87.

———. 2009. "The New Development Economics: We Shall Experiment, but How Shall We Learn?" In *What Works in Development? Thinking Big and Thinking Small*, edited by Jessica L. Cohen and William Easterly. Washington, DC: Brookings Institution Press.

———. 2014. "The Past, Present, and Future of Economic Growth." In *Towards a Better Global Economy: Policy Implications for Citizens Worldwide in the 21st Century*. New York: Oxford University Press.

Rodrik, Dani, and Arvind Subramanian. 2009. "Why Did Financial Globalization Disappoint?" *IMF Staff Papers* 56 (1): 112–38.

Rosenberg, Richard, 2010. "Does Microcredit Really Help Poor People?" CGAP Focus Note 59, CGAP, Washington, DC.

Rosenstein-Rodan, Paul N. 1943. "Problems of Industrialisation of Eastern and Southeastern Europe." *Economic Journal* 53 (210/211): 202–11.

Rostow, Walt W. 1962. *The Process of Economic Growth.* 2nd ed. New York: W. W. Norton.

Roubini, Nouriel, and Xavier Sala-i-Martin. 1992. "Financial Repression and Economic Growth." *Journal of Development Economics* 39 (1): 5–30.

Rousseau, Peter, and Paul Wachtel. 1998. "Financial Intermediation and Economic Performance: Historical Evidence from Five Industrialized Countries." *Journal of Money, Credit and Banking* 30 (4): 657–78.

Rousseau, Peter L., and Paul Wachtel. 2000. "Equity Markets and Growth: Cross-Country Evidence on Timing and Outcomes, 1980–1995." *Journal of Banking and Finance* 24 (12): 1933–57.

Sapienza, Paola. 2004. "The Effects of Government Ownership on Bank Lending." *Journal of Financial Economics* 72 (2): 357–84.

Satta, Tadeo A. 2002. "A Multidimensional Strategy Approach to Improving Small Businesses' Access to Finance in Tanzania." Institute for Development Policy and Management, University of Manchester.

Shaw, Edward S. 1973. *Financial Deepening in Economic Development.* New York: Oxford University Press.

Solow, Robert M. 2007. "The Last 50 Years in Growth Theory and the Next 10." *Oxford Review of Economic Policy* 23 (1): 3–14.

Srinivasan, Thirukodikaval N. 1985. "Neoclassical Political Economy, the State and Economic Development." *Asian Development Review* 3: 38–58.

Stigler, George J. 1971. "The Theory of Economic Regulation." *Bell Journal of Economics and Management Science* 2 (1): 3–21.

Stiglitz, Joseph E. 2008. "Is There a Post-Washington Consensus Consensus?" In *The Washington Consensus Reconsidered,* edited by Narcis Serra and Joseph E. Stiglitz. New York: Oxford University Press.

Tullock, Gordon. 1967. "The Welfare Costs of Tariffs, Monopolies and Theft." *Western Economic Journal* 5 (3): 224–32.

Williamson, John. 1990. "What Washington Means by Policy Reform." In *Latin American Adjustment: How Much Has Happened?* edited by John Williamson. Washington, DC: Institute for International Economics.

Williamson, John, and Molly Mahar. 1998. "A Review of Financial Liberalization." South Asia Region Internal Discussion Paper IDP-171, World Bank, Washington, DC.

World Bank. 1983. *World Development Report 1983.* Washington, DC: World Bank.

———. 1989. *World Development Report 1989.* Washington, DC: World Bank.

———. 2003a. *Colombia Rural Finance: Access Issues, Challenges and Opportunities.* Report 27269-CO. Washington, DC: World Bank.

———. 2003b. "Broadening Access to Financial Services among the Urban Poor: Mexico City's Unbanked." Draft Final Report, July. World Bank, Washington, DC.

———. 2005. *Economic Growth in the 1990s: Learning from a Decade of Reform.* Washington, DC: World Bank.

————. 2008. *Banking the Poor: Measuring Banking Access in 54 Economies*. Washington, DC: World Bank.

————. 2013a. *Global Financial Development Report 2013: Rethinking the Role of the State in Finance*. Washington, DC: World Bank.

————. 2013b. "Universal Financial Access Is Vital to Reducing Poverty, Innovation Key to Overcoming the Enormous Challenge, Says President Jim Yong Kim." Press Release, October 11.

————. 2014. *Global Financial Development Report 2014: Financial Inclusion*. Washington, DC: World Bank.

————. 2015. *Global Financial Development Report 2015/16: Long-Term Finance*. Washington, DC: World Bank.

Wright, Robert E. 2002. *The Wealth of Nations Rediscovered: Integration and Expansion in American Financial Markets, 1780–1850*. Cambridge: Cambridge University Press.

Wurgler, Jeffrey. 2000. "Financial Markets and the Allocation of Capital." *Journal of Financial Economics* 58 (1–2): 187–214.

Xu, Zhenhui. 2000. "Financial Development, Investment, and Economic Growth." *Economic Inquiry* 38 (2): 331–44.

CHAPTER 2

Conceptual Issues in Access to Finance

Introduction

This chapter discusses some conceptual issues in access to finance. In particular, the chapter presents a framework for studying problems of access to finance and their underlying causes, which is used throughout the book to analyze how the different experiences described might ameliorate these problems. Although the conceptual framework presented in this chapter can help readers understand how the different initiatives work and where their value added may lie, this framework is not required to understand the discussions in the other chapters. Readers who are less interested in theoretical issues can skip this chapter, without much loss of continuity, and jump to the discussion in chapter 3 of the different views on the role of the state in broadening access or the descriptions in chapters 4 through 8 of the different experiences in several countries.

This chapter begins by defining a problem of access to finance, and differentiating it from a mere lack of use of credit services. Next, the chapter analyzes the underlying causes of problems of access. Finally, the chapter discusses how the institutional environment affects access to finance by shaping financial arrangements and influencing the extent to which these arrangements can effectively overcome problems of access.

What Is a Problem of Access to Finance?

As described in chapter 1, in many developing countries a large fraction of firms and households do not receive credit services from formal financial intermediaries, with small and medium enterprises (SMEs) and low-income households typically being among those that display a lower rate of use of external financing. This low observed use of formal finance is often decried as a problem in the literature and in policy discussions.

However, to conclude that the low use of formal credit services by a certain fraction of firms and households in an economy actually constitutes a problem is not straightforward.[1] The low observed use of external finance may just be a consequence of demand factors. For instance, firms may not use credit simply because they do not need to borrow, either because they lack profitable investment opportunities or because they have enough funds available to finance their investment needs. In this case, the observed lack of use of credit cannot be considered a "problem" in the commonly used sense of the word, and artificially increasing the supply of credit to these firms might just result in a misallocation of resources.

The expansion of credit without sufficient regard for creditworthiness can affect financial stability, and might even lead to financial crises. A recent example in this regard might be the 2008–09 financial crisis in the United States. Several commentators have argued that the U.S. government's intervention in residential mortgage markets to increase access to housing finance for lower-income borrowers played a significant role in the rapid expansion of lower-quality (so-called subprime) mortgage lending in the run-up to the financial crisis. The collapse of the subprime market was a catalyst for the crisis.[2] The low observed use of credit by lower-income sectors might just reflect their lack of resources and investment opportunities, and not some underlying failure of financial markets. In such a case, the adequate policy solution might not be to artificially increase the provision of credit to these households, but rather to seek other means of reducing poverty.[3]

As this discussion highlights, a low observed use of credit and an actual problem of access to credit are two very different things. This distinction, unfortunately, has often been ignored in the literature and in policy discussions, and the failure to recognize it can lead to the wrong policy advice. Defining a problem of access to finance and differentiating it from a mere lack of use of credit requires understanding how capital allocation decisions are made and the underlying factors that can lead financial intermediaries to curtail lending to certain borrowers.

In a world with frictionless and complete markets, capital would seamlessly flow from those agents with excess funds to those with profitable investment projects, and there would be no problems of access to finance. In this setting, the choice between lending (saving) and borrowing would be determined purely by agents' risk and time preferences and investment opportunities. For instance, households whose preferred consumption path over time differed from their earnings time profile would save or borrow so as to achieve their desired consumption patterns (of course, subject to their intertemporal wealth constraint). In such a world, all profitable investment projects would get external funding. By "profitable projects," we mean those projects that generate returns meeting the market risk-adjusted cost of capital and that, therefore, agents would be willing to finance themselves if they had the required resources. In this world, investment decisions would be independent from consumption and financing decisions.[4] Some agents' lack of credit use would not constitute a problem because it would just reflect a lack of borrowing needs. Households that did not borrow for consumption smoothing would be those whose desired consumption time path matched their earnings time profile. Firms that did not borrow for investment would be those that lacked investment projects or had enough internal funds to finance them. Firms and households would face no credit constraints, and capital would be channeled to its most productive uses.[5]

But problems of access do arise in some well-defined sense in the real world and are linked to frictions that prevent the seamless flow of capital from agents with excess funds to those with profitable investment projects. Frictions introduce a wedge between the expected internal rate of return of investment projects (that is, the return generated by the projects' fundamentals) and the rate of return that external financiers require to finance them. The existence of this wedge implies that it is cheaper for firms to finance investment projects from internal funds than to rely on external finance. As a result, investments will depend on the availability of internal funds and not just on business opportunities, with financially constrained firms and households bypassing profitable investment opportunities that would have been financed if internal funds were available. In this situation, it will be difficult to decouple investment decisions from financing and consumption decisions.

On the basis of these arguments, we adopt a working definition of a problem of access to finance to conduct our study: a *problem of access to finance* exists when an investment project that would be internally financed by the agent (that is, the firm or individual) if she had the required resources does not get external financing. As mentioned above, this occurs because there is a wedge between the expected internal rate of return of the project and the rate of return that external investors require to finance it. This wedge is mainly introduced by two well-known constraints, namely, *principal–agent problems* and *transaction costs*.

Our working definition of a problem of access abstracts from any factors that might affect the opportunity cost of funds. For example, a reduction in macroeconomic volatility may reduce the opportunity cost of funds in the economy, increasing the number of profitable projects and the amount of financial contracting. However, this will not necessarily increase the fraction of profitable projects that get external financing; a lower cost of capital does not imply a lower wedge between the internal rate of return for investment projects and the return required by external financiers. Although, in this example, there would be an increase in the observed use of financial services and potentially major welfare gains, it would not necessarily entail a mitigation of problems of access according to our definition. In effect, our definition does not focus on the number of projects that are profitable or on the number of projects that receive external financing, per se. An increase in those numbers might be beneficial to society but is outside the scope of our definition.

The existence of a problem of access to finance is, in most cases, a rational response by economic agents to existing frictions in an economy. As discussed below, difficulties in mitigating information asymmetries and enforcing contracts can lead creditors to curtail lending to some potential borrowers with profitable investment projects. Extending credit to these firms or households may not constitute a prudent use of resources given the difficulties and costs of assessing their creditworthiness, monitoring their actions, or enforcing repayment. Consider, for instance, the case of a lender granting a loan. Even if the lender can perfectly identify those borrowers with profitable investment projects, she might not be able to monitor their actions after disbursing the loan. In this situation, borrowers may have incentives to use borrowed funds for riskier projects or may just run away with the money. Facing this problem, a profit-maximizing lender might decide not to lend. According to our working definition, this constitutes a problem of access to finance because borrowers with profitable investment projects are not receiving external financing. But it is clear that the decision by the financier not to lend is fully rational and economically efficient, given the constraints she faces.[6] Addressing problems of access, therefore, requires ameliorating these constraints.

What Causes Problems of Access to Finance?

The two fundamental elements that introduce the wedge between the internal rate of return on investment projects and the rate of return that external investors require to finance them are, as mentioned above, principal–agent problems and transaction costs.[7] These elements generate problems of access to finance. We now turn to a discussion of each of these elements.[8]

Principal–Agent Problems

Consider principal–agent problems first. A debt contract is a promise between two agents to exchange current resources for future ones. In this contract, the lender or creditor transfers resources in the present to the borrower or debtor. The borrower uses these resources to finance investments or smooth consumption and commits to returning the resources to the creditor at some point in the future, typically including (in addition to the original amount lent) an interest payment or premium that reflects the opportunity cost for the creditor of relinquishing the resources for the duration of the contract. The temporal nature of the debt contract introduces uncertainty about the returns to the lender. Whether or not the borrower will repay in full is not known at the time the contract is written and is likely to depend both on the borrower's actions and on the realized state of the world, given the stochastic nature of project returns.

In this situation, information asymmetries and difficulties in monitoring borrower actions and enforcing contracts can generate conflicts of interest between the lender (the *principal*) and the borrower (the *agent*). These principal–agent problems can arise at different points in the debt transaction. First, prior to extending the loan, the creditor may have less information than potential borrowers about the quality of their investment projects and their willingness to repay. This information asymmetry can give rise to an *adverse selection* problem. Second, after the loan has been disbursed, borrower actions can affect the returns from the investment project and therefore the probability of repayment. The lender might have imperfect information regarding these actions, and it may be costly to monitor borrowers and enforce contracts. This can give rise to an *ex ante moral hazard* problem. Finally, after project returns have been realized, the borrower might have incentives to claim that these returns were low and therefore not repay the loan in full. The creditor may not be able to perfectly observe the magnitude of the realized returns and might face high monitoring and contract enforcement costs. This can give rise to an *ex post moral hazard* problem. We now describe in more detail each of these problems and their effects on the functioning of credit markets.[9]

Adverse Selection

The adverse selection (also called *hidden type*) problem arises in a situation where potential borrowers differ in terms of their credit quality (because of differences in their investment projects or their willingness to repay) and this information is not symmetrically shared; borrowers have better information regarding their credit quality than creditors do, and creditors cannot credibly extract or verify this information before granting a loan.[10] Because creditors cannot perfectly determine the quality of each potential borrower, they will end up charging the same lending interest rate to borrowers of different qualities, although it would be optimal to charge higher rates to riskier borrowers to offset higher expected credit losses.[11] In this situation, changes to the contracted lending rate can affect the overall riskiness of the pool of potential borrowers. In particular, as lending rates increase, better-quality borrowers may drop out of the market. This is the adverse selection effect.

Adverse selection arises because debt contracts are subject to limited liability; that is, if project returns are below contracted debt repayments, creditors can seize only the realized returns and debtors are not required to compensate them for the difference. This implies that lenders bear the downside risk, whereas all project returns above the loan repayment obligation accrue to the borrowers.[12] In this situation—and in most states of the world—a higher lending rate negatively affects safer borrowers, who know that there is a high probability that they will repay their loans, more than it affects riskier borrowers, who anticipate that they will not repay. In the extreme case, a borrower who knows that she will never repay the loan, and does not face any penalties in case of default, is basically unaffected by the contracted lending rate and therefore would be willing to borrow at almost any rate.[13]

In the presence of adverse selection, increases in the contracted lending rate beyond a certain level can lead to a decrease in the expected return to creditors because the higher rate leads to a riskier borrower pool and higher credit losses (Stiglitz and Weiss 1981). Hence, creditors will not increase the lending rate above this threshold, even though demand for credit might exceed supply at this rate. In the absence of adverse selection, the excess demand for credit would lead to an increase in the lending rate until credit supply equals credit demand. But, faced with adverse selection, creditors will not increase the lending rate because this would reduce their expected returns. Instead, they will curtail lending to some potential borrowers. This implies that credit markets will not clear (that is, at the prevailing lending rate, demand for credit will exceed supply) and there will be credit rationing in equilibrium: some loan applicants will be denied credit, although they are observationally indistinguishable from those applicants that receive loans and would be willing to pay a higher rate than that charged by creditors.[14] Credit rationing constitutes a problem of access to finance according to our working definition because borrowers with investment projects whose expected returns exceed the market risk-adjusted cost of capital do not get external financing.

This situation is illustrated in figure 2.1. In the presence of asymmetric information, increases in the contracted lending rate do not necessarily translate into proportional increases in the expected return to creditors, because a higher rate reduces the average quality of the borrower pool. This can result in a nonmonotonic credit supply curve, as illustrated by curve S in figure 2.1. Above a certain contracted lending rate (r^*), the revenue increase resulting from an increase in the lending rate is fully offset by the larger expected credit losses due to the higher probability of default. At least two possible types of equilibrium might arise in this situation. First, if the credit demand curve crosses the credit supply curve (S) before this curve reaches its maximum at r^*, the credit market will clear and there will be no credit rationing. This is illustrated by demand curve D_1 in figure 2.1. In this case, the equilibrium is determined as usual by the point at which the credit supply and the credit demand curves intersect, which implies that the market interest rate will be equal to r and the amount of credit will be Q. Credit supply and credit demand will be equal, and there will be no credit rationing in equilibrium. However, it is possible that the supply and demand curves will not intersect,

FIGURE 2.1 Adverse selection and credit rationing

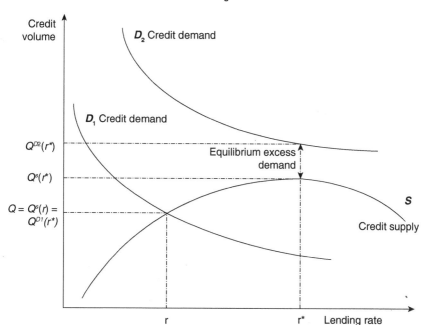

Note: The credit supply curve is given by S. Above a certain contracted lending rate (r*), the revenue increase resulting from an increase in the lending rate is fully offset by the higher expected credit losses due to the higher probability of default. So the credit supply curve is nonmonotonic. At least two possible equilibria may arise. First, if the credit demand curve is given by D_1 then the equilibrium is determined by the point at which the credit supply and the credit demand curves intersect, which implies that the market interest rate will be equal to r and the amount of credit will be Q. Credit supply and credit demand will be equal and there will be no credit rationing in equilibrium. Credit demand curve D_2 illustrates the alternative scenario: the supply and demand curves do not intersect, so creditors will fix their lending rate at r^* and markets will not clear: demand for credit will exceed supply and there will be credit rationing in equilibrium.

as illustrated by credit demand curve D_2. In this situation, creditors will fix their lending rate at r^* and markets will not clear; demand for credit will exceed supply—as shown by the difference between $Q^{D2}(r^*)$ and $Q^S(r^*)$—and there will be credit rationing in equilibrium.

Faced with the prospect of adverse selection, creditors have incentives to try to credibly extract or verify borrowers' private information regarding their credit quality. Creditors can invest in information acquisition, for instance by investigating the credit history of loan applicants, analyzing their business prospects and management quality, and establishing long-term relationships with borrowers that might allow them to gather information about their credit quality over time. Creditors can also use nonprice characteristics of the debt contract to try to determine credit quality and screen out lower-quality borrowers. For instance, creditors could offer a set of debt contracts with different combinations of lending rates and collateral requirements to try to induce borrowers to reveal their credit quality.[15]

Ex Ante Moral Hazard

The ex ante moral hazard (also called *hidden action*) problem arises in a situation where noncontractible actions taken by borrowers after funds are disbursed, but before project returns are realized, can affect the expected return to lenders.[16] Even if lenders are able to perfectly observe the credit quality of potential borrowers before granting a loan, once funds are disbursed, borrowers might take actions that reduce the probability of repayment, such as investing resources in riskier activities, exerting less effort, or diverting funds to private uses. If creditors cannot perfectly observe borrower actions or cannot costlessly enforce contracts, then they may not be able to completely prevent such behavior.[17]

Ex ante moral hazard problems can lead to credit rationing in equilibrium in a manner similar manner to adverse selection. In particular, higher lending rates might eventually result in lower expected returns to creditors by affecting borrowers' behavior. Limited liability implies that borrowers are effectively insured against downside risk while retaining all investment project returns in excess of their repayment obligations. Higher lending rates reduce the returns that borrowers receive in case of success (that is, with no default) and therefore might induce borrowers to undertake projects with lower probabilities of success but higher payoffs when successful (Jensen and Meckling 1976; Stiglitz and Weiss 1981; Bester and Hellwig 1987). Higher lending rates might also discourage borrowers from exerting effort and increase incentives for borrowers to divert funds to private uses (Watson 1984; Clemenz 1986; Black and de Meza 1992). Thus, higher contracted lending rates can reduce the probability of repayment, potentially resulting in a non-monotonic relationship between lending rates and expected returns to creditors, as in the case of adverse selection described above. In this situation, it will not be profitable for creditors to increase the lending rate above a certain threshold, even though demand for credit may exceed supply at this rate, leading to credit rationing in equilibrium.

Faced with the prospect of ex ante moral hazard, creditors can try, first, to design debt contracts that reduce borrower incentives to take actions that decrease the probability of repayment and, second, to monitor borrowers after disbursing loans. Creditors can include covenants in debt contracts, that is, clauses that require the borrower to take or refrain from taking various actions, reducing the scope for opportunistic behavior.[18] Effective use of covenants to align incentives requires lenders to monitor borrower compliance and to be able to enforce contracts in case of noncompliance. Requiring borrowers to post collateral—that is, assets that can be seized by the lender if the borrower fails to pay back in full—might also help deal with ex ante moral hazard problems. Collateral requirements imply that borrowers face a cost in case of default and therefore can reduce their incentives to take actions that decrease the probability of repayment, such as undertaking riskier projects or exerting less effort. Creditors can also try to align incentives by imposing costs of nonrepayment on debtors through other mechanisms, such as taking control of investment projects, denying access to future financing, or imposing nonpecuniary sanctions in case of default.[19]

Ex Post Moral Hazard

The ex post moral hazard (also called *enforcement*) problem arises in a situation where, after project returns are realized, creditors cannot costlessly enforce repayment. Even if lenders are able to perfectly observe the credit quality of potential borrowers before granting a loan and thus can ensure that borrower actions after the disbursement of funds are fully consistent with the lenders' objectives, borrowers could claim, once project returns are realized, that returns were low and default or could just take the money and run. Creditors that cannot perfectly observe project returns or cannot costlessly enforce contracts may not be able to prevent borrowers from engaging in strategic default, that is, defaulting when they have the ability to repay.[20] In the extreme case, where no repayment can be legally enforced and borrowers face no cost of default, there will be no point in granting a loan because borrowers will never pay it back.

Ex post moral hazard problems can lead to credit rationing in equilibrium, even if creditors are able to observe project returns and enforce repayment by incurring some costs, as shown by Williamson (1987).[21] As long as the borrower pays back in full, the lender will not need to verify the outcome of the project and incur any costs. But if the borrower defaults, it might be optimal for the lender to verify the project outcome and seize any realized returns. The threat of verifying the outcome in case of default and seizing any returns can induce borrowers to repay in case of success.[22] In this situation, increases in the lending rate beyond a certain level might lead to a decrease in the expected return to creditors. A higher lending rate implies that, everything else being equal, there are more states of the world where project returns will be below contracted debt repayments and borrowers will default, leading lenders to incur verification costs. Therefore, an increase in the lending rate not only raises lenders' revenue but also increases expected verification costs.[23] This can result in a nonmonotonic relationship between lending rates and expected returns for creditors, potentially leading to credit rationing, similar to the cases of adverse selection and ex ante moral hazard described above.

Faced with the prospect of ex post moral hazard, creditors can try to impose some costs of default on borrowers to induce them to repay when the project is successful. Collateral might be an effective mechanism to reduce incentives for strategic default because creditors can seize the pledged assets in case of nonrepayment. Borrowers considering whether to default when the investment project is successful will compare the value of the collateral to the required debt repayments and will repay as long as the former exceeds the latter.[24] This implies that, if collateral requirements are the only mechanism to induce repayment, the value of the collateral that borrowers can pledge imposes an upper bound on the amount they can credibly commit to repaying and therefore on the amount creditors will be willing to lend them. Creditors can also try to reduce incentives for strategic default by denying access to future financing to defaulting borrowers or imposing some nonpecuniary sanctions in case of nonrepayment.[25] If creditors cannot legally enforce repayment, borrowers will pay back when the project is successful only when the perceived costs of default exceed debt repayment obligations.

It is worth mentioning that, even if principal–agent problems do not lead to credit rationing in equilibrium, they can still result in a problem of access to finance according to our working definition. As described above, lenders might be able to ameliorate principal–agent problems by investing resources in screening and monitoring borrowers and by adjusting some of the nonprice characteristics of the debt contract, such as collateral requirements, loan size, and maturity. Although these mechanisms can be effective in dealing with agency problems, they can also result in the denial of credit to some borrowers with profitable projects.

Consider, for instance, the use of monitoring to address the ex ante moral hazard problem. Lenders might be able to reduce borrower incentives to engage in opportunistic behavior by undertaking costly monitoring activities. If monitoring allows them to perfectly align incentives, there will be no credit rationing in equilibrium. But there will still be a problem of access to finance according to our working definition. Lenders in a competitive market will charge a lending rate equal to the risk-adjusted cost of capital plus the monitoring costs. Agents with profitable investment projects whose return is below this level (but above the risk-adjusted cost of capital) will not receive any loans, although these projects would have been internally financed if agents had the required resources.

Consider also the use of collateral to deal with ex post moral hazard problems. If lenders cannot enforce repayment after project returns are realized, they might require borrowers to post collateral to induce them to repay. Although collateral can be an effective mechanism to eliminate strategic default, its use implies that borrowers without enough assets to pledge as collateral will not receive a loan, even though they may have profitable investment projects. This constitutes a problem of access to finance according to our working definition.

Transaction Costs

Lending transactions require engaging in activities—such as disbursing funds, receiving payments, and maintaining borrower records—that entail monetary costs. Creditors might also need to incur operating costs not directly related to a specific transaction, such as maintaining a brick-and-mortar infrastructure to reach potential borrowers. These monetary costs associated with lending transactions, which we define as transaction costs, can result in a problem of access to credit according to our working definition.[26]

To remain profitable, creditors need to adjust their lending rates to cover all the monetary costs associated with conducting financial transactions and maintaining lender operations. This introduces a wedge between the (expected) internal rate of return of investment projects and the rate of return that external investors require to finance them. For instance, if transaction costs are fixed, lenders in a competitive market will charge a lending rate equal to the risk-adjusted cost of capital plus the average transaction costs. Agents with profitable investment projects whose returns are below this level will not receive credit in equilibrium, although these projects would have been internally financed if agents had the required resources, resulting in a problem of access according to our working definition.[27]

This situation is illustrated in figure 2.2. The credit supply curve S_1 represents the expected return to creditors, which, in the absence of transaction costs and principal–agent problems, is driven by the opportunity costs of capital.[28] This curve crosses the credit demand curve D (which represents the expected return of investment projects by borrowers), resulting in an equilibrium lending rate of r_1 and a lending amount of Q_1. Now, if there were transactions costs, creditors would need to adjust their lending rates to cover these costs. This would result in a rightward shift of the credit supply curve from S_1 to S_2 (for each amount lent, creditors need to charge a higher lending rate to cover the transaction costs).[29] The equilibrium amount lent and lending rate would change to Q_2 and r_2, respectively. Note that this situation constitutes a problem of access according to our definition because agents with investment projects whose return is above the cost of capital (that is, those borrowers between Q_2 and Q_1) will not receive any loans, although these projects would have been internally financed if agents had the required resources.

It is worth stressing that transaction costs constitute real economic costs; therefore, the decision by lenders to charge a higher lending rate to cover these costs leads to efficient outcomes, given the constraints faced by agents in

FIGURE 2.2 Transaction costs in credit markets

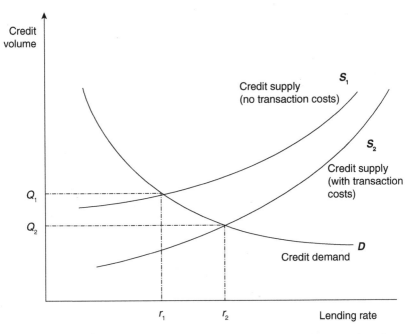

Note: This figures illustrates the impact of transaction costs on credit markets. The curve S_1 represents the credit supply curve in the abscence of transaction costs. This curve crosses the credit demand curve D, resulting in an equilibrium lending rate of r_1 and a lending amount of Q_1. With transaction costs the supply curve shifts downward, from S_1 to S_2 (for each amount lent, creditors need to charge a higher lending rate to cover the transaction costs). The equilibrium amount lent and lending rate change to Q_2 and r_2, respectively.

the economy.[30] This outcome can be considered nonoptimal only in comparison with a (hypothetical) situation in which transaction costs were lower. Addressing a problem of access in this case would require reducing these costs.

Institutions and Access to Finance

Why Institutions Matter for Access

The frictions that give rise to problems of access to finance described in the previous section create incentives for the emergence of specialized financial intermediaries. In a world with frictionless and complete markets, agents with excess funds would directly channel these resources to those agents that require funding to finance profitable projects and there would be no need for financial intermediaries.[31] However, in the presence of principal–agent problems and transaction costs, financial intermediaries can generate value by mitigating these frictions.[32] For instance, financial intermediaries can reduce the costs of acquiring and processing information. Without intermediaries, each investor would face the large (and mostly fixed) costs of evaluating business conditions, firms, managers, and so forth when deciding where to invest. Financial intermediaries may undertake the task of researching investment opportunities, exploiting economies of scale, and economizing on information acquisition costs, and can therefore contribute to reducing information asymmetries and adverse selection problems. Similarly, financial intermediaries may take on the role of "delegated monitors" for financiers relative to firms, providing an effective means for investors to (indirectly) monitor and influence how firms use external financing, thus ameliorating moral hazard problems. Moreover, financial institutions can reduce the transaction costs associated with collecting savings from disparate investors, thereby exploiting economies of scale and overcoming investment indivisibilities.

Although financial intermediaries can help deal with principal–agent problems and transaction costs, thereby ameliorating problems of access to finance, the extent to which these intermediaries can effectively deal with these frictions, as well as the specific financial arrangements that will emerge, depend critically on the institutional framework of the economy.[33]

Financial contracting depends on the certainty of the legal rights of creditors, stockholders, and borrowers and the predictability and speed with which these rights can be enforced. The extent to which the legal claims and rights of external financiers can be upheld is key in dealing with principal–agent problems. For instance, creditors must be able to enforce debt covenants in a timely manner to prevent opportunistic behavior by borrowers. Creditors must also be able to appropriate the assets pledged as collateral in case of default to align incentives. This requires not only well-defined property rights over these assets but also collateral repossession procedures that allow ownership transfers at a cost commensurate with the value of the lending transaction. Efficient legal rules and procedures that allow for the timely, efficient, and impartial enforcement of financial contracts can help ameliorate principal–agent problems and thus contribute to reducing problems of access, according to our working definition.

In environments with weak public institutions, contract writing and enforcement are difficult and publicly available information tends to be scarce. As a result, financiers may need to resort to alternative mechanisms to help reduce information asymmetries and align incentives. One such mechanism is relationship-based arrangements. If agents have repeated dealings, these interactions may reduce information asymmetries because agents can collect information about each other over the course of their business transactions, and the relationship itself can help align incentives, through the threat of termination in case of opportunistic behavior.[34] Parties will honor agreements (even in the absence of written contracts) to ensure a stream of future business within the relationship and to maintain their reputations.[35] When institutions are weak, relationship-based arrangements can, at least partly, serve as substitutes for legal rules and courts in supporting contracting.[36] These arrangements can take many forms. For instance, credit networks based on reputational mechanisms have long been observed in different parts in the world.[37] Fafchamps (2004) and Biggs and Shah (2006) describe how interfirm networks based on a common ethnicity in Africa facilitate information transmission and provide credible enforcement mechanisms, increasing access to trade credit in an environment with weak public institutions.

Financial intermediaries may also establish close relationships with borrowers through repeated interactions. For instance, banks can collect information about their borrowers through a variety of contacts over time—such as providing loans, monitoring debt covenants, and offering deposits and other financial services—thereby reducing information asymmetries. Because this information is not fully available to external financiers, this gives the "inside" bank a competitive advantage, allowing it to offer financing to those borrowers that it identifies as being creditworthy at better terms (for example, lower lending rates, lower collateral requirements, larger amounts) than it offers other potential lenders. This competitive advantage also allows the bank to exert some control over these borrowers—because it would be costly for them to switch lenders—which might help to limit opportunistic behavior.[38] This suggests that relationship lending can be an effective way of dealing with principal–agent problems in situations where information is not widely available and contract enforcement is difficult.[39]

Another relationship-based arrangement to deal with agency problems in financial contracting is related lending, which involves financial intermediaries extending credit to parties closely related to their owners and managers, such as firms owned by them, their families and clans, or their friends and business associates. Also, banks might directly own shares in some of the firms to which they lend. Related lending can contribute to reducing information asymmetries because bankers are likely to have better information about related borrowers than unrelated ones. On the other hand, related lending might allow insiders (bank owners and directors) to expropriate minority shareholders and depositors by channeling bank resources to projects with lower returns. Historical evidence from developed countries suggests that, despite their potential drawbacks, related lending practices can help to cope with a deficient informational and contractual environment.[40]

Relationship-based arrangements can be effective in dealing with adverse selection and moral hazard problems in environments with weak public institutions, but by definition can work only within a circumscribed network of participants. Informal enforcement mechanisms that rely on repeated interactions and/or reputational concerns might substitute legal rules and courts in supporting contracting but are difficult to extend to a large group; additional participants are likely to be less well-connected, and therefore maintaining the relationship will be less valuable to them, reducing their incentives to avoid opportunistic behavior.[41] Relationship-based financing arrangements cause creditors and debtors to stick with established relationships rather than looking for new partners, thereby creating barriers to entry. The lack of reliable public information on borrowers in countries with weak institutions reinforces the narrowness of the group that can have access to finance. When adequate mechanisms for information transmission are not available, a financier's primary sources of information are personal relationships or business transactions. This suggests that, in environments with weak public institutions, access to credit is likely to be restricted to those with connections, excluding outsiders with profitable investment projects.

As discussed above, collateral is another way of mitigating agency problems in all institutional environments—by pledging some assets, borrowers put their own resources at risk, which helps align their incentives with those of the creditor. However, the effectiveness of collateral as a mechanism for dealing with principal–agent problems depends on the cost and complexity of securing a loan, as well as on how difficult it is for lenders to appropriate assets in case of default. In an environment where property rights are poorly defined, it will be difficult to legally enforce secured loans (de Soto 2000). This problem is usually compounded by the lack of adequate property registries, which makes it difficult for creditors to track the ownership and pledging of assets. Moreover, seizing and selling collateral in case of default requires time-consuming and costly legal procedures in environments where legal rules and courts are not efficient.

All these factors reduce the (expected) value of collateral from the lender's perspective and therefore can lead to higher collateral requirements. For instance, banks in several African countries typically require collateral value to represent at least 150 percent of the amount lent (World Bank 2004). Moreover, these problems are likely to affect movable assets relatively more, leading lenders to rely almost exclusively on fixed collateral (typically, real estate).[42] As this discussion makes clear, the use of collateral can be an effective mechanism to deal with agency problems in principle; however, in environments with weak public institutions, it can result in the exclusion of a significant fraction of borrowers with profitable projects who lack enough fixed collateral. This exclusion disproportionally affects lower-income households and SMEs, which usually do not own land or buildings.

In contrast, in environments with strong public institutions, financiers can rely on efficient legal rules and procedures and publicly available information to ameliorate principal–agent problems. Institutions that provide credible, impartial, and low-cost third-party contract enforcement (such as courts) reduce the need for relationship-based enforcement mechanisms, allowing financiers to engage in so-called arm's-length financing, that is, financing based on legally enforceable impersonal contracts.[43] In addition, reliable disclosure and accounting standards, as well as efficient information-sharing mechanisms such as credit registries, reduce the costs of assessing and monitoring borrowers, diminishing the value of relationship-specific information and allowing borrowers to tap a wider circle of potential financiers. As a result, in countries with strong institutional environments, personalized relationships matter less and the market becomes a more important medium for conducting financial transactions, increasing the informational content of price signals and enabling a more efficient allocation of resources (Rajan and Zingales 2001). Well-defined property rights and low-cost and timely collateral repossession procedures facilitate secured lending transactions, reducing uncertainty and increasing the (expected) value of collateral for financiers, thus allowing them to reduce collateral requirements. In sum, a strong institutional environment reduces the need to rely on relationship-based financing arrangements and fixed collateral to deal with agency problems, allowing firms and households with profitable investment projects to overcome the disadvantages that would otherwise arise from the lack of collateral or personalized connections.

Empirical Evidence on the Link between Institutions and Finance

A growing empirical literature on law and finance provides evidence consistent with the idea that a better institutional environment facilitates the extent to which financial intermediaries can deal with market frictions, fostering financial development and broadening access to finance.[44] For instance, research shows that countries with legal frameworks that facilitate the establishment and enforcement of collateral and protect the rights of creditors in case of bankruptcy tend to have more developed credit markets, better firm access to credit, longer loan maturities, and lower lending interest rates (La Porta et al. 1997; Levine, Loayza, and Beck 2000; Djankov, McLiesh, and Shleifer 2007; Qian and Strahan 2007; Bae and Goyal 2009; Haselmann, Pistor, and Vig 2010; Fan, Titman, and Twite 2012). Cross-country evidence also shows that, in countries with better credit information–sharing systems, credit markets are more developed and firms report lower financing obstacles (Jappelli and Pagano 2002; Love and Mylenko 2003; Detragiache, Gupta, and Tressel 2005; Djankov, McLiesh, and Shleifer 2007; Martinez Peria and Singh 2014). Moreover, better institutions and information-sharing systems seem to disproportionately improve access to finance for smaller firms and those with less fixed collateral (Claessens and Laeven 2003; Beck, Demirgüç-Kunt, and Maksimovic 2005; Galindo and Micco 2005; Liberti and Mian 2010; Love, Martinez Peria, and Singh 2013; Claessens, Ueda, and Yafeh 2014).

The literature has also analyzed the impact of the institutional environment on equity markets, finding that countries where the legal rights of minority shareholders are better protected tend to have more developed stock markets (La Porta et al. 1997; Levine 2003; Djankov et al. 2008; Laeven 2014). Cross-country evidence also suggests that more transparent accounting standards are associated with deeper stock markets (La Porta et al. 1997; Levine 2003). Moreover, the literature finds evidence that better legal protection of minority shareholder rights is associated with higher firm valuations, lower ownership concentration, higher dividend payouts, lower benefits of control, more accurate share prices, and more efficient investment, consistent with the idea that a better legal framework makes it easier for small shareholders to monitor managers and reduce opportunistic behavior (La Porta et al. 1998, 2000, 2002; Claessens, Djankov, and Lang 2000; Claessens et al. 2002; Nenova 2003; Dyck and Zingales 2004; McLean, Zhang, and Zao 2012).

Figure 2.3 illustrates the relation between financial development and the legal framework for financial transactions. Panel a shows that countries with laws that better protect the rights of creditors against defaulting debtors have more developed credit markets, as measured by bank credit to the private sector over gross domestic product (GDP). Panel b shows that countries where securities regulations require more extensive disclosure tend to have more developed stock markets, as measured by market capitalization over GDP.

FIGURE 2.3 Relation between financial market development and legal framework

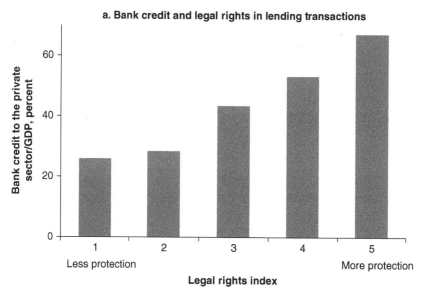

a. Bank credit and legal rights in lending transactions

(continued on next page)

b. Stock market capitalization and disclosure requirements

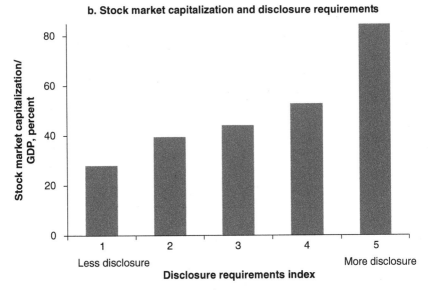

Sources: World Bank Doing Business Database, Global Financial Development Database.
Note: Panel a shows the average ratio of bank credit supplied to the private sector to GDP for different country groupings. Countries are grouped in five categories based on the degree to which collateral and bankruptcy laws protect the rights of borrowers and lenders, as measured by the legal rights index from the World Bank's Doing Business Database. The data cover 151 countries. Panel b shows the average ratio of stock market capitalization to GDP for different country groupings. Countries are grouped in five categories based on their disclosure requirements of related-party transactions, as measured by the extent of disclosure index from the World Bank's Doing Business Database. The data cover 75 countries. Country-level data on financial development variables are averages for the 1990-2012 period.

Conclusions

This chapter presents a conceptual framework for analyzing problems of access to finance and their underlying causes, which we use throughout the book to assess how the different experiences described might ameliorate these problems.

On the basis of our discussion of how capital allocation decisions are made, we adopt a working definition of a problem of access to finance. According to our definition, a *problem of access to finance* exists when an investment project that would be internally financed by the agent if she had the required resources does not get external financing. This occurs because there is a wedge between the expected internal rate of return of the project and the rate of return that external investors require to finance it. This wedge causes external financing to be costlier than internal funding. As a result, investment decisions depend not only on business opportunities but also on the availability of internal funds, with financially constrained firms and households bypassing profitable investment opportunities. This wedge is mainly introduced by two well-known constraints, namely, *principal–agent problems* and *transaction costs.*

Principal–agent problems and transaction costs are pervasive features of any real economy. Therefore, problems of access to finance, at least according to our working definition, will always exist in the real world. The exclusion of some borrowers with profitable projects from financial markets because of transaction costs or difficulties in acquiring information and enforcing contracts is a rational response by economic agents to these frictions and can be considered nonoptimal or inefficient only in comparison to a (hypothetical) situation in which these frictions were lower. Thus, the relevant question when assessing different mechanisms to ameliorate problems of access is how well these mechanisms can deal with principal–agent problems and transaction costs and reduce their effects on access to finance.

The institutional framework of the economy affects information flows, transaction costs, and contract enforcement. Therefore, institutions can have a significant impact on the type of financial contracts and intermediaries that emerge, as well as on the extent to which these arrangements can effectively overcome problems of access. Strong public institutions reduce the need to rely on relationship-based financial arrangements and fixed collateral to deal with agency problems, allowing financiers to engage in arm's-length financing. This allows firms and households with profitable investment projects to overcome the disadvantages that would otherwise arise because of their lack of collateral or personalized connections.

Several relevant issues for the analysis of the different experiences described throughout this book, as well as for the discussion of the role of the state in fostering access to finance, emerge from the conceptual discussion in this chapter. First, even with a clear conceptual definition of what a problem of access entails, it is difficult to identify a problem of access in practice and differentiate it from the mere lack of demand for external financing. In other words, data might show that some households or firms in the economy do not receive credit, but this might reflect either supply or demand factors. This implies that the observation of a low use of formal financing by a particular group of agents by itself cannot be considered an indication of a problem of access to finance. Conversely, observing that a given policy intervention increases the amount of financial contracting in the economy is not a sufficient condition for concluding that it effectively reduces a problem of access. For instance, all the additional financing generated by the intervention might be channeled to projects whose returns are below the risk-adjusted cost of capital, resulting in a misallocation of resources.

Second and closely related to the previous point, the exclusion of particular groups of borrowers from credit markets is, in most cases, a rational response by lenders to the existing frictions in the economy. Therefore, policy interventions will succeed in ameliorating problems of access only to the extent that they contribute to reducing those frictions.

Finally, the view that financial development is closely related to institutional development implies that, like any process of institutional evolution, financial development is characterized by "path dependence" (North 1990).[45] Path dependence reflects the fact that institutional arrangements are self-reinforcing (although not always efficient) because of substantial increasing returns—the large setup costs of new institutions, the subsequent lowering of uncertainty and transaction and information costs, and the associated spillovers and externalities for contracting. An important corollary of path dependence is that an isolated legal or regulatory feature that might be functional under a given institutional matrix and at a given stage of financial development might have unintended effects when transplanted to another institutional milieu.[46] Another important implication is that, like any process of institutional change, financial development is likely to be a slow process, typically requiring a long gestation period before producing visible dividends. Moreover, the view that financial development is closely related to institutional development implies that significant attention should be paid to the political economy of finance. Institutional change requires compensating those that lose from the change or overcoming their resistance through the political process. Therefore, a good understanding of the political economy of finance is likely to be a key complement to the technical soundness of any proposed policy reform. We explore some of these issues in more detail in chapters 3 and 9.

Notes

1. Although the discussion in this chapter focuses on access to credit services, a similar distinction between the lack of use and a problem of access can be applied to all financial services. However, the exact definition of a problem of access, as well as its underlying causes, will vary depending on the financial services being analyzed. See Beck and de la Torre (2007) for an analysis of conceptual issues in access to payment and savings services.

2. See, for example, Calomiris and Wallison (2008), Whalen (2008), Greenspan (2010), Pinto (2010), Rajan (2010), Conard (2012), and Wallison (2014), among others, for arguments that U.S. government intervention in the residential mortgage market played a key role in the growth of subprime lending and the financial crisis. Several commentators have challenged this view (see, among many others, Coleman, LaCour-Little, and Vandell 2008; Jaffee 2010; Thomas and Van Order 2011; Financial Crisis Inquiry Commission 2011; Krugman and Wells 2011; Min 2011; Avery and Brevoort 2015).

3. Whether credit provision is an adequate tool for poverty reduction is a hotly contested issue, as the debate surrounding the impact of microcredit highlights. Microcredit proponents argue that the provision of microloans to low-income borrowers contributes to poverty reduction (see, for instance, Daley-Harris 2003; Littlefield,

Morduch, and Hashemi 2003; Yunus 2003; and Dunford 2006). On the other hand, some authors have questioned whether microcredit constitutes an adequate poverty reduction strategy, arguing that access to credit might not be the binding constraint for the poor (Adams and Von Pischke 1994; Dichter 2006; Karnani 2007). The empirical evidence invoked by microcredit supporters in most cases is largely based on anecdotal evidence, descriptive studies, and impact studies that fail to disentangle causation from correlation. Several recent studies have tried to overcome this limitation and identify the causal effect of microcredit by using randomized experiments. These studies tend to find little or no effect of microcredit on income and poverty but find that micro loans help households to cope with income shocks and to better manage risks. This suggests that microcredit can have a positive effect, but this is not coming through poverty reduction, as microcredit proponents claim. See Attanasio et al. (2015) and Banerjee, Karlan, and Zinman (2015) for overviews of randomized experiments analyzing the effects of microcredit. We discuss some of these issues in more detail in chapter 8.

4. The conclusion that firms' investment decisions are independent from their financing decisions and from the preferences of their owners was first established for the case of an economy with perfect markets and no uncertainty by Irving Fisher in his *Theory of Interest* (1930). This result, known as Fisher's Separation Theorem, implies that firms should focus on maximizing the net present value of their profits. Miller and Modigliani (1961, 1963) and Modigliani and Miller (1958) extend Fisher's analysis to a world with uncertainty and show that, in the absence of taxes, bankruptcy costs, and market imperfections, the value of the firm is unaffected by its capital structure and dividend policy. This in effect implies that investment decisions are independent from financing decisions because the value of the firm only depends on its profit stream. Stiglitz (1969, 1974, 1979) and Duffie (1992) show that Modigliani and Miller's results also hold under more general conditions.

5. These conclusions would hold even if there were uncertainty and agents differed in their preferences and beliefs. As long as there are no transaction costs, information (whether perfect or imperfect) is symmetrically shared among all the agents in the economy, and contracts over all possible states of nature can be costlessly written and enforced, the observed lack of use of credit will reflect only the lack of borrowing needs. Of course, the level of uncertainty in the economy, as well as agents' endowments and preferences, will affect the risk-adjusted rate of return and which agents get credit in equilibrium. But all the households and firms that want to borrow at the prevailing market rate of return (subject to meeting their intertemporal wealth constraints) would be able to do so. See Arrow (1953), Debreu (1959), and Radner (1982) for analyses of general equilibrium under conditions of uncertainty.

6. In the situation described, the outcome will be that, in equilibrium, less credit will be provided relative to a situation where monitoring is costless. But this outcome might be constrained Pareto efficient; that is, it may not be possible to make someone better off without making someone else worse off, once existing frictions (in this case, monitoring costs) in the economy are taken into account. In this situation, state intervention in the allocation of credit might not improve efficiency, unless the public sector has some advantage relative to private financiers in dealing with existing market frictions.

7. Although the term "transaction costs" is widely used in the literature, there is significant debate regarding what these costs actually entail (see Allen 1999 and Klaes 2008 for overviews of alternative definitions). For analytical purposes, we adopt a relatively narrow definition of transaction costs. According to our definition, these costs encompass the direct monetary costs associated with lending transactions, such as the cost of processing payments, and the general costs of lender operations, such as the expenses associated with maintaining physical outlets. We differentiate these transaction costs from information acquisition and contract enforcement costs that give rise to principal–agent problems. Namely, transaction costs encompass all the costs, apart from their cost of capital, that financiers face when engaging in lending transactions, even if there are no principal–agent problems.

8. Although the discussion in this section focuses on debt contracts, both for expositional purposes and because debt financing is typically the major source of external funding for households and firms, principal–agent problems and transaction costs are present in all types of transactions in which an agent raises external financing.

9. Although adverse selection and moral hazard are conceptually different problems, it is very difficult to distinguish them empirically in credit markets, as discussed by Karlan and Zinman (2009).

10. The canonical analysis of adverse selection problems is due to Akerlof (1970), who shows how ex ante information asymmetries between buyers and sellers can affect the market equilibrium.

11. If creditors could perfectly observe the credit quality of potential borrowers, there would be no problem of adverse selection because they would charge a different lending rate to each borrower depending on her quality (for example, in a competitive credit market, the lending rate charged to each borrower would be such that the expected return to the creditor would equal the risk-adjusted opportunity cost of capital). Creditors might be able to classify borrowers into different credit risk categories on the basis of observable characteristics, charging higher lending rates to riskier groups and the same rate to all borrowers in each group. However, adverse selection problems can still arise in this situation because creditors cannot observe borrower-specific credit quality and, therefore, the higher-quality borrowers in each category might have incentives to opt out of credit markets.

12. Pledging assets as collateral means that, even in the presence of limited liability, debtors face at least part of the downside risk, as creditors can seize the collateral if debtors do not repay their loans in full. Also, lenders might be able to impose some nonpecuniary costs of default on borrowers.

13. Note that asymmetric information is necessary for adverse selection problems to arise. If information were symmetrically shared among creditors and potential borrowers, there would be no problem of adverse selection, even if credit quality were uncertain. Adverse selection arises because creditors can observe only the average credit quality of the borrower pool (or the average credit quality of different groups of borrowers), whereas borrowers have private information regarding their quality. Therefore, less-risky borrowers might opt out of credit markets if the lending rate is too high for them, given their quality. If information, although imperfect, were symmetrically shared,

this problem would not arise. Borrowers would make similar assumptions regarding their credit quality as creditors (that is, assume that their credit quality is the average for the whole borrower pool or for their risk category) and therefore they would have no incentives to drop out of the market.

14. Credit rationing is defined as a situation where some borrowers' demand for credit is turned down, even though these borrowers would be willing to pay the required lending rate and to comply with all the required nonprice elements of the loan contract, such as collateral requirements (see Freixas and Rochet 2008). Following Keeton (1979), the literature distinguishes between two types of credit rationing. Type I rationing occurs when all borrowers within a group are completely or partially rationed (for example, all borrowers receive smaller loan amounts than what they demand at the going lending rate). Type II rationing occurs when, within a group that is homogenous from the lender's perspective, some randomly selected borrowers receive the full amount of the loan they demand whereas others are completely denied credit. The discussion in this chapter focuses mostly on Type II credit rationing because this has received more attention in the literature, but principal–agent problems can result in both types of rationing—for example, Jaffee and Russell (1971) analyze how adverse selection can lead to Type I rationing; Aghion and Bolton (1997) analyze the case of ex ante moral hazard; and Gale and Hellwig (1985) discuss the case of ex post moral hazard.

There is a significant debate in the literature regarding the generalizability of the result of credit rationing in equilibrium obtained by Stiglitz and Weiss (1981). For instance, de Meza and Webb (1987) and Bernanke and Gertler (1990) show that, under different assumptions regarding the distribution of project returns, information asymmetries can actually result in a positive selection effect, with increases in the lending rate leading to improvements in the quality of the borrower pool. As a result, in equilibrium there is excessive lending relative to the social optimum instead of credit rationing, with some nonprofitable projects obtaining financing.

15. There is a significant debate in the literature regarding whether collateral is a good screening mechanism (see, for instance, Benjamin 1978; Stiglitz and Weiss 1981; Besanko and Thakor 1987; and Bester 1987). Coco (2000) and Rodriguez-Mesa (2004) review the literature on the use of collateral to address principal–agent problems. Also, creditors could try to use loan size as a screening device by offering a schedule of loans of different sizes at different lending rates (Bester 1985; Milde and Riley 1988; Innes 1991).

16. Ex ante moral hazard problems arise in a situation where borrower actions are not contractible, but, once project returns are realized, lenders can costlessly verify whether projects were successful or not and enforce repayment. The converse situation (in which borrower actions are contractible but lenders cannot perfectly enforce repayment) can give rise to problems of ex post moral hazard.

17. If borrower actions were perfectly observable (not only by creditors but also by a third party such as courts) and complete contracts (that is, contracts contingent on all possible states of the world) could be costlessly written and enforced, there would be no ex ante moral hazard problems because the debt contract would specify the exact actions to be taken by creditors, eliminating any conflicts of interest.

18. Although, in principle, if complete contracts could be written and enforced, covenants would specify the exact actions to be taken by debtors in all possible states of the world, in practice covenants typically take the form of simple rules that can be easily verified and enforced by a third party. Moreover, although covenants can reduce the scope for opportunistic behavior by borrowers, they come at a cost because they reduce borrower flexibility to take some actions that might be value increasing. See Smith and Warner (1979), Berlin and Mester (1992), and Rajan and Winton (1995) for analyses of the use of debt covenants.

19. The threat of excluding borrowers from further lending can be an effective mechanism to align incentives in an environment where there are only a few creditors that can coordinate among themselves. However, it is not clear that this threat can be enforced when there are many potential lenders because competition is likely to undercut lenders' ability to coordinate on excluding a defaulting borrower from credit markets (Bulow and Rogoff 1989a; Chari and Kehoe 1993; Kehoe and Levine 1993; Bond and Krishnamurthy 2004; Krueger and Uhlig 2006).

   The threat of violence and resorting to physical intimidation and punishment are commonly observed devices used by loan sharks. In the case of formal, legally enforceable debt contracts, the extent to which lenders can resort to imposing nonpecuniary penalties on defaulters to align incentives is likely to be limited, given that in most countries these types of penalties are illegal (Bond and Newman 2009). However, nonpecuniary punishments for default were quite common in the past. For instance, the penalty for bankruptcy in Ancient Rome was slavery or being cut to pieces (Djankov 2009). In the United Kingdom and the United States, imprisonment for insolvent debtors was legal until the nineteenth century (Welch 1995; Mann 2002). Also, the literature on microfinance has highlighted the role of social sanctions in reducing moral hazard in group lending transactions. See chapter 8 for a discussion.

20. If project returns were perfectly observable (not only by debtors but also by a third party such as courts) and contracts could be costlessly enforced, there would be no ex post moral hazard problems.

21. Williamson's (1987) analysis builds on the concept of costly state verification—that is, that verification (or disclosure) of project outcomes by an outsider is costly—developed by Townsend (1979) and Gale and Hellwig (1985).

22. The situation where the lender verifies and seizes returns can be interpreted as bankruptcy, and the verification costs as bankruptcy costs faced by lenders.

23. In this situation, increases in the lending rate do not affect investment project returns because there are no ex ante moral hazard problems. If there were no verification costs, the higher probability of default resulting from increases in the lending rate would not affect the expected returns to lenders because default would be costless and lenders would just appropriate all realized project returns in case of default. In this case, increases in the contracted lending rate would lead to revenue increases only for lenders and there would be no credit rationing.

24. Note that what matters from borrowers' perspective is not necessarily the market value of the assets pledged as collateral but rather the (subjective) value that they assign to those assets (Barro 1976; Benjamin 1978). Most assets used as collateral

tend to be more highly valued by borrowers than by lenders (Lacker 2001). Selling these assets therefore implies a welfare loss, even in the absence of repossession and liquidation costs.

25. The question of how to ensure repayment when debt contracts suffer from limited enforceability has been widely discussed in the literature on sovereign debt because countries typically cannot credibly pledge assets as collateral and lenders to sovereign nations have little legal recourse in case of nonpayment. Some arguments have stressed the role of reputational concerns in ensuring repayment (Eaton and Gersovitz 1981; Cole and Kehoe 1998; Kletzer and Wright 2000). Others have focused on penalties outside of the debt contract itself in case of default, ranging from trade sanctions to military interventions, as the main incentive for repaying sovereign debt (Bulow and Rogoff 1989a, 1989b; Kaletsky 1985; Rose 2005).

26. As mentioned above, for analytical purposes we adopt a relatively narrow definition of transaction costs, which encompass the direct monetary costs associated with lending transactions, and differentiate these costs from information acquisition and contract enforcement costs that give rise to principal–agent problems.

27. Apart from this direct effect, transaction costs can also result in a problem of access to finance in the presence of asymmetric information and/or enforcement problems by making principal–agent problems more acute. Consider, for instance, ex ante moral hazard problems. An increase in average transaction costs will result in an increase in the lending rate that creditors need to charge to remain profitable. This higher lending rate might increase borrower incentives to engage in opportunistic behavior, reducing the probability of repayment and potentially resulting in equilibrium credit rationing.

28. We assume an increasing marginal opportunity cost of capital because it might be costlier for financiers to relinquish larger amounts of funds (for example, they might need to give up projects with higher returns as the amount lent increases). The conclusions would be the same if we assumed a constant opportunity cost of capital.

29. We assume that transaction costs are a fixed amount per unit lent, which results in a nonparallel rightward shift of the credit supply curve, as shown in figure 2.2. Similar results would be obtained if we made other assumptions regarding the nature of transaction costs (for example, if we assumed that transaction costs are proportional to the amount lent, the credit supply curve would shift rightward in a parallel fashion and all the results would hold).

30. In the situation described, the outcome will be that, in equilibrium, less credit will be provided relative to a situation without transaction costs. But this outcome will be constrained Pareto efficient; that is, it will not be possible to make someone better off without making someone else worse off, once existing frictions (in this case, transaction costs) in the economy are taken into account.

31. Fama (1980) shows that, if agents have access to perfect (that is, complete and frictionless) capital markets, the existence of financial intermediaries has no effect on resource allocation and the economy's equilibrium.

32. A large theoretical literature shows that information acquisition, transaction, and contract enforcement costs create incentives for the emergence of financial

intermediaries. See Levine (1997, 2005) and Freixas and Rochet (2008) for reviews of this literature.

33. Institutions have been broadly defined in the economics literature as the "rules of the game," which constrain the behavior of agents in an economy. North (1993), for instance, defines institutions as "the humanly devised constraints that structure human interaction. They are made up of formal constraints (rules, laws, constitutions), informal constraints (norms of behavior, conventions, and self imposed codes of conduct), and their enforcement characteristics. Together they define the incentive structure of societies and specifically economies."

34. A large literature on game theory analyzes how repeated interactions between agents might enable punishment and reward mechanisms that prevent or limit opportunistic behavior and support cooperation. See Mailath and Samuelson (2006) for a review of this literature.

35. Relationship-based agreements are strengthened when they are embedded in social or business networks because these networks facilitate information sharing and raise the costs of noncompliance through reputational mechanisms. An agent's compliance record can be shared among network members, and opportunistic behavior can result in collective punishment, such as the group's refusal to do business again with an agent that misbehaves or the imposition of social sanctions.

36. Even in economies with effective legal systems, contracting relies not only on legal rules and courts but also on interfirm relationships. However, in these economies, relationship-based agreements are typically not designed to replace formal legal enforcement, but rather to supplement the legal system in facilitating contracting (see, for example, Macaulay 1963; Galanter 1981; Baker, Gibbons, and Murphy 1994; and Mann 1998). See also Johnson, McMillan, and Woodruff (2002) for evidence on the relative importance of courts and relationships in enforcing contracts.

37. There is a great deal of fascinating literature on how agency problems have been dealt with through relationship-based arrangements in earlier stages of financial development. For example, Greif (1993) provides an illuminating analysis of how the Maghribi traders were able to monitor agents involved in distant trading by forming a community of merchants who were mutually bound by a set of rules (the Merchant's Law). Milgrom, North, and Weingast (1990), Greif, Milgrom, and Weingast (1994), and Greif (2001) also show that reputational mechanisms played a significant role in dealing with principal–agent problems and facilitating trade in Europe in the medieval period.

38. The ability of the bank to obtain proprietary information gives it some market power over its customers. This might not only help to prevent opportunistic borrower behavior but also increases the bank's incentives to collaborate with borrowers because the continuation of the relationship is valuable from its perspective. On the other hand, the limitation of competition implicit in a lending relationship can also impose some costs on firms because the inside bank could try to exploit its information monopoly. See Degryse, Kim, and Ongena (2009) and Kysucky and Norden (2016) for reviews of the empirical literature on relationship lending; Freixas and Rochet (2008) present an overview of the theoretical literature.

39. Relationship lending is typically considered the main lending technique to reach SMEs, even in environments with good public institutions, given that these firms tend to be less transparent, have limited credit histories, and usually have little or no viable collateral. However, as discussed by Berger and Udell (2006) and de la Torre, Martinez Peria, and Schmukler (2010), other lending techniques are also used to reach these firms, provided that the relevant legal framework is in place.

40. See Aoki, Patrick, and Sheard (1994) for the case of Japan; Lamoreaux (1994) and Cantillo Simon (1998) for the United States; Fohlin (1998) for Germany; and Calomiris (1995) for a comparison of the experiences of Germany and the United States.

    Maurer and Haber (2007) analyze the rapid expansion of bank lending to the textile industry in Mexico between 1876 and 1911, which was mostly accounted for by lending to insiders. They show that, because of certain rules of the game—which required lenders to have substantial own resources at risk, enabled minority shareholders to monitor controlling shareholders, and boosted reputation effects—such related lending did not degenerate into looting or the misallocation of credit. La Porta, Lopez-de-Silanes, and Zamarripa (2003), in contrast, illustrate the negative effects of related lending by showing that, in present day Mexico, related borrowers have been 33 percent more likely to default on their debts than unrelated ones and recovery rates have been 30 percent lower for related loans than for unrelated ones.

41. The literature shows that informal enforcement mechanisms can work within stable and cohesive groups (see, for example, Bernstein 1992, 2001; Greif 1993; Rauch 2001; and Casella and Rauch 2002). However, the quality of information and the possibility of credibly punishing opportunistic behavior tend to decrease as the size of the group increases. The contrasting studies of two merchant groups by Greif (1994, 1997) clearly illustrate this problem. Similarly, the case studies by Ostrom (1990) show that small group size is an important condition for successfully solving collective action dilemmas. See also Dixit (2004) for a formal model that characterizes the maximum size of self-enforcing groups.

42. Despite titling and foreclosure problems that limit the use of real estate as collateral in many countries, property rights for real estate are typically better defined than those for other assets. Also, real estate is less subject to moral hazard problems than moveable assets, and there are usually active secondary real estate markets, which allow creditors to sell these assets in case of repossession at a relatively low cost. See Rodriguez-Mesa (2004) for a discussion of the relative advantages of different types of assets as collateral.

43. North (1990) emphasizes the need for credible, low-cost, and formal third-party enforcement mechanisms to enable the expansion of impersonal exchange and argues that the lack of such mechanisms (in particular, effective state enforcement through coercion) is one of the main drivers of low economic growth and inefficiency in developing countries.

44. See Beck and Levine (2005) and La Porta, Lopez-de-Silanes, and Shleifer (2008) for earlier reviews of this literature. Although the cross-country literature documents a positive relation between the institutional environment and financial development,

establishing causality is not straightforward. For instance, countries that have more active financial markets may develop supporting laws and regulations as a result. Also, the institutional environment may actually proxy for other variables that affect financial development, such as culture (Guiso, Sapienza, and Zingales 2004, 2006), religion (Stulz and Williamson 2003), and political factors (Hellwig 2000; Pagano and Volpin 2005; Roe 2000). Several studies have tried to ameliorate these concerns by moving away from cross-sectional evidence and analyzing the effects of changes in legal rules on financial markets, finding evidence of a positive association between improvements in shareholder and creditor rights protection, as well as the efficiency of the judicial system, and financial development (see, for example, Linciano 2003; Djankov, McLiesh, and Shleifer 2007; Chemin 2009; Haselmann, Pistor, and Vig 2010; and Nenova 2012).

45. Empirical studies suggest that legal traditions help explain cross-country differences in investor protection laws, contracting environment, and financial development (see, for example, Beck, Demirgüç-Kunt, and Levine 2003; Levine 1998, 1999; and La Porta et al. 1997, 1998), with countries of English legal origin having better creditor and shareholder rights protection and more developed financial markets. This evidence suggests the existence of a high level of path dependence in financial development. However, other researchers reject the view that legal origin is a central determinant of investor protection and stress the role of politics in determining regulations and contract enforcement (see, for example, Roe 1994; Pagano and Volpin 2001; Rajan and Zingales 2003; and Roe and Siegel 2009).

46. Several case studies highlight the problems that arise when introducing new institutions that do not interact well with existing ones. For instance, although the literature emphasizes the role of formal land titling in providing secured property rights to expand the set of assets that can be legally pledged as collateral, Shipton (1988) and Ensminger (1997) show how formal titling in Kenya failed to achieve this objective because existing informal rights could not be overridden. Similarly, Kranton and Swamy (1999) show how arrangements for arm's-length bank lending in India undermined informal arrangements that served other useful aims, such as insurance. See Dixit (2009) for further discussion. Also, using a repeated-game framework, the theoretical literature shows that a partial improvement to a weak formal enforcement arrangement can worsen the performance of existing informal enforcement mechanisms, by reducing the costs of cheating (Baker, Gibbons, and Murphy 1994; Dixit 2004).

References

Adams, Dale W., and J. D. Von Pischke. 1994. "Micro-Enterprise Credit Programs: Deja Vu." In *Financial Landscapes Reconstructed: The Fine Art of Mapping Development*, edited by J.F.A. Bouman and Otto Hospes, chapter 9. London: Westview.

Aghion, Philippe, and Patrick Bolton. 1997. "A Theory of Trickle-Down Growth and Development." *Review of Economic Studies* 64 (2): 151–72.

Akerlof, George A. 1970. "The Market for Lemons: Quality Uncertainty and the Market Mechanism." *Quarterly Journal of Economics* 84: 488–500.

Allen, Douglas W. 1999. "Transaction Costs." In *Encyclopedia of Law and Economics*, vol. 1, 893–926. Cheltenham: Edward Elgar.

Aoki, Masahiko, Hugh Patrick, and Paul Sheard. 1994. "The Japanese Main Bank System: An Introductory Overview." In *The Japanese Main Bank System: Its Relevance for Developing and Transforming Economies*, edited by Masahiko Aoki and Hugh Patrick. New York: Oxford University Press.

Arrow, Kenneth J. 1953. "Le Role des Valeurs Boursieres pour la Repartition la Meilleur des Risques." Paris, International Colloquium on Econometrics, Centre National de la Recherche Scientifique. Also in English as "The Role of Securities in the Optimal Allocation of Risk-Bearing," *Review of Economic Studies* 31 (2; April 1964): 91–96.

Attanasio, O., B. Augsburg, R. De Haas, E. Fitzsimons, and H. Harmgart. 2015. "The Impacts of Microfinance: Evidence from Joint-Liability in Mongolia." *American Economic Journal: Applied Economics* 7 (1): 90–122.

Avery, Robert B., and Kenneth P. Brevoort. 2015. "The Subprime Crisis: Is Government Housing Policy to Blame?" *Review of Economics and Statistics* 97 (2): 352–63.

Bae, Kee-Hong, and Vidhan K. Goyal. 2009. "Creditor Rights, Enforcement, and Bank Loans." *Journal of Finance* 64 (2): 823–60.

Baker, George, Robert Gibbons, and Kevin J. Murphy. 1994. "Subjective Performance Measures in Optimal Incentive Contracts." *Quarterly Journal of Economics* 109 (4): 1125–56.

Banerjee, A., D. Karlan, and J. Zinman. 2015. "Six Randomized Evaluations of Microcredit: Introduction and Further Steps." *American Economic Journal: Applied Economics* 7 (1): 1–21.

Barro, Robert J., 1976. "Perceived Wealth in Bonds and Social Security and the Ricardian Equivalence Theorem: Reply to Feldstein and Buchanan." *Scholarly Articles* 3612770. Department of Economics, Harvard University.

Beck, Thorsten, and Augusto de la Torre. 2007. "The Basic Analytics of Access to Financial Services." *Financial Markets, Institutions and Instruments* 16 (2): 79–116.

Beck, Thorsten, Asli Demirgüç-Kunt, and Ross Levine. 2003. "Law, Endowments, and Finance." *Journal of Financial Economics* 70 (2): 137–81.

Beck, Thorsten, Asli Demirgüç-Kunt, and Vojislav Maksimovic. 2005. "Financial and Legal Constraints to Growth: Does Firm Size Matter?" *Journal of Finance* 60 (1): 137–77.

Beck, Thorsten, and Ross Levine. 2005. "Legal Institutions and Financial Development." In *Handbook of New Institutional Economics*, edited by Claude Ménard and Mary M. Shirley. New York: Springer.

Benjamin, Daniel K. 1978. "The Use of Collateral to Enforce Debt Contracts." *Economic Inquiry* 16 (3): 333–59.

Berger, Allen N., and Gregory F. Udell. 2006. "A More Complete Conceptual Framework for SME Finance." *Journal of Banking and Finance* 30 (11): 2945–66.

Berlin, Mitchell, and Loretta J. Mester. 1992. "Debt Covenants and Renegotiation." *Journal of Financial Intermediation* 2 (2): 95–133.

Bernanke, Ben, and Mark Gertler. 1990. "Financial Fragility and Economic Performance." *Quarterly Journal of Economics* 105 (1): 87–114.

Bernstein, Lisa. 1992. "Opting Out of the Legal System: Extralegal Contractual Relations in the Diamond Industry." *Journal of Legal Studies* 21 (1): 115–57.

———. 2001. "Private Commercial Law in the Cotton Industry: Creating Cooperation through Rules, Norms, and Instutions." *Michigan Law Review* 99 (7): 1724–90.

Besanko, David, and Anjan V. Thakor. 1987. "Collateral and Rationing: Sorting Equilibria in Monopolistic and Competitive Credit Markets." *International Economic Review* 28 (3): 671–89.

Bester, Helmut. 1985. "Screening vs. Rationing in Credit Markets with Imperfect Information." *American Economic Review* 75 (4): 850–55.

———. 1987. "The Role of Collateral in Credit Markets with Imperfect Information." *European Economic Review* 31 (4): 887–99.

Bester, Helmut, and Martin Hellwig. 1987. "Moral Hazard and Equilibrium Credit Rationing: An Overview of the Issues." In *Agency Theory, Information, and Incentives*, edited by Günter Bamberg and Klaus Spremann. New York: Springer-Verlag.

Biggs, Tyler, and Manju Kedia Shah. 2006. "African SMES, Networks, and Manufacturing Performance." *Journal of Banking and Finance* 30 (11): 3043–66.

Black, Jane and David de Meza. 1992. "Diversionary Tactics: Why Business Loans Are So Safe." Discussion Papers in Economics 9/92, University of Exeter.

Bond, Philip, and Arvind Krishnamurthy. 2004. "Regulating Exclusion from Financial Markets." *Review of Economic Studies* 71 (3): 681–707.

Bond, Philip, and Andrew F. Newman. 2009. "Prohibitions on Punishments in Private Contracts." *Journal of Financial Intermediation* 18 (4): 526–40.

Bulow, Jeremy, and Kenneth Rogoff. 1989a. "A Constant Recontracting Model of Sovereign Debt." *Journal of Political Economy* 97 (1): 155–78.

———. 1989b. "Sovereign Debt: Is to Forgive to Forget?" *American Economic Review* 79 (1): 43–50.

Calomiris, Charles W. 1995. "The Costs of Rejecting Universal Banking: American Finance in the German Mirror, 1870–1914." In *Coordination and Information: Historical Perspectives on the Organization of Enterprise*, edited by Naomi R. Lamoreaux and Daniel M. G. Raff. Cambridge, MA: National Bureau of Economic Research.

Calomiris, Charles W., and Peter J. Wallison. 2008. "Blame Fannie Mae and Congress for the Credit Mess." *Wall Street Journal*, September 23.

Cantillo Simon, Miguel. 1998. "The Rise and Fall of Bank Control in the United States: 1890–1939." *American Economic Review* 88 (5): 1077–93.

Casella, Alessandra, and James E. Rauch. 2002. "Anonymous Market and Group Ties in International Trade." *Journal of International Economics* 58 (1): 19–47.

Chari, Varadarajan V., and Patrick J. Kehoe. 1993. "Sustainable Plans and Mutual Default." *Review of Economic Studies* 60 (1): 175–95.

Chemin, Matthieu. 2009. "Do Judiciaries Matter for Development? Evidence from India." *Journal of Comparative Economics* 37 (2): 230–50.

Claessens, Stijn, Simeon Djankov, Joseph P. H. Fan, and Larry H. P. Lang. 2002. "Disentangling the Incentive and Entrenchment Effects of Large Shareholdings." *Journal of Finance* 57 (6): 2741–71.

Claessens, Stijn, Simeon Djankov, and Larry H. P. Lang. 2000. "The Separation of Ownership and Control in East Asian Corporations." *Journal of Financial Economics* 58 (1–2): 81–112.

Claessens, Stijn, and Luc Laeven. 2003. "Financial Development, Property Rights, and Growth." *Journal of Finance* 58 (6): 2401–436.

Claessens, Stijn, Kenichi Ueda, and Yishay Yafeh. 2014. "Institutions and Financial Frictions: Estimating with Structural Restrictions on Firm Value and Investment." *Journal of Development Economics* 110 (September): 107–22.

Clemenz, Gerhard. 1986. "The Impact of Imperfect Monitoring on the Efficiency Wage Hypothesis." *Empirica* 13 (2): 203–19.

Coco, Giuseppe. 2000. "On the Use of Collateral." *Journal of Economic Surveys* 14 (2): 191–214.

Cole, Harold L., and Patrick J. Kehoe. 1998. "Models of Sovereign Debt: Partial versus General Reputations." *International Economic Review* 39 (1): 55–70.

Coleman, Major, Michael LaCour-Little, and Kerry Vandell. 2008. "Subprime Lending and the Housing Bubble: Tail Wags Dog?" *Journal of Housing Economics* 17 (4): 272–90.

Conard, Edward. 2012. *Unintended Consequences: Why Everything You've Been Told about the Economy Is Wrong.* New York: Penguin Group.

Daley-Harris, Sam. 2003. *State of the Microcredit Summit Campaign Report 2003.* Washington, DC: Microcredit Summit Campaign.

Debreu, Gérard. 1959. *Theory of Value.* New York: John Wiley & Sons.

Degryse, Hans, Moshe Kim, and Steven Ongena. 2009. *Microeconometrics of Banking: Methods, Applications and Results.* New York: Oxford University Press.

de la Torre, Augusto, Maria Soledad Martinez Peria, and Sergio L. Schmukler. 2010. "Bank Involvement with SMEs: Beyond Relationship Lending." *Journal of Banking and Finance* 34 (9): 2280–93.

de Meza, David, and David C. Webb. 1987. "Too Much Investment: A Problem of Asymmetric Information." *Quarterly Journal of Economics* 102 (2): 281–92.

Detragiache, Enrica, Poonam Gupta, and Thierry Tressel. 2005. "Finance in Lower-Income Countries: An Empirical Exploration." Working Paper WP/05/167. International Monetary Fund, Washington, DC.

de Soto, Hernando. 2000. *The Mystery of Capital: Why Capitalism Triumphs in the West and Fails Everywhere Else.* New York: Basic Books.

Dichter, Thomas. 2006. "Hype and Hope: The Worrisome State of the Microcredit Movement." Unpublished manuscript.

Dixit, Avinash. 2004. *Lawlessness and Economics. Alternative Modes of Governance.* Princeton, NJ: Princeton University Press.

———. 2009. "Governance Institutions and Economic Activity." *American Economic Review* 99 (1): 5–24.

Djankov, Simeon. 2009. "The Regulation of Entry: A Survey." *World Bank Research Observer* 24 (2): 183–203.

Djankov, Simeon, Caralee McLiesh, and Andrei Shleifer. 2007. "Private Credit in 129 Countries." *Journal of Financial Economics* 84 (2): 299–329.

Djankov, Simeon, Rafael La Porta, Florencio Lopez-de-Silanes, and Andrei Shleifer. 2008. "The Law and Economics of Self-Dealing." *Journal of Financial Economics* 88 (3): 430–65.

Duffie, Darrell. 1992. "Modigliani-Miller Theorem." In *The New Palgrave Dictionary of Money and Finance,* edited by Peter Newman, Murray Milgate, and John Eatwell, 715–18. London: Macmillan Press.

Dunford, Christopher. 2006. "Evidence of Microfinance's Contribution to Achieving the Millennium Development Goals." Paper prepared for Global Microcredit Summit, Halifax, November.

Dyck, Alexander, and Luigi Zingales. 2004. "Private Benefits of Control: An International Comparison." *Journal of Finance* 59 (2): 537–600.

Eaton, Jonathan, and Mark Gersovitz. 1981. "Debt with Potential Repudiation: Theoretical and Empirical Analysis." *Review of Economic Studies* 48 (2): 289–309.

Ensminger, Jean. 1997. "Changing Property Rights: Reconciling Formal and Informal Rights to Land in Africa." In *The Frontiers of the New Institutional Economics*, edited by John N. Drobak and John V. C. Nye, 165–96. San Diego: Academic Press.

Fafchamps, Marcel. 2004. *Market Institutions in Sub-Saharan Africa: Theory and Evidence*. Cambridge, MA: MIT Press.

Fama, Eugene F. 1980. "Banking in the Theory of Finance." *Journal of Monetary Economics* 6 (1): 39–57.

Fan, Joseph P. H., Sheridan Titman, and Garry Twite. 2012. "An International Comparison of Capital Structure and Debt Maturity Choices." *Journal of Financial and Quantitative Analysis* 47 (1): 23–56.

Financial Crisis Inquiry Commission. 2011. *The Financial Crisis Inquiry Report: Final Report of the National Commission on the Causes of the Financial and Economic Crisis in the United States*. Washington, DC: U.S. Government Publishing Office.

Fisher, Irving. 1930. *The Theory of Interest*. New York: Macmillan.

Fohlin, Caroline. 1998. "Financing Decisions and Corporate Capital Structure in the Later Stages of the German Industrialization." Working Paper 1030. Division of the Humanities and Social Sciences, California Institute of Technology, Pasadena.

Freixas, Xavier, and Jean-Charles Rochet. 2008. *Microeconomics of Banking*. Cambridge, MA: MIT Press.

Galanter, Marc. 1981. "Justice in Many Rooms: Courts, Private Ordering, and Indigenous Law." *Journal of Legal Pluralism* 13 (19): 1–47.

Gale, Douglas, and Martin Hellwig. 1985. "Incentive-Compatible Debt Contracts: The One-Period Problem." *Review of Economic Studies* 52 (4): 647–63.

Galindo, Arturo, and Alejandro Micco. 2005. "Creditor Protection and Credit Volatility." Research Department Publications 4401. Research Department, Inter-American Development Bank, Washington, DC.

Greenspan, Alan. 2010. "The Crisis." *Brookings Papers on Economic Activity*, Spring: 201–46.

Greif, Avner. 1993. "Contract Enforceability and Economic Institutions in Early Trade: the Maghribi Traders' Coalition." *American Economic Review* 83 (3): 525–48.

———. 1994. "Trading Institutions and the Commercial Revolution in Medieval Europe." In *Economics in a Changing World: Proceedings of the Tenth World Congress of the International Economic Association, Moscow—Volume 1. System Transformation: Eastern and Western Assessments*, 115–125. IEA Conference Volume, no. 107.

———. 1997. "Reputation and Coalitions in Medieval Trade: Evidence on the Maghribi Traders." In *Reputation: Studies in the Voluntary Elicitation of Good Conduct*, edited by Daniel B. Klein, 137–63. Ann Arbor: University of Michigan Press.

———. 2001. "Impersonal Exchange and the Origin of Markets: From the Community Responsibility System to Individual Legal Responsibility in Pre-Modern Europe."

In *Communities and Markets*, edited by M. Aoki and Y. Hayami. New York: Oxford University Press.

Greif, Avner, Paul Milgrom, and Barry R. Weingast. 1994. "Coordination, Commitment, and Enforcement: The Case of the Merchant Guild." *Journal of Political Economy* 102 (4): 745–76.

Guiso, Luigi, Paola Sapienza, and Luigi Zingales. 2004. "The Role of Social Capital in Financial Development." *American Economic Review* 94 (3): 526–56.

Guiso, Luigi, Paola Sapienza, and Luigi Zingales. 2006. "Does Culture Affect Economic Outcomes?" *Journal of Economic Perspectives* 20 (2): 23–48.

Haselmann, Rainer, Katharina Pistor, and Vikrant Vig. 2010. "How Law Affects Lending." *Review of Financial Studies* 23 (2): 549–80.

Hellwig, Martin. 2000. "Banken Zwischen Politik und Markt: Worin Besteht die Volkswirtschaftliche Verantwortung der Banken?" *Perspektiven Der Wirtschaftspolitik* 1 (3): 337–56.

Innes, Robert. 1991. "Investment and Government Intervention in Credit Markets When There Is Asymmetric Information." *Journal of Public Economics* 46 (3): 347–81.

Jaffee, Dwight. 2010. "The Role of the GSEs and Housing Policy in the Financial Crisis." Testimony before the Financial Crisis Inquiry Commission, February 25.

Jaffee, Dwight M., and Thomas Russell. 1976. "Imperfect Information, Uncertainty, and Credit Rationing." *Quarterly Journal of Economics* 90 (4): 651–66.

Jappelli, Tullio, and Marco Pagano. 2002. "Information Sharing, Lending and Defaults: Cross-Country Evidence." *Journal of Banking & Finance* 26 (10): 2017–45.

Jensen, Michael C., and William H. Meckling. 1976. "Theory of the Firm: Managerial Behavior, Agency Costs and Ownership Structure." *Journal of Financial Economics* 3 (4): 305–60.

Johnson, Simon, John McMillan, and Christopher Woodruff. 2002. "Courts and Relational Contracts." *Journal of Law, Economics, and Organization* 18 (1): 221–77.

Kaletsky, Anatole. 1985. *The Costs of Default.* New York: Twentieth Century Fund.

Karlan, Dean, and Jonathan Zinman. 2009. "Observing Unobservables: Identifying Information Asymmetries With a Consumer Credit Field Experiment." *Econometrica* 77 (6): 1993–2008.

Karnani, Aneel. 2007. "Microfinance Misses Its Mark." *Stanford Social Innovation Review* 5 (3): 34–40.

Keeton, William R. 1979. *Equilibrium Credit Rationing.* New York: Garland.

Kehoe, Timothy J., and David K. Levine. 1993. "Debt-Constrained Asset Markets." *Review of Economic Studies* 60 (4): 865–88.

Klaes, Matthias. 2008. "History of Transaction Costs." In *The New Palgrave Dictionary of Economics*, 2nd edition, edited by Steven N. Durlauf and Lawrence E. Blume. New York: Palgrave Macmillan.

Kletzer, Kenneth M., and Brian D. Wright. 2000. "Sovereign Debt as Intertemporal Barter." *American Economic Review* 90 (3): 621–39.

Kranton, Rachel E., and Anand V. Swamy. 1999. "The Hazards of Piecemeal Reform: British Civil Courts and the Credit Market in Colonial India." *Journal of Development Economics* 58 (1): 1–24.

Krueger, Dirk, and Harald Uhlig. 2006. "Competitive Risk Sharing Contracts with One-sided Commitment." *Journal of Monetary Economics* 53 (7): 1661–91.

Krugman, Paul, and Robin Wells. 2010. "The Slump Goes On: Why?" *New York Review of Books*, September 30.

Kysucky, Vlado, and Lars Norden. 2016. "The Benefits of Relationship Lending in a Cross-Country Context: A Meta-Analysis." *Management Science* 62 (1): 90–110.

Lacker, Jeffrey M. 2001. "Collateralized Debt as the Optimal Contract." *Review of Economic Dynamics* 4 (4): 842–59.

Laeven, Luc. 2014. "The Development of Local Capital Markets: Rationale and Challenges," Working Paper No. 14/234, International Monetary Fund, Washington, DC.

Lamoreaux, Naomi R. 1994. *Insider Lending: Banks, Personal Connections, and Economic Development in Industrial New England*. NBER Series on Long-Term Factors in Economic Development. Cambridge: Cambridge University Press.

La Porta, Rafael, Florencio Lopez-de-Silanes, and Andrei Shleifer. 2008. "The Economic Consequences of Legal Origins." *Journal of Economic Literature* 46 (2): 285–332.

La Porta, Rafael, Florencio Lopez-de-Silanes, Andrei Shleifer, and Robert W. Vishny. 1997. "Legal Determinants of External Finance." *Journal of Finance* 52 (3): 1131–50.

———. 1998. "Law and Finance." *Journal of Political Economy* 106: 1113–55.

———. 2000. "Investor Protection and Corporate Governance." *Journal of Financial Economics* 58 (1–2): 3–27.

———. 2002. "Investor Protection and Corporate Valuation." *Journal of Finance* 57 (3): 1147–70.

La Porta, Rafael, Florencio Lopez-de-Silanes, and Guillermo Zamarripa. 2003. "Related Lending." *Quarterly Journal of Economics* 118 (1): 231–68.

Levine, Ross. 1997. "Financial Development and Economic Growth: Views and Agenda." *Journal of Economic Literature* 35 (2): 688–726.

———. 1998. "The Legal Environment, Banks, and Long-Run Economic Growth." *Journal of Money, Credit and Banking* 30 (3): 596–613.

———. 1999. "Law, Finance, and Economic Growth." *Journal of Financial Intermediation* 8 (1-2): 8–35.

———. 2003. "Stock Market Liquidity and Economic Growth: Theory and Evidence." In *Finance, Research, Education and Growth*, edited by Luigi Paganetto and Edmund S. Phelps, 3–24. New York: Palgrave Macmillan.

———. 2005. "Finance and Growth: Theory and Evidence." In *Handbook of Economic Growth*, edited by Philippe Aghion and Steven N. Durlauf, 865–934. Amsterdam: Elsevier.

Levine, Ross, Norman Loayza, and Thorsten Beck. 2000. "Financial Intermediation and Growth: Causality and Causes." *Journal of Monetary Economics* 46 (1): 31–77.

Liberti, Jose M., and Atif R. Mian. 2010. "Collateral Spread and Financial Development." *Journal of Finance* 65 (1): 147–77.

Linciano, Nadia. 2003. "Non-Voting Shares and the Value of Control: The Impact of Corporate Regulation in Italy." EFA 2003 Annual Conference Paper 400, EMFA 2003 Helsinki Meetings.

Littlefield, Elizabeth, Jonathan Murdoch, and Syed Hashemi. 2003. "Is Microfinance an Effective Strategy to Reach the Millennium Development Goals?" CGAP Focus Note 24, Consultative Group to Assist the Poor, Washington, DC, January.

Love, Inessa María Soledad Martínez Pería, and Sandeep Singh. 2013. "Collateral Registries for Movable Assets: Does Their Introduction Spur Firms' Access to Bank Finance?" Policy Research Working Paper 6477, World Bank, Washington, DC.

Love, Inessa, and Nataliya Mylenko. 2003. "Credit Reporting and Financing Constraints." Policy Research Working Paper 3142, World Bank, Washington, DC.

Macaulay, Stewart. 1963. "Non-Contractual Relations in Business: A Preliminary Study." *American Sociological Review* 28 (1): 55–67.

Mailath, George J., and Larry Samuelson. 2006. *Repeated Games and Reputations: Long-Run Relationships.* New York: Oxford University Press.

Mann, Bruce H. 2002. *Republic of Debtors: Bankruptcy in the Age of American Independence.* Cambridge, MA: Harvard University Press.

Mann, Ronald J. 1998. "Verification Institutions in Commercial Transactions." Unpublished manuscript. University of Michigan Law School, Ann Arbor.

Martinez Peria, Maria Soledad, and Sandeep Singh. 2014. "The Impact of Credit Information Sharing Reforms on Firm Financing." Policy Research Working Paper 7013, World Bank, Washington, DC.

Maurer, Noel, and Stephen Haber. 2007. "Related Lending and Economic Performance: Evidence from Mexico." *Journal of Economic History* 67 (3): 551–81.

McLean, R. David, Tianyu Zhang, and Mengxin Zhao. 2012. "Why Does the Law Matter? Investor Protection and Its Effects on Investment, Finance, and Growth." *Journal of Finance* 67 (1): 313–50.

Milde, Hellmuth, and John G. Riley. 1988. "Signaling in Credit Markets." *Quarterly Journal of Economics* 103 (1): 101–29.

Milgrom, Paul R., Douglass C. North, and Barry R. Weingast. 1990. "The Role of Institutions in the Revival of Trade: The Law Merchant, Private Judges, and the Champagne Fairs." *Economics and Politics* 2 (1): 1–23.

Miller, Merton H., and Franco Modigliani. 1961. "Dividend Policy, Growth, and the Valuation of Shares." *Journal of Business* 34 (4): 411–33.

———. 1963. "Corporate Income Taxes and the Cost of Capital: A Correction." *American Economic Review* 53 (3): 433–43.

Min, David. 2011. "For the Last Time, Fannie and Freddie Didn't Cause the Housing Crisis." *The Atlantic,* December 16.

Modigliani, F., and Merton H. Miller. 1958. "The Cost of Capital, Corporation Finance and the Theory of Investment." *American Economic Review* 48 (3): 261–97.

Nenova, Tatiana. 2003. "The Value of Corporate Voting Rights and Control: A Cross-Country Analysis." *Journal of Financial Economics* 68 (3): 325–51.

———. 2012. "Takeover Laws and Financial Development." Working Paper 68845. World Bank, Washington, DC.

North, Douglas. 1990. *Institutions, Institutional Change, and Economic Performance.* Cambridge: Cambridge University Press.

North, Douglass C. 1993. "Prize Lecture: Economic Performance through Time." Nobel Foundation, December 9.

Ostrom, Elinor. 1990. *Governing the Commons: The Evolution of Institutions for Collective Action.* Cambridge: Cambridge University Press.

Pagano, Marco, and Paolo Volpin. 2001. "The Political Economy of Finance." *Oxford Review of Economic Policy* 17 (4): 502–19.

———. 2005. "The Political Economy of Corporate Governance." *American Economic Review* 95 (4): 1005–30.

Pinto, Edward. 2010. "Triggers of the Financial Crisis." Memorandum to Staff of Financial Crisis Inquiry Commission.

Qian, Jun, and Philip Strahan. 2007. "How Law and Institutions Shape Financial Contracts: The Case of Bank Loans." *Journal of Finance* 62 (6): 2803–34.

Radner, Roy. 1982. "Equilibrium Under Uncertainty." In *Handbook of Mathematical Economics*, edited by Kenneth J. Arrow and Michael D. Intriligator, vol. II, chapter 20. Amsterdam: North-Holland.

Rajan, Raghuram G. 2010. *Fault Lines: How Hidden Fractures Still Threaten the World Economy*. Princeton, NJ: Princeton University Press.

Rajan, Raghuram G., and Andrew Winton. 1995. "Covenants and Collateral as Incentives to Monitor." *Journal of Finance* 50 (4): 1113–46.

Rajan, Raghuram G., and Luigi Zingales. 2001. "Financial Systems, Industrial Structure, and Growth." *Oxford Review of Economic Policy* 17 (4): 467–82.

———. 2003. "The Great Reversals: The Politics of Financial Development in the Twentieth Century." *Journal of Financial Economics* 69 (1): 5–50.

Rauch, James E. 2001. "Business and Social Networks in International Trade." *Journal of Economic Literature* 39 (4): 1177–203.

Rodriguez-Mesa, J., 2004. "Debtor Enhancement Policies." Presentation at the Inter-American Development Bank Conference on Financial Products and Poverty Reduction in Latin America and the Caribbean, Washington, DC, September 30 to October 1.

Roe, M. 1994. *Strong Managers and Weak Owners: The Political Roots of American Corporate Finance*. Princeton, NJ: Princeton University Press.

Roe, Mark. 2000. "Political Preconditions to Separating Ownership from Corporate Control." *Stanford Law Review* 53: 539–606.

Roe, M. J., and J. Siegel. 2009. "Finance and Politics: A Review Essay Based on Kenneth Dam's Analysis of Legal Traditions in the Law-Growth Nexus." *Journal of Economic Literature* 47: 781–800.

Rose, Andrew K. 2005. "One Reason Countries Pay Their Debts: Renegotiation and International Trade." *Journal of Development Economics* 77 (1): 189–206.

Shipton, Parker. 1988. "The Kenyan Land Tenure Reform: Misunderstanding in the Public Creation of Private Property." In *Land and Society in Contemporary Africa*, edited by Richard E. Downs and Stephen P. Reyna, 91–135. Hanover, NH: University Press of New England.

Smith, Clifford W., Jr., and Jerold B. Warner. 1979. "On Financial Contracting: An Analysis of Bond Covenants." *Journal of Financial Economics* 7 (2): 117–61.

Stiglitz, Joseph E. 1969. "A Re-Examination of the Modigliani-Miller Theorem. *American Economic Review* 59 (5): 784–93.

———. 1974. "On the Irrelevance of Corporate Financial Policy." *American Economic Review* 64 (6): 851–66.

———. 1979. "Equilibrium in Product Markets with Imperfect Information." *American Economic Review* 69 (2): 339–45.

Stiglitz, Joseph E., and Andrew Weiss. 1981. "Credit Rationing in Markets with Imperfect Information." *American Economic Review* 71 (3): 393–410.

Stulz, Rene M., and Rohan Williamson. 2003. "Culture, Openness, and Finance." *Journal of Financial Economics* 70 (3): 313–49.

Thomas, Jason, and Robert Van Order. 2011. "A Closer Look at Fannie Mae and Freddie Mac: What We Know, What We Think We Know and What We Don't Know." Unpublished manuscript.

Townsend, Robert M. 1979. "Optimal Contracts and Competitive Markets with Costly State Verification." *Journal of Economic Theory* 21 (2): 265–93.

Wallison, Peter J. 2014. "Dissent from the Majority Report of the Financial Crisis Inquiry Commission." In *Dodd–Frank Wall Street Reform and Consumer Protection Act: Purpose, Critique, Implementation Status and Policy Issues*, chapter 18. Singapore: World Scientific Publishing."

Watson, Harry S. 1984. "Credit Markets and Borrower Effort." *Southern Economic Journal* 50 (3): 802–13.

Welch, K.D. 1995. "Bankruptcy, Debtors' Prison, and Collateral in Optimal Debt Contracts." Unpublished manuscript.

Whalen, Richard Christopher. 2008. "The Subprime Crisis: Cause, Effect and Consequences." *Journal of Affordable Housing and Community Development Law* 17 (3): 219–35.

Williamson, Stephen D. 1987. "Costly Monitoring, Loan Contracts, and Equilibrium Credit Rationing." *Quarterly Journal of Economics* 102 (1): 135–45.

World Bank. 2004. *World Development Report 2005: A Better Investment Climate for Everyone.* Washington, DC: World Bank.

Yunus, Muhammad. 2003. *Banker to the Poor: Micro-Lending and the Battle Against World Poverty.* New York: PublicAffairs.

CHAPTER 3

The Role of the State in Broadening Access

Introduction

This chapter discusses the role of the state in broadening access to finance. In particular, the chapter analyzes the two contrasting views that have dominated the debate regarding the appropriate role of the state in fostering access and their policy prescriptions. It also describes an emerging third view, which seems to be behind some recent innovative experiences to broaden access, like the ones described in this book.

Given the potential benefits of access-enhancing financial development, a relevant question is whether state intervention to broaden access to finance is warranted, and, if so, what form this intervention should take. Although most economists would agree that the state can play a significant role in fostering financial development and broadening access, the specific nature of its involvement has been a matter of much debate. Opinions on this issue tend to be polarized in two highly contrasting but well-established views: the *interventionist* and the *laissez-faire* views. The interventionist view argues that problems of access to finance result from widespread market failures that cannot be overcome in underdeveloped economies by market forces. Therefore, the state is called upon to have an intense, hands-on involvement in mobilizing and allocating financial resources. In contrast, the laissez-faire view contends that governments can do more harm than good by intervening directly in the allocation of financial resources and argues that government efforts should instead be deployed toward improving the enabling environment, which will help reduce agency problems and transaction costs and mitigate problems of access.

A third view seems to be emerging in the middle ground between the two dominating views, favoring restricted state interventions in nontraditional ways. This third view, which we denominate *pro-market activism*, seems to be behind some innovative programs to broaden access to finance, like the ones described in this book. This view is closer to the laissez-faire view, to the extent that it recognizes a limited role for the state in financial markets and acknowledges that institutional efficiency is the best way to achieve high-quality financial development over the long run. However, it does not exclude the possibility that some direct state interventions to broaden access might be warranted. The adequate role of the state, according to this view, is to complement private financiers, rather than replace them, by focusing on areas where the state might have some relative advantages in addressing problems of access.

The rest of this chapter begins with a discussion of the rationale for state intervention in the financial sector. We then analyze the interventionist view and its policy prescriptions, the laissez-faire view and associated policies, and the emerging pro-market activism view. The final section concludes.

The Rationale for State Intervention in the Financial Sector

As discussed in chapter 1, economic theory and empirical evidence suggest that access-enhancing financial development can yield significant welfare gains. Given these potential benefits, a relevant question, especially in countries with underdeveloped financial systems, is whether state intervention to foster financial development and broaden access is warranted, and, if so, what form this intervention should take.

Arguments for state intervention in the financial sector typically focus on (i) the need to maintain the safety and soundness of the financial system, given the large costs and externalities generated by financial crises; (ii) imperfections in financial markets arising from information asymmetries and enforcement problems; (iii) externalities generated by the provision of financial services; and (iv) the state's potential advantage in risk bearing.[1]

The first set of arguments is typically invoked to justify government supervision and regulation of financial intermediaries and markets. These arguments are in most cases driven by financial stability concerns, rather than developmental considerations.[2] Although the overall role of the state in the financial system is the subject of much debate, there is a widespread consensus on the need for regulation and supervision of financial intermediaries and markets. Debates in this regard focus on how best to design regulations and supervisory arrangements to ensure the safety and soundness of the financial system. The global financial crisis highlighted major shortcomings in regulation and supervision and in national and international arrangements for crisis management and surveillance, reopening debates in all these areas. A discussion of all these issues is beyond the scope of this book.[3] We focus our discussion on the last three sets of arguments, which are directly related to financial development and access to finance.

Information asymmetries and difficulties in monitoring borrower actions and enforcing contracts affect the functioning of financial markets and can result in the exclusion of particular groups of borrowers. A debt contract is a promise between two agents to exchange current resources for future resources. The temporal nature of the debt contract introduces uncertainty about the returns to the lender. Whether the borrower will repay in full is not known at the time the contract is written and is likely to depend both on borrower actions and on the realized state of the world. In this situation, information asymmetries and difficulties in monitoring borrower actions and enforcing contracts can generate conflicts of interest between the lender (the *principal*) and the borrower (the *agent*). As discussed in chapter 2, these principal–agent problems can lead creditors to deny financing to some borrowers with profitable projects, rationing credit below the socially optimal level.[4]

However, the fact that information and contract enforcement are costly does not, in and of itself, imply that state intervention in financial markets is warranted. First, private agents have incentives to collect information and devise mechanisms to overcome principal–agent problems. The key question in this regard is whether private intermediaries and markets can do this efficiently. Some arguments stress that information may have some public good characteristics, such as nonrivalries in consumption and nonexcludability, and as a result private financial intermediaries might underinvest in information acquisition.[5] For instance, private intermediaries may not find it optimal to screen and finance some new borrowers because, once these borrowers obtain a good credit history, they can get credit from other intermediaries who will not bear the initial screening costs and potential credit losses.[6] However, mechanisms to generate and distribute information about borrowers, such as credit rating agencies, have emerged privately, suggesting that markets can, at least partly, overcome the public good problem.

Second, even if private financiers cannot effectively address principal–agent problems and allocate resources efficiently, the direct intervention of the state in financial markets can be justified in economic terms only if the state can actually improve on private outcomes. This would require the public sector to have some advantage relative to private financial intermediaries in dealing with information and enforcement problems. As we have argued elsewhere (Anginer, de la Torre, and Ize 2014), this can be the case in the presence of collective action frictions (such as coordination failures or free-rider problems), which might prevent private parties from creating mechanisms to deal with agency problems. For instance, setting up a credit bureau requires extensive coordination among lenders—not easily achieved when individual lenders can capture monopoly rents by not sharing their private information.[7] In this situation, the state could overcome coordination problems among private intermediaries by creating incentives for information sharing or—in extreme cases—by mandating that lenders share borrower information. State intervention in this case can improve on market outcomes not because the state has an advantage in directly dealing with agency frictions but rather because it can better resolve the collective action problems that undermine the market's ability to overcome agency frictions. On the other hand, if the only sources of market failure are information asymmetries and enforcement problems (that is, if there are no collective action frictions), direct intervention in financial markets by the state would improve on market outcomes only if the state has an advantage relative to private intermediaries in collecting and processing information about borrowers, monitoring them, and enforcing contracts, something that cannot be claimed in general.[8]

Another set of arguments for state intervention in financial markets focuses on the potential externalities associated with the provision of financial services to certain groups.[9] Externalities create a divergence between private and social benefits (or private and social costs). Private financiers focus on the expected returns they receive and therefore have little incentive to finance socially profitable but financially unattractive investments. As a result, projects with positive externalities, for which social returns exceed private returns, might not get enough funding, resulting in a suboptimal resource allocation. For instance, private creditors may find it unattractive to finance infant industries or industries that are not particularly profitable but are considered of national interest, such as airlines or oil refineries. Similarly, private banks might not find it profitable to open branches in rural and isolated areas because they fail to internalize the positive externalities on growth and poverty reduction generated by the provision of financial services in those areas. In the presence of externalities, private financial intermediaries will not allocate resources to those projects with the highest social returns, and state intervention to encourage financing to projects with high social returns (and discourage financing to those with low social returns) could increase welfare.[10]

The last set of arguments for state intervention in the financial sector focuses on the state's potential advantage in risk bearing. Arrow and Lind (1970) argue that the state's intertemporal tax and borrowing capacity gives it a unique ability to spread risk across large populations, and as a result the social cost of risk tends to zero.[11] This implies that the state has an advantage relative to the (risk-averse) private sector in risk bearing because the private risk premium will be too high. This provides a rationale for state intervention in financial markets through credit guarantees or other risk-bearing mechanisms to encourage financing for risky projects (Anginer, de la Torre, and Ize 2014).[12]

Although the arguments discussed above may justify state intervention in financial markets, in most cases they do not provide clear guidance on the specific nature of this intervention. Consider, for instance, the case of externalities. If firms in sectors with large positive externalities do not receive enough credit, because private financial intermediaries fail to internalize these externalities, there are several ways the government could try to address this problem. The government could provide incentives for private banks to lend to these firms, for instance by funding loans to them at below-market rates, lowering capital requirements on these loans, or offering (subsidized) partial credit guarantees. The government could also establish lending requirements, mandating private intermediaries to lend to firms in sectors with positive externalities, or could provide credit directly to these firms through state-owned banks. Which specific intervention will have a larger effect in terms of increasing financing to excluded borrowers is likely to depend on the government's ability to provide incentives and monitor private intermediaries relative to its ability to monitor its own agents (for example, state-owned banks), its ability to deal directly with principal–agent problems, the level of financial development, and the institutional framework of the economy, among other factors.[13]

The specific nature of state intervention in financial markets to broaden access to finance has been a matter of much debate. As discussed in the introduction, opinions on this matter tend to be polarized in two highly contrasting well-established views: the *interventionist* and the *laissez-faire* views. We now turn to a more detailed characterization of each view and associated policy prescriptions.

The Interventionist View

The interventionist view can be traced back to the 1950s and dominated financial development policy thinking at least until the middle to late 1970s. This view regards problems of access to finance as resulting from widespread market failures that cannot be overcome in underdeveloped economies by leaving markets forces alone.[14] For the proponents of this view, it is less important to gain an adequate understanding of why private markets fail than to recognize that they do fail, and badly. The key contention, therefore, is that expanding access to finance beyond the narrow circle of privileged borrowers—mainly large firms and well-off households—requires the active intervention of the state. This view emphasizes the state's role in addressing market failures and calls for direct state involvement in mobilizing and allocating financial resources, with the state becoming a substitute for (rather than a complement to) private intermediaries and markets.

The interventionist view is closely related to the prevailing thinking during the 1950s and 1960s about the role of the state in the development process. The early development literature drew attention to the constraints imposed by limited capital accumulation and argued that markets tend to work inadequately in developing countries (see, for example, Rosenstein-Rodan 1943; Hirschman 1958; Gerschenkron 1962; Rostow 1962).[15] Consistent with this view, the growth strategies of most developing countries in the 1950s and 1960s focused on accelerating capital accumulation and technological adoption through direct state intervention. The role of the state was to take the "commanding heights" of the economy and allocate resources to those areas believed to be most conducive to long-term growth. This led to import substitution policies, state ownership of firms, subsidization of infant industries, central planning, and a wide range of state interventions and price controls. Confidence in state intervention was, at least partially, based on its perceived success in expanding production during World War II and its role in the reconstruction of Europe and Japan. Moreover, memories of the Great Depression made policy makers skeptical about the functioning of markets.

One of the main access-broadening instruments promoted by proponents of the interventionist view was the direct provision of financial services through state-owned financial institutions. State ownership was expected to overcome market failures in financial markets, enhancing savings mobilization, allocating funds to projects with high social returns, and making financial services affordable to larger parts of the population. This led to the nationalization of the largest, and in some cases all, commercial banks in many developing countries, as well as the creation of development finance institutions, such as agricultural banks and housing finance companies, to provide long-term financing to particular sectors. As a result, state ownership of financial institutions expanded significantly. By the 1970s, the state owned on average about 35 percent of the assets of the ten largest banks in developed countries and 66 percent in developing countries (excluding communist countries, where banks were fully state owned). As illustrated in figure 3.1, although state ownership of banks in developing countries was widespread, there were large variations across countries, with the proportion of total bank assets held by state-owned banks in 1970 ranging from about 24 percent in Thailand to 100 percent in Ecuador, India, and Tanzania. State-owned financial institutions became key policy vehicles used by governments to pursue their social and developmental agenda through the administered allocation of credit, typically on a subsidized basis, to sectors deemed by the government to be of priority.

Apart from the direct provision of credit at subsidized interest rates through state-owned financial institutions, another widespread policy instrument to increase financing to sectors perceived as being rationed out of credit markets was the imposition of directed lending requirements, which mandated that private banks allocate a certain share of their funds (or even absolute amounts) to specific sectors or regions. In Brazil, for example, commercial banks were required to allocate between 20 and 60 percent (depending on bank size) of their demand deposits to agriculture. In India, 50 percent of bank deposits had to be invested in

FIGURE 3.1 State bank ownership across selected countries, 1970 and 2010

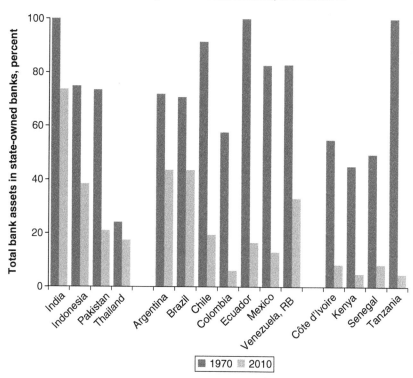

Sources: La Porta, Lopez-de-Silanes, and Shleifer 2002; World Bank 2011 Bank Regulation and Supervision Survey.
Note: This figure shows the extent of state bank ownership for selected developing countries in 1970 and 2010.
For 1970, the data displayed are the fraction of the total assets of the ten largest banks in each country that was held
by state-owned banks. Data correspond in most cases to 1970; when data for this year were not available, data for
the closest year available are reported. For 2010, data show the fraction of the total banking system's assets that was
in banks that were state-controlled (e.g., where the state owned 50 percent or more equity).

government bonds at below-market rates, and most of the remaining funds had to
be directed to priority sectors like agriculture and small firms, with only about
20 percent of bank resources being freely allocated. In Thailand, bank branches
established outside Bangkok after 1975 were subject to "local lending requirements," mandating them to lend at least 60 percent of their deposit resources
locally (Booth et al. 2001). Credit quotas on private financiers were expected to
help channel funds to priority sectors or regions that otherwise might not receive
adequate financing because of information asymmetries or the failure of private
intermediaries to internalize the positive externalities of lending to them.

Another commonly used tool was the regulation of interest rates. Governments
often established preferential rates for lending to priority sectors, which were
significantly lower than those on regular loans. In Colombia, for example,

interest rates on directed credit were, on average, about 12 percentage points lower than those on nonpreferential credit over the period 1983–87 (World Bank 1990a). In the case of Turkey, this differential averaged 36 percentage points between 1980 and 1982 (World Bank 1989). A variation of this tool was the establishment of interest rate ceilings on deposits or loans, which could apply across the board or vary by sector or type of loan. Interest rate controls were expected to result in lower financing costs and greater access to credit.[16]

Many developing countries also established refinance schemes, which allowed commercial banks to discount loans to selected sectors on attractive terms. According to the World Bank (1989), for instance, in a sample of 65 developing countries, over half had export refinance schemes. Moreover, most countries operated several schemes, typically directed to different sectors. Bangladesh, for example, had 12 refinancing schemes, and the Indonesian Central Bank operated 32 different schemes.

The extensive regulation of the banking sector resulted in a pervasive influence of the state on credit allocation in many developing countries. In Colombia, for example, directed credit accounted on average for more than 60 percent of total credit provided by commercial banks and financial corporations to industry and mining between 1984 and 1987 (World Bank 1990b). In Brazil, government credit programs represented over 70 percent of credit outstanding in 1987 (World Bank 1989). In the case of the Republic of Korea, the ratio of directed credit to total credit reached 60 percent at the end of the 1970s (Booth et al. 2001).

The general experience with state ownership of financial institutions in developing countries has not been successful. Cross-country evidence shows that greater state participation in bank ownership tends to be associated with lower levels of financial development, less credit for the private sector, lower banking sector outreach, wider intermediation spreads, greater credit concentration, slower economic growth, less fiscal discipline, and a higher incidence of financial crises (Barth, Caprio, and Levine 2001, 2004; Caprio and Honohan 2001; Caprio and Martinez Peria 2002; La Porta, Lopez-de-Silanes, and Shleifer 2002; IDB 2005; Beck, Demirgüç-Kunt, and Martinez Peria 2007; Gonzalez-Garcia and Grigoli 2013).[17] The evidence also suggests that state-owned commercial banks operating in developing countries have lower profitability than comparable private banks, as well as lower interest margins, higher overhead costs, and a higher fraction of non-performing loans (Micco, Panizza, and Yañez 2007; IDB 2005).[18]

The interpretation of the cross-country evidence described above in terms of causality is quite difficult, however. The association between state bank ownership and poor financial development and macroeconomic performance could stem either from the need for more state intervention in countries with lower financial and economic development or from a negative impact of public banks.[19] Similarly, analyzing the profitability of state-owned banks does not provide conclusive evidence regarding their performance. State-owned banks could in effect be less profitable than private banks either because they are not meant to maximize profits but rather pursue broader social objectives (hence, often investing in financially unprofitable projects with positive externalities) or because they are managed less effectively than private institutions and their lending is driven by political motivations.

Detailed within-country studies of state-owned banks point to a negative effect of state ownership of financial institutions on financial development and provide evidence of political manipulation of their lending. For instance, Cole (2009a) analyzes the effects of bank nationalization in India and finds that, although there is a large increase in credit to rural borrowers in areas with more nationalized banks, this increase does not lead to improved agricultural outcomes. Moreover, his results suggest that state bank ownership is associated with a lower quality of financial intermediation and a misallocation of resources. Using detailed loan-level data from Pakistan, Khwaja and Mian (2005) find that politically connected firms obtain larger and cheaper loans from state-owned banks (but not from private ones) and default on these loans more frequently than nonconnected borrowers. They estimate that the economy-wide costs of the resulting misallocation of resources could reach almost 2 percent of gross domestic product (GDP) every year.

Cole (2009b) also presents evidence of political manipulation of lending in India, with state-owned banks increasing agricultural lending substantially in tightly contested districts during electoral years.[20] The election-year increase in government lending is associated with higher default rates and does not have a measurable effect on agricultural output. Evidence from Brazil also shows that lending from state-owned banks is channeled to regions where incumbents aligned with the national government face stronger political competition (Carvalho 2014) and to firms that donate to the electoral campaigns of winning candidates (Claessens, Feijen, and Laeven 2008; Lazzarini et al. 2011). Political manipulation of state bank lending is not restricted to developing countries: Sapienza (2004) presents evidence that state-owned banks serve as a mechanism for political patronage in Italy.

The perceived failure of state ownership of financial institutions in developing countries contrasts with historical evidence suggesting that development banks played an important role in the rapid industrialization of continental Europe and Japan (Gershenkron 1952; Cameron 1953, 1961).[21] It is also worth noting that, although the general experience with state ownership of financial institutions in developing countries has not been successful, these institutions are highly heterogeneous, both across and within countries. Detailed case studies highlight some success stories, such as the Village Bank system of Bank Rakyat in Indonesia (Yaron, Benjamin, and Charitonenko 1998) and the Bank for Agriculture and Agricultural Cooperatives in Thailand (Townsend and Yaron 2001).[22]

The generally negative experience with state-owned financial institutions in developing countries can be ascribed, to a large extent, to incentive and governance problems. These institutions usually lack disciplining devices, such as active profit-maximizing shareholders, and in many cases face a soft budget constraint. The large pockets of the government mean that losses can be easily made up. Because many development finance institutions are financed through budgetary transfers, rather than through deposits, they tend to have a weak sense of the actual cost of capital. Moreover, because state-owned financial institutions are supposed to maximize broader social objectives, credit losses can always be blamed on the need to finance financially unprofitable projects with positive externalities, rather than on bad loan origination. These incentive and governance problems have led to such recurrent problems as wasteful administrative expenditures, overstaffing, political manipulation of lending, plain corruption, and capture by powerful special interests. As a result, public financial institutions have frequently failed to reach their target clientele, with larger and more influential borrowers usually being favored. For instance, over 60 percent of the loans made by the rural finance credit program in Brazil were allocated to the largest 2 percent of borrowers in the program, whereas the smallest 75 percent of borrowers received only 6 percent of loans (World Bank 2005a).

In many cases, public banks have also been characterized by poor loan origination and even poorer loan collection, thereby fostering a nonpayment culture. The World Bank (1989), for example, reports that a study of 18 development finance institutions in developing countries found that on average 50 percent of their loans were in arrears. Low repayment rates, coupled with interest rate subsidies and high administrative expenses, resulted in large financial losses for state-owned financial institutions and the need for recurrent recapitalizations. In 2001, the Brazilian government absorbed the nonperforming loan portfolios of two public banks (Banco do Brasil and Caixa Economica Federal) at a net cost of about 6 percent of GDP (Micco and Panizza 2005). In Mexico, the government had to recapitalize Banrural, a development bank that provides financing to the rural sector, with about US$1.1 billion in 1999, even after having significantly downscaled its operations in previous years (Brizzi 2001).[23]

The experience with directed lending programs has also been relatively unsuccessful in most developing countries (World Bank 1989, 2005a). Although some East Asian economies—like Japan, Korea, and Taiwan, China—achieved some success with directed lending to manufacturing and export-oriented sectors, in most developing countries the results have been poor.[24] Directed credit programs have often failed to reach their intended beneficiaries, usually favoring larger and more influential borrowers within priority sectors.[25] Lenders have misclassified loans to provide credit to other sectors, and borrowers have diverted credit to other uses. Directed credit programs have often been used not to correct market failures but to provide funds to politically connected sectors and firms. Once established, directed credit programs have created a strong constituency of beneficiaries, making it very difficult for governments to downscale or eliminate these programs, regardless of how inefficient or costly they were. The cost of subsidies on directed credit programs has often been substantial. In Brazil, for example, this cost was estimated at between 7 and 8 percent of GDP in 1987. In Korea, the subsidy provided by directed credit was approximately 1 percent of GDP during the 1980s (Booth et al. 2001). Directed lending requirements in many cases left little power or responsibility for credit allocation to private banks, resulting in low investments in credit assessment and monitoring. Also, extensive refinance schemes at low interest rates reduced the incentives for financial institutions to mobilize resources on their own, leading to a lower level of financial intermediation.

Direct state intervention in the operation of financial markets—through directed lending programs, interest rate controls, entry restrictions, and high reserve requirements—has been found to have significant costs in terms of economic efficiency and growth and to stifle, rather than promote, financial development. These policies were initially challenged by Goldsmith (1969) and later by Shaw (1973) and McKinnon (1973), who coined the term "financial repression" to describe them. Goldsmith (1969) argues that the main impact of financial repression is to reduce the marginal productivity of capital. Because interest rate controls keep rates below their equilibrium level, high-quality projects with higher returns do not get financed. McKinnon (1973) and Shaw (1973) focus on two additional channels. First, financial repression reduces the efficiency of the banking sector in allocating savings because bankers do not ration credit according to price criteria. Second, by maintaining interest rates below their market equilibrium, financial repression can reduce the savings level. These two channels have a negative impact on growth because too little will be saved and those savings will not be allocated to the projects with the highest returns.[26] Financial development is also likely to suffer under these conditions because the low return on financial assets encourages savers to keep their savings outside the financial system.

The Laissez-Faire View

Mostly as a reaction to the aforementioned problems of state-owned banks and direct state intervention in the financial sector, a second, entirely opposite view has gained ground over the years: the laissez-faire view. This view also stems from an increasing awareness of the role of institutions in financial development. The laissez-faire view contends that, because of incentive issues, bureaucrats will never be good bankers and that governments can do more harm than good by intervening directly in credit allocation and pricing. According to this view, market failures in the financial sector may exist but are not as pervasive as assumed by proponents of the interventionist view, and private parties by themselves, given well-defined property rights and good contractual institutions, can address most of these problems. Additionally, the costs of government failures are likely to exceed those of market failures, rendering direct interventions at best ineffective and, in many cases, counterproductive. Therefore, this view recommends that governments exit from bank ownership and lift restrictions on the allocation of credit and the determination of interest rates. Instead, the argument goes, government-friendly efforts should be deployed toward improving the enabling environment—for example, by providing a stable macroeconomic framework, enhancing creditor and shareholder rights and their enforceability, upgrading prudential regulation, modernizing accounting practices, and promoting the expansion of reliable debtor information systems (Caprio and Honohan 2001; Rajan and Zingales 2001; Klapper and Zaidi 2005; World Bank 2005a, 2013, 2015).

The laissez-faire view is consistent with the general shift in thinking about the role of the state in the development process in recent decades. The experiences of developing countries in the 1970s and 1980s showed that widespread state intervention in the economy—through trade restrictions, state ownership of firms, financial repression, price controls, and foreign exchange rationing—resulted in the waste of large resources and impeded, rather than promoted, economic growth. Confidence in the ability of government to foster economic development diminished dramatically, as growing evidence showed that government failure was widespread in developing countries and in many cases outweighed market failure (see, for example, Krueger and Tuncer 1982; World Bank 1983; Srinivasan 1985; and Krueger 1990).[27] This led economists and policy makers to conclude that constraining the role of the state in the economy and eliminating the distortions associated with protectionism, subsidies, and state ownership were essential to fostering growth.[28] Much of this vision was reflected in the so-called Washington Consensus and guided most of the reform programs during the 1990s.[29] Governments focused on creating a stable macroeconomic environment by reducing fiscal deficits and improving monetary policies. Countries privatized state-owned enterprises, deregulated domestic industries, eliminated quantitative restrictions and licensing requirements, and dismantled agricultural marketing boards and other state monopolies. Many countries also reduced tariffs and other restrictions on imports and liberalized regulations on foreign investment. Starting in the late 1990s, the focus of the reforms turned away from macroeconomic stabilization and liberalization and shifted toward improving the institutional environment (World Bank 1999, 2002), consistent with the growing empirical evidence on the impact of institutions on economic development.[30]

The failure of financial repression policies led many countries to liberalize their financial systems, reducing direct state involvement in the allocation and pricing of credit. Financial liberalization was carried out on both the domestic and the external fronts. Liberalization policies on the domestic front included the elimination or downscaling of directed lending programs, the reduction of reserve requirements, and the deregulation of interest rates. On the external front, many countries lifted restrictions on foreign borrowing by financial institutions and corporations and dismantled controls on foreign exchange and capital transactions. Despite stops, gaps, and some reversals, the process of financial liberalization advanced throughout much of the world in recent decades.[31]

Countries in all income groups have liberalized their financial systems, although developed countries were among the first to start this process and have remained more liberalized than lower-income economies (figure 3.2). In developing countries, the pace and timing of financial liberalization have differed across regions. In Latin America, Argentina, Chile, and Uruguay liberalized their financial systems in the late 1970s but reversed these reforms in the aftermath of the 1982 debt crisis, and financial systems remained repressed during most of the 1980s. Latin American countries then carried out substantial financial liberalizations in the late 1980s and early 1990s. In the case of East Asia, the liberalization process was more gradual. A number of countries started slowly rationalizing their directed credit programs and liberalizing their interest rates during the 1980s, and the process in many cases stretched for over a decade.

The financial liberalization process was accompanied by a significant privatization of state-owned banks, driven by fiscal considerations and the changing view about the role of the state in the economy.[32] From 1985 to 2000 more than 50 countries carried out bank privatizations, totaling 270 transactions and raising over US$119 billion (Boehmer, Nash, and Netter 2005). Although the process started in higher-income countries, developing countries quickly followed suit. Figure 3.3 illustrates the bank privatization process in developing countries and shows the significant differences in the timing and pace of privatization across regions. Latin American countries were among the first to embark on large-scale bank privatization programs in the early 1990s. The worldwide bank privatization trend intensified in the second half of the 1990s, when transition countries started privatizing financial institutions. In the case of Asian countries, the bank privatization process started later, but significantly intensified from 2005 onward, driven mostly by the privatization of some Chinese state-owned financial institutions. The privatization wave has resulted in a significant reduction in state bank ownership, as illustrated in figure 3.1. However, the presence of the public sector in the banking systems of developing countries remains quite significant. In 2010, the share of the total banking system assets held by state-owned banks averaged about 11 percent across high-income countries, compared to an average of 17 percent for low- and

FIGURE 3.2 Evolution of financial liberalization, selected regions

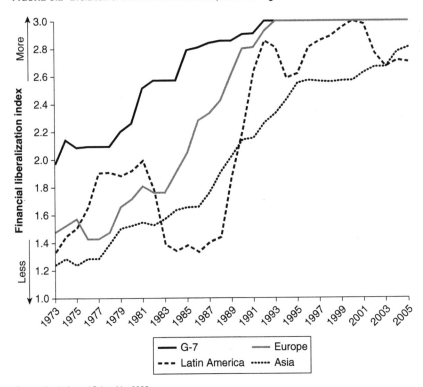

Source: Kaminsky and Schmukler 2008.
Note: This figure shows the extent of financial liberalization across regions. The liberalization index is calculated as the simple average of three indices (liberalization of the capital account, domestic financial sector, and stock market) that range between 1 and 3, where 1 means no liberalization and 3 means full liberalization. These data are then aggregated as the simple average between countries of each region. G-7 is the average of Canada, France, Germany, Italy, Japan, the United Kingdom, and the United States. Latin America is the average of Argentina, Brazil, Chile, Colombia, Mexico, Peru, and República Bolivariana de Venezuela. Asia is the average of Hong Kong, China; Indonesia; the Republic of Korea; Malaysia; the Philippines; Taiwan, China; and Thailand. Europe is the average of Denmark, Finland, Ireland, Norway, Portugal, Spain, and Sweden. Figures correspond to annual averages calculated from monthly data.

middle-income countries. Furthermore, in 20 percent of the 76 developing countries for which information is available, the state controls banks accounting for a third of total banking system assets or more, compared to just three high-income countries where this is the case.

The laissez-faire view led to a barrage of reforms aimed at creating the proper institutions and infrastructure for financial markets to flourish. Governments tried to mitigate principal–agent problems in credit markets by reforming bankruptcy laws and enacting new legislation regarding creditor rights. Several countries introduced simplified collateral enforcement procedures, allowing secured

FIGURE 3.3 Cumulative amount raised through bank privatization in developing countries

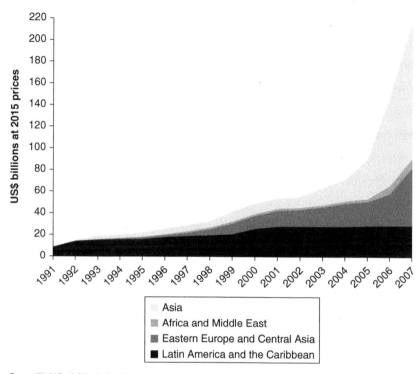

Source: World Bank Privatization Database.
Note: This figure shows the cumulative amount raised through the privatization of state-owned financial institutions in developing countries in billion U.S. dollars at 2015 prices.

creditors to repossess collateral through out-of-court mechanisms. In some countries, governments also modified collateral laws to broaden the types of assets that can be legally pledged as collateral. These reforms were complemented in many cases by the creation of registries for moveable property, which make it easier for creditors to track the ownership and pledging of assets.[33]

Several countries also tried to improve information sharing among lenders by fostering the development of private credit bureaus.[34] Credit bureaus make borrowers' loan repayment history available to different lenders, facilitating information exchange and reducing screening costs. Credit bureaus also increase incentives for repayment; borrowers know that their reputations will be shared among different creditors.[35] Governments tried to create a supportive environment for private credit bureaus by enacting data protection and credit reporting laws that facilitate information sharing. This has led to a significant expansion of private credit bureaus in recent decades. As illustrated in figure 3.4, the number of developing countries with an active private credit bureau increased from only 8 in 1985 to 23 in 2000, and 47 in 2012. Private credit bureaus covered about 19 percent of the adult population of low- and middle-income countries in 2015, up from less than 6 percent in 2004. In many cases, governments also established public credit registries.[36] As shown in figure 3.4, 36 developing countries established a public credit registry between 1990 and 2012.

Enticed by the potential benefits, governments also implemented several reforms aimed at fostering securities market development.[37] In particular, governments created domestic securities and exchange commissions, developed the regulatory and supervisory framework, and took important strides

FIGURE 3.4 Evolution of credit-reporting institutions in developing countries

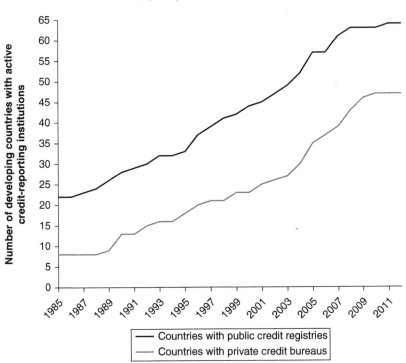

Sources: Djankov, McLiesh, and Shleifer 2007; World Bank 2013 Credit Reporting Database.
Note: This figure shows the evolution of the number of developing countries with different credit-reporting institutions. Public credit registries are databases managed by a government agency, usually the central bank or the superintendent of banks, which collect information on the standing of borrowers in the financial system and make it available to financial intermediaries. A private credit bureau is a private firm or nonprofit organization that provides credit information on consumers and/or firms for a variety of uses. Data only include countries for which we have information on the year when credit-reporting institutions became active.

toward establishing and improving the basic infrastructure for securities market operations. Moreover, many countries tried to improve corporate governance practices by introducing new standards in a number of different areas, including voting rights, tender procedures, and the structure of the board of directors.[38] Some countries also improved accounting and disclosure standards and enacted new insider trading regulations.[39]

Despite the intense reform effort, in most developing countries the observed outcomes in terms of financial development and access to finance have failed to match the (high) initial expectations of reform. Although financial systems in many developing countries have deepened over the past decades, with financial markets becoming more complete and bond and equity markets gaining ground compared to the banking sector, in most cases there has been little convergence toward the levels of financial development observed in more developed countries (World Bank 2005b; Dorrucci, Meyer-Cirkel, and Santabarbara 2009; de la Torre, Ize, and Schmukler 2012; Allen et al. 2014). Several countries experienced a strong growth in deposit volumes during the 1990s, but this growth failed to translate into an increase of similar magnitude in credit for the private sector (Hanson 2003). And, in many of those countries where credit for the private sector did expand, a large fraction of this increase was accounted for by consumer credit (including credit card lending), with corporate financing lagging behind (BIS 2005; IMF 2006).[40] Similarly, although domestic securities markets in many emerging economies have expanded in recent decades, they remain relatively small and illiquid in most cases, and their performance in terms of broadening access to finance to many corporations has been disappointing (de la Torre and Schmukler 2004; Didier, Levine, and Schmukler 2015). Moreover, access to long-term financial instruments remains quite limited in most developing countries (World Bank 2015).

Despite a general perception that the reforms have had little success, academic research suggests that reforms did in fact have a positive impact on financial development and macroeconomic outcomes. For instance, the empirical evidence suggests that domestic financial sector reforms—including the liberalization of interest rate controls, the elimination or downscaling of directed lending programs, and reductions in state ownership of banks— have led to a deepening of domestic financial markets, lower credit constraints (especially for small and medium enterprises, SMEs), and a more efficient allocation of capital across firms and industries (see, for example, Jaramillo, Schiantarelli, and Weiss 1996; Galindo, Micco, and Ordoñez 2002; Laeven 2003; Galindo, Schiantarelli, and Weiss 2007; Abiad, Oomes, and Ueda 2008; Tressel 2008; and Tressel and Detragiache 2008). Christiansen, Schindler, and Tressel (2013) find that domestic financial sector liberalization has significant growth effects for middle-income countries, particular by increasing productivity growth.[41] Regarding the impact of other reforms, Djankov, McLiesh, and Shleifer (2007), for instance, find that improvements in creditor rights and the introduction of information-sharing systems are associated with increases in credit to the private sector. Similarly, Martinez Peria and Singh (2014) find that, after the introduction of a credit bureau, firm access to finance improves, interest rates decrease, and loan maturities increase. De la Torre, Gozzi, and Schmukler (2007) find that securities markets reforms tend to be followed by significant increases in stock market capitalization, trading, and capital-raising activity.[42]

The contrast between the empirical evidence and the general perception that reforms were ineffective might be explained by excessively high expectations at the beginning of the reform process.[43] The gap between expectations and outcomes can also be, at least partly, ascribed to a combination of insufficient reform implementation and impatience.[44] In effect, despite what many claim, key reforms were in some cases not even initiated, whereas other reforms were often implemented incompletely or inconsistently. In many cases, laws were approved but not duly implemented or adequately enforced. Policy makers have been too impatient, often expecting results to materialize sooner than warranted. Although the expectation of a rapid payoff might be justified with respect to some first-generation reforms, more complex second-generation reforms have long gestation periods.[45]

Moreover, the positive view on the effects of domestic financial sector reforms is somewhat clouded by the large increase in financial fragility experienced by developing countries in the 1980s and 1990s, which was linked in many cases to poorly designed or sequenced financial liberalization (Caprio and Summers 1993; Stiglitz 1994).[46] Indeed, financial liberalization has been found to lead to credit expansions, which, in the absence of adequate supervisory and regulatory frameworks, can fuel financial instability (Demirgüç-Kunt and Detragiache 1999, 2005; Kaminsky and Reinhart 1999; Mendoza and Terrones 2008, 2014). This suggests that the benefits of financial liberalization may need to be weighed against its potential costs in terms of financial fragility. Regardless of its underlying causes, the general perception of a lack of results from the reform process has led to reform fatigue and increasing pressures for governments to take on a more active role.

The global financial crisis has brought to the forefront the discussion on the role of the state in the financial sector. The crisis has highlighted significant failures in private contracting in financial markets, reigniting the debate about the costs and benefits of financial liberalization and giving greater credence to the idea that active state involvement in the financial sector can be beneficial. Direct state intervention in financial markets has expanded significantly since the crisis as governments around the world have taken over troubled financial institutions and pursued a variety of strategies to ramp up financing to the private sector (World Bank 2013). Several countries have relied on state-owned banks to compensate for the slowdown in credit provision by private banks.[47] For instance, in Brazil state-owned banks played a countercyclical role during the crisis, significantly expanding their lending to the private sector and acquiring ownership stakes and loan portfolios from private financial institutions that faced liquidity problems (Bonomo, Brito, and Martins 2015; Coleman and Feler 2015). In Mexico, development banks increased lending to private firms and established temporary guarantee programs to help firms roll over short-term debt and commercial paper (Sidaoui, Ramos-Francia, and Cuadra 2011). In China, state-owned banks played a key role in the stimulus package launched by the government, rapidly expanding credit during the crisis (IMF 2011). Development banks in several European countries—including Austria, Bulgaria, Germany, Italy, Lithuania, and Spain—also played a countercyclical role during the crisis, increasing their lending, extending their scope to reach new sectors and groups of borrowers, and taking on new activities (Wruuck 2015).

Several countries (including Canada, Chile, Finland, France, Germany, Greece, Japan, Korea, Malaysia, the Netherlands, and the United States) relied heavily on public credit guarantee schemes to compensate for the reduction in private bank lending.[48] In many countries, existing guarantee programs were ramped up, with increases in the total amount of funds available, the number of eligible firms, the percentage of the loan guaranteed, or the size of the guaranteed loans. In other countries, such as Ireland and the United Kingdom, new programs were introduced. The countercyclical use of credit guarantee schemes during the financial crisis led to a significant increase in their scale and scope. For instance, data for credit guarantee schemes in 18 European countries with available information show that the total value of outstanding guarantees grew by almost 38 percent between 2008 and 2010 (from about €56.1 billion to €77.1 billion), with the number of SMEs benefiting from these guarantees increasing from €1.5 million to more than €2.7 million over the same period (AECM 2013). Credit guarantee schemes in Latin America experienced an even larger expansion in terms of volume, with the total value of outstanding guarantees more than doubling between 2008 and 2010, from US$8.8 billion to US$19.3 billion (REGAR 2012).[49]

Although the crisis has highlighted many of the fault lines in the laissez-faire view, reigniting the debate on the need for direct state intervention in financial markets, it is fair to say that the laissez-faire view still seems to be the predominant view on the role of the state in financial development, at least among those in the economics profession (World Bank 2013, 2015). Despite this widespread support, the policy prescriptions associated with the laissez-faire view are not free of problems. Improving the enabling environment is easier said than done. Even if we knew exactly what needed to be done, and in what sequence, there is no denying that actual reform implementation would face glitches and would likely be affected by the two-steps-forward-one-step-back phenomenon. But because there is no simple ex ante formula to achieve access-enhancing financial development, the reality is that we do not know with precision all that needs to be done. Financial development is not amenable to one-size-fits-all or a "template" approach, not least because of its evolutionary, path-dependent nature, as discussed in chapter 2. A good enabling environment is in effect the historical result of a complicated and rather delicate combination of mutually reinforcing institutional innovations and market dynamics, which cannot be transplanted at will from one country to another. Hence, financial reforms that are partial, inadequately complemented, or wrongly sequenced can lead to dysfunctional yet self-reinforcing institutional hybrids, which might be subsequently hard to dislodge.

Given these characteristics of the institutional reform process, considerable time might elapse before most emerging economies can develop an adequate enabling environment and see significant results in terms of broader access to credit. Even innovative solutions like microfinance that, at least partly, help overcome institutional deficiencies are unlikely to broaden access significantly in the short term.[50] It seems rather naive to expect governments to remain completely disengaged from any direct intervention geared at broadening access during the long transition to a developed financial system. For one, governments are likely to face increasing political pressures to do something. As mentioned above, there is a growing disillusionment with the reform process, as reforms have failed to meet the (possibly excessive) initial expectations, and the global financial crisis has raised significant questions about the benefits of financial liberalization. Whether or not this disillusionment is warranted, reform fatigue is in any case likely to boost pressures for state intervention. Second, a quick state withdrawal from financial markets may not be feasible in many countries because the state is still actively involved in the financial system. This involvement has actually increased since the global financial crisis. Existing state-owned financial institutions have incentives to continue intervening in financial markets; in many cases closing these institutions or significantly downscaling their operations might not be politically feasible or even desirable, given existing links among markets and institutional arrangements. Finally, one could reasonably argue that certain direct state interventions can help smooth the transition toward a developed financial system or even speed it up, without distracting from the long-run policy objective of institutional reform.

If one thinks in terms of nonconflicting long- and short-run policy objectives, it is possible to rationalize some recent experiences of state intervention like the ones described in this book into a third, middle-ground view, which we denominate pro-market activism. We now turn to the characterization of this view.

The Pro-Market Activism View

The pro-market activism view is an emerging view that seems to be behind a series of recent state interventions to broaden access to finance. Given that this view is relatively recent and not yet fully articulated, it is difficult to fully characterize it. It might be easier to understand it by contrasting it with the two well-established views described above. In contrast to the interventionist view, the pro-market activism view does not assume that market failures are widespread and that direct state involvement in mobilizing and allocating financial resources is warranted. Much to the contrary, this view argues that markets can and do broaden access to finance and that therefore the state should focus on promoting the development of deep and efficient financial markets. The appropriate role of the state, according to this view, is to complement private financiers by focusing on areas where the state might have some relative advantages, rather than to replace them.

This view recognizes that direct state intervention might be warranted under some conditions and in some cases, but argues that careful analyses should precede any intervention. Interventions should be directed at addressing the underlying causes of problems of access, not at increasing the use of financial services per se, and can only be justified if they can do this in a cost-effective manner. According to the pro-market activism view, state interventions should be designed to complement (rather than displace) market-based financial contracting and facilitate the development of financial markets through the adequate choice of instruments (for example, subsidies, loans, guarantees) and institutions (for example, private financial intermediaries, state-owned banks). This view is well aware of the risks of direct state involvement in the allocation and pricing of credit and therefore tends to favor a wide range of instruments beyond lending when designing interventions.

In a sense, the pro-market activism view is closer to the laissez-faire view because it contends that governments' main focus should be to forge ahead with the task of improving the enabling environment for financial markets. However, in contrast with that view, it recognizes that there might be room for well-designed, restricted state interventions to address specific problems. Although the laissez-faire view rightfully emphasizes that the public sector in most cases has little or no advantage relative to private financial intermediaries in addressing principal–agent problems and allocating credit, it tends to understate the relevance of market failures and coordination problems that might prevent the private sector from addressing problems of access. The pro-market activism view contends, instead, that there is a role for government in overcoming coordination failures and helping private financiers develop solutions to address the underlying causes of problems of access. It contends also that, under some circumstances, it may also be warranted for the government to take on credit risk, preferably sharing it with the private sector and ensuring that government risk-taking activities, again, complement (rather than distort) market activity. According to this view, it seems unrealistic and unwarranted in good logic for governments to focus solely on the enabling environment and to remain completely disengaged from any direct intervention to broaden access during the long transition to a developed financial system.

Thus, the main message of pro-market activism is that there is indeed a market-friendly role for the visible hand of the state to promote access in the short run while the fruits of ongoing institutional reform are still unripe. The important qualifier is, however, that the state needs to be highly selective in its interventions, always trying to ensure that they work with the market, never against it. There must be mechanisms in place to prevent political capture. Pro-market activism, moreover, favors a policy strategy that explicitly creates room for a process of discovery and learning by doing. Interventions should be designed to complement institutional reform efforts and can actually be useful in providing authorities firsthand understanding of what legislation or enforcement mechanisms are missing for certain innovations to take off. For pro-market activism, the ultimate goal is to foster the broadening of access in ways that simultaneously create financial markets where they are missing and enhance the functioning of existing ones.

To a large extent, the evolution of policy thinking about the role of the state in broadening access to finance over the last decades mirrors the evolution of thinking about economic development policies more broadly. From this perspective, the pro-market activism view can be seen as part of an emerging view on development policies, based on the experience of recent decades. Although still far from providing completely coherent, fully articulated thinking, this view tends to argue that a good enabling environment, although a necessary condition for sustainable long-term growth, is not enough to initiate the development process and that selective state interventions to address specific market failures and help jump-start economic growth are required.[51] For instance, the World Bank (2004) argues that reviewing the experience of the 1990s "confirms the importance for growth of fundamental principles: macro-stability, market forces in the allocation of resources, and openness" but also shows that "selective government interventions can contribute to growth when they address market failures, are carried out effectively, and are subject to institutional checks." This view is more nuanced than previous development views in its take on the role of government in the development process, recognizing that the market is the basic mechanism for resource allocation but that governments can play a significant role in addressing coordination failures, knowledge spillovers, and possibly also high risk aversion, all of which can constrain the birth and expansion of new (higher-productivity) sectors.[52]

This emerging view calls for policy diversity, selective and modest reforms, and experimentation. In fact, its salient characteristic may be recognition of the need to avoid one-size-fits-all strategies and to follow a more targeted approach, taking into account country specificities.[53] The lack of clear guidelines regarding what works in igniting growth calls for more nuanced policy prescriptions and an experimentalist approach to development policies, based on relatively narrow targeted policy interventions that create room for a process of trial and error to identify what works and what does not in a particular institutional setting.[54] Although a more nuanced approach to development policies is warranted, it is worth pointing out that this view runs the risk of degenerating into an "anything-goes" approach. A major challenge for this view is translating its recommendations into specific operational guidelines for promoting development, without degenerating into a rigid blueprint. Moreover, a key question among policy makers is whether direct state interventions to broaden access can actually be designed in such a way as to avoid the government failures that have accompanied many previous attempts at intervention.

Conclusions

This chapter discusses the two contrasting views that have dominated the debate regarding the adequate role of the state in broadening access to finance. The interventionist view argues that active, direct state involvement in mobilizing and allocating financial resources, including state ownership of banks, is needed to broaden access to finance as private markets fail to expand access. In contrast, the laissez-faire view contends that governments can do more harm than good by intervening directly in the financial system and argues that government efforts should focus instead on improving the enabling environment, which will help reduce agency problems and transaction costs and mitigate problems of access.

Some recent initiatives to broaden access to finance can be rationalized by an emerging middle-ground view, which we denominate pro-market activism. In a sense, this view is closer to the laissez-faire view, to the extent that it recognizes a limited role for government in financial markets and acknowledges that institutional efficiency is the best way to achieve healthy financial development over the long haul. However, it contends that there might be room for well-designed, restricted state interventions to address specific problems and help private financiers develop solutions to address the underlying causes of problems of access.

The main message of pro-market activism is that there is a role for the visible hand of the government in promoting access in the short run, while the fruits of ongoing institutional reform are still unripe. However, the government must be highly selective in its interventions, always trying to ensure that they promote the development of deep domestic financial markets, rather than replace them. Interventions should be directed at addressing the underlying causes of problems of access, not at increasing the use of financial services per se, and can only be justified if they can do this in a cost-effective manner.

The pro-market activism approach to financial development, if warranted, must understand the idiosyncrasies of institutional arrangements and market conditions in each country, and the specific ways in which access problems arise in that context, not only because well-designed and efficient institutions are the first-best solutions but also because guaranteeing that eventual interventions do not conflict with the long-run objective of institutional reform will crucially hinge on the quality and extent of such understanding.

For all its potential appeal, pro-market activism raises many questions. Are there actually cases where state interventions do not displace financial market activity, but rather crowd it in? Even if there is strong economic rationale for interventions, how can we make sure that potential costs of government failure do not exceed the costs of market failures? In other words, can direct interventions indeed be designed so as to avoid the policy failures that have accompanied many previous attempts at intervention and to ensure that at least no harm is done? If a given state intervention is efficient, in the sense that it leads to greater, mutually beneficial financial contracting without any (explicit or hidden) subsidies, why don't private financial intermediaries take the initiative? Is direct state intervention actually necessary or, given the right incentives, would private financial intermediaries take the initiative?

Although it is very difficult to provide definite answers to these questions, we try to address them in the rest of this book by analyzing a number of recent initiatives to broaden access to finance in Latin America, which seem to be driven by the pro-market activism view. It is necessary to stress that we do not attempt to make a comprehensive assessment of these interventions or to claim that they have been successful. Rather, we use them to illustrate how pro-market activism has worked in practice and to understand to what extent actual experiences have conformed to the stylized description of this view presented in this chapter. These experiences also highlight potential problems in the design and implementation of these types of interventions. This analysis can provide a better understanding of whether the pro-market activism view can actually constitute a viable alternative to broaden access to finance in developing countries.

Notes

1. See Stiglitz (1994) for a discussion of the main arguments for state intervention in the financial sector. Besley (1994) presents a critical review of these arguments, with a focus on rural credit markets. See also de la Torre, Ize, and Schmukler (2012) for a discussion of these issues.

2. Financial stability may contribute to financial development because a more stable financial system may increase investor confidence, leading to more resources being channeled through financial intermediaries.

3. See Claessens and Kodres (2014) for an overview of the regulatory responses to the global financial crisis.

4. Credit rationing is defined as a situation where some borrowers' demand for credit is turned down, even though these borrowers would be willing to pay the required lending rate and to comply with all the required nonprice elements of the loan contract, such as collateral requirements.

5. A good is nonrival in consumption if the consumption of the good by one individual does not detract from that of another individual. Nonexcludability means that it is very costly to exclude anyone from enjoying the good.

6. Additionally, because the likelihood of default increases with the amount borrowed, further borrowing by the debtor may have a negative impact on the first creditor (Arnott and Stiglitz 1991).

7. See World Bank (2013) for a discussion of how coordination problems and monopoly rents may affect the emergence of credit bureaus. Bruhn, Farazi, and Kanz (2013) find that private credit bureaus are less likely to emerge in countries with highly concentrated banking systems because large banks stand to lose more monopoly rents from sharing their extensive borrower information with smaller players.

8. Some authors argue that the state could have an advantage in dealing with information asymmetries and contract enforcement problems because government agencies might be able to cross-check information with official records and compel the disclosure of information that is not available to private parties (Stiglitz 1994); but whether this is actually true in practice is debatable (Besley 1994).

9. An externality is defined as a situation where the well-being of a consumer or the production possibilities of a firm are directly affected by the actions of another agent in the economy.

10. The fact that a given sector generates positive externalities does not necessarily imply that state intervention to encourage financing to this sector is warranted. There are many other ways in which the state could foster the development of sectors with positive externalities, such as tax credits and direct subsidies, and access to credit might not be the binding constraint preventing their development.

11. There is significant debate in the literature regarding the validity of the Arrow-Lind result that the social cost of risk tends to zero as the state spreads the risk associated with investment projects among a large population. Foldes and Rees (1977) argue that, under a more realistic formulation of fiscal policy, this result holds only under very stringent assumptions, and therefore the practical circumstances in which the Arrow-Lind conclusions apply are extremely restricted. Gardner (1979) shows that the Arrow-Lind results hold only if the investment risk is arbitrarily small. From a different perspective, Klein (1996) argues that, if the state's advantage did not lie purely in its coercive taxation powers (that is, its capacity to oblige taxpayers to bear risk through the tax system), then markets would be able to spread risk just as efficiently.

12. Anginer, de la Torre, and Ize (2014) argue that uninternalized externalities or principal-agent problems alone do not justify risk taking by the government in the form of loans or credit guarantees. For the latter to be market-friendly interventions, the comparative advantage of the government in risk spreading could be deployed to deal with high risk aversion, especially in underdeveloped markets where the opportunities for risk dispersion are limited. The loans or credit guarantees could be priced to cover expected losses in an actuarially fair manner. However, an appropriate monitoring framework would need to be in place to neutralize the moral hazard associated with government-issued loans or credit guarantees, which otherwise would unduly erode market discipline.

13. The literature on contracting discusses the conditions under which state ownership could be preferable to contracting and regulation of private firms. See Shleifer (1998) for a review of this literature and IDB (2005) for a discussion of how these arguments apply to banking.

14. Gerschenkron (1962) was one of the first authors to argue that the private sector alone is not able to overcome problems of access to finance in a weak institutional environment.

15. The arguments made by these early authors have been formalized in several theoretical papers (see, for example, Murphy, Shleifer, and Vishny 1989; and Hoff and Stiglitz 2001).

16. Broadening access to credit was not the only reason for the imposition of interest rate controls and directed lending requirements. Strict regulation of the banking system was also expected to give monetary authorities better control over the money supply and provide the government with easily accessible resources to finance public expenditures. See Roubini and Sala-i-Martin (1992) for further discussion of these issues.

17. The IDB (2005) revises the empirical evidence on the impact of state-owned banks and finds that, although the result that these banks have a negative impact is not as strong as previous research suggests, there is no indication that state ownership has a positive effect. It concludes that public banks, at best, do not play much of a role in financial development. See Andrianova, Demetriades, and Shortland (2010) and Korner and Schnable (2011) for further cross-country analyses of the effects of state bank ownership on financial development and macroeconomic outcomes.

18. In contrast with the observed lower profitability and efficiency of state-owned commercial banks in developing countries, the empirical evidence suggests that in developed countries, there are no significant differences in performance between public and private banks (see, for example, Altunbas, Evans, and Molyneux 2001; and Micco, Panizza, and Yañez 2007).

19. Galindo and Micco (2004) try to address the problem of causality by analyzing within-country differences in industry growth. They find that the development of private financial intermediaries is associated with a higher growth rate of industries that rely more on external finance and have less collateral, whereas public bank ownership has no effect on the growth of these industries.

20. Dinç (2005) shows that increased lending by state-owned banks during election years is not specific to India, but is also observed in a sample of 19 emerging markets (but not in industrial countries). Micco, Panizza, and Yañez (2007) show that these results hold for a much larger sample of developing countries and that the increased lending by state-owned banks during election years is associated with a decrease in their interest rate margins and profitability.

21. Armendáriz de Aghion (1999) compares the successful development banking experience of Credit Nationale in France with the relatively unsuccessful experience of Nacional Financiera in Mexico before the 1990s. She argues that the requirement to engage in cofinancing arrangements with private financial intermediaries in the case of Credite Nationale and the type of state involvement (subsidized credit and loan guarantees in the case of France, direct ownership in Mexico) are among the factors that explain the contrasting results.

22. Following Yaron (1992), these papers use a comprehensive framework to evaluate the performance of development banks and their lending programs, mainly in terms of the outreach to their targeted clientele and the degree to which their operations are dependent on subsidies.

23. Banrural was liquidated in 2003, at an estimated fiscal cost of about US$3.5 billion, and was replaced by a new rural finance entity, Financiera Rural. The total cost of state intervention in the rural financial system in Mexico, mostly through different development banks, during the 1983–92 period has been estimated at approximately US$28.5 billion, 80 percent of which is associated with interest rate subsidies. The annual average of these costs represents about 13 percent of agricultural GDP (Brizzi 2001).

24. See World Bank (1993) for a description of the experience of East Asian countries with directed credit. Also, Vittas and Cho (1996) try to extract the main lessons from this experience and conclude that directed credit programs should be small, narrowly focused, and of limited duration. Several authors (see, for example, World Bank 1993; Cho 1997; Santomero 1997; and Vittas 1997) point out that the relative success of directed credit programs in East Asian countries was achieved at the expense of a slower development of more complete financial markets.

25. Zia (2008) analyzes detailed loan-level data from the directed lending program for exporting firms in Pakistan and finds that about half of the subsidized funds went to large, financially unconstrained firms that did not need them.

26. A number of cross-country studies have attempted to measure the impact of financial repression on growth. Most of these papers use real interest rates (or variables based on threshold values of real interest rates) to measure financial repression because controls on lending and deposit rates typically resulted in low or negative real interest rates in many developing countries (Agarwala 1983; Gelb 1989). These studies tend to find a negative relation between financial repression and economic growth (see, for example, Lanyi and Saracoglu 1983; World Bank 1989; Roubini and Sala-i-Martin 1992; and Easterly 1993).

27. The theoretical literature also started to focus on the causes of government failure, such as rent seeking and capture by special interests (see, for example, Buchanan 1962; Tullock 1967; Stigler 1971; and Krueger 1974).

28. The view that better policies would lead to higher growth was also motivated by endogenous growth theories developed by Lucas and Romer in the mid-1980s, which imply that government policies can influence not just countries' income level but also their steady-state growth rates. This literature provided the foundation for empirical work based on cross-country regressions to analyze the effects of policies on growth, which was started by Barro (1991). Temple (1999), Durlauf, Johnson, and Temple (2005), and Easterly (2005) provide critical surveys of this literature. See also Rodrik (2012).

29. The term "Washington Consensus" was coined by Williamson (1990). See Birdsall, de la Torre, and Valencia Caicedo (2011) for an analysis of reforms implemented in Latin America following the Washington Consensus. World Bank (2005b) reviews the reforms implemented in developing countries during the 1990s and discusses the resulting policy lessons.

30. See, for example, Hall and Jones (1999), Acemoglu, Johnson, and Robinson (2001), Easterly and Levine (2003), and Rodrik, Subramanian, and Trebbi (2004).

31. See Williamson and Mahar (1998) for an overview of the financial liberalization process around the world.

32. See Megginson (2005) for a review of the empirical literature on bank privatization.

33. Reports from the World Bank's Doing Business project present detailed accounts of recent reforms to collateral laws and procedures around the world (see, for example, World Bank 2016).

34. The World Bank Group has supported the development of credit-reporting systems around the world for more than a decade. See IFC (2006) for an overview of experiences in developing private credit bureaus. The World Bank's *General Principles for Credit Reporting* (World Bank 2011) provide international standards for credit reporting systems' policy and oversight.

35. McIntosh and Wydick (2004) show that the total effect of credit bureaus can be decomposed into two separate effects (a screening effect and an incentive effect) and that credit bureaus can improve access to financing for low-income borrowers. Cross-country evidence shows that, in countries with better credit-information-sharing systems, credit markets are more developed and firms report lower financing obstacles (Jappelli and Pagano 2002; Love and Mylenko 2003; Djankov, McLiesh, and Shleifer 2007; Tasić and Valev 2008; Martinez Peria and Singh 2014).

36. Public credit registries are databases managed by a government agency, usually the central bank or the superintendent of banks, which collect information on the standing of borrowers in the financial system and make it available to financial intermediaries. A private credit bureau is a private firm or nonprofit organization that provides credit information on consumers and/or firms for a variety of uses. Unlike public registries, private bureaus usually gather information from nonbank lenders and public sources, distribute more data, and offer a broader range of services to lenders, such as credit scoring.

37. See de la Torre and Schmukler (2004) and de la Torre, Ize, and Schmukler (2012) for descriptions of the evolution of securities markets and related reforms in recent decades, with a focus on Latin America.

38. See Capaul (2003) for an overview of corporate governance reforms in Latin America.

39. Bhattacharya and Daouk (2002) find that 39 developing countries established insider trading regulations between 1990 and 1998.

40. Beck et al. (2012) find that the growth effect of financial deepening is driven by business lending, rather than household credit.

41. In contrast with the empirical evidence for a positive effect of domestic financial sector liberalization, the evidence on the effects of liberalizing cross-border financial transactions is much less conclusive. See, for example, Prasad, Rajan and Subramanian (2007), Aizenman and Sushko (2011), and Aizenman, Jinjarak, and Park (2013) for recent empirical analyses of the links between financial globalization and growth. Several explanations have been posited to account for the lack of robust evidence in this regard. For instance, different forms of financial integration may have different effects. Consistent with this hypothesis, studies focusing on equity market liberalizations typically find significant positive effects of integration on investment and growth (Henry 2000a, 2000b; Bekaert, Campbell, and Lundblad 2003, 2005). Other arguments have focused on the existence of threshold effects, whereby international financial integration has a positive effect on financial development and growth only in countries that have a certain level of financial and institutional development (Dell'Ariccia et al. 2008; Klein and Olivei 2008; Kose et al. 2009). See Eichengreen (2001), Henry (2007), and Rodrik and Subramanian (2009) for reviews of the literature on the costs and benefits of capital account liberalization.

42. Several papers analyze the effects of changes in legal rules on financial markets, finding evidence of a positive association between improvements in shareholder and creditor rights protection, as well as the efficiency of the judicial system, and financial development (see, for example, Linciano 2003; Chemin 2009; Haselmann, Pistor, and Vig 2010; and Nenova 2012).

43. Loayza, Fajnzylber, and Calderón (2005) analyze the growth outcome of the reforms of the 1990s in Latin America and find that most countries experienced growth rates consistent with the extent of the reforms. However, the estimated payoffs of the reforms in many cases are quite small, suggesting that initial expectations may have been overly optimistic. Lora, Panizza, and Quispe-Agnoli (2004) analyze the causes of reform fatigue in Latin America and conclude that this phenomenon is driven by the moderate observed effects of reforms on growth and productivity and the gap between these outcomes and the expectations initially created by the reformers.

44. Renditions of this view, in the more general context of assessing the impact of reforms on economic development, can be found in World Bank (1997), Fernandez Arias and Montiel (2001), Krueger (2004), and Singh et al. (2005).

45. In general terms, first-generation reforms were those taken as part of the initial wave of efforts to regain macroeconomic stability while deregulating the economy. In the financial sector, first-generation reforms focused mainly on liberalizing the domestic financial market and allowing cross-border capital mobility. Second-generation reforms concern the subsequent wave of reforms that are, by and large, much more intensive in institution building. In the financial sector, these entail, for instance, strengthening prudential oversight and transparency,

improving creditor rights, enhancing corporate governance practices and minority shareholder protection, and modernizing market infrastructures.

46. A pioneering investigation into the links between liberalization and financial crises is the classic paper by Carlos Diaz-Alejandro (1983), aptly titled "Good-Bye Financial Repression, Hello Financial Crash." A number of theoretical papers show that financial liberalization may be associated with crises (see, for example, McKinnon and Pill 1997; Allen and Gale 2000; Bacchetta and van Wincoop 2000; and Calvo and Mendoza 2000).

47. Micco and Panizza (2006) analyze the behavior of bank lending over the business cycle using bank-level data for 119 countries for the 1995–2002 period and find that state-owned bank lending is less procyclical than lending by private banks. Bertay, Demirgüç-Kunt, and Huizinga (2015) analyze the more recent period from 1999 to 2010 and also find evidence that state bank lending is less procyclical than private bank lending, especially in countries with good governance. Cull and Martinez Peria (2013) study the impact of bank ownership on credit growth during the financial crisis and find that, although the behavior of state-owned banks in Eastern Europe did not differ significantly from that of private domestic banks, state-owned banks in Latin America behaved in a countercyclical manner, expanding credit at a faster pace than private banks during the crisis. De Luna-Martinez and Vicente (2012) conduct a survey of development banks around the world and find that most of the development banks in their sample increased lending in a countercyclical manner during the crisis. As a result, the combined loan portfolio of development banks increased by 36 percent between 2007 and 2009 (from US$1.2 trillion to US$1.6 trillion), compared to an increase of only 10 percent in private bank lending in the countries surveyed.

48. Credit guarantee schemes are mechanisms in which a third party—the guarantor—pledges to repay some or the entire loan amount to the lender in case of borrower default. The guarantor assumes part or all of the credit risk, reducing the risk faced by financial intermediaries and thus making it possible for firms to obtain credit or improve the terms and conditions under which they can borrow. See OECD (2010, 2012, 2013) and World Bank (2013) for discussions on the use of public credit guarantee schemes as countercyclical tools during the financial crisis. Chapter 7 discusses the role of credit guarantee schemes in broadening access.

49. Note that these figures include data on both public and private credit guarantee schemes, including mutual guarantee associations (MGAs), in which firms deposit money into a fund that guarantees loans to members from financial institutions. In most countries, the government gives significant support to private guarantee schemes, providing funding and offering counterguarantees. Data for European countries cover selected credit guarantee schemes in Austria, Belgium, the Czech Republic, Estonia, France, Germany, Greece, Hungary, Italy, Latvia, Lithuania, Poland, Portugal, Romania, Spain, Slovakia, Slovenia, and Turkey.

50. See chapter 8 for an overview of microfinance and its role in broadening access.

51. Different renditions of this view, which tend to differ on how significant market failures are and the extent and nature of government interventions required to

overcome them, have been presented by Rodrik (2002, 2006, 2009), Hausmann and Rodrik (2003, 2006), World Bank (2005b), Stiglitz (2008), Lin (2012), and Lin, Monga, and Stiglitz (2015), among many others.

52. This emerging development policy view has reignited interest in industrial policies (that is, policies by which the government attempts to shape the sectorial allocation of the economy), as way to foster the development of higher-productivity sectors and jump-start the development process. These policies had become discredited following the failure of import substitution policies and the perception that they often involved political favoritism, wasted resources, rent seeking, and corruption. Governments in developing (and developed) countries were not particularly good at picking winners, and, as a result, industrial policies ended up favoring less productive firms and leading to the emergence of industrial lobbies. It remains to be seen whether this emerging view can avoid the pitfalls that have characterized industrial policies in the past. IDB (2015) presents a framework for rethinking industrial policies. Harrison and Rodriguez-Clare (2010) review theoretical models of industrial policy and the empirical evidence on its effects.

53. This view regarding the lack of clear policy guidelines to ignite growth and the need for pragmatism and context-specific policies is perhaps best represented by the Commission on Growth and Development (2008) report. Similar views have been expressed by a wide spectrum of economists (see, for example, Easterly 2001; Lindauer and Pritchett 2002; Harberger 2003; Barcelona Development Agenda 2004; Rodrik 2006, 2014; and Solow 2007). The literature on cross-country growth regressions yields similar conclusions. The empirical evidence shows that growth rates are not persistent over time (Easterly et al. 1993), rejecting the hypothesis that differences in growth rates across countries can be explained by very persistent country characteristics, and also fails to identify any time-varying variables (such as policies) that are robustly related to growth (Levine and Renelt 1992; Durlauf, Johnson, and Temple 2005; Ciccone and Jarocinski 2010).

54. For further discussion of this issues see, for instance, Rodrik (2009, 2010) and Hausmann, Rodrik, and Velasco (2010).

References

Abiad, Abdul, Nienke Oomes, and Kenichi Ueda. 2008. "The Quality Effect: Does Financial Liberalization Improve the Allocation of Capital?" *Journal of Development Economics* 87 (2): 270–82.

Acemoglu, Daron, Simon Johnson, and James A. Robinson. 2001. "The Colonial Origins of Comparative Development: An Empirical Investigation." *American Economic Review* 91: 1369–401.

Agarwala, Ramgopal. 1983. "Price Distortions and Growth in Developing Countries." World Bank Staff Working Paper 575, World Bank, Washington, DC.

AECM (European Association of Mutual Guarantee Societies). 2013. *Statistics AECM 2012.* Brussels: AECM.

Aizenman, J., Y. Jinjarak, and D. Park. 2013. "Capital Flows and Economic Growth in the Era of Financial Integration and Crisis, 1990–2010." *Open Economies Review* 24 (3): 371–96.

Aizenman, J., and V. Sushko. 2011. "Capital Flow Types, External Financing Needs, and Industrial Growth: 99 Countries, 1991–2007." NBER Working Paper No. 17228, National Bureau of Economic Research, Cambridge, MA.

Allen, Franklin, and Douglas Gale. 2000. "Financial Contagion." *Journal of Political Economy* 108 (1): 1–33.

Allen, Franklin, Elena Carletti, Robert Cull, Qian Jun, Lemma Senbet, and Patricio Valenzuela. 2014. "The African Financial Development and Financial Inclusion Gaps." Policy Research Working Paper 7019, World Bank, Washington, DC.

Altunbas, Yener, Lynne Evans, and Philip Molyneux. 2001. "Bank Ownership and Efficiency." *Journal of Money, Credit and Banking* 33 (4): 926–54.

Andrianova, Svetlana, Panicos Demetriades, and Anja Shortland. 2010. "Is Government Ownership of Banks Really Harmful to Growth?" Discussion Paper 987, DIW Berlin, German Institute for Economic Research.

Anginer, Deniz, Augusto de la Torre, and Alain Ize. 2014. "Risk-Bearing by the State: When Is It Good Public Policy?" *Journal of Financial Stability* 10: 76–86.

Armendáriz de Aghion, Beatriz. 1999. "Development Banking." *Journal of Development Economics* 58 (1): 83–100.

Arnott, Richard, and Joseph Stiglitz. 1991. "Equilibrium in Competitive Insurance Markets with Moral Hazard." NBER Working Paper 3588, National Bureau of Economic Research, Cambridge, MA.

Arrow, Kenneth J., and Robert C. Lind. 1970. "Uncertainty and the Evaluation of Public Investment Decisions." *American Economic Review* 60 (3): 364–78.

Bacchetta, Philippe, and Eric van Wincoop. 2000. "Does Exchange Rate Stability Increase Trade and Welfare?" *American Economic Review* 90 (5): 1093–1109.

Barcelona Development Agenda. 2004. Consensus Document Resulting from Forum Barcelona 2004, Barcelona, Spain, September 24–25.

Barro, Robert J. 1991. "Economic Growth in a Cross-Section of Countries." *Quarterly Journal of Economics* 106 (2): 407–43.

Barth, James R., Gerard Caprio, and Ross Levine. 2001. "Banking Systems around the Globe: Do Regulation and Ownership Affect Performance and Stability?" In *Prudential Regulation and Supervision: Why Is It Important and What Are the Issues?* edited by Frederic S. Mishkin, chap. 2. Cambridge, MA: National Bureau of Economic Research.

———. 2004. "Bank Regulation and Supervision: What Works Best?" *Journal of Financial Intermediation* 13 (2): 205–48.

Beck, Thorsten, Berrak Büyükkarabacak, Felix Rioja, and Neven Valev. 2012. "Who Gets the Credit? And Does It Matter? Household vs. Firm Lending across Countries." *B.E. Journal of Macroeconomics* 12 (1).

Beck, Thorsten, Asli Demirgüç-Kunt, and Maria Soledad Martinez Peria. 2007. "Reaching Out: Access to and Use of Banking Services across Countries." *Journal of Financial Economics* 85 (1): 234–66.

Bekaert, Geert, Campbell R. Harvey, and Christian T. Lundblad. 2003. "Equity Market Liberalization in Emerging Markets." *Journal of Financial Research* 26 (3): 275–99.

———. 2005. "Does Financial Liberalization Spur Growth?" *Journal of Financial Economics* 77 (1): 3–56.

Bertay, Ata C., Asli Demirgüç-Kunt, and Harry Huizinga. 2015. "Bank Ownership and Credit Over the Business Cycle: Is Lending by State Banks Less Procyclical?" *Journal of Banking and Finance* 50: 326–339.

Besley, Timothy. 1994. "How Do Market Failures Justify Interventions in Rural Credit Markets?" *World Bank Research Observer* 9: 27–47.

Bhattacharya, Utpal, and Hazem Daouk. 2002. "The World Price of Insider Trading." *Journal of Finance* 57: 75–108.

Birdsall, Nancy, Augusto de la Torre, and Felipe Valencia Caicedo. 2011. "The Washington Consensus: Assessing a Damaged Brand." In *The Oxford Handbook of Latin American Economics*, edited by José Antonio Ocampo and Jaime Ros. New York: Oxford University Press.

BIS (Bank for International Settlements). 2005. *Bank for International Settlements 75th Annual Report*. Basel: BIS.

Boehmer, Ekkehart, Robert C. Nash, and Jeffry M. Netter. 2005. "Bank Privatization in Developing and Developed Countries: Cross-Sectional Evidence on the Impact of Economic and Political Factors." *Journal of Banking and Finance* 29: 1981–2013.

Bonomo, Marco, Ricardo Brito, and Bruno Martins. 2015. "Macroeconomic and Financial Consequences of the Post-Crisis Government-Driven Credit Expansion in Brazil." Working Paper IDB-WP-551, Inter-American Development Bank, Washington, DC.

Booth, Laurence, Varouj Aivazian, Asli Demirgüç-Kunt, and Vojislav Maksimovic. 2001. "Capital Structure in Developing Countries." *Journal of Finance* 56: 87–129.

Brizzi, Adolfo. 2001. "Rural Development and Agriculture." In *Mexico: A Comprehensive Development Agenda for the New Era*, edited by Marcelo M. Guigale, Olivier Lafourcarde, and Vinh H. Nguyen, chap. 15. Washington, DC: World Bank.

Bruhn, Miriam, Subika Farazi, and Martin Kanz. 2013. "Bank Competition, Concentration, and Credit Reporting." Policy Research Working Paper 6442, World Bank, Washington, DC.

Buchanan, James M. 1962. "Politics, Policy, and the Pigovian Margins." *Economica* 29: 17–28.

Calvo, Guillermo A., and Enrique G. Mendoza. 2000. "Rational Contagion and the Globalization of Securities Markets." *Journal of International Economics* 51(1): 79–113.

Cameron, Rondo E. 1953. "The Credit Mobilier and the Economic Development of Europe." *Journal of Political Economy* 61 (6): 461–88.

———. 1961. *France and the Economic Development of Europe, 1800–1914*. Princeton, NJ: Princeton University Press.

Capaul, Mierta. 2003. *Corporate Governance in Latin America*. Washington, DC: World Bank.

Caprio, Gerard, and Patrick Honohan. 2001. *Finance for Growth: Policy Choices in a Volatile World*. New York: Oxford University Press for World Bank.

Caprio, Gerard, and Maria Soledad Martínez Pería. 2002. "Avoiding Disaster: Policies to Reduce the Risk of Banking Crisis." In *Monetary Policy and Exchange Rate Regimes: Options for the Middle East*, edited by E. Cardoso and A. Galal. Cairo: Egyptian Center for Economic Studies.

Caprio, Gerard, and Lawrence H. Summers. 1993. "Finance and Its Reform: Beyond Laissez-Faire." Policy Research Working Paper 1171, World Bank, Washington, DC.

Carvalho, Daniel. 2014. "The Real Effects of Government-Owned Banks: Evidence from an Emerging Market." *Journal of Finance* 69 (2): 577–609.

Chemin, Matthieu. 2009. "Do Judiciaries Matter for Development? Evidence from India." *Journal of Comparative Economics* 37 (2): 230–50.

Cho, Yoon J. 1997. "Credit Policies and the Industrialization of Korea." In *Policy-Based Finance and Market Alternatives: East Asian Lessons for Latin America and the Caribbean*, edited by Kim B. Staking. Washington, DC: Inter-American Development Bank.

Christiansen, Lone, Martin Schindler, and Thierry Tressel. 2013. "Growth and Structural Reforms: A New Assessment." *Journal of International Economics* 89 (2): 347–56.

Ciccone, Antonio, and Marek Jarocinski. 2010. "Determinants of Economic Growth: Will Data Tell?" *American Economic Journal: Macroeconomics* 2 (4): 222–46.

Claessens, Stijn, Erik Feijen, and Luc Laeven. 2008. "Political Connections and Preferential Access to Finance: The Role of Campaign Contributions." *Journal of Financial Economics* 88 (3): 554–80.

Claessens, Stijn, and Laura Kodres. 2014. "The Regulatory Responses to the Global Financial Crisis: Some Uncomfortable Questions." IMF Working Paper 14/46, International Monetary Fund, Washington, DC.

Cole, Shawn A. 2009a. "Financial Development, Bank Ownership, and Growth: Or, Does Quantity Imply Quality?" *Review Of Economics and Statistics* 91 (1): 33–51.

———. 2009b. "Fixing Market Failures or Fixing Elections? Elections, Banks, and Agricultural Lending in India." *American Economic Journal Applied Economics* 1 (1): 219–50.

Coleman, Nicholas S., and Leo Feler. 2015. "Bank Ownership, Lending, and Local Economic Performance during the 2008–2010 Financial Crisis." *Journal of Monetary Economics* 71: 50–66.

Commission on Growth and Development. 2008. *The Growth Report: Strategies for Sustained Growth and Inclusive Development*. Washington, DC: World Bank.

Cull, Robert, and María Soledad Martinez Peria. 2013. "Bank Ownership and Lending Patterns during the 2008–2009 Financial Crisis: Evidence from Latin America and Eastern Europe." *Journal of Banking and Finance* 37 (12): 4861–78.

de la Torre, Augusto, Juan C. Gozzi, and Sergio L. Schmukler. 2007. "Stock Market Development under Globalization: Whither the Gains from Reforms?" *Journal of Banking and Finance* 31 (6): 1731–54.

de la Torre, Augusto, Alain Ize, and Sergio L. Schmukler. 2012. *Financial Development in Latin America and the Caribbean: The Road Ahead*. Washington, DC: World Bank.

de la Torre, Augusto, and Sergio L. Schmukler. 2004. "Coping with Risks through Mismatches: Domestic and International Financial Contracts for Emerging Economies." *International Finance* 7 (3): 349–90.

de Luna-Martinez, Jose, and Carlos Leonardo Vicente. 2012. "Global Survey of Development Banks." Policy Research Working Paper 5969, World Bank, Washington, DC.

Dell'Ariccia, Giovanni, Julian di Giovanni, Andre Faria, Ayhan Kose, Paolo Mauro, Jonathan Ostry, Martin Schindler, and Marco Terrones. 2008. "Reaping the Benefits of Financial Globalization." IMF Occasional Paper 264, International Monetary Fund, Washington, DC.

Demirgüç-Kunt, Asli, and Enrica Detragiache. 1999. "Financial Liberalization and Financial Fragility." In *Annual World Bank Conference on Development Economics 1998*, edited by Boris Pleskovic and Joseph Stiglitz. Washington, DC: World Bank.

———. 2005. "Cross-Country Empirical Studies of Systemic Bank Distress: A Survey." IMF Working Paper 05/96, International Monetary Fund, Washington, DC.

Díaz-Alejandro, Carlos. 1983. "Good-Bye Financial Repression, Hello Financial Crash." *Journal of Development Economics* 19: 1–24.

Didier, Tatiana, Ross Levine, and Sergio L. Schmukler. 2015. "Capital Market Financing, Firm Growth, and Firm Size Distribution." Policy Research Working Paper 7353, World Bank, Washington, DC.

Dinç, I. Serdar. 2005. "Politicians and Banks: Political Influences on Government-Owned Banks in Emerging Markets." *Journal of Financial Economics* 77 (2): 453–79.

Djankov, Simeon, Caralee McLiesh, and Andrei Shleifer. 2007. "Private Credit in 129 Countries." *Journal of Financial Economics* 84 (2): 299–329.

Dorrucci, Ettore, Alexis Meyer-Cirkel, and Daniel Santabarbara. 2009. "Domestic Financial Development in Emerging Economies: Evidence and Implications." Occasional Paper Series 102, European Central Bank, Frankfurt.

Durlauf, Steven N., Paul A. Johnson, and Jonathan R. W. Temple. 2005. "Growth Econometrics." In *Handbook of Economic Growth*, edited by Philippe Aghion and Steven N. Durlauf, vol. 1, chap. 8. Amsterdam: Elsevier.

Easterly, William. 1993. "How Much Do Distortions Affect Growth?" *Journal of Monetary Economics* 32: 187–212.

———. 2001. "The Lost Decade: Developing Countries' Stagnation in Spite of Policy Reform 1980–1990." *Journal of Economic Growth* 6: 135–57.

———. 2005. "National Policies and Economic Growth: A Reappraisal." In *Handbook of Economic Growth*, edited by Philippe Aghion and Steven N. Durlauf, vol. 1, chap. 15. Amsterdam: Elsevier.

Easterly, William, Michael Kremer, Lant Pritchett, and Lawrence H. Summers. 1993. "Good Policy or Good Luck?" *Journal of Monetary Economics* 32 (3): 459–83.

Easterly, William, and Ross Levine. 2003. "Tropics, Germs, and Crops: How Endowments Influence Economic Development." *Journal of Monetary Economics* 50: 3–40.

Eichengreen, Barry. 2001. "Capital Account Liberalization: What Do Cross-Country Studies Tell Us?" *World Bank Economic Review* 15 (3): 341–65.

Fernandez-Arias, Eduardo, and Peter Montiel. 2001. "Reform and Growth in Latin America: All Pain and No Gain?" *IMF Staff Papers* 48: 522–46.

Foldes, Lucien P., and Ray Rees. 1977. "A Note on the Arrow-Lind Theorem." *American Economic Review* 67 (2): 188–93.

Galindo, Arturo, and Alejandro Micco. 2004. "Do State-Owned Banks Promote Growth? Cross-Country Evidence for Manufacturing Industries." *Economics Letters* 84 (3): 371–76.

Galindo, Arturo, Alejandro Micco, and Guillermo Ordoñez. 2002. "Financial Liberalization: Does It Pay to Join the Party?" *Economia* 3(1): 231–61.

Galindo, Arturo, Fabio Schiantarelli, and Andrew Weiss. 2007. "Does Financial Liberalization Improve the Allocation of Investment? Micro-evidence from Developing Countries." *Journal of Development Economics* 83 (2): 562–87.

Gardner, Roy. 1979. "The Arrow-Lind Theorem in a Continuum Economy." *American Economic Review* 69 (3): 420–22.

Gelb, Alan H. 1989. "Financial Policies, Growth, and Efficiency." Policy Research Working Paper 202, World Bank, Washington, DC.

Gershenkron, Alexander. 1952. "Economic Backwardness in Historical Perspective." In *The Progress of Underdeveloped Areas*, edited by Bert F. Hoselitz. Chicago: University of Chicago Press.

———. 1962. *Economic Backwardness in Historical Perspective: A Book of Essays.* Cambridge, MA: Harvard University Press.

Goldsmith, Raymond W. 1969. *Financial Structure and Development.* New Haven, CT: Yale University Press.

González-García, Jesús, and Francesco Grigoli. 2013. "State-Owned Banks and Fiscal Discipline." IMF Working Paper 13/206, International Monetary Fund, Washington, DC.

Hall, Robert E., and Charles I. Jones. 1999. "Why Do Some Countries Produce So Much More Output per Worker Than Others?" *Quarterly Journal of Economics* 114: 83–116.

Hanson, James A. 2003. "Banking in Developing Countries in the 1990s." Policy Research Working Paper 3168, World Bank, Washington, DC.

Harberger, Arnold C. 2003. "Foreword." In *Latin American Macroeconomic Reforms: The Second Stage*, edited by José Antonio González, Vittorio Corbo, Anne O. Krueger, and Aaron Tornell. Chicago: University of Chicago Press.

Harrison, Ann, and Andrés Rodríguez-Clare. 2010. "Trade, Foreign Investment, and Industrial Policy." In *Handbook of Development Economics Volume 5*, edited by Dani Rodrik and Mark Rosenzweig. Amsterdam: Elsevier.

Haselmann, Rainer, Katharina Pistor, and Vikrant Vig. 2010. "How Law Affects Lending." *Review of Financial Studies* 23 (2): 549–80.

Hausmann, Ricardo, and Dani Rodrik. 2003. "Economic Development as Self-Discovery." *Journal of Development Economics* 72 (2): 603–33.

———. 2006. "Doomed to Choose: Industrial Policy as Predicament." Discussion Paper, Harvard University, Cambridge, MA.

Hausmann, Ricardo, Dani Rodrik, and Andres Velasco. 2008. "Growth Diagnostics." In *The Washington Consensus Reconsidered: Towards a New Global Governance*, edited by J. Stiglitz and N. Serra. New York: Oxford University Press.

Henry, Peter Blair. 2000a. "Stock Market Liberalization, Economic Reform, and Emerging Market Equity Prices." *Journal of Finance* 55 (2): 529–64.

———. 2000b. "Do Stock Market Liberalizations Cause Investment Booms?" *Journal of Financial Economics* 58 (1–2): 301–34.

———. 2007. "Capital Account Liberalization: Theory, Evidence, and Speculation." *Journal of Economic Literature* 45 (4): 887–935.

Hirschman, Albert O. 1958. *The Strategy of Economic Development.* New Haven, CT: Yale University Press.

Hoff, Karla, and Joseph E. Stiglitz. 2001. "Modern Economic Theory and Development." In *The Future of Development Economics in Perspective*, edited by Gerald M. Meier and Joseph E. Stiglitz. New York: Oxford University Press.

IDB (Inter-American Development Bank). 2005. *Economic and Social Progress Report (IPES) 2005: Unlocking Credit: The Quest for Deep and Stable Bank Lending.* Washington, DC: IDB.

———. 2015. *Rethinking Productive Development, Sound Policies and Institutions for Economic Transformation.* Washington, DC: IDB.

IFC (International Finance Corporation). 2006. "Credit Bureau Knowledge Guide." International Finance Corporation, Washington, DC.

IMF (International Monetary Fund). 2006. *Global Financial Stability Report: Market Developments and Issues—September 2006*. Washington, DC: IMF.

———. 2011. "People's Republic of China: Financial System Stability Assessment," IMF, Washington, DC.

Jappelli, Tullio, and Marco Pagano. 2002. "Information Sharing, Lending and Defaults: Cross-Country Evidence." *Journal of Banking & Finance* 26 (10): 2017–45.

Jaramillo, Fidel, Fabio Schiantarelli, and Andrew Weiss. 1996. "Capital Market Imperfections Before and After Financial Liberalization: An Euler Equation Approach to Panel Data for Ecuadorian Firms." *Journal of Development Economics* 51 (2): 367–386.

Kaminsky, Graciela L., and Carmen M. Reinhart. 1999. "The Twin Crises: The Causes of Banking and Balance of Payments Problems." *American Economic Review* 89 (4): 473–500.

Kaminsky, Graciela, and Sergio L. Schmukler. 2008. "Short Run Pain, Long-Run Gain: Financial Liberalization and Stock Market Cycles." *Review of Finance* 12 (2): 253–92.

Khwaja, Asim Ijaz, and Atif Mian. 2005. "Do Lenders Favor Politically Connected Firms? Rent Provision in an Emerging Financial Market." *Quarterly Journal of Economics* 120 (4): 1371–411.

Klapper, Leora, and Rida Zaidi. 2005. *A Survey of Government Regulation Intervention in Financial Markets*. Washington, DC: World Bank.

Klein, Michael. 1996. "Risk, Taxpayers, and the Role of the Government in Project Finance." Policy Research Working Paper 1688, World Bank, Washington, DC.

Klein, Michael W., and Giovanni P. Olivei. 2008. "Capital Account Liberalization, Financial Depth, and Economic Growth." *Journal of International Money and Finance* 27 (6): 861–75.

Korner, Tobias, and Isabel Schnabel. 2011. "Public Ownership of Banks and Economic Growth: The Impact of Country Heterogeneity." *Economics Of Transition* 19 (3): 407–41.

Kose, M. Ayhan, Eswar Prasad, Kenneth Rogoff, and Shang-Jin Wei. 2009. "Financial Globalization: A Reappraisal." *IMF Staff Papers* 56 (1): 8–62.

Krueger, Anne O. 1974. "The Political Economy of the Rent-Seeking Society." *American Economic Review* 64 (3): 291–303.

———. 1990. "Government Failures in Development." *Journal of Economic Perspectives* 4 (3): 9–23.

———. 2004. "Meant Well, Tried Little, Failed Much: Policy Reforms in Emerging Market Economies." Remarks at the Roundtable Lecture at the Economic Honors Society, New York University, March 23.

Krueger, Anne O., and Baran Tuncer. 1982. "An Empirical Test of the Infant Industry Argument." *American Economic Review* 72 (5): 1142–52.

Laeven, Luc. 2003. "Does Financial Liberalization Reduce Financial Constraints?" *Financial Management* 32 (1): 5–35.

Lanyi, Anthony, and Rsudu Saracoglu. 1983. "The Importance of Interest Rates in Developing Economies." *Finance and Development* 20: 20–23.

La Porta, Rafael, Florencio Lopez-de-Silanes, and Andrei Shleifer. 2002. "Government Ownership of Banks." *Journal of Finance* 57 (1): 265–301.

Lazzarini, Sergio G., Aldo Musacchio, Rodrigo Bandeira-de-Mello, and Rosilene Marcon. 2015. "What Do State-Owned Development Banks Do? Evidence from BNDES, 2002–2009." *World Development* 66: 237–53

Levine, Ross, and David Renelt. 1992. "A Sensitivity Analysis of Cross-Country Growth Regressions." *American Economic Review* 82 (4): 942–63.

Lin, Justin Yifu. 2012. *New Structural Economics: A Framework for Rethinking Development and Policy.* Washington, DC: World Bank.

Lin, Justin Yifu, Celestin Monga, and Joseph E. Stiglitz. 2015. "Introduction: The Rejuvenation of Industrial Policy." In *The Industrial Policy Revolution I: The Role of Government Beyond Ideology*, edited by Joseph E. Stiglitz and Justin Yifu Lin. New York: Palgrave Macmillan.

Linciano, Nadia. 2003. "Non-Voting Shares and the Value of Control: The Impact of Corporate Regulation in Italy." EFA Annual Conference Paper 400, EFMA Helsinki Meetings.

Lindauer, David L., and Lant Pritchett. 2002. "What's the Big Idea? The Third Generation of Policies for Economic Growth." *Journal of LACEA Economia* 3 (1): 1–28.

Loayza Norman, Pablo Fajnzylber, and César Calderón. 2005. *Economic Growth in Latin America and the Caribbean: Stylized Facts, Explanations, and Forecasts.* Washington, DC: World Bank.

Lora, Eduardo, Ugo Panizza, and Myriam Quispe-Agnoli. 2004. "Reform Fatigue: Symptoms, Reasons, and Implications." *Federal Reserve Bank of Atlanta Economic Review* 89 (2): 1–28.

Love, Inessa, and Nataliya Mylenko. 2003. "Credit Reporting and Financing Constraints." Policy Research Working Paper 3142, World Bank, Washington, DC.

Martinez Peria, María Soledad, and Sandeep Singh. 2014. "The Impact of Credit Information Sharing Reforms on Firm Financing." Policy Research Working Paper 7013, World Bank, Washington, DC.

McIntosh, Craig, and Bruce Wydick. 2004. "A Decomposition of Screening and Incentive Effects in Credit Information Systems." University of California at San Diego.

McKinnon, Ronald I. 1973. *Money and Capital in Economic Development.* Washington, DC: Brookings Institution Press.

McKinnon, Ronald I., and Huw Pill. 1997. "Credible Economic Liberalizations and Overborrowing." *American Economic Review* 87 (2): 189–93.

Megginson, William L. 2005. "The Economics of Bank Privatization." *Journal of Banking and Finance* 29 (8): 1931–80.

Mendoza, Enrique, and Marco Terrones. 2008. "An Anatomy of Credit Booms: Evidence from Macroeconomic Aggregates and Firm Level Data." NBER Working Paper 14049, National Bureau of Economic Research, Cambridge, MA.

———. 2014. "An Anatomy of Credit Booms and their Demise." In *Capital Mobility and Monetary Policy*, edited by M. Fuentes, C. Raddatz, and C. Reinhart. Santiago: Central Bank of Chile.

Micco, Alejandro, and Ugo Panizza. 2005. "Public Banks in Latin America." Background Paper Prepared for the Conference *Public Banks in Latin America: Myths and Reality.* Washington, DC: Inter-American Development Bank.

———. 2006. "Bank Ownership and Lending Behavior." *Economics Letters* 93: 248–54.

Micco, Alejandro, Ugo Panizza, and Monica Yañez. 2007. "Bank Ownership and Performance: Does Politics Matter?" *Journal of Banking and Finance* 31 (1): 219–41.

Murphy, Kevin M., Andrei Shleifer, and Robert W. Vishny. 1989. "Industrialization and the Big Push." *Journal of Political Economy* 97 (5): 1003–26.

Nenova, Tatiana. 2012. "Takeover Laws and Financial Development." Working Paper 68845, World Bank, Washington, DC.

OECD (Organisation for Economic Co-operation and Development). 2010. *Assessment of Government Support Programmes for SMEs' and Entrepreneurs' Access to Finance during the Crisis.* Paris: OECD.

———. 2012. *Financing SMEs and Entrepreneurs. An OECD Scoreboard 2012.* Paris: OECD.

———. 2013. *SME and Entrepreneurship Financing: The Role of Credit Guarantee Schemes and Mutual Guarantee Societies in Supporting Finance for Small and Medium-Sized Enterprises.* Paris: OECD.

Prasad, E. S., Rajan, R. G., and A. Subramanian. 2007. "Foreign Capital and Economic Growth." NBER Working Paper No. 13619, National Bureau of Economic Research, Cambridge, MA.

Rajan, Raghuram G., and Luigi Zingales. 2001. "Financial Systems, Industrial Structure, and Growth." *Oxford Review of Economic Policy* 17 (4): 467–82.

REGAR (Red Iberoamericana de Garantias). 2012. *Situacion de los Sistemas de Garantia en Iberoamerica Año 2012: Tendencias y Perspectivas desde el Conocimiento de la Actividad.* Rio de Janeiro: REGAR.

Rodrik, Dani. 2002. "After Neo-Liberalism, What?" *Economic Times,* November 19.

———. 2006. "Goodbye Washington Consensus, Hello Washington Confusion? A Review of the World Bank's Economic Growth in the 1990s: Learning from a Decade of Reform." *Journal of Economic Literature* 44 (4): 973–87.

———. 2009. "The New Development Economics: We Shall Experiment, but How Shall We Learn?" In *What Works in Development? Thinking Big and Thinking Small,* edited by Jessica L. Cohen and William Easterly. Washington, DC: Brookings Institution Press.

———. 2010. "Diagnostics Before Prescription." *Journal of Economic Perspectives* 24 (3): 33–44.

———. 2012. "Why We Learn Nothing from Regressing Economic Growth on Policies." *Seoul Journal of Economics* 25 (2): 137–51.

———. 2014. "The Past, Present, and Future of Economic Growth." In *Towards a Better Global Economy: Policy Implications for Citizens Worldwide in the 21st Century.* New York: Oxford University Press.

Rodrik, Dani, and Arvind Subramanian. 2009. "Why Did Financial Globalization Disappoint?" *IMF Staff Papers* 56 (1): 112–38.

Rodrik, Dani, Arvind Subramanian, and Francesco Trebbi. 2004. "Institutions Rule: The Primacy of Institutions over Geography and Integration in Economic Development." *Journal of Economic Growth* 9 (2): 131–65.

Rosenstein-Rodan, Paul N. 1943. "Problems of Industrialisation of Eastern and Southeastern Europe." *Economic Journal* 53 (210/211): 202–11.

Rostow, Walt W. 1962. *The Process of Economic Growth.* 2nd ed. New York: W. W. Norton.

Roubini, Nouriel, and Xavier Sala-i-Martin. 1992. "Financial Repression and Economic Growth." *Journal of Development Economics* 39 (1): 5–30.

Santomero, Anthony M. 1997. "Effective Financial Intermediation." In *Policy-Based Finance and Market Alternatives: East Asian Lessons for Latin America and the Caribbean*, edited by Kim B. Staking. Washington, DC: Inter-American Development Bank.

Sapienza, Paola. 2004. "The Effects of Government Ownership on Bank Lending." *Journal of Financial Economics* 72 (2): 357–84.

Shaw, Edward S. 1973. *Financial Deepening in Economic Development.* New York: Oxford University Press.

Shleifer, Andrei. 1998. "State versus Private Ownership." *Journal of Economic Perspectives* 12 (4): 133–50.

Sidaoui, J., M. Ramos-Francia, and G. Cuadra, 2011. "The Global Financial Crisis and Policy Response in Mexico." In *The Global Crisis and Financial Intermediation in Emerging Market Economies.* Basel: Bank for International Settlements.

Singh, Anoop, Agnès Belaisch, Charles Collyns, Paula De Masi, Reva Krieger, Guy Meredith, and Robert Rennhack. 2005. "Stabilization and Reform in Latin America: A Macroeconomic Perspective of the Experience since the 1990s." IMF Occasional Paper 238, International Monetary Fund, Washington, DC.

Solow, Robert M. 2007. "The Last 50 Years in Growth Theory and the Next 10." *Oxford Review of Economic Policy* 23 (1): 3–14.

Srinivasan, Thirukodikaval N. 1985. "Neoclassical Political Economy, the State and Economic Development." *Asian Development Review* 3: 38–58.

Stigler, George J. 1971. "The Theory of Economic Regulation." *Bell Journal of Economics and Management Science* 2 (1): 3–21.

Stiglitz, Joseph E. 1994. "The Role of the State in Financial Markets." In *Proceedings of the World Bank Annual Conference on Development Economics, 1993: Supplement to The World Bank Economic Review and The World Bank Research Observer*, 19–52. Washington, DC.

———. 2008. "Is There a Post-Washington Consensus Consensus?" In *The Washington Consensus Reconsidered*, edited by Narcis Serra and Joseph E. Stiglitz. New York: Oxford University Press.

Tasić, Nikola, and Neven Valev. 2008. "The Maturity Structure of Bank Credit: Determinants and Effects on Economic Growth." Andrew Young School of Policy Studies Research Paper Series 08-12, Atlanta: Georgia State University.

Temple, Jonathan. 1999. "The New Growth Evidence." *Journal of Economic Literature* 37 (1): 112–56.

Townsend, Robert M., and Jacob Yaron. 2001. "The Credit Risk-Contingency System of an Asian Development Bank." *Economic Perspectives–Federal Reserve Bank of Chicago* 25 (3): 31–48.

Tressel, Thierry. 2008. "Unbundling the Effects of Reforms." Unpublished manuscript. International Monetary Fund, Washington, DC.

Tressel, Thierry, and Enrica Detragiache. 2008. "Do Financial Sector Reforms Lead to Financial Development? Evidence from a New Dataset." IMF Working Paper 08/265, International Monetary Fund, Washington, DC.

Tullock, Gordon. 1967. "The Welfare Costs of Tariffs, Monopolies and Theft." *Western Economic Journal* 5 (3): 224–32.

Vittas, Dimitri. 1997. "Policy-Based Finance: Application of East Asian Lesson to the America." In *Policy-Based Finance and Market Alternatives: East Asian Lessons for Latin America and the Caribbean*, edited by Kim B. Staking. Washington, DC: Inter-American Development Bank.

Vittas, Dimitri, and Yoon Je Cho. 1996. "Credit Policies: Lessons from Japan and Korea." *World Bank Research Observer* 11 (2): 277–98.

Williamson, John. 1990. "What Washington Means by Policy Reform." In *Latin American Adjustment: How Much Has Happened?* edited by John Williamson. Washington, DC: Institute for International Economics.

Williamson, John, and Molly Mahar. 1998. "A Review of Financial Liberalization." South Asia Region Internal Discussion Paper IDP-171, World Bank, Washington, DC.

World Bank. 1983. *World Development Report 1983*. Washington, DC: World Bank.

———. 1989. *World Development Report 1989*. Washington, DC: World Bank.

———. 1990a. *Colombia Industrial Competition and Performance. Report 7921-Co*. Washington, DC: World Bank.

———. 1990b. *Colombia Industrial Restructuring and Development Project*. Washington, DC: World Bank.

———. 1993. *The East Asian Miracle: Economic Growth and Public Policy*. Washington, DC: World Bank.

———. 1997. *The Long March: A Reform Agenda for Latin America and the Caribbean in the Next Decade*. Washington, DC: World Bank.

———. 1999. *World Development Report 1999*. Washington, DC: World Bank.

———. 2002. *World Development Report 2002*. Washington, DC: World Bank.

———. 2004. "The Growth Experience. What Have We Learned from the 1990s?" Background Note Prepared by PREM, World Bank, Washington, DC.

———. 2005a. *World Development Report 2005*. Washington, DC: World Bank.

———. 2005b. *Economic Growth in the 1990s: Learning from a Decade of Reform*. Washington, DC: World Bank.

———. 2011. *General Principles for Credit Reporting*. Washington, DC: World Bank.

———. 2013. *Global Financial Development Report 2013: Rethinking the Role of the State in Finance*. Washington, DC: World Bank.

———. 2014. *Global Financial Development Report 2014: Financial Inclusion*. Washington, DC: World Bank.

———. 2015. *Global Financial Development Report 2015/16: Long-Term Finance*. Washington, DC: World Bank.

———. 2016. *Doing Business 2017—Equal Opportunity for All*. Washington, DC: World Bank.

Wruuck, Patricia. 2015. *Promoting Investment and Growth: The Role of Development Banks in Europe*. Frankfurt: Deutsche Bank.

Yaron, Jacob. 1992. "Assessing Development Financial Institutions: A Public Interest Analysis." World Bank Discussion Paper 174, World Bank, Washington, DC.

Yaron, Jacob, McDonald Benjamin, and Stephanie Charitonenko. 1998. "Promoting Efficient Rural Financial Intermediation." *World Bank Research Observer* 13 (2): 147–70.

Zia, Bilal H. 2008. "Export Incentives, Financial Constraints, and the (Mis)Allocation of Credit: Micro-Level Evidence from Subsidized Export Loans." *Journal of Financial Economics* 87 (2): 498–527.

CHAPTER 4

Structured Finance: FIRA's Experience in Mexico

Introduction

This chapter describes the experience of FIRA (Fideicomisos Instituidos en Relación con la Agricultura, or Agriculture-Related Trust Funds), a Mexican development finance institution that has arranged tailor-made structured finance transactions to facilitate access to credit for borrowers in the agriculture, livestock, and fishing sectors.

Structured finance differs from conventional on-balance-sheet financing (such as loans, equity, and bonds) and encompasses a very wide range of financial market transactions. In general terms, structured finance can be defined as a form of financial intermediation that involves the pooling of financial claims and the subsequent sale to investors of securities backed by these assets. An owner (called the *originator*) transfers assets to a third party (commonly referred to as a *special purpose vehicle*, or SPV). The SPV then sells securities to investors representing claims on the cash flow generated by the underlying assets. Usually several classes of securities with different risk and return characteristics are issued.

Structured finance transactions have several features that make them attractive to investors and issuers and can help deal with information asymmetries and transaction costs. First, asset pooling allows investors to diversify their risk exposure and increases the size of transactions, reducing costs and improving liquidity in secondary markets. Second, the transfer of the underlying assets to the SPV means that those assets are not part of the originating company's estate in case of bankruptcy. In principle, this delinks the performance of the securities from that of the originator; the return to investors depends on the cash flow generated by the underlying assets, and not on the overall performance of the originator.

Third, structured finance transactions can complete financial markets by creating securities with specific risk–return profiles that are not offered by existing financial instruments. Finally, structured finance allows participants to isolate the different risks of the underlying assets and allocate them to those parties best equipped or more willing to deal with them.

Structured finance transactions originated with the sale of residential mortgage-backed securities (MBS) in the United States in the 1970s. Over the following decades, the global structured finance market grew significantly, both in terms of the volume of issuances and the variety of assets securitized. The expansion of structured finance transactions can be ascribed to a large extent to the significant flexibility of this financial instrument, which can be tailored to meet a wide variety of investor and issuer needs.

The rapid growth of worldwide structured finance markets came to a halt during the global financial crisis. The crisis highlighted significant flaws in structured finance markets and their regulatory framework, prompting many people to reassess the costs and benefits of structured finance. Incentive and information problems among different participants in structured transactions resulted in poor loan origination and excessive risk taking. In addition, high transaction complexity made many structured finance securities difficult to value and susceptible to sudden changes in risk perception. The financial crisis showed that, despite the potential benefits described above, without proper incentives and regulations structured finance can lead to risk concentration and even be a source of financial instability. In contrast to the negative view of structured finance that prevailed in the immediate aftermath of the crisis, regulators and market participants have since reassessed its benefits, highlighting its role in mobilizing illiquid assets, allocating risk, and expanding access to credit.

This chapter describes the experience of FIRA in Mexico, which has arranged tailored structured finance transactions for private financial intermediaries to provide financing to borrowers in the agriculture, livestock, and fishing sectors. In particular, we describe two structured finance transactions arranged by FIRA that rely on two different types of instruments: asset-backed securities (ABS) and collateralized loan obligations (CLOs). FIRA's ABS transactions are designed to transform movable assets, such as commodity inventories, into viable collateral for financial institutions through the securitization of loans backed by these assets. These transactions involve an operational agent, usually a large commercial firm, that shares the risk, screens producers, and provides an outlet for collateral liquidation in case of default. In turn, FIRA's CLO transactions are designed to provide working capital financing. In these transactions, a large commercial firm acts as originator, granting working capital loans to its suppliers, which are then transferred to an SPV. Securities backed by this asset pool are sold to investors. FIRA's ABS and CLO transactions have several built-in mechanisms to align incentives and reduce adverse selection and moral hazard.

FIRA's experience with structured finance transactions is an example of the move of some development finance institutions away from traditional credit operations and toward pro-market interventions. FIRA's main role in structured finance transactions is not to lend directly to producers but rather to play a "catalytic" role, acting as an arranger to promote coordination among industry stakeholders and financial intermediaries to overcome informational and enforcement problems.[1] These types of transactions differ from the role of the state as a direct provider of financial services because, in principle, FIRA does need to be part of the financial contract or take counterparty risk. Analyzing this experience not only sheds light into how pro-market interventions work in practice but can also help us understand the challenges faced in their implementation.

The remainder of this chapter is organized as follows. The next section presents a general overview of structured finance transactions, focusing on how they help overcome barriers to access to finance, expanding the discussion from this introduction. The following section then describes two structured finance transactions arranged by FIRA in Mexico. The final section concludes with a discussion of these experiences and their implications for the debate on the role of the state in fostering access, as well as the insights they might provide about how pro-market interventions work in practice.

Structured Finance

Accurately defining structured finance is quite difficult because even among market practitioners there is no agreement on exactly what it encompasses.[2] As mentioned above, structured finance can be broadly defined as a form of financial intermediation based upon securitization technology. In its simplest form, it is a process by which present or future receivables are pooled and securities representing claims on the cash flow generated by these assets are sold to investors.[3] The owner (*originator*) transfers assets to a third party (*special purpose vehicle* or *SPV*), which can be a corporation, trust, or any other independent legal entity. The SPV in turn issues securities backed by the asset pool. Typically, several classes of securities (called *tranches*) with distinct risk–return profiles are issued.[4] For instance, securities with different degrees of seniority and exposure to credit risk might be created, with junior or so-called *equity* tranches bearing the majority of the risk by absorbing initial losses in the asset pool and more senior tranches being relatively isolated from credit risk because they face only residual losses. The proceeds from the sale of securities are used to pay the originator for the assets transferred to the SPV. In principle, almost any type of financial claims or rights to receive a future payment can be securitized. The main requirements for securitization are that the receivables must be amenable to rigorous credit and statistical performance analysis and that they should be easily separated from the originator. Also, large pools of homogeneous receivables are usually required to facilitate risk assessment, achieve economies of scale, and diversify idiosyncratic risks.

Structured finance transactions involve several different participants. Typically, these include the *originator*, which originates the underlying assets in the course of its regular business activities or purchases them in the market; the *arranger*, which sets up the structure and markets the securities; the *servicer*, which collects payments and tracks the performance of the asset pool; the *trustee*, which oversees cash distributions to investors and monitors compliance with deal documentation; and, in some cases, *financial guarantors,* which provide credit guarantees for certain tranches. For example, in the case of transactions that include non-traded loans in the asset pool, the originator is typically a commercial bank or financial company. The arranger in most cases is an investment bank or the asset management arm of a financial conglomerate. In the case of MBS, governmental or quasi-governmental entities—such as the Government National Mortgage Association (GNMA, also called Ginnie Mae) or the Federal Home Loan Mortgage Corporation (FHLMC, commonly called Freddie Mac) in the United States—might also act as arrangers. The role of servicer, which is particularly important for transactions that include a large number of loans in the asset pool, is usually undertaken by the originating financial institution or by a specialized company. Trustees tend to be law firms or legal units within financial institutions. Credit enhancements, when required, are typically provided by commercial guarantee companies, which in most cases are specialized insurance firms. In the case of MBS, government-sponsored housing finance enterprises or similar entities might also act as guarantors.

Structured finance operations originated in the sale of residential MBS by government-sponsored enterprises in the United States during the 1970s. The first transactions were the sales of mortgage pass-through certificates, guaranteed by Ginnie Mae in 1970. These early operations were followed by the sale of whole loan pools by Freddie Mac and the Federal National Mortgage Association (FNMA, or Fannie Mae) in the late 1970s and early 1980s.[5] During this period, mortgage pass-through certificates were the most common form of MBS. Pass-throughs are securities backed by a pool of mortgages in which all principal and interest payments from the underlying loans (less a servicing fee) are passed directly to investors every month. The cash flow from these securities can vary from month to month, depending on the actual prepayment rate of the underlying mortgages. A major innovation in the MBS market occurred in 1983, when Freddie Mac issued the first collateralized mortgage obligations (CMOs). The main difference between CMOs and mortgage pass-throughs is that, whereas in mortgage pass-throughs all investors participate proportionally in the cash flow from the underlying mortgage pool, in CMOs several classes of securities are issued, each giving investors rights to a different component of the cash flow. In this way, investors can select those securities that most closely meet their maturity and cash flow requirements.[6] In 1985, Sperry Corporation (a large U.S. equipment and electronics company) issued the first ABS involving nonmortgage assets, with a US$192.5 million securitization of computer lease receivables, marking the beginning of diversification in terms of underlying assets and deal structures. Over the following decades, the structured finance market expanded significantly in terms of the assets securitized, ranging from cash instruments (for example, loans, bonds, credit card receivables, intellectual property rights, and utility receivables) to synthetic exposures (for example, credit default swaps), although MBS still account for the large majority of transactions.[7]

The significant flexibility of structured finance transactions in terms of maturity profile, security design, and underlying asset types made them increasingly popular among issuers and investors. Structured finance appealed strongly to investors searching for higher-yielding, safe-rated, fixed-income instruments and also helped banks decrease their funding costs by allowing them to move assets off balance sheet and reduce their regulatory capital requirements.[8] As a result, structured finance transactions experienced significant growth in developed countries since the mid-1990s, with the total amount outstanding growing nearly fivefold between 1996 and 2007 and reaching almost US$13 trillion in 2007, the vast majority of which was accounted for by the United States (figure 4.1). Issuance of

FIGURE 4.1 Evolution of structured finance markets

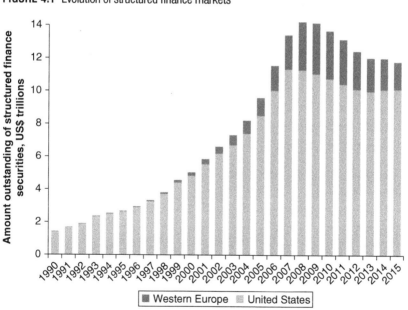

Source: Securities Industry and Financial Markets Association (SIFMA).
Note: This figure shows the evolution of the amount outstanding of structured finance securities in Western European countries and the United States for the period 1990–2015 in trillion dollars. Data for European countries include retained deals.

private-label securitizations in the United States (that is, structured finance transactions excluding securities backed by government-sponsored agencies) soared from negligible volumes in the mid-1990s to a peak of more than US$2 trillion in 2006 (figure 4.2, panel a). Before the global financial crisis, structured finance had become a key funding source for consumer and mortgage lending in many developed countries, providing between 20 and 60 percent of the funding for new residential mortgages originated in the United States, Western Europe, Japan, and Australia (IMF 2009).

The global financial crisis caused an effective breakdown of structured finance markets.[9] Problems started in 2007, with structured finance instruments that included U.S. subprime (lower credit quality) mortgages in their asset pools. Default rates on these loans soared as a long period of housing price appreciation came to a halt, leading to large losses in the value of related structured finance instruments and a loss of investor confidence in structured finance products in general. This was magnified by illiquidity in financial markets and high transaction complexity, which made many structured finance securities difficult to value and susceptible to sudden changes in risk perception.

As a result, activity in structured finance markets came to a halt. Issuance volumes in the United States dropped by almost 50 percent between 2006 and 2008 (figure 4.2, panel a). Moreover, reflecting a generalized loss of investor confidence in the sector, most of the remaining issuance activity was accounted for by MBS underwritten by government-sponsored housing finance agencies. Some segments of the structured finance market, most notably ABS backed by auto loans and consumer credit, have recovered since the crisis, but overall issuance volumes remain below precrisis levels. In the case of Europe, where there is no government-sponsored agency MBS market, issuance volumes have been significantly lower since the crisis, with only US$235 billion of structured finance securities issued in 2015, about 40 percent of the precrisis annual issuance volume (figure 4.2, panel b).[10]

In the case of emerging markets, the development of structured finance markets started relatively slowly in the mid-1990s and was initially hampered by the lack of adequate legal frameworks.[11] Activity in many local structured finance markets decreased during the global financial crisis but has grown significantly since then, with increasing volumes and diversification in terms of structures and the types of assets securitized. This recent expansion has been spurred both by yield-seeking investors in an environment of low interest rates and by regulatory reforms aimed at developing legal and financial frameworks for structured transactions in several countries. Among emerging economies, the Republic of Korea has historically been one the largest structured finance markets, with total securitization issuance reaching about US$48.2 billion in 2013. China's structured finance market has grown exponentially in recent years as a result of government efforts to foster its development, with total issuance volume reaching over US$34 billion in 2014, more than twice the total cumulative amount issued between 2005 and 2013.[12]

FIGURE 4.2 Evolution of structured finance issuance activity

a. Gross structured finance issuance, United States

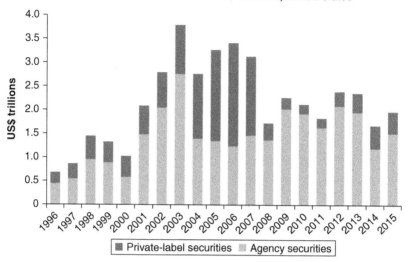

Private-label securities   Agency securities

b. Gross structured finance issuance, Western Europe

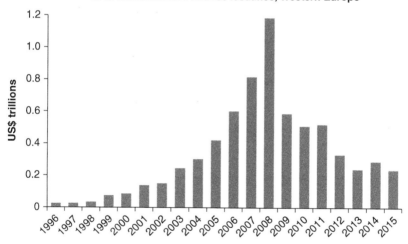

Source: SIFMA.

Note: This figure shows the evolution of the gross amount issued of structured finance securities for selected countries. Panel a displays data for the United States, and panel b for Western European countries. Agency securities include mortgage-backed securities and collateralized mortgage obligations issued by Fannie Mae (Federal National Mortgage Association), Freddie Mac (Federal Home Loan Mortgage Corporation) and Ginnie Mae (National Mortgage Association). Private label securities include nonagency mortgage-related securities and asset-backed securities. Data for European countries include retained deals.

In Latin America, structured finance issuance was initially dominated by cross-border transactions, but domestic markets have grown significantly, with Brazil and Mexico having the largest markets. Transactions backed by mortgages or mortgage-related assets are the most popular type of structured finance deals in Latin American markets, followed by consumer loan securitizations.

The prevailing view on structured finance before the financial crisis stressed its benefits in terms of mobilizing illiquid assets, improving risk allocation, and expanding access to credit (Shin 2009). The global financial crisis highlighted significant flaws in structured finance markets and their regulatory framework, giving rise to an opposite view, which stressed how incentive and information problems in the securitization process resulted in poor loan origination and excessive risk taking, increasing financial fragility. In this regard, structured finance, like other forms of financial innovation, has both benefits and risks, and is not necessarily good or bad per se. In contrast to the negative view of structured finance that prevailed in the immediate aftermath of the crisis, regulators and market participants have since reassessed its benefits. International organizations and national authorities in several countries have stressed the need to reestablish well-functioning structured finance markets in order to improve risk allocation, complete financial markets, and help expand access to credit (IMF 2009; FSB 2010; Bank of England and ECB 2014; European Investment Bank 2014; European Commission 2015).[13]

As described above, structured finance transactions involve three main features: (i) the pooling of assets; (ii) the transfer of the asset pool from the originator to a finite-lived stand-alone entity (the SPV); and (iii) the tranching of securities that are backed up by the asset pool. Each of these features generates benefits for issuers and investors and helps deal with information asymmetries and transaction costs, which generate problems of access to credit.[14]

Pooling can improve the liquidity of many types of assets by increasing the number of potential investors (Duffie and Garleanu 2001). For instance, the number of investors interested in buying a particular consumer loan might be quite small, so it would be too costly and time-consuming to try to sell this type of asset individually in the market. Pooling a large number of homogeneous assets (structured transactions in many cases include several tens of thousands of loans in the asset pool) and selling shares in the pool to investors significantly reduces transaction costs by increasing the size of issues. Pooling also allows investors to diversify their risk exposure because they do not face the idiosyncratic risk of an individual asset (for example, a particular loan), but rather the overall risk of the asset pool. As a result, more investors are willing to buy the securities and liquidity is improved.

The transfer of assets from the originator to the SPV provides collateral for the transaction. This transfer also delinks the performance of the instrument from that of the originator; payments to investors, in principle, depend only on the cash flow generated by the underlying asset pool, not on the performance of the originating firm.[15] For example, in the case of MBS, the cash flow that investors receive depends only on the principal and interest payments of those particular mortgages included in the asset pool. The performance of the remaining mortgage portfolio of the originator and any of its other business activities does not affect the cash flow accruing to investors. This feature of structured finance transactions reduces information requirements because investors do not need to assess the overall business prospects of the originating firm, only the quality of the underlying assets used in the transaction. Another advantage of transferring assets to the SPV is that it is a bankruptcy-remote entity, in the sense that, if the originator files for bankruptcy, the assets in the pool do not come under court jurisdiction. For instance, in the case of MBS, the mortgages are removed from the books of the originating financial institution and the SPV is their legal owner. This represents a significant advantage in countries with weak creditor rights and cumbersome and costly bankruptcy procedures.[16] All these benefits taken together make it possible to issue securities with well-defined risk characteristics and returns that might be more predictable than those of the originator. As a result, the credit risk of the transaction might be lower than that of the originating firm, lowering the cost of accessing external financing.

As described above, tranching consists of slicing the cash flows generated by the underlying asset pool into different components, according to factors such as credit risk, maturity, and duration. This allows issuers to create several classes of securities with distinct risk–return profiles. Tranching is used in many cases to create a subset of securities with a higher credit rating than the average rating of the underlying collateral pool by prioritizing payments to the different tranches, so that more senior tranches face only residual credit losses.[17] As emphasized by Mitchell (2005), in a world of perfect capital markets, without informational asymmetries and transaction costs, tranching would not add any value relative to directly selling shares in the asset pool because the structure of liabilities would be irrelevant.[18] Therefore, market imperfections are required for tranching to add value.

One imperfection that can be addressed by tranching is market incompleteness. If markets are complete, then every pattern of cash flow can be generated by some combination of existing securities, and creating new securities does not add value to investors. On the other hand, if markets are not complete, then tranching might add value by creating securities whose cash flows in certain states of nature cannot be spanned by existing assets. Investors benefit from the increased investment opportunities and therefore would be willing to pay a premium for these new securities.

Another market imperfection that can be addressed by creating new securities through tranching is segmentation across investor groups. Segmentation might arise because of investment mandates, differential tax rates, or regulations that constrain the set of securities in which different investor groups can invest.[19] For example, some institutions are allowed to hold only investment-grade or highly rated assets. Other asset managers, such as high-yield mutual funds, must focus on non-investment-grade securities. These types of restrictions limit the access of particular investor groups to some securities or cash flows that might be desirable. In this situation, tranching can add value by creating securities that are tailored to the meet the needs of specific investor groups, providing the desired cash flows without violating the constraints they face (Oldfield 2000). For instance, the investment-grade tranche of a consumer loan securitization might provide cash flows under different economic conditions that meet the particular demands of a certain investor group and that are not available through combinations of existing investment-grade securities.

Structured finance can also generate benefits by unbundling traditional functions performed by lenders and allowing market participants to separate and assign the risks present in a transaction. In structured finance operations, the traditional lending role performed by financial institutions can be unbundled into several subfunctions—such as loan origination, funding, servicing, and guaranteeing—which can be contracted out separately to specialized firms. This can generate significant benefits because these firms might develop more specialized knowledge and might be able to reap economies of scale. Structured finance also permits the unbundling of the risks of the underlying assets into their different components, such as credit risk, interest rate risk, and liquidity risk, as well as allowing investors to slice these risks in different ways through tranching. This facilitates risk transfer, resulting in a better allocation of risks among market participants.

Despite the potential benefits of structured finance transactions in overcoming problems of access to finance, without proper incentives and regulations, principal–agent problems between the different parties involved in these transactions can lead to poor loan origination and excessive risk taking, as became clear during the global financial crisis.[20] First, consider moral hazard. Asset securitization separates the functions of loan origination and funding. This might reduce lenders' incentives to carefully screen and monitor borrowers because most of the credit risk is transferred to investors.[21] A way of ameliorating this problem is shifting part of the credit risk back to the originator. This can be achieved, for instance, if the originator retains the first losses in the asset pool (Pennacchi 1988; Gorton and Pennacchi 1995).[22] Reputational concerns can also reduce moral hazard, especially in transactions that include only assets originated by a single institution.

Adverse selection problems can also arise in structured finance transactions, because the originator and/or the arranger might have private information on the quality of the underlying assets. In this case, they might select to transfer lower-quality assets to the SPV, retaining those of higher quality in their balance sheets. To reduce this problem, risk-averse investors and those with less information can purchase senior tranches (those that are more protected from default and face only residual losses), which are less affected by adverse selection. Also, the originator, the arranger, and the servicer might retain subordinated exposure (that is, the first losses in the pool) to align incentives. Reputational concerns can also help reduce strategic adverse selection.

Apart from these principal–agent problems, the complexity of structured finance transactions might increase opacity in some cases, making it more difficult for investors to accurately assess risks and value securities.[23] Evaluating the risk of structured finance instruments requires not only assessing the credit risk of the underlying asset pool but also taking into account how the different transaction features affect the distribution of cash flows from the asset pool to the different tranches. Tranching adds additional layers between the performance of the underlying assets and the returns from the different securities created, making it more difficult to assess the risk-and-return profiles of these securities.[24] In principle, this problem can be ameliorated by using simpler standardized structures, with a smaller number of tranches and fewer contractual features, which can be more easily evaluated by investors.[25]

Structured finance transactions require an appropriate legal framework that facilitates the securitization process and accommodates the numerous legal relationships that must be established for these transactions to work. The lack of such a framework is one of the main factors behind the sparse development of structured finance markets in many developing countries. Structured finance requires legal provisions that facilitate the creation of bankruptcy-remote entities and allow originators to transfer assets to the SPV in a cost-effective manner, while providing the necessary protection for the securitization to be successful. Moreover, taxation, accounting, and regulatory issues can affect structured financing transactions by determining their costs and implications for originators.[26]

Since the mid-1990s, governments in several developing countries have implemented reforms to create an adequate enabling environment for structured finance transactions, including improvements in the overall legal and judicial framework and the introduction of regulations specifically aimed at facilitating the securitization process. In some countries—most notably Korea, Malaysia, and Mexico—governments have taken a more active role, trying to stimulate the issuance of MBS through the creation of institutions similar to the government-sponsored housing finance enterprises in the United States. Although it is still too early to reach a conclusive judgment regarding the effectiveness of these efforts, in most cases they have had a relatively modest impact so far.[27]

In this chapter we analyze another type of state intervention, illustrated by the experience of FIRA in Mexico. In particular, we analyze structured finance transactions arranged by public development finance institutions. These transactions usually differ from typical structured finance operations, requiring tailor-made structures and using underlying assets that are more difficult to securitize.

Another example of direct public sector involvement in structured finance transactions is the support provided by international development agencies to structured finance deals by microfinance institutions in recent years.[28] International donors and development finance institutions have played a key role in fostering structured finance issues by microfinance institutions, arranging microloan securitizations, buying equity or junior tranches in these transactions, and providing credit enhancements.

We now turn to the description of two of FIRA's structured finance transactions. In the final section, we will discuss the main insights regarding the functioning of pro-market interventions that emerge from these experiences, as well as some of the arguments that might support these types of state interventions.

FIRA's Structured Finance Transactions

FIRA is a second-tier development finance institution created by the Mexican government in 1954 to provide financial services and technical assistance to the agriculture, livestock, fishing, forestry, and agribusiness sectors. It provides a wide range of services, including second-tier lending, rediscounting of agricultural credit portfolios, partial credit guarantees, and technical assistance, and also operates several subsidy programs.

Historically, state intervention in rural finance markets in Mexico has been widespread. FIRA was one of the main agents for public provision of financial services to the rural sector, together with Banco Nacional de Credito Rural (Banrural).[29] State intervention consisted primarily of the provision of directed credit at lower-than-market interest rates and subsidized credit guarantees. This type of intervention was characterized by high administrative costs, widespread strategic defaults induced by debt-forgiveness programs, and failure to reach the intended clientele, resulting in significant fiscal drains. The estimated total cost of state intervention in rural credit markets in Mexico reached about US$28.5 billion between 1983 and 1992, 80 percent of which corresponds to transfers to state-owned financial institutions (World Bank 2001). Budget transfers to FIRA, to cover operating costs and losses, amounted to approximately US$1.3 billion between 1986 and 1991 (World Bank 1993). FIRA also received off-budget subsidies, in the form of lending at below-market rates from the Bank of Mexico, worth about US$2.2 billion during this period, implying total government support of about US$3.5 billion.

In the mid-1990s, the Mexican government decided to terminate financial transfers to FIRA, having determined that its lending activities would need to be financed from its own operations and balance sheet.[30] The Bank of Mexico made a one-time loan to FIRA to provide it with additional capital, which was repaid in full by 2013. At the same time, new management was brought in and significant changes to FIRA's operations and strategy were implemented

(Austin, Chu, and Reavis 2004). FIRA's new strategy focused on establishing strategic partnerships between large agribusiness companies and primary producers and creating new financial and risk management instruments that might be attractive for financial intermediaries. Moreover, FIRA's risk management, finance, and strategic management capabilities were strengthened, and new human resource management policies were introduced. FIRA significantly reduced its interest rate subsidies, with the spread between its lending rate and interbank rates decreasing from over 7 percent in 1998 to less than 2 percent by 2004. FIRA had total assets of US$7.7 billion at the end of 2014, with its loan portfolio reaching US$6 billion and a total value of outstanding credit guarantees of about US$3 billion. FIRA's second-tier lending and credit guarantees accounted for 68 percent of total commercial bank financing to the primary sector in Mexico in 2014 and reached almost 1 million borrowers.

FIRA has used tailor-made structured finance transactions to facilitate access to credit in the agriculture, livestock, and fishing sectors. FIRA has arranged structured finance transactions that rely on two different types of instruments: asset-backed securities (ABS) and collateralized loan obligations (CLO). FIRA's ABS transactions are usually designed to transform movable assets, such as commodity inventories, into viable collateral for financial institutions. These transactions involve the securitization of loans backed by movable collateral and the sale of participations in the trust fund that owns these loans to investors, typically financial institutions. They also involve an operational agent, usually a large commercial firm, which shares the risk, screens producers, monitors inventories, and provides an outlet for the liquidation of the collateral in case of default. FIRA's CLO transactions, in turn, are usually designed to provide working capital financing; that is, there is no physical collateral. In this type of transaction, a large commercial firm acts as originator, granting working capital loans to its suppliers. These credit rights are then transferred to an SPV, and securities backed by this asset pool are issued. To align incentives and reduce adverse selection and moral hazard problems, various participants in the supply chain provide guarantees to cover eventual credit losses.

Next, we describe two specific transactions arranged by FIRA, which illustrate how structured finance can address problems of access to finance and might also shed light on the role played by FIRA. We first describe a CLO transaction implemented to provide financing to shrimp producers and then an ABS transaction designed to channel credit to sugar mills.

A CLO Transaction to Provide Financing to Shrimp Producers

The shrimp industry was one of the many industries affected by Mexico's financial crisis in 1994–95 and the subsequent contraction in credit to the private sector.[31] As bank lending to the industry decreased, trade credit became the primary source of financing for shrimp producers. Shrimp farms can obtain credit from feed suppliers, usually paying 50 percent of their input purchases upfront and 50 percent within seven months, but this covers only a relatively small fraction of their total operating costs.[32] Furthermore, this trade credit is restricted by the lack of access to external finance by feed suppliers and also exposes them to high credit risk. Shrimp distributors are another potential source of working capital financing for shrimp producers. However, the contraction in bank lending to the sector following the crisis limited distributors' ability to grant credit to producers.

In this context, FIRA designed a CLO transaction to provide working capital financing to shrimp producers in collaboration with Ocean Garden, the largest shrimp distributor in Mexico.[33] The general structure is summarized in figure 4.3. Shrimp producers sign supply contracts with Ocean Garden to deliver a certain amount of shrimp at a future date at an agreed-on price. Ocean Garden pays a portion of these contracts (typically 75 percent) in advance to provide producers with working capital. These loans have a maturity of 180 days, renewable for another 90 days. The interest rate on these loans is determined by Ocean Garden based on the credit quality of each producer. Ocean Garden has historical data on the performance of shrimp producers, allowing it to construct credit histories, and has also developed a credit-scoring system to evaluate their creditworthiness. This implies that producers have an incentive to meet their obligations to maintain a good track record and obtain lower interest rates in future transactions.

FIGURE 4.3 FIRA's CLO transaction in the shrimp industry

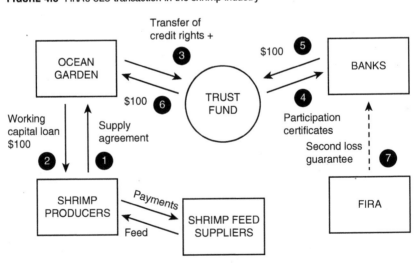

Note: This figure describes the functioning of FIRA's CLO transaction to provide financing to shrimp producers.

The working capital loans made by Ocean Garden are then transferred to an SPV, which sells participations to investors, mostly commercial banks. Ocean Garden acts not only as originator but also as servicer, responsible for transferring payments to the SPV once producers deliver their production and repay their loans.

This structured finance transaction ameliorates information asymmetries by outsourcing the screening of small producers to a large commercial firm like Ocean Garden that has an informational advantage relative to financial intermediaries. A significant problem in this type of structured finance transaction is strategic adverse selection, that is, the fact that, if the originator can choose which assets to transfer to the SPV, it might transfer those with lower credit quality, retaining higher-quality assets on its balance sheet. Also, given that most of the credit risk is transferred to investors, the originator might have fewer incentives to carefully screen and monitor borrowers. Anticipating these problems, investors who have less information about the quality of the assets might not be willing to invest or might ask for a premium to compensate them.

This particular transaction has several built-in mechanisms to ameliorate these problems. First, because Ocean Garden signs supply agreements with the producers, it depends on the fulfillment of these agreements for its future sales, and therefore has incentives to adequately screen and monitor producers. Second, to further reduce incentive compatibility problems, different industry participants share part of the risk of the transaction by providing liquid (cash) guarantees to cover credit losses. Shrimp producers and suppliers of shrimp feed provide liquid guarantees that cover credit losses up to 24 percent. These guarantees are linked to specific loans and cover only the default of a particular producer, creating incentives for the shrimp feed suppliers to screen and monitor shrimp producers. Feed producers agree to provide guarantees because this scheme implies a lower credit risk exposure for them than directly granting trade credit to shrimp producers, as was the norm before this transaction. Also, by helping their clients improve their access to credit, suppliers benefit from an increased demand for their products.

Ocean Garden provides a general guarantee that covers all credit losses up to 25 percent of the total asset pool. Once these guarantees are exhausted, investors start facing credit losses. This happens when total losses exceed about 32 percent. FIRA estimates that historical credit losses in the shrimp industry average about 4.2 percent per year, with a maximum observed level of 27 percent; hence, these guarantees are expected to cover all credit losses under most circumstances. Credit losses not covered by these liquid guarantees are divided between FIRA (90 percent) and the banks that purchase the securities (10 percent), as shown in table 4.1. Thus, the total net risk exposure of the banks that purchase the securities in this scheme is 5.1 percent, whereas that of FIRA is 45.9 percent, in both cases after first losses.

TABLE 4.1 Distribution of credit losses in FIRA's CLO transaction in the shrimp industry

Percentage of nonperforming loans	Shrimp and feed producer guarantees (*)	Ocean Garden guarantee	FIRA guarantee	Bank credit losses
10	2.4	7.6	0.0	0.0
20	2.4	7.6	0.0	0.0
30	2.4	7.6	0.0	0.0
40	2.4	2.2	4.9	0.5
50	2.4	0.0	6.8	0.8
60	2.4	0.0	6.8	0.8
70	2.4	0.0	6.8	0.8
80	2.4	0.0	6.8	0.8
90	2.4	0.0	6.8	0.8
100	2.4	0.0	6.8	0.8
Total risk exposure	**24.0**	**25.0**	**45.9**	**5.1**

Note: This table shows the distribution of credit losses among participants in FIRA's CLO transaction in the shrimp sector depending on the overall share of nonperfoming loans in the asset pool.
* These guarantees are loan specific.

As described above, FIRA acts not only as an arranger for the transaction (charging a fee of 0.75 percent for this service) but also as a financial guarantor, covering second losses (charging a 1 percent premium for the provision of its guarantee). Furthermore, because FIRA is a second-tier lending institution, it requires all banks that participate in this transaction to use its funding to purchase the securities issued by the SPV. The provision of credit by FIRA is not key for the functioning of the program and, as discussed in the section below, seems to be a consequence of institutional incentives, given that FIRA's performance is assessed on the basis of the volume of its loan disbursements.

This structured finance transaction presents several advantages in terms of dealing with problems of access to credit. First, as mentioned above, the participation of a large commercial firm like Ocean Garden that has a better knowledge of small producers ameliorates information problems. Second, pooling loans to several producers reduces transaction costs and allows investors to diversify their risk exposure. This financing scheme involves about 150 small shrimp producers. Securing credit for each of these producers individually would be too costly for financial institutions; but through the pooling of working capital loans, it is possible to achieve economies of scale and reduce costs. The process also allows financial institutions to diversify their risk exposure as they face the aggregate credit risk of all participating shrimp producers, rather than the risk of a particular producer.[34]

Another advantage of this transaction is that financial institutions do not face Ocean Garden's credit risk because the supply contracts are removed from its balance sheet and their ownership is transferred to the SPV. This means that, if Ocean Garden files for bankruptcy, the assets in the pool do not come under court jurisdiction.[35] This type of transaction also allows smaller, mostly urban banks to provide financing to the fishing sector, helping them to diversify their loan portfolio. Finally, this transaction generates a more efficient and transparent distribution of risks. As mentioned above, before the creation of this scheme, shrimp producers relied mostly on trade credit from their suppliers, who in many cases faced significant credit constraints themselves. In contrast, this CLO transaction profits from the informational advantages of industry players without requiring them to act as financiers. It also increases transparency, by making clear the risk faced by each party and the corresponding compensation.

FIRA has arranged similar CLO transactions to provide financing to small producers in other sectors—including wheat, corn, and sorghum production—using large commercial firms as originators.

ABS Transactions to Provide Financing to Sugar Mills

Mexico is a significant producer, consumer, and exporter of sugar. Historically, state intervention in the sugar industry has been very extensive, resulting in a series of policies that regulate the market and attempt to protect sugar producers. See box 4.1 for a description of some of these policies and the evolution of the Mexican sugar industry. These policies shift a significant part of industry risk to sugar mills and reduce their ability to adjust to market conditions. In 2001, sugar mills faced a significant credit crunch, partly as a legacy of the 1994–95 financial crisis that had led to large increases in interest rates, resulting in unsustainable debt burdens for mills that were already highly indebted, and partly as a consequence of overproduction and increased competition from corn fructose imported from the United States.

In this context, FIRA designed an ABS transaction to provide financing to sugar mills, with the collaboration of Cargill Mexico. The general structure is summarized in figure 4.4. Sugar mills store their sugar inventories in warehouses previously selected and authorized by Cargill. Cargill then gives credit to the sugar mills by making a repurchase agreement (repo) for the certificates of deposit issued by these warehouses.[36] These loans are for an amount equivalent to 80 percent of the value of the sugar inventories stored in the warehouse and have a maturity of 45 days, renewable for successive periods of 45 days, up to a maximum of 270 days. The implicit interest rate on these loans is equal to LIBOR (London Interbank Offered Rate) plus 4.75 percentage points, without any

BOX 4.1 The Mexican sugar industry

Mexico is a significant producer, consumer, and exporter of sugar. It is the sixth-largest sugarcane and sugar producer in the world, accounting for about 3 percent of world sugarcane production in 2012. The Mexican sugar industry accounted for about 0.4 percent of gross domestic product in 2012, generating directly over 900,000 jobs and indirectly about 2.2 million. Historically, state intervention in this sector has been very extensive. This has translated into a series of policies that regulate the sugar market and attempt to protect sugarcane producers, resulting at times in the expropriation and state ownership of sugar mills.

Until the 1970s, Mexican sugar mills were mostly privately owned. Nonetheless, the government actively intervened in the industry. Beginning in the 1930s, the government worked with mills to regulate the domestic sugar market via the Comisión Estabilizadora del Mercado de Azúcar (Commission to Stabilize the Sugar Market). The authorities also introduced two legal measures that, to a large extent, have shaped the industry's structure and evolution. In 1944, the government issued a decree (Decreto Cañero, Sugarcane Grower Decree) that regulates relations between sugar mills and sugarcane producers.[a] This decree required farms operating close to sugar mills to produce only sugarcane and also mandated sugar mills to buy all of these farms' output. This requirement in effect created a captive market for farmers, leading to a significant increase in the area dedicated to sugarcane production. The decree also established a pricing formula for sugarcane purchases by mills. In addition to the Decreto Cañero, the government also imposed a set of contractual obligations for sugar mills in their relations with workers (Contrato Ley) that are far more rigorous than those in other industries.

The government's intervention in the sugar industry in effect restricted mills' ability to adjust their purchases to market conditions, transferring most of the industry risk to these firms. Prices were regulated along the entire industry chain, and there was little relation between the price paid to producers for sugarcane and wholesale sugar prices. Price controls at the consumer level were used to maintain low prices, whereas the price paid to producers was increased to stimulate production. Furthermore, the Decreto Cañero provided incentives for farmers to maximize their production, irrespective of whether mills could sell their sugar at a profit or not. This industry structure resulted in significant financial difficulties for mills. In 1971, the Mexican government decided to take over those mills that were in financial trouble, and by the mid-1980s it owned about three-fourths of the sugar mills in the country.

The government maintained control of most of the industry for the following two decades. Sugar production increased significantly during this period, growing from 2.2 million tons in 1970 to 3.5 million tons in 1989, primarily as a result of a large expansion in the area dedicated to sugarcane production led by small producers. State-owned sugar mills were overstaffed, and productivity levels declined. Subsidies to the sugar sector grew continuously over this period, and by 1988 they represented about one-fourth of the annual budget of the secretary of agriculture.

In the late 1980s, the government decided to privatize publicly owned mills and announced some measures to liberalize the sugar market. Given the high degree of political intervention in the sector and the financial difficulties faced by sugar mills, the government encouraged private investor participation by allowing the purchase of mills through highly leveraged operations. The government also established import tariffs of 10 and 15 percent for raw and refined sugar, respectively, to protect the sector from foreign competition. However, despite these tariffs, imports grew exponentially

(continued on next page)

BOX 4.1 The Mexican sugar industry *(continued)*

between 1989 and 1991. The 1994–95 financial crisis had a significant impact on the industry because the resulting increase in interest rates led to unsustainable debt burdens for already highly leveraged mills. In September 1995, a debt-restructuring package worth US$1.3 billion was offered through Financiera Nacional Azucarera (FINASA), a government-owned bank focused on the sugar sector (Larson and Borrell 2001).

The Mexican government also tried to support the sugar industry by keeping domestic prices above world prices, limiting imports through high tariffs, and regulating the amount of sugar sold in the domestic market. In 1997, the government started to coordinate with mills the amount of sugar that could be sold domestically, in effect establishing the quantity that had to be exported or held in stock. Export quotas were divided among mills on a pro rata basis, and the government imposed penalties to discourage firms from selling assigned export quotas in the local market.

Despite these efforts, most mills continued to face significant financial difficulties, not only because of their high debt burdens but also as a result of high sugarcane production and increased competition from sugar substitutes, especially high fructose corn syrup imported from the United States.[b] In 2001, as financial difficulties in the sugar industry became more acute, the Mexican government decided to take over those mills that were in the worst financial condition. It expropriated 27 of the 61 sugar mills in the country, which represented about 60 percent of total sugar production at the time.[c]

a. There have been several decrees replacing the original Decreto Cañero, but they have maintained a relatively similar structure to regulate relations between sugar mills and sugarcane producers. A significant change introduced in 1991 was linking the price paid to sugarcane producers to the official price of sugar and allowing price differentiation depending on the quality of sugarcane. In 2005, the government derogated the latest version of Decreto Cañero, but the Mexican Congress created a new sugar sector law that includes most of the old principles governing relations between industry participants.

b. Mexico has been involved in a trade dispute with the United States over the interpretation of the North American Free Trade Agreement (NAFTA) in its application to the sugar and high fructose corn syrup industries. In 1997, Mexico imposed antidumping duties on U.S. exports of high fructose corn syrup, which were subsequently lifted following adverse rulings from the World Trade Organization (WTO) and the NAFTA dispute settlement panels. In 2002, the Mexican government imposed a 20 percent tax on all beverages sweetened with high fructose corn syrup. This tax was subsequently declared in violation of WTO rules. See Haley and Suarez (1999) and Shwedel and Ampudia (2004) for more discussion of this issue.

c. The Mexican Supreme Court has since declared this expropriation unconstitutional, ordering that the mills be returned to their owners.

differentiation across mills. Cargill then creates a funded participation program backed by the pool of certificates of deposit and sells participations to investors, mostly commercial banks.

Cargill acts as a servicer in this transaction. It is in charge of evaluating, selecting, and monitoring warehouses and is also responsible for transferring payments to the fund when sugar mills cancel their loans. Cargill also administers a margin call system that is designed to protect investors from fluctuations in sugar prices. When the ratio of the market price of the sugar stored in the warehouse to the

FIGURE 4.4 FIRA's ABS transaction in the sugar industry

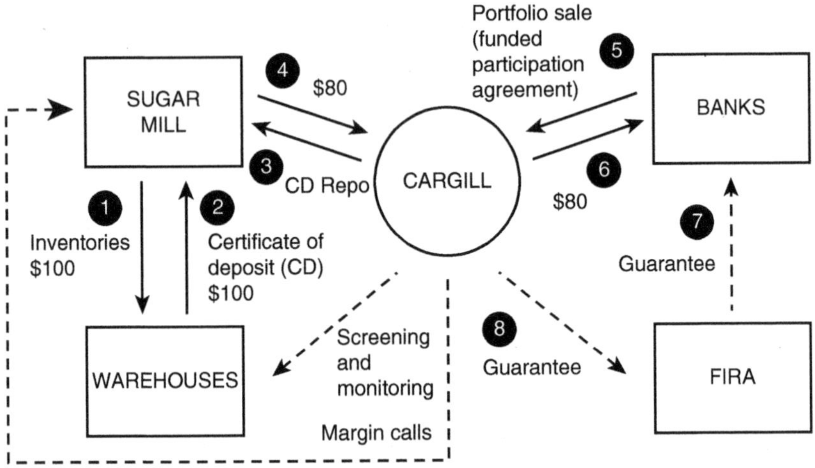

Note: This figure describes the functioning of FIRA's ABS transaction to provide financing to sugar mills.

value of the loan falls below 1.25, Cargill issues a margin call requiring the mill to deposit additional sugar in the warehouse (or to provide cash guarantees) to restore this ratio. Mills have three business days to fulfill the margin call—otherwise they are declared in default and their inventories are liquidated.[37]

FIRA acts as an arranger in this transaction and also provides a credit guarantee covering 96 percent of the total value of the financing provided by commercial banks. FIRA charges a 1 percent premium for the provision of this guarantee. To reduce its risk exposure, FIRA has an agreement with Cargill, which commits to purchasing any repossessed inventories from FIRA in case of default. Under this agreement, Cargill covers 80 percent of the total credit losses, reducing FIRA's exposure to 16 percent of the total credit provided through this transaction. Cargill charges a 2.5 percent fee for providing this guarantee and acting as a servicer. The fact that FIRA provides the guarantee to banks and then gets a guarantee from Cargill, instead of Cargill directly providing the guarantee to banks, is explained by regulatory arbitrage. Because FIRA is a public sector institution, capital requirements on bank loans guaranteed by FIRA are lower than those on loans guaranteed by a private party. It is also a consequence of institutional incentives, as discussed in more detail in the next section, because FIRA is evaluated on the basis of the amount of guarantees and loans it provides. Similar to the case of the CLO transaction described above, FIRA requires all banks to use its second-tier lending to purchase the participations in the fund.

This structured finance transaction facilitates access to finance for sugar mills by transforming their inventories into viable collateral for financial transactions. The use of these inventories as collateral for traditional commercial lending faces several difficulties. First, movable collateral such as sugar inventories is difficult to secure. Sugar mills could pledge their inventories as collateral and then easily sell those inventories without lenders knowing about it. In the case of Mexico, this problem was compounded by the lack of a reliable warehousing market that could guarantee the value and quality of the stored inventories. Cargill's know-how in selecting and monitoring commodity warehouses is key in this respect.

Second, sugar prices are very volatile and there are no derivatives markets for sugar in Mexico.[38] As a result, using sugar inventories as collateral would expose financial institutions to significant price risk. The system of margin calls managed by Cargill was established to address this problem. This system ensures that the value of the inventories pledged as collateral maintains a constant relation with the amount borrowed.

Finally, another problem with using sugar inventories as collateral is the potential high cost of repossession and liquidation. Banks are unlikely to have the required knowledge to participate directly in sugar markets and therefore face a high cost of selling sugar inventories in case of repossession. In this ABS transaction, Cargill's participation addresses this problem by providing an outlet for the liquidation of the sugar inventories. As described above, in case of default, FIRA can sell 80 percent of the repossessed sugar inventories to Cargill. Moreover, the use of a repurchase agreement reduces repossession costs because it effectively transfers legal ownership of the inventories to Cargill, eliminating the need to face the cumbersome and lengthy collateral repossession process when default occurs.

In addition to addressing the problems related to collateral, this structured finance transaction also reduces transaction costs by pooling loans to several sugar mills (27 in total). Pooling also allows financial institutions to diversify their risk exposure because they do not face the idiosyncratic risk of a specific mill, but rather the aggregate risk of lending to all the mills included in the scheme. Furthermore, this transaction increases transparency by making clear the amount and type of risk that each party bears and the corresponding compensation. Cargill takes 80 percent of the credit risk and acts as a servicer, obtaining a 2.5 percent fee. FIRA takes 16 percent of the credit risk and charges 1 percent for its guarantee. In addition, it charges 0.09 percentage point over LIBOR for its second-tier funding. Investors take 4 percent of the credit risk and obtain an intermediation margin of 1.16 percent. Overall, sugar mills pay an interest equal to LIBOR plus 4.75 percentage points.

FIRA has arranged similar ABS transactions to channel credit for rural producers in other sectors, including corn, shrimp, sorghum, wheat, and cattle.

Policy Discussion and Conclusions

FIRA's experience with structured finance transactions raises a number of interesting issues that deserve further discussion. We first briefly analyze some of the salient design features of FIRA's transactions and then discuss some arguments that might provide support to this type of state intervention. We end with a discussion of some open questions regarding these transactions. We believe that a better understanding of these issues can yield significant insights for the debate on the role of the public sector in broadening access and can also help in understanding the potential value added of this type of intervention. We return to some of these issues in chapter 9.

There are several features of FIRA's structured finance transactions that in our view provide relevant insights into how pro-market interventions might work in practice and how they are shaped by institutional constraints and incentives.

First, as described above, FIRA not only acts as an arranger in these transactions but also provides credit guarantees and second-tier lending to the participating financial institutions. This bundling of several different products (for example, arranger services, credit guarantees, and lending) reduces transparency, making it difficult to assess the benefits and pricing of each product, and carries the risk of distorting incentives. The provision of credit guarantees and second-tier lending by FIRA as part of the structured finance transactions seems to be, to a large extent, the result of institutional incentives; because FIRA is evaluated on the basis of its loan disbursements and the volume of guarantees it provides, it has incentives to structure its operations around these financial products. This suggests that, as institutions move toward more catalytic interventions, where the main role of the state is to foster contracting among private parties, new performance metrics and evaluation procedures will be necessary. This requires moving away from measures based on the volume of credit and/or guarantees provided and focusing instead on the amount of financial intermediation promoted and the impact of interventions on those firms and households that receive financing. These new performance criteria are more difficult to design and measure than traditional ones, and it might take time and a process of trial and error to find the correct indicators to evaluate specific interventions.

Second, FIRA provides guarantees that cover most of the credit risk faced by investors in its structured finance transactions. In the transactions described in this chapter, FIRA's guarantees limit the credit risk exposure of participating banks to only about 5 percent of the total amount lent. Although, in more recent structured transactions, FIRA has reduced the level of credit enhancement it provides, the credit risk faced by participating financial institutions remains quite low. FIRA reduces its risk exposure by purchasing guarantees from private parties and only taking second losses, decreasing the amount of risk shifting to the public sector that actually takes place. Interviews with banks that participate in FIRA's structured transactions suggest that the high level of credit enhancement provided by FIRA is explained not by banks' risk aversion but rather by regulatory arbitrage. Capital requirements for loans guaranteed by FIRA are lower than those for loans with no guarantees and loans with private guarantees. Banks would be willing to take on more credit risk, but this would lead to higher lending costs because lower FIRA guarantees would mean higher capital requirements.

Third, the investors in the structured finance transactions described are only commercial banks—although, in principle, participations in these transactions could be sold to other investor groups, such as insurance companies, mutual funds, and pension funds. This could help broaden the investor base and might also foster the development of nonbank intermediaries. The exclusive participation of banks in these transactions is partly a consequence of the institutional design because FIRA is a second-tier financial institution that provides guarantees and lending to commercial banks. FIRA's mandate has been modified to allow it to include other financial intermediaries and investors in its transactions.

FIRA's structured finance transactions are designed to involve private financial institutions in the provision of financing to the agriculture, livestock, and fishing sectors. In principle, at least, private financial intermediaries could have arranged these types of transactions. In fact, as mentioned above, Mexico has one of the most active structured finance markets in Latin America. Therefore, some might question whether FIRA's involvement in directly arranging these transactions is actually necessary. At the time that the transactions described in this chapter were implemented, private sector firms were not providing structured finance to the sugar and shrimp sectors, and producers in both industries had limited access to formal financing. It is difficult to pinpoint exactly why financial intermediaries were not exploiting a potentially profitable opportunity. One possible explanation is that the structured finance transactions designed by FIRA require the involvement of several different industry players, and coordination failures among private parties might make it difficult for these types of arrangements to emerge privately. In this situation, there can be a role for a public institution like FIRA to intervene, to the extent that it might have a relative advantage in overcoming coordination problems.

Another possible explanation for why private financial intermediaries did not arrange similar structured finance transactions despite their potential profitability is that the securitization of the type of assets used in FIRA's transactions requires specialized knowledge and using tailor-made structures. Private financial intermediaries might lack incentives to incur the upfront costs of learning about new sectors and devising less standardized transactions because, once their efforts prove to be successful, others can easily reproduce them (Stiglitz 1987; Besley 1994). In this situation, there might be a role for the public sector to promote innovation in financial markets. FIRA's structured finance transactions could have a demonstration effect, showing that these types of operations can be profitable and fostering private financial intermediaries to develop similar structures.

Even if there are relevant arguments to justify FIRA's intervention, some valid questions concerning its structured finance transactions still remain. First, it is not clear to what extent FIRA's interventions actually foster financial market development because they seem to leave very little room for private financial intermediation. As described above, FIRA not only acts as an arranger in its structured finance transactions but also grants second-tier financing to banks and provides them with credit guarantees that significantly reduce their risk exposure. The fact that banks face only residual credit risk can reduce incentives to improve their risk assessment capabilities and develop adequate knowledge in lending to the primary sector. Furthermore, the provision of credit guarantees by FIRA might prevent the development of an active private guarantee market.

Second, even if there is a role for the public sector in fostering financial innovation, this could be achieved in different ways. It is not clear whether the direct intervention of a state-owned financial institution like FIRA in the development and provision of new financial products is the best option. Alternatively, the government could provide a subsidy to investment banks or other private financial intermediaries to arrange the kind of operations brokered by FIRA. A possible rationale for FIRA's direct involvement is that, as mentioned above, it may have some advantages relative to private intermediaries in arranging these transactions, given its specialized industry knowledge and closer relation with the different industry players. Moreover, it may be difficult for the state to contract private financial intermediaries to develop financial innovations, given that by definition new financial products are unknown a priori and therefore this objective is not easily contractable and monitorable.[39] In this situation, as discussed in more detail in chapter 9, institutions like FIRA could play a role in promoting financial innovation by actively seeking new opportunities and identifying obstacles to financial contracting. Further research is necessary to determine whether this could be an effective model to foster innovation in financial markets and address problems of access to finance.

Third, FIRA's interventions might be viewed as second-best solutions that can cause the public sector to deviate from its basic and unique function as provider of an adequate enabling environment for financial contracting. Arguably, it would be better to improve the collateral market by fostering the development of a reliable warehousing system and improving collateral repossession laws and judicial procedures, instead of devising an ABS transaction to circumvent the problems of using inventories as collateral. However, both measures are not necessarily mutually exclusive. The ABS transaction developed by FIRA may be a short-term solution, whereas the warehousing market takes time to develop. Also, this ABS scheme may contribute to the development of the warehousing market by providing adequate incentives to warehouses and may help authorities to understand which regulations or enforcement mechanisms are necessary for this market to develop.

Finally, the case of the ABS transaction described in the previous section raises some questions regarding the motivations for FIRA's interventions. As described in box 4.1, the Mexican sugar sector is highly politicized and state intervention in the industry has been widespread. It is thus natural to question whether FIRA's ABS transaction was developed just as a means to channel financing to a politically connected sector without addressing an actual problem of access to finance. Although political motivations likely played an important role in the development of this particular operation, this does not necessarily imply that ABS transactions are not useful instruments for dealing with problems of access. Similar structured finance transactions have been used to provide financing to producers in other sectors—including corn, wheat, sorghum, shrimp, and cattle—which are not as politically connected as the sugar industry. Nevertheless, this experience highlights the risk that political motivations, and not the need to address problems of access, may drive public sector interventions. Although different institutional mechanisms may be designed to try to isolate the operations of development finance institutions from political influence, these mechanisms cannot guarantee independence. Therefore, the extent to which pro-market interventions can be implemented without undue political influence is likely to ultimately depend on the will of political stakeholders. This might be a significant constraint for replicating these experiences, especially in countries that lack an adequate institutional and political environment.

To conclude, FIRA's structured finance transactions are interesting examples of the emerging new types of public sector interventions aimed at increasing access to finance, which entail a move away from traditional public lending operations. FIRA's main role in these transactions has been acting as arranger, promoting the coordination among different industry stakeholders and financial intermediaries. Further research is necessary to adequately identify the extent to which these structured finance transactions are efficient instruments to overcome problems of access to credit and how these interventions can be designed to ensure that they do not displace market activity and to minimize any distortions.

Notes

1. As discussed in detail later in the chapter, FIRA typically plays multiple roles in structured finance transactions, mostly as a result of institutional incentives.

2. See Davis (2005) for a survey of alternative definitions of structured finance.

3. Structured finance transactions that include existing receivables (for example, loans, leases, intellectual property rights) in the asset pool are usually referred to as *asset backed*, and transactions that use receivables to be generated in the future arising from the originator's business activities (for example, future toll collections from a toll road operator; future credit card receivables generated by an airline) are called *future flow* transactions.

4. Some authors (for example, Alles 2001 and BIS 2005) differentiate between securitization, which involves only the pooling and transfer of assets to a third party and subsequent issuance of securities, and structured financing, which also involves the creation of different classes of securities. In keeping with common usage, we use the term "structured finance" to refer to both types of instruments.

5. Fannie Mae (created in 1938) and Freddie Mac (created in 1970) are government-sponsored enterprises chartered by the U.S. Congress to provide financing for single-family and multifamily housing.

6. CMOs were originally developed to address the problems generated by prepayment risk, that is, the risk arising from the fact that homeowners tend to refinance their mortgages when interest rates are lower, which translates into prepayment of MBS principal, forcing investors to reinvest their returned funds at lower rates. The first CMOs were structured so as to reduce the prepayment risk faced by certain tranches, by shifting prepayment variability to more junior tranches. The growth of the U.S. market for CMOs was subsequently fostered by the Tax Reform Act of 1986, which provided favorable tax treatment for MBS.

7. In synthetic securitization structures, financial institutions transfer the credit risk of the asset pool to the SPV by means of credit derivatives, such as credit default swaps (contracts between two parties in which one party, the seller or writer, offers the other, the buyer, insurance against default of the underlying assets in return for periodic payments), instead of directly transferring ownership of the assets, as in traditional securitizations.

8. See Jones (2000), CGFS (2005), IMF (2009), and Hull and White (2012), among others, for discussions of the main drivers of the precrisis expansion of structured finance markets.

9. See Borio (2008), Caballero and Krishnamurthy (2008), *The Economist* (2009), Gorton (2008), BIS (2009), Brunnermeier (2009), and Thakor (2015), among many others, for overviews of the global financial crisis.

10. The data on structured finance issuance for European countries include retained issues, that is, structured finance transactions that are not placed in the market but rather created by banks to be used as collateral for accessing funding from the European Central Bank. If retained issues are excluded, figures for European countries are significantly lower.

11. See IOSCO (2010) for a general overview of structured finance markets and their regulatory frameworks in emerging economies.

12. China initially launched a pilot asset securitization program in 2005, which allowed some banks to issue ABS. This program was put on hold during the global financial crisis and was restarted in 2011, when the government expanded the program to new sectors, such as nonbank financial intermediaries, and increased the aggregate issuance volume allowed.

13. Governments, international regulators, and industry standard-setters have launched a variety of regulatory initiatives aimed at addressing incentive and information problems in the securitization process. BCBS (2011) provides an overview of postcrisis regulatory initiatives related to structured finance markets. In some cases, governments have also intervened directly in structured finance markets, purchasing certain types of ABS and/or providing guarantees to foster the securitization of some

types of underlying assets, such as loans to small and medium enterprises (SMEs). See Aiyar et al. (2015) for a discussion of initiatives aimed at fostering the securitization of SME loans.

14. See Mitchell (2005) for a detailed analysis of the benefits of structured finance.

15. In many structured finance transactions, originators provide credit enhancements, which protect investors from reductions in the value of the underlying assets. Originators may also provide liquidity backstops to protect investors from rollover risk in those transactions in which the securities issued by the SPV have a shorter maturity than the underlying assets. These types of guarantees imply that at least part of the risk remains with the originator, and thus the performance of the securities is not completely delinked from that of the originator. Shin (2009) and Acharya et al. (2013) argue that this incomplete risk transfer played a significant role in the global financial crisis. In those transactions where the originator remains as the servicer, its performance could affect the cash flow accruing to investors.

16. Gorton and Souleles (2007) argue that SPVs create value by minimizing the deadweight costs of bankruptcy. Ayotte and Gaon (2011) show that separating the creditors of the SPV from the originating firm can limit expropriation in bankruptcy.

17. See CGFS (2005) for a discussion of the role of credit ratings in structured finance.

18. This is an application of the Modigliani–Miller theorem, which states that—in the absence of taxes, bankruptcy costs, and market imperfections—the value of a firm is unaffected by its capital structure (Modigliani and Miller 1958).

19. Restrictions on the set of securities in which asset managers can invest may arise endogenously to solve principal–agent problems between investors and portfolio managers (Titman 2002; Cantor 2004).

20. See Riddough (1997), De Marzo and Duffie (1999), De Marzo (2005), and Gorton and Souleles (2007) for analyses of issues related to asymmetric information in structured finance transactions. Ashcraft and Schuermann (2008) present an extensive analysis of the incentive and information problems that arise throughout the long chains from origination to investment in structured finance transactions (such as originators, arrangers, guarantors, rating agencies, and asset managers), with a focus on the U.S. subprime mortgage market. A large literature discusses how incentive and information problems in structured finance resulted in poor loan origination and excessive risk taking in the run-up to the global financial crisis (see, among many others, IMF 2009; Paligorova 2009; BCBS 2011; and Segoviano et al. 2013).

21. Mian and Sufi (2009), Keys et al. (2010), Purnanandam (2011), Demyanyk and Van Hemert (2011), and Dell'Ariccia, Igan, and Laeven (2012) present empirical evidence suggesting that securitization reduced incentives for U.S. mortgage originators to adequately screen borrowers, leading to a worsening in credit quality in the run-up to the crisis. In contrast to these findings, Albertazzi et al. (2011) analyze the case of Italy and find that banks were able to effectively overcome the negative effects of asymmetric information in the securitization market by selling less opaque loans, retaining equity tranches, and building up a reputation for good lending standards.

22. In the aftermath of the financial crisis, several countries introduced regulations requiring originators to retain a portion of their issues in order to help align incentives.

·For instance, the Dodd–Frank Act in the United States and the Capital Requirement Directive (CRD II) in Europe require issuers to retain an ownership interest of at least 5 percent in the assets they securitize. See Fender and Mitchell (2009) for a theoretical analysis of the effects of different retention mechanisms on the incentives of originators to screen borrowers.

23. See Cousseran et al. (2005) and Fender and Mitchell (2005) for discussions of the sources of complexity in structured finance transactions and the resulting risks.

24. Several authors have argued that the complexity of structured finance transactions, especially those transactions involving tranches of other structured deals in the asset pool, made it difficult for investors to accurately assess their risk, resulting in an overreliance on credit ratings and unexpected credit losses during the 2007–09 financial crisis (see, for example, ECB 2008; Gorton 2008; and BIS 2009).

25. Since the financial crisis, national authorities and international regulators have launched a variety of initiatives aimed at increasing simplicity, transparency, and comparability of structured finance transactions in order to make it easier for both investors and supervisors to asses their risks. See, for instance, Bank of England and ECB (2015); BCBS and IOSCO (2015); European Commission (2015); and Jobst (2015).

26. See Alles (2001) for more discussion of these issues.

27. See Chiquier, Hassler, and Lea (2004) for an earlier review of the experience of emerging markets with the issuance of MBS.

28. Chapter 8 discusses the role of microfinance in improving access to financial services.

29. Banrural was liquidated in 2003, at an estimated fiscal cost of about US$3.5 billion, and was replaced by a new rural finance entity, Financiera Rural.

30. The subsidy programs operated by FIRA are still financed through budget transfers.

31. See chapter 5 for a brief description of the evolution of the Mexican financial system after 1994.

32. Feed represents about 60 percent of the total operating costs of shrimp farms.

33. Ocean Garden handled approximately two-thirds of Mexico's shrimp exports when this structured finance transaction was first conducted. The firm was owned by the Mexican government and was privatized in 2006.

34. Although it is possible to conceive an alternative scheme in which various banks could provide credit directly to shrimp producers with a guarantee from either Ocean Garden or FIRA (or both), this would be more costly for lenders and would increase banks' exposure to the idiosyncratic risk of each individual producer.

35. However, returns to investors in this transaction could be affected if Ocean Garden went bankrupt because it would be necessary to find a new outlet to sell the production already contracted for with shrimp producers.

36. A repurchase agreement is an agreement whereby one party sells an asset to another at a certain price with the commitment to buy back the asset at a later date for another price. A repo is legally a sale and subsequent repurchase, effectively transferring the property of the asset to the creditor. However, from an economic perspective, it is similar to a secured loan.

37. FIRA estimates that, given the historical volatility of sugar prices, the maximum expected loss during a three-day period, at a 95 percent confidence level, is 2.82 percent.

38. Hedging price risk in international derivatives markets is not feasible, given that sugar markets are highly protected and segmented, and therefore prices may evolve differently across countries.

39. The literature on contracting discusses the conditions under which state ownership could be preferable to contracting with and regulation of private firms. See Shleifer (1998) for a review of this literature, and IDB (2005) for a discussion of how these arguments apply to banking.

References

Acharya, Viral V., Philipp Schnabl, and Gustavo Suarez. 2013. "Securitization Without Risk Transfer." *Journal of Financial Economics* 107: 515–36.

Aiyar, S., A. Al-Eyd, B. Barkbu, and A. Jobst. 2015. "Revitalizing Securitization for Small and Medium-Sized Enterprises in Europe." IMF Staff Discussion Note 15/07, International Monetary Fund, Washington, DC.

Albertazzi, Ugo, Ginette Eramo, Leonardo Gambacorta, and Carmelo Salleo. 2011. "Securitization Is Not That Evil After All." BIS Working Papers No 341, Bank for International Settlements, Basel.

Alles, Lakshman. 2001. "Asset Securitization and Structured Finance: Future Prospects and Challenges for Emerging Market Countries." IMF Working Paper 01/147, International Monetary Fund, Washington, DC.

Ashcraft, Adam B., and Til Schuermann. 2008. "Understanding the Securitization of Subprime Mortgage Credit." *Foundations and Trends in Finance* 2 (3): 191–309.

Austin, James E., Michael Chu, and Cate Reavis. 2004. "FIRA: Confronting the Mexican Agricultural Crisis." Harvard Business School Case 304-032. March.

Ayotte, Kenneth, and Stav Gaon. 2011. "Asset-Backed Securities: Costs and Benefits of Bankruptcy Remoteness." *Review of Financial Studies* 24 (4): 1299–1335.

Bank of England and ECB (European Central Bank). 2014. "The Case for a Better Functioning Securitisation Market in the European Union." Discussion paper, Bank of England and ECB.

———. 2015. "Joint Response from the Bank of England and the European Central Bank to the Consultation Document of the European Commission: An EU Framework for Simple, Transparent and Standardised Securitisation." Bank of England and ECB.

BCBS (Basel Committee on Banking Supervision). 2011. "Report on Asset Securitisation Incentives." Bank for International Settlements, Basel.

BCBS (Basel Committee on Banking Supervision) and IOSCO (International Organization of Securities Commissions). 2015. "Criteria for Identifying Simple, Transparent and Comparable Securitisations." Bank for International Settlements, Basel.

Besley, Timothy. 1994. "How Do Market Failures Justify Interventions in Rural Credit Markets?" *World Bank Research Observer* 9 (1): 27–47.

BIS (Bank for International Settlements). 2005. *Bank for International Settlements 75th Annual Report.* Basel: BIS.

———. 2009. *Bank for International Settlements 79th Annual Report 2008/09*. Basel: BIS.

Borio, Claudio. 2008. "The Financial Turmoil of 2007–?: A Preliminary Assessment and Some Policy Considerations." BIS Working Papers 251, Bank for International Settlements, Basel.

Brunnermeier, Markus K. 2009. "Symposium: Early Stages of the Credit Crunch: Deciphering the Liquidity and Credit Crunch 2007–2008." *Journal Of Economic Perspectives* 23 (1): 77–100.

Caballero, Ricardo J., and Arvind Krishnamurthy. 2008. "Collective Risk Management in a Flight to Quality Episode." *The Journal of Finance* 63 (5): 2195–230.

Cantor, Richard. 2004. "An Introduction to Recent Research on Credit Ratings." *Journal of Banking And Finance* 28 (11): 2565–73.

CGFS (Committee on the Global Financial System). 2005. "The Role of Ratings in Structured Finance: Issues and Implications." CGFS Papers no. 23, Bank for International Settlements, Basel, January.

Chiquier, Loic, Olivier Hassler, and Michael Lea. 2004. "Mortgage Securities in Emerging Markets." Policy Research Working Paper 3370, World Bank, Washington, DC.

Cousseran, Pierre Olivier, Keith Hall, Isabel von Koeppen, Yoshinori Nakata, and Erin Stuart. 2005. "Non-Credit Risks in Structured Finance Transactions and the Role of Rating Agencies." Background note for the Committee on the Global Financial System (CGFS) Working Group on Ratings in Structured Finance.

Davis, Henry A. 2005. "The Definition of Structured Finance: Results from a Survey." *Journal of Structured Finance* 11: 5–10.

Dell'Ariccia, Giovanni, Deniz Igan, and Luc Laeven. 2012. "Credit Booms and Lending Standards: Evidence from the Subprime Mortgage Market." *Journal of Money, Credit and Banking* 44 (3): 367–84.

De Marzo, Peter M. 2005. "The Pooling and Tranching of Securities: A Model of Informed Intermediation." *Review of Financial Studies* 18 (1): 1–35.

De Marzo, Peter M., and Darrell Duffie. 1999. "A Liquidity-Based Model of Security Design." *Econometrica* 67 (1): 65–99.

Demyanyk, Y., and O. Van Hemert. 2011. "Understanding the Subprime Mortgage Crisis." *Review of Financial Studies* 24 (6): 1848–80.

Duffie, Darrell, and Nicolae Garleanu. 2001. "Risk and Valuation of Collateralized Debt Obligations." *Financial Analysts Journal* 57 (1): 41–59.

ECB (European Central Bank). 2008. *Financial Stability Review—June 2008*. Frankfurt: ECB.

The Economist. 2009. "When a Flow Becomes a Flood." January 22.

European Commission. 2015. "An EU Framework for Simple, Transparent and Standardised Securitisation." European Commission, Brussels, February.

European Investment Bank. 2014. *Unlocking Lending in Europe*. Luxembourg: European Investment Bank.

Fender, Ingo, and Janet Mitchell. 2005. "Structured Finance: Complexity, Risk and the Use of Rating." *BIS Quarterly Review*, June.

———. 2009. "Incentives and Tranche Retention in Securitisation: A Screening Model." Working Paper No 289, Bank for International Settlements, Basel.

FSB (Financial Stability Board). 2010. "Progress Since the Washington Summit in the Implementation of the G20 Recommendations for Strengthening Financial Stability." Report of the Financial Stability Board to G20 Leaders, Basel, FSB.

Gorton, Gary B. 2008. "The Subprime Panic." *European Financial Management* 15 (1): 10–46.

Gorton Gary B., and George G. Pennacchi. 1995. "Bank and Loan Sales: Marketing Nonmarketable Assets." *Journal of Monetary Economics* 35 (3): 389–411.

Gorton Gary B., and Nicholas S. Souleles. 2007. "Special Purpose Vehicles and Securitization." In *The Risks of Financial Institutions*, edited by Mark Carey and René M. Stulz. National Bureau of Economic Research Conference Report. Chicago: University of Chicago Press.

Haley, Stephen, and Nydia Suarez. 1999. "U.S.-Mexico Sweetener Trade Mired in Dispute." U.S. Department of Agriculture (USDA) Economic Research Service, *Agricultural Outlook (September)*: 17–20.

Hull, J., and A. White. 2012. "Ratings, Mortgage Securitizations, and the Apparent Creation of Value." In *Rethinking the Financial System*, edited by Alan Blinder, Andrew Lo, and Robert Solow, chap. 7. New York: Russell Sage Foundation.

IDB (Inter-American Development Bank). 2005. "Economic and Social Progress Report (IPES) 2005: Unlocking Credit: The Quest for Deep and Stable Bank Lending." IDB, Washington, DC.

IMF (International Monetary Fund). 2009. *Global Financial Stability Report.* Washington, DC: IMF.

IOSCO (International Organization of Securities Commissions), 2010. "Securitization and Securitized Debt Instruments in Emerging Markets." IOSCO, Madrid.

Jobst, A. 2015. "Proposed Attributes of High-Quality Securitization in Europe 1, Annex II of Revitalizing Securitization for Small and Medium-Sized Enterprises in Europe." IMF Staff Discussion Note 15/07, International Monetary Fund, Washington, DC.

Jones, D. 2000. "Emerging Problems with the Basel Capital Accord: Regulatory Capital Arbitrage and Related Issues." *Journal of Banking and Finance* 24 (1–2): 35–58.

Keys, Benjamin, Tanmoy Mukherjee, Amit Seru, and Vikrant Vig. 2010. "Did Securitization Lead to Lax Screening? Evidence from Subprime Loans." *Quarterly Journal of Economics* 125 (1): 307–62.

Larson, Donald F., and Brent Borrell. 2001. "Sugar Policy and Reform." Policy Research Working Paper 2602, World Bank, Washington, DC.

Mian, Atif, and Amir Sufi. 2009. "The Consequences of Mortgage Credit Expansion: Evidence from the US Mortgage Default Crisis." *Quarterly Journal of Economics* 124 (4): 1449–96.

Mitchell, Janet. 2005. "Financial Intermediation Theory and Implications for the Sources of Value in Structured Finance Markets." Working Paper 71, National Bank of Belgium, Brussels.

Modigliani, F., and Merton H. Miller. 1958. "The Cost of Capital, Corporation Finance and the Theory of Investment." *American Economic Review* 48 (3): 261–97.

Oldfield, George S. 2000. "Making Markets for Structured Mortgage Derivatives." *Journal of Financial Economics* 57 (3): 445–71.

Paligorova, T. 2009. "Agency Conflicts in the Process of Securitization." *Bank of Canada Review* Autumn: 33–47.

Pennacchi, George G. 1988. "Loan Sales and the Cost of Bank Capital." *Journal of Finance* 43 (2): 375–96.

Purnanandam, A. 2011. "Originate-to-Distribute Model and the Subprime Mortgage Crisis." *Review of Financial Studies* 24 (6): 1881–915.

Riddough, Timothy J. 1997. "Optimal Design and Governance of Asset-Backed Securities." *Journal of Financial Intermediation* 6 (2): 121–52.

Segoviano, M., B. Jones, P. Lindner, and J. Blankenheim, 2013. "Securitization: Lessons Learned and the Road Ahead." IMF Working Paper 255/13, International Monetary Fund, Washington, DC.

Shin, H. S. 2009. "Securitisation and Financial Stability." *Economic Journal* 119 (536): 309–32.

Shleifer, Andrei. 1998. "State versus Private Ownership." *Journal of Economic Perspectives* 12 (4): 133–50.

Shwedel, Kenneth, and Alejandro Ampudia. 2004. "Trade Disputes in an Unsettled Industry: Mexican Sugar." In *Keeping the Borders Open*, edited by R. M. A. Loyns, Karl Meilke, Ronald D. Knutson, and Antonio Yunez-Naude. Proceedings of the 8th Agricultural and Food Policy Systems Information Workshop. Winnipeg: Friesen Printers.

Stiglitz, Joseph E. 1987. "Technological Change, Sunk Costs, and Competition." *Brookings Papers on Economic Activity* 18 (3): 883–937.

Thakor, A. J. 2015. "The Financial Crisis of 2007–09: Why Did It Happen and What Did We Learn?" *Review of Corporate Finance Studies* 4 (2): 115–205.

Titman, Sheridan. 2002. "The Modigliani and Miller Theorem and the Integration of Financial Markets." *Financial Management* 31 (1): 101–15.

World Bank. 1993. *The East Asian Miracle: Economic Growth and Public Policy.* Washington, DC: World Bank.

———. 2001. *Mexico Rural Finance: Savings Mobilization Potential and Deposit Instruments in Marginal Areas.* Report 21286-ME. Washington, DC: World Bank.

CHAPTER 5

An Online Platform for Reverse Factoring Transactions: NAFIN's Experience in Mexico

Introduction

This chapter describes the experience of Nacional Financiera (NAFIN), a Mexican development bank that created an online platform for financial intermediaries to provide factoring services to small and medium enterprises (SMEs).

Small businesses in many countries face difficulties in financing their entire production cycle because bank credit is usually not fully available (at least at desired conditions) and most buyers typically take between 30 and 90 days to pay their suppliers. After delivery, sellers issue an invoice, recorded as an account receivable by the seller and an account payable by the buyer. But sellers need to continue financing their operations after delivery of their products, even if buyers have not yet repaid them. This has led to the emergence of factoring.

Factoring is a type of asset-based financing whereby firms sell their accounts receivable at a discount to a third party (called the *factor*) and receive immediate cash. Factoring is an asset sale, not a loan. There is no debt repayment and no additional liabilities on the supplier's balance sheet.

Factoring is one of the oldest types of commercial finance and has existed in various forms for many centuries. In recent decades, it has experienced significant growth, becoming an important source of short-term working capital financing for SMEs in both developed and developing countries. Factoring seems to have an advantage relative to other forms of commercial lending in providing financing to informationally opaque firms. The key element in this regard is that the credit risk of factoring transactions is primarily determined by the quality of the receivables rather than the creditworthiness of the firm seeking financing. Financial firms have only to evaluate the quality of these underlying assets. As a consequence, factoring can allow small opaque firms, whose clients might be large creditworthy firms, to gain access to credit.

Factoring can be more attractive in countries with weaker institutional environments because it tends to make less intensive use of judicial systems and bankruptcy laws and procedures than traditional forms of financing. Factoring is an asset sale, not a loan; if a firm goes bankrupt, its factored receivables are not part of its bankruptcy estate, and it avoids the need for costly and lengthy bankruptcy procedures. However, creditor rights and contract enforcement are not irrelevant for factoring: they affect factors' ability to collect payment from buyers. Also, in many developing countries the lack of good credit information systems makes it very difficult for factors to accurately assess the credit quality of a supplier's receivables portfolio, hampering the development of factoring markets.

This chapter describes the experience of NAFIN's reverse factoring program in Mexico. In 2001, NAFIN created an Internet-based infrastructure to facilitate factoring transactions. The program works by creating chains between "large buyers" and their suppliers. The buyers that participate in the program, typically large creditworthy firms, must invite suppliers to join their chain. The program allows small suppliers to use their receivables from these large buyers to obtain working capital financing through factoring operations with participating financial institutions. Almost all components of the transaction take place online, reducing costs and making operations almost instantaneous. The program has several built-in mechanisms to deal with information asymmetries and reduce fraud. NAFIN was responsible for the development, production, and marketing costs of the electronic system and is in charge of its operation, but does not provide factoring services directly. Private financial intermediaries carry out all factoring transactions. The program has been quite successful, and NAFIN has entered into agreements with regional development banks to implement similar schemes in several Latin American countries.

NAFIN's reverse factoring program is an example of the recent move of some development finance institutions away from traditional credit operations and toward pro-market interventions. As described above, NAFIN's main role in the program is not to lend directly to SMEs but rather to play a "catalytic" role, providing a platform for financial transactions to take place.[1] NAFIN's case also illustrates how technology can be leveraged to overcome barriers to access to finance. Analyzing this experience not only sheds light on how pro-market interventions work in practice but can also help us understand the challenges that development finance institutions might face in their implementation.

The rest of this chapter is organized as follows. The next section, "How Does Factoring Work?" presents a general overview of factoring, focusing on how it helps overcome barriers to access to finance for SMEs, expanding the discussion from this introduction. Then we describe NAFIN's reverse factoring program. The final section concludes with a discussion of this experience and its implications for the debate on the role of the state in fostering access, as well as the insights it might provide regarding how pro-market interventions actually work.

How Does Factoring Work?

As described above, factoring is a form of commercial finance whereby a firm sells the collection rights of its accounts receivable to a third party in exchange for immediate cash. There are usually three parties in a factoring transaction: the *supplier*, the *buyer*, and the *factor*, typically a specialized financial firm. A standard factoring operation works in the following way. First, the supplier receives a purchase order from the buyer and, upon delivery, issues an invoice, recorded as an account receivable by the supplier and an account payable by the buyer. The supplier then sells this account receivable to the factor at a discount (equal to interest plus service fees) in exchange for immediate cash. When the receivable is due, the buyer pays its debt directly to the factor, who is the legal owner of the receivable.

Although factoring is one of the oldest types of commercial finance and has existed in various forms since the development of commerce and trade, it has experienced significant growth in both developed and developing countries over the last decades.[2] Between 2001 and 2015, total worldwide factoring volume more than doubled in real terms, reaching over €2.5 trillion (US$2.4 trillion) at the end of this period (figure 5.1, panel a). Factoring seems to have weathered the global financial crisis much better than other forms of financing, with worldwide volume experiencing a small decrease in 2009 and quickly resuming its growth thereafter. The worldwide expansion of factoring transactions actually accelerated in the aftermath of the crisis because increased risk aversion among financial intermediaries led to a shift in financing to SMEs from overdraft/unsecured credit facilities to receivables-based factoring, which was perceived as less risky (FCI 2015). In terms of geographical distribution, Europe is the largest factoring market, accounting for about two-thirds of worldwide factoring volumes in 2015, followed by Asia, with 25 percent of total volume. When analyzing cross-country differences, the most active markets (scaling factoring turnover by the size of the economy, as measured by gross domestic product, GDP) are located in France, Italy, and the United Kingdom (figure 5.1, panel b). Factoring is still relatively underdeveloped in most developing countries, but, as figure 5.1 (panel a) shows, transaction volume in those countries has grown exponentially in recent decades, increasing more than tenfold in real terms between 2001 and 2015.[3] Factoring is

FIGURE 5.1 Factoring market development

a. Evolution of worldwide factoring volume

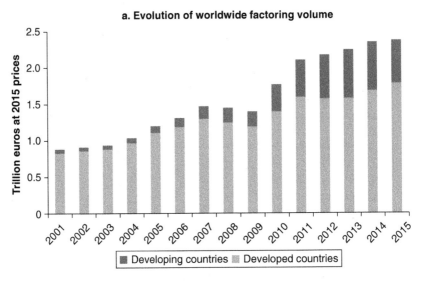

b. Annual factoring volume

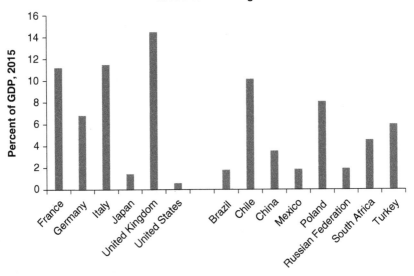

Sources: Factors Chain International, World Economic Outlook (IMF).
Note: Panel a shows the evolution of total factoring volume in developing and developed countries for the period 2004–15 in trillion euros at 2015 prices. Panel b shows factoring volume as a percentage of GDP for G-7 economies and selected developing countries in 2015. Developed countries correspond to high-income economies according to the World Bank classification. Developing countries correspond to low- and middle-income economies according to the World Bank classification.

now a widely used practice and can take a variety of different forms, depending on the characteristics of the firms involved and their financial needs.

Factoring transactions can be done on either a *nonrecourse* or a *recourse* basis. In nonrecourse transactions, the factor assumes most of the credit risk because it has no right to recourse against the supplier in case the buyer defaults. Thus, the credit risk the factor faces is solely that of the buyer. Recourse factoring, on the other hand, allows the factor to make claims against the supplier for any payment deficiency. As a result, the factor faces credit losses only if the supplier cannot compensate for the buyer's failure to pay, resulting in a lower credit risk (other things being equal). In either case, the factor typically does not advance the full amount to be paid for the receivables, holding a percentage as a reserve in case of default. Therefore, even in nonrecourse factoring there is risk sharing between the factor and the supplier.

Factoring can be viewed as a bundling of three different services (Berger and Udell 2006). The first is financing. Factors purchase accounts receivable from suppliers, giving them access to immediate cash to finance their production cycle. The second one is credit-assessment services. Firms that use factoring are essentially outsourcing the evaluation of the credit quality of their buyers to the factoring firm. Factors might have some advantages in credit assessment, because of their specialized knowledge, economies of scale, and better access to credit information (including their own proprietary databases on buyer performance). Finally, factoring also involves collection services. Factors are in charge of collecting current accounts and delinquent accounts and pursuing collections through the judicial system when needed. Again, factoring allows firms to effectively outsource the collection of their trade receivables to factors, which have more expertise in this area and can reap economies of scale.

The fact that factoring is an asset sale, not a loan, differentiates it from other forms of commercial financing. In traditional commercial lending, the main source of repayment is the cash flow generated by the borrower's operations. Although borrowers may pledge some collateral, this is viewed as only a secondary source of repayment. Therefore, access to commercial finance is based mostly on the perceived creditworthiness of the borrower. In the case of factoring, the borrower's viability and creditworthiness, although not irrelevant, tend to be of secondary importance because the credit risk of the operation is mostly that of the accounts receivable themselves.[4]

Factoring can ameliorate problems of access to credit by reducing information asymmetries. As mentioned above, the credit risk of factoring transactions is primarily based on the quality of the receivables rather than the creditworthiness of the firm seeking financing. Financial firms need to evaluate only the quality of these underlying assets and not the business prospects of the borrower, reducing information requirements. As a consequence, factoring allows small, informationally opaque firms, whose clients might be larger creditworthy firms, to gain access to credit (Berger and Udell 2006). Factoring also reduces moral hazard; in most cases, when the accounts receivable are due, the factor collects directly from the buyer, eliminating the possibility of borrowers diverting funds to other uses.

Factoring tends to make less intensive use of the contractual and institutional environment than other forms of financing, making it relatively more attractive in countries with weak commercial laws and enforcement (Klapper 2006). Conventional forms of lending require secured lending laws, proper collateral registries, and quick and efficient judicial systems to enable collateral repossession in case of default. In contrast, these systems are not essential for factoring transactions because these transactions do not involve the use of collateral. Factoring also relies less heavily than traditional lending on the availability of good bankruptcy laws and procedures. Because it involves the purchase of accounts receivable by the factor, not the provision of a loan, the receivables become the property of the factor and are not affected by the bankruptcy of the supplier.

The fact that factoring makes less intensive use of the contractual framework does not imply, however, that the institutional environment has no relevance for its functioning. In ordinary factoring transactions, firms sell their complete portfolio of receivables, or a large part of it, to a particular factor. Most factors buy only large sets of receivables to reduce their exposure to any particular buyer and to achieve a minimum transaction size. This implies that factors must collect credit information on a large number of firms, which can be difficult to obtain in countries without good credit information systems. The lack of good historical credit information on the buyers results in a large credit risk exposure for factors. Because they affect factors' ability to collect payment from buyers, weak creditor rights and contract enforcement institutions can also hamper the success of factoring transactions.[5] Moreover, fraud—such as bogus receivables or nonexistent customers—is a significant problem in factoring transactions. A weak legal environment and lack of adequate registries and credit bureaus can make fraud more likely.

The development of factoring is also affected by specific legal, regulatory, and tax issues that go beyond the general institutional environment discussed above. A key legal issue for the success of factoring transactions is whether a country's commercial law recognizes factoring as an asset sale or not. Another important issue concerns the commercial status of the factoring industry, which in turn determines its regulatory and supervisory structure. In some countries factoring companies are regulated alongside other financial firms, such as banks and insurance companies, whereas in others they operate without any specific regulation. This determines the reporting requirements to which factoring companies are subject, as well as the extent to which prudential regulations are applied to these firms. In some countries, factoring transactions face additional legal hurdles, such as restrictions on the transfer of receivables or the need for debtor approval, which can limit the transferability of receivables (Milenkovic-Kerkovic and Dencic-Mihajlov 2012). In addition, stamp taxes on factored invoices and value-added taxes in some countries can make factoring transactions too costly.[6]

One mechanism to overcome some of the limitations of the contractual and informational environment is *reverse factoring*. In reverse factoring transactions, the factor purchases only accounts receivable issued by certain high-quality buyers. This ameliorates the problems generated by poor information infrastructures because factors need to collect information and estimate the credit risk of only some select buyers that are generally large, creditworthy firms, for which information is readily available. The credit risk faced by the factor will be that of these high-quality buyers. Moreover, by focusing on the accounts receivable from large, well-known firms, factors can reduce the possibility of fraud. These characteristics make reverse factoring particularly attractive for extending credit to SMEs in developing countries.

Reverse factoring can also provide benefits to both factors and buyers. Reverse factoring allows financial institutions to develop relationships with SMEs that have high-quality customers, which enables them to build credit histories on these firms and might lead to cross-selling opportunities. Buyers might be able to negotiate better terms with their suppliers, who obtain working capital financing. Buyers might also benefit by outsourcing their payables management because they have to deal only with a few factors, instead of myriad suppliers.

We now turn to the description of NAFIN's reverse factoring program. In the final section of the chapter, we discuss the main insights regarding the functioning of pro-market interventions that emerge from this experience, as well as some of the arguments that might support this type of state intervention.

NAFIN's Online Platform for Reverse Factoring Transactions

NAFIN is a Mexican development bank created in 1934 that provides commercial financing and credit guarantees. NAFIN was initially established to assist the Mexican government with the sale of bonds and to foster the development of the market for private securities. In 1941, NAFIN was transformed into a development bank with the mandate of providing financing to industries considered of national interest, such as sugar, pulp, textiles, cement, iron, and steel. Over time, NAFIN was entrusted with a wide range of functions extending beyond industrial finance, such as acting as the government's financial agent, providing financing for the construction of public utilities, and even acting as the main regulator of the stock exchange. Since the mid-1990s, NAFIN has increasingly moved away from direct lending, becoming mostly a second-tier financial institution. NAFIN is currently the second-largest public development bank in Mexico in terms of assets, with total assets of US$22.1 billion as of March 2016, which represents about 25 percent of the combined total assets of Mexican development banks.[7]

In 2015, NAFIN provided financing to the private sector for US$37 billion, with about half of this amount corresponding to second-tier lending and the rest consisting mostly of credit guarantees.

During the 1990s, NAFIN increasingly focused its activities on providing financing and guarantees to SMEs. This was, at least partly, a response to the reduction in bank financing for the private sector (and particularly SMEs) that followed the 1994–95 financial crisis, described in more detail in boxes 5.1 and 5.2 below.

BOX 5.1 Evolution of the Mexican banking sector since the 1994–95 crisis

Mexico experienced a severe financial crisis in 1994–95 that resulted in a significant contraction of the banking sector. As figure B5.1.1 shows, bank credit for the nonfinancial private sector decreased from 31 percent of GDP in 1994 to only 14 percent in 2003. Bank credit has partly recovered since, reaching 24 percent of GDP in 2015, but is still below its precrisis levels.

FIGURE B5.1.1 Evolution of the Mexican banking system

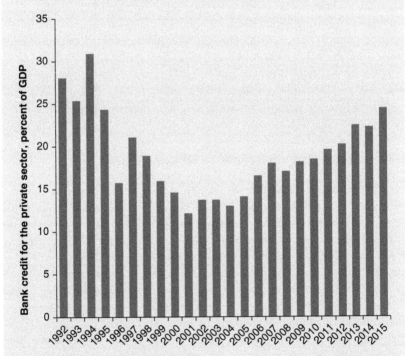

Source: World Bank World Development Indicators.
Note: This figure shows the evolution of bank credit to the private sector as a percentage of GDP in Mexico.

(continued on next page)

The financial crisis also resulted in a significant shift in the composition of commercial banks' credit portfolio, away from business lending and toward consumer and mortgage credit (figure B5.1.2). Although business lending has recovered in recent years, it accounted for only 55 percent of the total lending portfolio of commercial banks at the end of 2015, compared to 74 percent in 1994. The contraction in bank lending and the change in its composition have resulted in a significant reduction in total financing for the Mexican corporate sector, which decreased from 43 percent of GDP in 1994 to 21 percent in 2003, increasing since then to reach about 32 percent of GDP in 2015 (figure B5.1.3). Although there has been an increase in firms' access to domestic capital markets, facilitated by a supporting macroeconomic environment and financial reforms, this has not fully compensated for the decrease in banks' business lending.[a]

FIGURE B5.1.2 Composition of commercial bank lending in Mexico

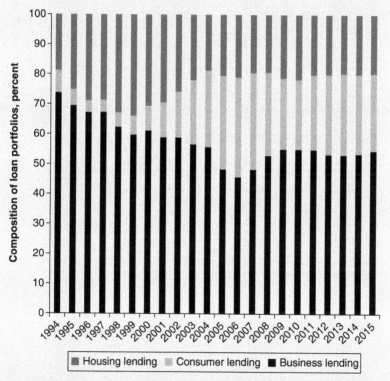

■ Housing lending ▨ Consumer lending ■ Business lending

Source: Bank of Mexico.
Note: This figure shows the evolution of the structure of lending to the private sector by commercial banks in Mexico. Only performing loans to the nonfinancial private sector are included in the analysis. Data correspond to December of each year.

(continued on next page)

FIGURE B5.1.3 Evolution of corporate sector financing in Mexico, by source

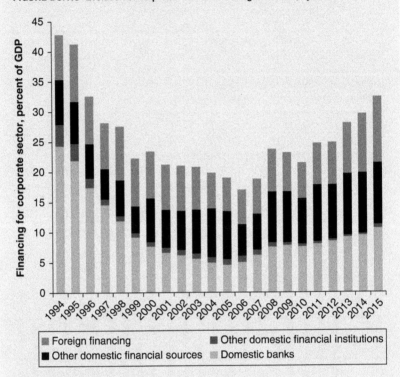

Foreign financing
Other domestic financial sources
Other domestic financial institutions
Domestic banks

Source: Bank of Mexico.
Note: This figure shows the evolution of corporate sector financing by source in Mexico, as a percentage of GDP. Data correspond to the last quarter of each year.

a. See IMF and World Bank (2007) for an overview of the evolution of financing for the private sector in Mexico since the 1994–95 financial crisis.

BOX 5.2 SMEs in Mexico

SMEs play a significant role in Mexico's economy, accounting for over 30 percent of total employment and 26 percent of gross output according to the 2014 Economic Census.[a] Access to finance for these firms is usually limited because of their lack of adequate collateral and financial and credit history information, which is partly a result of the high degree of informality in the economy. Governance problems arising from their family-based structure, weak creditor rights, and high contract enforcement costs, as well the high transaction costs of serving small borrowers, further contribute to their lack of access to finance.

(continued on next page)

BOX 5.2 SMEs in Mexico *(continued)*

SMEs were particularly affected by the contraction in bank business lending that followed the 1994–95 financial crisis, described in box 5.1 above. According to a quarterly survey conducted by the Bank of Mexico, the share of medium firms that reported using bank credit declined from about 40 percent in 1998 to 25 percent in 2009 (figure B5.2.1). In the case of small firms, a similar decline is visible, with the share of small firms that reported using bank credit decreasing from 29 percent to 17 percent over the same period. The 2014 Economic Census shows that the use of bank credit among SMEs has increased somewhat since 2009 but is still quite limited, with only 22 percent of small firms using commercial bank lending and the remainder relying on other sources—such as family loans, suppliers, partners, and savings banks—to finance their activities.

FIGURE B5.2.1 Access to credit for SMEs in Mexico

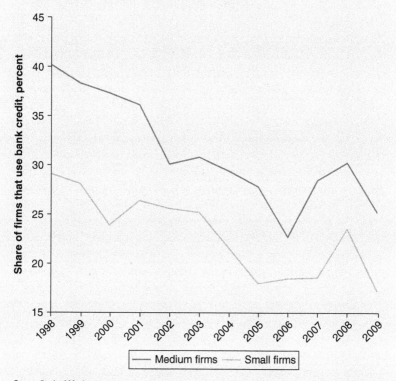

Source: Bank of Mexico.
Note: This figure shows the percentage of SMEs that report using bank credit according to a quarterly survey conducted by the Bank of Mexico between 1998 and 2009. Data correspond to the last quarter of each year. Small firms are those with sales of betweeen 1 million and 100 million Mexican pesos in 1997 (about US$126,000 to US$12.6 million). Medium firms are those with sales of between 100 million and 500 million Mexican pesos in 1997 (about US$12.6 million to US$63.1 million).

a. Small (medium) firms accounted for 15 (16) and 10 (17) percent of employment and gross output, respectively.

NAFIN's focus on SMEs was further boosted in the early 2000s, when it was given new management and direction, with the specific goal of using technology to provide SME financing, and complementing its lending with training and technical assistance. SMEs accounted for over 80 percent of NAFIN's outstanding loan and credit guarantee portfolio at the end of 2015. The reforms introduced in the early 2000s also included an amendment to NAFIN's charter mandating the preservation of its capital (which is achieved by targeting a nonnegative real return on equity), as well as increased operational autonomy and improved corporate governance and accountability.[8]

In 2001, in line with its new goals, NAFIN launched an innovative program called Cadenas Productivas (Productive Chains) to facilitate reverse factoring services to SMEs through an online platform. NAFIN was responsible for the development, production, and marketing costs of the electronic system and is in charge of its operation, but does not provide factoring services directly.

The Cadenas Productivas program works by creating chains between large buyers and their suppliers. The buyers that participate in the program must invite suppliers to join their chain. Buyers tend to be large creditworthy firms, and are required to have annual sales of more than US$16 million and an outstanding line of credit with at least one financial intermediary. Suppliers are typically small opaque firms that have difficulty accessing credit from commercial lending institutions. The program enables these firms to acquire working capital financing via factoring transactions with participating private financial institutions. All transactions are carried out on the electronic platform.

Figure 5.2 illustrates how the program works. NAFIN maintains a website with a dedicated webpage for each buyer. Once a supplier delivers goods to the buyer and issues an invoice, the buyer posts on its NAFIN webpage an online negotiable document equal to the amount that will be factored (usually 100 percent of the value of the receivable). Participating financial institutions that are willing to factor this particular receivable post their interest rate quotes for the transaction. The supplier can access this information and choose the best quote. Once the factor is chosen, the amount of the discounted receivable is transferred to the supplier's bank account. All factoring transactions are done without recourse, which implies that the credit risk factors face is solely that of the large buyers. The factor is paid directly by the buyer when the invoice is due.

NAFIN was responsible for the development, production, and marketing costs related to the electronic platform. It operates the system and also handles all the legal work, such as document transfers, preparing and signing documents, and so forth. NAFIN requires all participating financial institutions to use its second-tier funding to provide credit through the system. In fact, NAFIN does not charge a fee for the use of the electronic platform, but rather covers its costs with the interest it charges on its loans. The provision of credit by NAFIN is not key for the functioning of the program and, as discussed in the next section, seems

FIGURE 5.2 NAFIN reverse factoring transactions

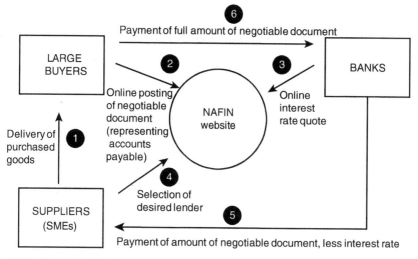

Note: This figure shows the functioning of a typical factoring transaction carried out on NAFIN's electronic platform.

to be a consequence of institutional incentives, given that NAFIN's performance is assessed on the basis of the volume of its loan disbursements.

NAFIN's decision to rely on a nonlending instrument to promote access to finance was, to a larger extent, driven by the fact that its lending strategy was no longer competitive (Naranjo 2005). NAFIN's traditional second-tier lending model was based on granting credit at longer maturities and lower costs than are typically available in the Mexican market, given its ability to obtain funding at sovereign interest rate levels. The larger the spread between sovereign and inter-bank rates, the more competitive NAFIN's lending was. Under this strategy, NAFIN promoted SME lending by providing credit to financial institutions at below-market interest rates. The subsidized rates were supposed to allow financial intermediaries to cover the transaction and informational costs associated with lending to SMEs. Improvements in macroeconomic conditions, accompanied by financial market reforms and the internationalization of the Mexican financial system, significantly reduced the spread between sovereign interest rates and interbank rates, making NAFIN's second-tier lending less attractive for financial intermediaries. The creation of an electronic platform for reverse factoring allowed NAFIN to increase demand for its funding, without having to rely on interest rate subsidies.

NAFIN's reverse factoring program has several built-in advantages in terms of dealing with informational asymmetries. First, as described above, buyers must invite their suppliers to join their chain and participate in the program. This effectively outsources screening to the buyers, who have an informational advantage relative to financial institutions. Buyers generally require suppliers to have a relationship of a minimum length and a good performance record before inviting them to participate in the program. Second, the use of reverse factoring reduces information requirements for participating financial institutions. Factors need only to collect credit information and estimate the credit risk of buyers, which are large, creditworthy firms that in many cases already have an ongoing business relationship with them. Third, the system increases information availability. Financial institutions can access historical information on the performance of suppliers, which helps in establishing credit histories and can provide cross-selling opportunities. Fourth, the program design also reduces operational risks and fraud. Only authorized individuals can access the system using equipment specifically designated for the program. Also, because the buyer (not the supplier) enters the receivables into the system, the supplier cannot submit bogus receivables or pledge the same receivables more than once. Finally, the program reduces moral hazard because the buyer pays directly to the factor, eliminating the possibility of suppliers diverting the funds to other uses.

The use of an electronic platform significantly reduces transaction costs and facilitates enforcement. The electronic platform allows NAFIN to capture economies of scale because most of the costs of the system are fixed and electronic access enables a large number of firms and financial institutions to participate. The platform also increases the speed of transactions; all transactions are completed within three hours and the funds are credited to the suppliers' accounts by close of business, providing them with immediate liquidity. Because almost all steps of the transaction take place electronically (over 98 percent of all services are provided online) and contracts are signed in advance, execution and enforcement are automatic. The online platform ensures that the transactions are followed through by all parties; given that the buyer posts the negotiable document in the system, the property of the receivable is unquestionable and the contracts signed by all participants also make all property transfers using NAFIN's platform certain and unquestionable. Furthermore, the use of an electronic system increases competition among financial intermediaries: once a transaction is posted online, all participating financial institutions can bid to factor it by posting an online quote. The electronic platform allows all banks to participate, giving national reach to smaller regional banks and providing suppliers from remote areas access to banks in financial centers.

The Cadenas Productivas program has been very successful. The program experienced a significant expansion between 2001 and 2010, with over 11 million factoring transactions totaling more than US$90 billion completed during this period. According to Klapper (2006), many of the suppliers that participate in the program had no access to external financing before, relying on trade credit and internal funds to finance their activities. In recent years, program growth has been slower because commercial banks have increasingly focused on SMEs and some banks have even developed proprietary electronic systems for factoring transactions. By the end of 2015, the Cadenas Productivas program encompassed more than 600 large private sector buyers and about 12,000 suppliers, with about 40 private financial institutions providing factoring services. In 2015, financing granted through NAFIN's online factoring transactions reached US$13.3 billion, accounting for about 70 percent of NAFIN's second-tier lending and 36 percent of its total financing to the private sector.

NAFIN has created a similar online reverse factoring program for government purchases. This program aims not only at improving access to finance for SMEs that are government suppliers but also at increasing transparency and efficiency in payments made by government entities and giving a greater participation to SMEs in public sector purchases. In 2007, the national government made it mandatory for all federal administration agencies to participate in this program, requiring them to post the accounts payable for all of their goods and services purchases online within a 15-day period of issuing an invoice. This program covered 268 government agencies in 2015 and provided financing to 6,647 government suppliers for a total amount of US$5.6 billion, accounting for about 42 percent of total financing provided through NAFIN's online factoring transactions.

NAFIN has also started to offer other products, like working capital loans and contract financing, leveraging its electronic platform and the information on the sales and payment history of suppliers generated by the Cadenas Productivas program. In NAFIN's working capital loans program, small firms that have actively participated in the Cadenas Productivas program as suppliers and are in good credit standing can access loans with a maturity of up to one year for a maximum amount of about US$200,000. NAFIN has also developed a contract-financing program for firms that receive federal government contracts. In these contract-financing operations, suppliers that receive a confirmed purchase order from the government to deliver goods in the future can obtain financing for up to 50 percent of the value of the contract. Loans have a maximum maturity of three years, and the loan repayment schedule is designed to match contract payments. The maximum loan amount is about US$3 million. This financing is intended to allow suppliers to purchase raw materials and other inputs needed to complete the government purchase order. In 2015, 44 loans totaling about US$14 million were granted through this program. NAFIN has also established a similar contract-financing program for SMEs that work as suppliers of Pemex (Petroleos de Mexico), Mexico's state-owned oil company. This program granted 33 loans in 2015, for a total amount of US$13 million.

NAFIN has entered into agreements with development banks in Latin America to create reverse factoring programs. NAFIN is currently working with the Central

American Bank for Economic Integration (a regional development bank) to develop reverse factoring systems in the region. NAFIN is also working with the Andean Development Corporation (a multilateral financial institution) to create similar reverse factoring systems in Colombia and Ecuador.

Policy Discussion and Conclusions

NAFIN's experience with its online platform for reverse factoring transactions raises a number of interesting issues that deserve further discussion. We first briefly analyze some of the salient design features of NAFIN's Cadenas Productivas program and then discuss some of the arguments that might support this type of state intervention. We end with a discussion of some open questions regarding this program. We believe that a better understanding of these issues can yield significant insights for the debate on the role of the state in broadening access and can also help in understanding the value added of this type of intervention. We return to some of these issues in chapter 9.

Several factors have contributed to the success of NAFIN's program. First, a key element in the program's success was the consistency between strategy and resource deployment. The creation of the Cadenas Productivas program required NAFIN to radically change its business model—from one focused on increasing the credit supply to SMEs through second-tier lending to banks to a wider, more encompassing model that had to affect the demand for funds by fostering financial transactions. The promotion of the factoring program had to be done primarily at the level of the SMEs and required different human and technical resources than acting as a second-tier bank, namely, a large retail sales staff and promotional resources. Deploying the required resources to encourage the participation of large buyers and SMEs and to educate them on how to take advantage of the program has been perhaps the main driver of the success of NAFIN's program.

Second, the success of the program depended on the availability of technology to implement the required electronic systems. The use of an online platform significantly reduces transaction costs. It also reduces the possibility of fraud and increases competition, by enabling different market participants to connect remotely. The development of the electronic platform was possible because of the availability of the required security and telecommunications technologies. The existence of an adequate legal framework for online transactions, which makes these transactions legally binding and enforceable, is also key.[9]

Finally, another element that contributed to the program's success was the use of a nonlending contract like factoring, which helps to overcome institutional deficiencies. As mentioned above, this type of financing tends to make less intensive use of judicial systems and bankruptcy laws and procedures than traditional forms of financing, making it more attractive in countries with weaker institutional environments.

A salient feature of the Cadenas Productivas program is that NAFIN requires all participating financial institutions to use its second-tier lending for conducting factoring transactions through the program and does not charge any fees for the use of the electronic platform, covering its costs with the interest it charges on its loans. This reduces transparency, making it difficult to evaluate whether the program's services are adequately priced, and carries the risk of distorting incentives. Similar to the case of FIRA (Fideicomisos Instituidos en Relación con la Agricultura) described in chapter 4, the requirement to use NAFIN's funding seems to be, to a large extent, the result of institutional incentives; because NAFIN is evaluated on the basis of the volume of its loan disbursements and guarantees provided, it has incentives to structure its programs around these products. In fact, as described above, the Cadenas Productivas program was partly developed as a way of increasing demand for NAFIN's second-tier lending, after NAFIN lost most of its cost advantage. NAFIN's experience suggests that, as institutions move toward more catalytic interventions, where the main role of the state is to foster contracting among private parties, new performance metrics and evaluation procedures will be necessary. This requires moving away from quantitative measures based on the volume of credit provided, and focusing instead on the amount of financial intermediation promoted and the impact of interventions on those firms and households that receive financing. These new performance criteria are more difficult to design and measure than traditional ones, and it might take time and a process of trial and error to find the correct indicators to evaluate specific interventions. Consistent with the need to move away from volume-based performance measures, in 2009 the Mexican government mandated development financial institutions to periodically publish indicators measuring their services to their target populations. In addition, the Ministry of Finance will conduct and publish independent evaluations on these institutions.

NAFIN's reverse factoring program aims at increasing access to credit by providing a platform for private parties to engage in financial contracting. In principle at least, this system could be developed and operated by a private firm. In fact, technological innovations have allowed new private companies in developed countries to offer similar services in recent years (*The Economist* 2017). Therefore, some might question whether NAFIN's intervention is actually necessary. One possible explanation for why private financial intermediaries did not create a similar platform despite its potential profitability is that coordination failures among private parties might prevent such a system from emerging. In particular, the system created by NAFIN presents significant participation externalities because the value of participating for buyers and suppliers increases with the number of financial institutions that take part, and vice versa.[10] This might give rise to a "chicken and egg" problem: to attract buyers and suppliers, the program needs a large base of registered financial intermediaries, but these will be willing to register only if they expect many firms to participate. Also, financial intermediaries—which are most likely the ones with the required know-how to create a program of this type—might not be willing to incur the initial development costs because then they would have to open the platform to their competitors in order to make it attractive for a large number of buyers and suppliers to join. Without a coordination mechanism for private parties, innovation might not take place. In this situation, there may be a role for a public institution like NAFIN to intervene, to the extent that it can overcome coordination problems and promote innovation. As mentioned above, in recent years some Mexican commercial banks have developed proprietary electronic systems to conduct factoring transactions, suggesting that NAFIN's program might have had a demonstration role, fostering innovation.

Even if there are relevant arguments to justify NAFIN's initial intervention, some valid questions concerning its reverse factoring program might remain. In the first place, some may question whether, after having successfully set up this platform, NAFIN's continued involvement is required. In principle, if the Cadenas Productivas program is commercially viable and does not require any subsidies, NAFIN could sell it to a private firm and move on to other activities. Whether NAFIN should continue operating the program or not depends ultimately on the relative efficiency of the private and public sectors in operating this type of program. Second, even if transferring the program to a private operator was deemed optimal, it is not clear under which conditions this transfer should take place and how to design an adequate regulatory framework to guarantee that the system fosters competition by continuing to provide access to all financial intermediaries on an equal footing. Furthermore, institutional incentives might make transferring the Cadenas Productivas to a private operator quite difficult. When a program is successful and profitable, the public institution in charge of the program does not have incentives to divest it because the program may represent a significant fraction of its franchise value. In the case of NAFIN, for instance, about 70 percent of its second-tier lending in 2015 and more than a third of its total financing to the private sector corresponded to factoring transactions originated from the Cadenas Productivas program. Transferring it to a private operator would mean losing a significant part of its business. In addition, the fact that NAFIN's reverse factoring program is not separate from the bank's other activities and lacks a clear market-based pricing makes transferring it to a private firm more difficult.

To conclude, NAFIN's reverse factoring program is an interesting example of the emerging new types of state interventions aimed at increasing access to finance, which entail a move away from traditional credit provision by state-owned banks. NAFIN's main role in this case was to act as a catalyst to jump-start financial contracting among private parties, by providing a platform to conduct factoring transactions. This experience also highlights how technology can be leveraged to overcome barriers to access to finance. Further research is necessary to adequately identify to what extent this type of public sector intervention constitutes an efficient instrument to overcome problems of access to finance, and how these types of programs can be designed to ensure that they do not displace market activity and to minimize any distortions.

Notes

1. NAFIN requires participating financial institutions to use its second-tier funding to finance the factoring operations. As discussed in the concluding section, this seems to be a consequence of institutional incentives and, in principle, is not required for the program to work.

2. Some scholars trace the origins of factoring to the Roman Empire (Rutberg 1994) or even further back, to the rule of Mesopotamian King Hammurabi (Papadimitriou, Phillips, and Wray 1994). See Hillyer (1939) for an account of the historical evolution of factoring since the 14th century.

3. See Bakker, Klapper, and Udell (2004) for an overview of worldwide factoring markets, with a focus on Eastern European countries. Klapper (2006) analyzes the country-level determinants of factoring market development.

4. The fact that factoring is an asset sale also differentiates it from traditional asset-based financing. In asset-based lending, the borrower pledges some asset as collateral (for example, inventories, equipment, or even accounts receivable), and this collateral is considered the primary source of repayment. The amount of credit extended is explicitly linked to the liquidation value of the pledged assets. However, the borrowing firm maintains ownership of these assets. In contrast, in factoring transactions the property of the underlying assets—accounts receivable—is transferred to the lender, which means that in case of bankruptcy they are not part of the firm's estate.

5. De la Torre, Martinez Peria, and Schmukler (2010), for example, analyze factoring penetration in Argentina and Chile and find that differences in legal provisions that affect factors' ability to collect from buyers play a significant role in explaining the higher use of factoring in Chile.

6. See Klapper (2006) for more discussion of these issues.

7. The Mexican National Banking and Securities Commission (CNBV) classifies six institutions as development banks: NAFIN; the infrastructure lender Banco Nacional de Obras y Servicios Públicos (Banobras); the export-focused Banco Nacional de Comercio Exterior (Bancomext); the mortgage agency Sociedad Hipotecaria Federal (SHF); the military financial institution Banco Nacional del Ejército, Fuerza Aérea y Armada (Banejército); and the development bank Banco del Ahorro Nacional y Servicios Financieros (Bansefi). These six institutions had total assets of about US$88.3 billion, as of March 2016.

8. See World Bank (2010) for an overview of the reforms to Mexican development financial institutions introduced in the early 2000s.

9. Having an electronic signature law might facilitate the functioning of this type of program, but is not a necessary condition. In fact, Mexico enacted its electronic signature law in 2003, after NAFIN's program had been operating for over two years.

All that is required for this type of program to work is for the law to recognize online contracts and transactions between private parties as legally binding and enforceable.

10. Participation externalities occur when the gains from participating in an activity depend on the number of other agents participating as well because agents may fail to take into account the fact that the social benefits of their participation exceed their private benefits (Diamond 1982; Pagano 1989).

References

Bakker, Marie, Leora Klapper, and Gregory Udell. 2004. "Financing Small and Medium-Size Enterprises with Factoring: Global Growth and Its Potential in Eastern Europe." Policy Research Working Paper 3342, World Bank, Washington, DC.

Berger, Allen N., and Gregory F. Udell. 2006. "A More Complete Conceptual Framework for SME Finance." *Journal of Banking and Finance* 30 (11): 2945–66.

de la Torre, Augusto, María Soledad Martínez Pería, and Sergio L. Schmukler. 2010. "Bank Involvement with SMEs: Beyond Relationship Lending." *Journal of Banking and Finance* 34 (9): 2280–93.

Diamond, Peter A. 1982. "Aggregate Demand Management in Search Equilibrium." *Journal of Political Economy* 90 (5): 881–94.

The Economist. 2017. "Every Little Helps. How Fintech Firms Are Helping to Revolutionise Supply-Chain Finance." January 14.

FCI (Factor Chain International). 2015. *Annual Review 2015.* Amsterdam: FCI.

Hillyer, William Hurd. 1939. "Four Centuries of Factoring." *Quarterly Journal of Economics* 53 (2): 305–11.

IMF (International Monetary Fund) and World Bank. 2007. *Mexico: Financial Sector Assessment Program Update: Technical Note—Financing of the Private Sector.* Washington, DC: IMF and World Bank.

Klapper, Leora. 2006. "The Role of Factoring for Financing Small and Medium Enterprises." *Journal of Banking and Finance* 30 (11): 3111–30.

Milenkovic-Kerkovic, Tamara, and Ksenija Dencic-Mihajlov. 2012. "Factoring in the Changing Environment: Legal and Financial Aspects." *Procedia-Social and Behavioral Sciences* 44: 428–35.

Naranjo, Martin. 2005. "NAFIN'S Reverse Factoring Program." Background paper prepared for this report. World Bank, Washington, DC.

Pagano, Marco. 1989. "Trading Volume and Asset Liquidity." *Quarterly Journal of Economics* 104 (2): 255–74.

Papadimitriou, Dimitri, Ronnie Phillips, and L. Randall Wray. 1994. "Community-Based Factoring Companies and Small Business Lending." Working Paper 108. Jerome Levy Economics Institute of Bard College, New York.

Rutberg, Sidney. 1994. *The History of Asset-Based Lending.* New York: Commercial Finance Association.

World Bank. 2010. *Reforms That Help Mexico's Development Finance Institutions Thrive.* Results Profile. Washington, DC: World Bank.

CHAPTER 6

Correspondent Banking Arrangements: The Experience of Brazil

Introduction

This chapter analyzes the use of partnerships between financial institutions and commercial entities for the distribution of financial services, referred to as *correspondent banking arrangements*. In particular, we discuss the experience of Brazil, where financial institutions have developed large networks of correspondent outlets, focusing on the case of two state-owned banks.

Correspondent arrangements are partnerships between banks and nonbanks with a significant network of outlets—such as convenience stores, post offices, drugstores, and supermarkets—to distribute financial services. Access to financial services in many developing countries is hampered by the lack of a widespread network of banking outlets because financial intermediaries do not find it profitable to operate branches in remote or sparsely populated areas. Correspondent banking arrangements aim at increasing financial services outreach by offering an alternative, less-costly channel for providing services in those areas. Opening a bank branch requires considerable investments in staffing, infrastructure, and equipment. In contrast, the initial investments required to provide financial services through an already-existing commercial outlet tend to be relatively low. Correspondent arrangements also allow banks to reduce the ongoing costs of providing financial services by sharing the point of sale with the retailer, using its staff and infrastructure.

Correspondent banking is not necessarily new. Postal savings banks, which have been functioning in different forms for centuries, might be considered an earlier form of correspondent banking. However, the current generation of correspondent arrangements differs from previous experiences both in terms of its business model and the range and scale of services provided, which are to a large extent enabled by the availability of new technologies. Correspondent banking outlets in most countries focus primarily on transaction and payment services—such as bill payment, collection services, and payment orders. Some outlets also offer banking services, such as opening accounts and making deposits and withdrawals, as well as collecting information for credit analysis and receiving and forwarding loan and credit card applications.

This chapter analyzes the experience of Brazil, which is widely regarded as a global leader in correspondent banking. Brazil was an early adopter of the correspondent banking model, and over time its financial institutions have developed large correspondent networks—with the number of outlets increasing from fewer than 14,000 at the end of 2000 to almost 210,000 by 2014. Correspondent arrangements have enabled a wide increase in the geographic penetration of financial services. At the end of 2000, almost 30 percent of Brazilian municipalities had no bank service outposts. By the end of 2003, the expansion of correspondent agreements had left no municipality without financial service outlets, with 1,600 municipalities being served exclusively by correspondents. Correspondent outlets were present in all but two of Brazil's 5,588 municipalities by 2014. Our analysis focuses on the experiences of Banco do Brasil and Caixa Econômica Federal (CEF), the two largest state-owned commercial banks in Brazil, which have established some of the largest banking correspondent networks in the country.

Correspondent banking constitutes an innovative alternative to traditional policies aimed at increasing financial services outreach. These policies have typically relied on state-owned banks operating branches in remote areas or have mandated private banks to operate in these areas, usually at a loss. The Brazilian government has played an important catalytic role in jump-starting the development of correspondent banking, not only by providing an adequate legal and regulatory framework but also by auctioning off the use of the post office network to distribute financial services. Moreover, the government has played a more direct role in the expansion of correspondent banking as state-owned commercial banks have established large correspondent networks. This extensive involvement might yield significant insights regarding the role of the state in fostering correspondent banking.

The remainder of this chapter is organized as follows. The next section expands the discussion from this introduction and presents an overview of correspondent banking arrangements, focusing on how they might contribute to increasing financial services outreach. After that, we describe Brazil's experience with correspondent banking, focusing on the cases of Banco do Brasil and CEF. We conclude with a discussion of this experience and its implications for the debate on the role of the state in fostering access to financial services.

Correspondent Banking Arrangements

Access to financial services in many developing countries is hampered by the lack of a widespread network of banking outlets. Indeed, data from the World Bank's Global Financial Inclusion Database (Global Findex) show that more than 20 percent of the adults in developing countries who do not have an account at a formal financial institution cite distance as one of the main reasons (Demirgüç-Kunt et al. 2015). In many rural areas there are no bank branches or other delivery channels for financial services; financial intermediaries do not find it profitable to operate in these areas because of their lower population densities and incomes. Global Findex data show that rural residents are three times more likely than urban residents to cite distance as a reason for not having an account. The lack of local banking outlets not only results in high transaction costs—because customers need to travel long distances to reach the nearest outlet—but can also increase informational problems: not having a local office makes it more difficult for financial institutions to gather information on business conditions and to develop close relations with borrowers. Moreover, being close to a retail service point can be especially important for the poor, who might find it more costly and difficult to travel long distances. Consistent with this argument, Global Findex data show that distance is significantly more likely to be cited as a barrier to having an account by less educated and poor adults (Allen et al. 2016).

Figure 6.1 illustrates the large differences in the geographic penetration of banking services across countries. Panel a shows that many developing countries lack widespread networks of banking outlets, with countries such as Argentina, Bolivia, Paraguay, and Peru having fewer than two commercial bank branches per 1,000 square kilometers, compared to over 50 branches per 1,000 square kilometers in Italy and Spain. Analyzing automated teller machine (ATM) densities across countries shows similar patterns (figure 6.1, panel b).[1] Of course, these indicators are only crude proxies for the geographic availability of banking services, because branches and ATMs are not evenly distributed across the country but rather tend to be concentrated in urban areas.[2] Indeed, data from the Financial Access Survey of the International Monetary Fund (IMF) show that, in 45 developing countries (out of 62 with data available), more than a third of all bank branches are located in the three largest cities in each country. Furthermore, even when a wide network is available, not all bank offices might offer the same services. For instance, Beck, Demirgüç-Kunt, and Martinez Peria (2008) conducted a survey of the largest banks in 62 countries and found that in many cases customers

FIGURE 6.1 Geographic penetration of banking services, selected developed and developing countries

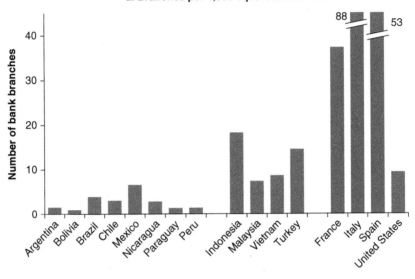

a. Branches per 1,000 square kilometers

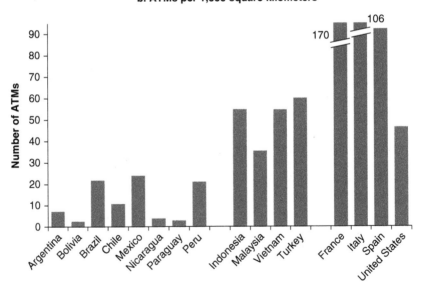

b. ATMs per 1,000 square kilometers

Source: IMF Financial Access Survey.
Note: Panel a shows the number of bank branches per 1,000 square kilometers in selected countries. Panel B shows the number of ATMs (automated teller machines) per 1,000 square kilometers in selected countries. Data correspond to 2015 or latest available.

must visit the head office to open an account or can submit loan applications only through certain branches. They also found some evidence that these restrictions tend to be higher in lower-income countries.

In many developing countries, the lack of a widespread network of banking outlets has been traditionally perceived to be the result of a market failure. Policy makers have argued that private banks do not find it profitable to open branches in rural and isolated areas because they fail to internalize the positive externalities on growth and poverty reduction generated by the provision of financial services in those areas. This argument has led to direct state interventions to expand the geographic outreach of banking services, through the direct provision of financial services by state-owned banks in remote areas or regulations mandating private banks to open branches in those areas. For instance, in India regulations required banks opening a new branch in an already-banked area to open branches in four unbanked locations. In addition, state-owned banks were mandated to open branches in previously unbanked areas. As a result, new bank branches were set up in 30,000 unbanked locations between 1969 and 1990 (Burgess and Pande 2005). Current regulations require all Indian banks to open 25 percent of their new branches in a given year in rural, unbanked areas. Similarly, several countries in Sub-Saharan Africa have introduced various measures to try to induce private banks to become more active in rural areas, such as requiring banks to open rural branches in exchange for licenses to open urban branches, auctioning subsidies for opening new branches in remote areas, and offering tax breaks. However, there is little evidence that these measures have significantly increased the geographic outreach of financial services (Meyer 2015).

Although state-owned banks and mandates for private banks to open branches in unbanked areas might help expand the geographic penetration of financial services in some cases, it is not clear whether this approach can increase access in a sustainable manner. Given the high recurring costs of operating bank branches in remote areas, these direct state interventions are likely to require permanent government subsidies (or cross-subsidies across activities conducted by private banks). In addition, it is not clear whether the services provided by full-fledged bank branches meet the needs of consumers in unbanked areas. This has led policy makers in several developing countries to increasingly turn to correspondent banking as a tool to extend financial services outreach over the last decades. As described in the introduction, correspondent banking refers to arrangements whereby banks outsource services typically undertaken at branches (such as making deposits and withdrawals, receiving loan applications, and paying bills) to nonfinancial firms with a significant network of outlets, such as lottery houses, post offices, supermarkets, convenience stores, and gas stations.[3] Correspondent banking arrangements aim at increasing financial services outreach by reducing the cost of providing these services in less-populated areas and in regions with low economic activity.

Correspondent banking is not necessarily new. Postal savings banks, which have been functioning in different forms for centuries, can be considered a form of correspondent banking.[4] The first national system of postal savings services was established in 1861 in the United Kingdom, and other countries soon adopted similar systems. According to estimates made by Clotteau and Measho (2016), over 90 percent of postal operators worldwide provide some financial services (remittances, government payments, insurance, current accounts, savings, and so on), either directly or in partnership with financial institutions. Postal networks typically offer savings services either through postal savings accounts—the proceeds of which are often invested in government bonds—or through the direct sale of Treasury bonds to the public. Postal savings services are very common in some developed countries, with the number of postal savings accounts in countries such as France, Germany, and Japan representing over 20 percent of the population.[5] Penetration in developing countries is much lower and shows large regional variations, with the number of postal savings accounts in East Asia and the Pacific representing over 60 percent of the population, compared to only 1 percent in Latin America (table 6.1). In many countries, postal networks have also established postal giro systems, which are retail payment systems based on written transfer orders submitted through post offices. These payment systems are still widely used today in Europe, Japan, and some developing countries. The increasing use of digital communications technologies and the resulting move away from traditional mail have led many postal operators to attempt to leverage their existing post office networks by expanding their financial service offerings in recent years (Berthaud and Davico 2013).

The current generation of correspondent arrangements differs from previous experiences in terms of its business model and the range and scale of services provided. A key difference between current correspondent banking arrangements and postal savings banks is that, in the former, the financial institution and its correspondents are clearly distinct entities that operate independently and enter into an agreement only to distribute financial services, whereas, in the latter, the financial services are directly provided by the post office itself or by an institution closely affiliated with it (usually established with the sole purpose of providing postal financial services). Moreover, modern correspondent banking arrangements differ in terms of the range, scale, and quality of services provided, which are to a large extent enabled by the availability of new technologies. As described above, postal bank services have traditionally focused on taking deposits, with some postal networks also offering money transfer facilities. In contrast, correspondent banking outlets typically provide a wide range of services. In most countries, these outlets focus primarily on transaction and payment services, such as bill payment, collection services, and payment orders, which include paying government

TABLE 6.1 Postal financial services, by region

Region	Fraction of postal services offering financial services (percent)	Number of accounts (million)	Accounts per capita (percent)
East Asia and Pacific	88	1,301	64
Eastern Europe and Central Asia	97	15	4
High-income OECD countries	85	205	19
Latin America and the Caribbean	89	8	1
Middle East and North Africa	100	72	18
South Asia	88	354	21
Sub-Saharan Africa	92	10	1
Total		1,965	27.3

Source: Clotteau and Measho 2016.
Note: Data correspond to 2015. OECD = Organisation for Economic Co-operation and Development.

benefits and pensions. Some outlets also offer banking services, such as opening accounts and making deposits and withdrawals, as well as collecting information for credit analysis and receiving and forwarding loan and credit card applications.

Correspondent banking transactions usually involve an intensive use of technology. To provide financial services, correspondent banking outlets must use a point of sale (POS) terminal, which is a device connected to a telephone line or other telecommunications network that can handle payments and other transactions. The device can be a card reader terminal, barcode scanner, mobile phone, personal computer, or any other hardware that can identify customers and handle payment transactions. POS devices must be electronically linked to the contracting financial institution to be able to send instructions for transferring value from one account to another. Transactions can be done either in real time or by periodically connecting to the network. In fact, a significant advantage of POS devices for serving rural areas is that they can work without always-on communication and electrical connections. Technological advances have played an important role in facilitating the development of correspondent banking through the reduction in the cost of POS terminals and the development of new products more suitable for remote areas, such as battery-powered, wireless POS devices.

Despite the important role of technology in correspondent banking arrangements, POS devices do not constitute banking channels by themselves.

An attendant is required to count and store cash, use the POS device to identify customers, and perform other related tasks. Attendants must also answer customer questions and provide information. Therefore, financial institutions must either provide their own staff for the operation of their correspondent outposts or, more commonly, train their correspondents' staffs to perform the necessary tasks and to provide information on their products.

Correspondent banking arrangements are partnerships between banks and nonbank entities that offer potential benefits to both parties. For banks, these arrangements offer the possibility of delivering their services to a larger client base at a relatively low cost because they avoid the cost of opening and maintaining branches. Opening a bank branch can be very costly, requiring considerable investments in staffing, infrastructure, equipment, and security for storing cash and valuables. In contrast, the initial investments required to provide banking services through an already-existing retail outlet can be significantly lower. For instance, in Peru, the estimated cost of establishing a bank branch is about US$200,000, whereas the initial investment required for a correspondent banking outlet is only US$5,000 (Prieto Ariza 2006). According to Kumar et al. (2005), in Brazil the initial investments required for establishing a new correspondent outpost can be as low as 0.5 percent of those for opening a new branch. Given this cost advantage, correspondent outlets can serve as branch substitutes in areas where the transaction volume might be too low to support a full-fledged branch, allowing financial institutions to expand their geographic outreach.

Correspondent banking also allows banks to reduce their operating costs by sharing the POS with the retailer and conducting all transactions online. Ongoing costs of operating correspondent outposts tend to be very low, especially when existing staff, infrastructure, and information and communications networks are used. In Pakistan, for instance, the average monthly operating costs of a correspondent agent are estimated to be about US$300, compared to US$28,000 for a bank branch (Ivatury and Mas 2008). In the case of Peru, estimates suggest that a cash transaction at a bank branch costs about US$0.85, compared to US$0.32 when the same transaction is carried out through a correspondent outlet (Almandoz 2006).

For commercial establishments, correspondent arrangements can lead to higher revenues. Providing financial services can increase store traffic, attracting new customers who might not only conduct financial transactions but also purchase other products. In addition, correspondent arrangements might allow stores to differentiate themselves from competitors and might bolster their reputation by being affiliated with a well-known financial institution. Moreover, financial transaction fees are typically shared between the financial institution and the correspondents, giving further incentives for commercial establishments to participate in these arrangements.

Despite these potential benefits, correspondent arrangements also raise some operational concerns for participating banks and commercial outlets.[6] Using a third party to handle cash on behalf of a bank can create a risk of fraud and theft. Evidence from Brazil suggests that this risk could be significant (Lyman, Ivatury, and Staschen 2006; CGAP and FGV 2010). Also, retail agents may lack experience in liquidity management, making it difficult and time-consuming. Ensuring there is sufficient cash in the till to meet customer withdrawals requires that agents balance several variables, including cash turnover, transaction processing time, and the periodicity of customers' cash needs, among others. Agents might also need to make frequent trips to the bank to deposit any excess cash generated by the financial transactions.[7] Moreover, correspondent banking arrangements could create reputational risks for banks if correspondents underperform. For instance, a bank's image might suffer if retail agents do not have enough cash at hand to meet customers' requests for withdrawals. Also, when providing services through correspondents, banks have less control over the customer experience. Staff members of third-party retail outlets with a limited understanding of financial products and services could provide a lower quality of customer service than at bank branches. From the perspective of retail outlets, processing financial transactions can be time-consuming, taking staff time away from regular activities, and might take up too much store space. Also, although increased foot traffic from financial transactions can lead to more product sales, it might also inconvenience store customers.

Correspondent banking can play a significant role in expanding the outreach of financial services. As mentioned above, these arrangements allow banks to provide services in remote or sparsely populated areas at significantly lower costs than opening and maintaining a full branch. In addition, even in areas with bank branches, correspondent arrangements can help increase financial inclusion by allowing banks to target new customer segments, such as low-income customers, that have lower transaction amounts and therefore might not be profitably served through more expensive channels. Correspondent outlets can also be an effective way of providing services to people who are not familiar with traditional banking facilities. Financially excluded sectors usually prefer using services provided by retail outlets they know, instead of visiting a bank branch (Lyman, Ivatury, and Staschen 2006).

Despite its potential as a tool for increasing the outreach of financial services, correspondent banking has some limitations. The international experience with correspondent arrangements suggests that customers tend to use agents mostly for making payments and sending transfers, not for savings or credit—even when these services are available (Ivatury and Mas 2008; Oxford Policy Management 2011; AFI 2012). In the case of savings services, most customers of correspondent outlets tend to time their deposits to coincide with their payments, leaving near-zero balances in their accounts, or do not even open an account through this channel. Credit services, in turn, cannot be easily standardized and provided though POS devices because they require appraising the credit quality of potential borrowers. Correspondents might not be an optimal channel for reaching new borrowers because their staff members might have a limited understanding of financial products and might also bias their referrals in favor of good commercial customers, rather than seeking out the best potential borrowers. These problems are compounded by a lack of credit histories for most customers of correspondent outlets and by the limited experience of financial institutions in lending to this customer group, which makes it more difficult to use automatic credit scoring methods.

Correspondent banking arrangements can be seen as part of an approach by financial institutions in many countries to provide financial services at a lower cost through "branchless banking," by leveraging new technologies to record and communicate transaction information (Lyman, Ivatury, and Staschen 2006; Mas 2008a). Apart from correspondent banking, another salient example of this approach is mobile money (usually referred to as m-money), which involves the transfer of money through mobile phones.[8] M-money allows account holders to pay bills, make deposits, and conduct other transactions using a mobile phone, eliminating the need for a physical branch infrastructure. The significant growth of mobile phone penetration in many developing countries has made m-money an increasingly viable tool for expanding financial services outreach in these countries. Global Findex data show that m-money provides millions of people with a way to pay bills and send or receive money. In Sub-Saharan Africa, almost a third of account holders, or 12 percent of adults, reported having an m-money account (World Bank 2014). And, in five countries in the region (Côte d'Ivoire, Somalia, Tanzania, Uganda, and Zimbabwe), more adults reported having an m-money account than an account at a financial institution.

Brazil—widely regarded as a global leader in correspondent banking arrangements—was an early adopter of the correspondent banking model, and over time its financial institutions have developed large correspondent networks covering almost all of the country's 5,588 municipalities. Partly motivated by Brazil's perceived success in creating wide-reaching, branchless financial service delivery channels, several developing countries started adopting correspondent banking arrangements in the mid-2000s, with varying degrees of success. These include, for instance, Bolivia, Chile, Colombia, Ecuador, Mexico, and Peru in Latin America; Kenya, Nigeria, South Africa, Tanzania, and Uganda in Africa; and Bangladesh, India, and Pakistan in South Asia.[9] By 2015, at least six countries had correspondent banking networks with more than 100,000 agents (Dias, Staschen, and Noor 2015).[10]

We now turn to the description of correspondent banking in Brazil, focusing in particular on the experiences of Banco do Brasil and CEF, the two largest state-owned commercial banks in the country. In the final section, we discuss the main insights emerging from these experiences regarding the potential of correspondent banking to increase financial services outreach and the role of the state in fostering these arrangements.

Correspondent Banking in Brazil

Since the early 2000s, Brazil has undergone a process of financial deepening and broadening of access to financial services, supported by a stable macroeconomic environment and improvements in the legal and informational framework for financial contracting.[11] According to estimates from the Brazilian Central Bank, the fraction of adults who have a relationship with a formal financial institution increased from about 61 percent in 2005 to 85 percent in 2014. This growing fraction of the population is served by a denser network of financial service providers, as the number of banking dependencies (including branches and other bank service outposts) increased from fewer than 28,000 in 2005 to almost 39,000 in 2014.[12]

Despite the significant improvements in terms of financial sector penetration, the availability of bank services in Brazil still presents wide regional disparities, with many areas having no bank branches. Banking facilities tend to be concentrated in the richer southern region, which has about 19.2 branches per 100,000 people, compared to 8.9 and 9.5 branches per 100,000 people in the poorer northern and northeastern regions, respectively (figure 6.2, panel a). Similar regional disparities in the availability of financial services are visible when considering all bank dependencies (including branches and other banking service outposts) and when analyzing penetration per square kilometer (figure 6.2, panel b). Out of a total of 5,588 municipalities, more than 1,900—arguably the poorest and least populated—had no bank branches at the end of 2014. Moreover, 241 municipalities had no banking dependencies or ATMs. These wide geographic disparities in the availability and use of banking services can be ascribed, to a large extent, to differences in income levels and population densities across regions (Kumar 2005).

Like many countries, Brazil traditionally relied on state-owned banks to extend outreach and provide financial services in remote areas. However, in many areas this strategy did not prove effective in extending financial services. In the late 1990s, some Brazilian banks started to develop physical outlets that were not considered branches, to avoid restrictive regulations and labor laws that resulted in high fixed costs for opening new branches.

In 1999, the Central Bank of Brazil officially recognized these agreements by allowing banks to formally enter into contracts with nonfinancial firms as correspondents to offer payment and deposit services as well as limited credit services. Initially, the regulations permitted the establishment of correspondent outlets only

FIGURE 6.2 Commercial bank penetration in Brazil, by region

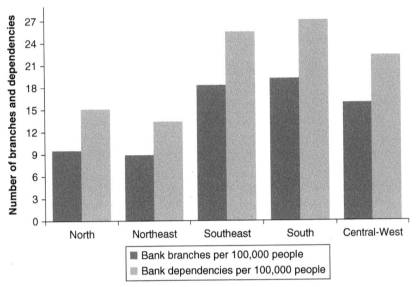

a. Commercial bank penetration per 100,000 people

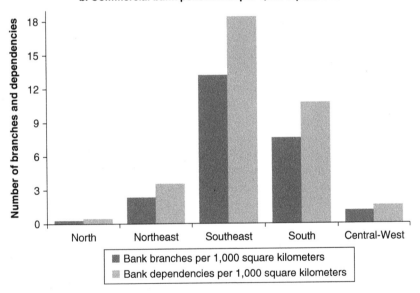

b. Commercial bank penetration per 1,000 square kilometers

Source: Banco Central do Brasil 2015.
Note: This figure shows the number of commercial bank branches and dependencies divided by population (panel a) and by area (panel b) for different Brazilian regions. Data on dependencies include commercial bank branches and other banking service outposts. Data correspond to 2014.

in municipalities without bank branches, requiring banks to close down the correspondent within 180 days if a branch was subsequently opened in the area. This restriction was dropped in 2000, facilitating the expansion of correspondent arrangements. Subsequent central bank regulations have expanded the range of services that can be provided by correspondents and have allowed nonbank financial institutions—such as investment banks, financial companies, and savings and loans associations—to establish correspondent arrangements.

These regulatory changes were followed by an impressive growth in correspondent banking arrangements. The number of correspondent outlets increased from fewer than 14,000 at the end of 2000 to more than 207,000 in 2014 (figure 6.3).[13] Correspondents have constituted the main avenue for the expansion of financial services outreach and currently represent over 70 percent of all financial service points in the country. At the end of 2000, 1,659 municipalities had no bank services

FIGURE 6.3 Evolution of financial service points in Brazil, by type

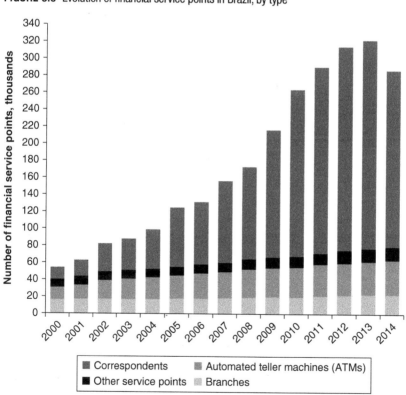

Sources: Brazilian Bank Federation (FEBRABAN); Central Bank of Brazil.
Note: This figure shows the evolution of the number of financial service points in Brazil for the period 2000–14.

(branches or bank service outposts) of any kind. By the end of 2003, the expansion of correspondent agreements had left no municipality without financial service outlets, with over 1,600 municipalities being served exclusively by correspondents. Correspondent outlets were present in all but two of Brazil's 5,588 municipalities by 2014. The growth of correspondent outlets has resulted in a reduction of the average distance to the nearest banking service outlet, from 53 kilometers in 1999 to about 3 kilometers.

There are currently over 200 financial institutions providing financial services through correspondent outlets. The financial institutions with the largest correspondent networks are Bradesco (the fourth-largest bank in the country, with total assets of about US$430 billion at the end of 2014) and two state-owned commercial banks (Banco do Brasil and CEF). Correspondent agents conducted almost 4 billion transactions in 2014, up from fewer than 3 billion in 2010. This represents about 17 percent of banking transactions conducted in physical outlets and 8 percent of all banking transactions, including those conducted through remote channels, such as Internet banking, call centers, and mobile phone banking. Correspondent agents have gradually expanded the range of services provided, increasingly moving into more complex banking services, such as making deposits and withdrawals, opening accounts, and providing credit. However, bill payments still constitute the lion's share of services provided by correspondents, accounting for about 70 percent of all correspondent transactions in 2014. About 67 percent of Brazilian households report paying at least one bill at a banking correspondent, and this figure reaches 79 percent in the case of unbanked households (Sanford and Cojocaru 2013). Correspondent outlets are also an important channel for the distribution of government benefits. More than 8 million monthly benefits of the Bolsa Família program, a conditional cash-transfer program that reaches about 13 million poor families, were distributed through correspondent agents in 2012, accounting for more than 60 percent of this program's payments.

Correspondent outlets in rural areas tend to handle more withdrawals and deposits as a proportion of their transactions than do those in urban areas, suggesting that agents may play a role in extending banking service outreach to those areas (CGAP 2010b). Moreover, there is some evidence that correspondent banking serves historically excluded populations because customers using correspondent outlets are more likely to be poor, female, less educated, and from a smaller town, and to live in the lower-income northeast region (Sanford and Cojocaru 2013). About 6 percent of Brazilian households report accessing a loan from a bank, microfinance organization, government program, or credit cooperative through a banking correspondent, and this figure reaches 18 percent for residents of small towns in the northeast.

A key factor behind the rapid expansion of correspondent banking in Brazil has been the creation of an adequate legal framework for these types of arrangements (CGAP 2010b; Nakane and Rocha 2012). As mentioned above, the Brazilian authorities have enacted a series of regulations clarifying the nature of the services provided, the institutions involved, and the resulting reporting obligations. Regulations allow virtually any entity to be an agent. Most agents are commercial establishments, such as grocery and drug stores, notaries, post offices, and lottery outlets. In order to prevent fraud and to increase consumer confidence, individuals may not be agents.[14] Initially, Central Bank authorization was needed for a financial institution to hire an agent, but this is no longer required. Financial institutions need only to register their agents online. Although regulations allow agents to work for several financial institutions, the three banks with the largest correspondent networks have exclusivity agreements with their correspondent agents. This might raise some concerns about potential barriers to entry into correspondent banking.

Regulations allow correspondent agents to perform the following activities: current and savings account deposits, withdrawals, and transfers; bill payments; receiving, reviewing, and forwarding applications for account opening, loans, and credit cards; preliminary credit assessment; loan collections; and international transfers. The contracting financial institution is fully responsible for the services provided by the correspondent agents. Regulations require financial institutions to control the activities of their agents by setting transaction limits and to ensure compliance with all applicable laws and regulations. Because of security concerns, banks typically establish very low limits on the cash that agents can have on hand; as a result, some agents have to go to the bank several times per day. According to the regulations, correspondent agents cannot charge fees to customers for providing financial services, but they receive commissions for their services from the contracting bank.

Several additional factors beyond the development of an adequate regulatory framework have also contributed to the expansion of banking correspondents in Brazil. First, the cost of opening and operating new branches in Brazil is quite high because of strict labor laws, strong unions, and high regulatory requirements in terms of security and infrastructure. Correspondents do not face all of these regulations, making them an attractive alternative for banks trying to expand their service networks. Additionally, utility bill payment is considered a bank service in Brazil and cannot be done at nonbank outlets, providing a captive market of transactions for banking correspondents (Ivatury and Mas 2008). Moreover, Brazilian banks are relatively technologically advanced, partly as a consequence of the years of high inflation, when rapid recording and synchronization of bank transactions was required. This facilitated correspondent arrangements because banks already had in place most of the technological infrastructure required for the fast and reliable processing of transactions.

The Brazilian government also played a more direct role in fostering the expansion of correspondent banking networks by auctioning off the rights to provide financial services through post offices. The state-owned postal service (Empresa Brasileira de Correios e Telegrafos) conducted a competitive public tender bidding process in 2001, which was won by Bradesco. Bradesco paid about US$85 million for the exclusive rights to distribute financial services through post offices across Brazil until 2009 (subsequently extended until 2011), and also agreed to pay the postal service a share of the fees generated by the financial transactions carried out through this channel. Under the terms of the contract, Bradesco was required to give priority to providing financial services through post offices in municipalities without banking service outlets. The post office already had a well-developed technological platform and communications network, making any needed incremental investments by Bradesco relatively small.

Bradesco created a subsidiary, Banco Postal, to operate its correspondent service in post offices. Banco Postal provides a wide range of banking services, including bill payments, checking and savings accounts, deposits, withdrawals, account balances, credit cards, and loans. Bradesco's contract with the postal service expired in 2011, and a new bidding process was carried out. Banco do Brasil paid an initial fee of US$1.8 billion for the exclusive right to distribute financial services through post offices until 2016.[15] Banco Postal had 6,155 correspondent outlets at the end of 2015, serving 94 percent of Brazilian municipalities. About 1,600 Banco Postal outlets were located in municipalities that lacked a bank branch. Banco Postal had about 2 million current account holders in 2015 and seems to be serving historically financially excluded populations, with 35 percent of its account holders having at most primary education.

Next, we describe in more detail the experience of the two largest state-owned commercial banks in Brazil, Caixa Econômica Federal and Banco do Brasil, with the use of correspondent banking arrangements. As mentioned above, these institutions are among the main players in the correspondent banking industry, having the second- and third-largest correspondent networks in the country, respectively, as of the end of 2015.

Caixa Econômica Federal

Caixa Econômica Federal (CEF) is a government-owned financial institution created in 1861 to foster national savings. Over the years, CEF has incorporated other functions, such as housing and urban development financing and managing several government funds and programs. Currently, CEF is the largest agent in the local mortgage market and the third-largest commercial bank in Brazil, with assets representing 14 percent of total banking system assets at the end of 2014.

CEF was the first Brazilian bank to establish correspondent banking arrangements. CEF started its correspondent banking operations when it was appointed by the Brazilian federal government as its exclusive agent for the distribution of social benefits, such as school grants and income subsidies, throughout the country. To achieve national penetration, CEF established a partnership with the association of lottery houses to use its network to distribute benefits, thus taking advantage of already-existing infrastructure. After the aforementioned regulatory changes, which formally recognized correspondent banking relations and enabled their expansion, CEF decided to convert lottery houses into correspondents and increased the range of services offered through them to include withdrawals, deposits, account balance inquiries, and statement services. To successfully deliver financial services through lottery houses, CEF had to develop a new technological platform because the terminals used by these outlets were not compatible with the new financial services offered.

Although CEF initially used only lottery houses as correspondents, over time it has also established correspondent agreements with other types of outlets, such as supermarkets, general stores, bakeries, and gas stations. The initial investments required to set up correspondent outlets in lottery shops tend to be relatively small, given that most lottery houses already have adequate transaction and communications systems, but local retailers require larger investments, such as for POS terminals and communications equipment.

CEF delivers its financial services through correspondents under the brand name Caixa Aqui. CEF does not consider its correspondent network a separate business segment, but rather a delivery channel for its financial services. Therefore, there is no distinction between an account opened at a CEF branch and a Caixa Aqui outlet, and all CEF customers are considered Caixa Aqui customers, and vice versa. Caixa Aqui offers a wide range of payment services to its customers, such as receiving social benefits and paying utilities, taxes, and credit card bills. Moreover, clients can make deposits and withdrawals from their checking and savings accounts, check account statements, and make transfers between CEF accounts. In certain correspondent outlets, consumers can apply to open checking and savings accounts and to obtain credit cards and loans. Services provided by Caixa Aqui are characterized by simplified application procedures to target a segment of the population that may be less acquainted with banking operations.

Caixa Aqui offers simplified checking and savings accounts, called Caixa Fácil, which can be opened using only a photo ID and tax identification number, without proof of residence or income, as required for standard account openings.[16] Only customers who do not have an active account in another institution can open and maintain this simplified account. The account balance and monthly movements cannot exceed 3,000 Brazilian reals (about US$870), and up to four withdrawals and four balance inquiries are allowed per month. All operations are done using a debit card. There is no maintenance fee, and CEF charges only for transactions that exceed the monthly limits. Opening a Caixa Fácil account allows customers to access other financial services offered by Caixa Aqui, such as loans, credit cards, and insurance. Lending is still a small share of Caixa Aqui's operations, with most of its transactions concentrated in payment and banking services.

In 2009, CEF launched a program in collaboration with the Ministry for Social Development to open Caixa Fácil accounts for recipients of the Bolsa Família program, a conditional cash-transfer program that provides monthly allowances to over 13 million poor families and is distributed by CEF. The Bolsa Família program is distributed through an electronic card that recipients can use to withdraw benefits at CEF's branches and correspondent agents. Funds not withdrawn within 90 days are returned to the government. This system does not provide an effective savings mechanism and does not grant recipients access to financial services. In 2009, the Bolsa Família law was amended to allow recipients who so choose to have their benefits directly deposited in a Caixa Fácil account.[17] This change has the objective of fostering financial inclusion by allowing Bolsa Família recipients to save part of their benefits in a bank account and to access all financial services provided through the Caixa Fácil account.[18] More than 2 million accounts had been opened through this program by the end of 2012, representing about 15 percent of Bolsa Família beneficiary families.

CEF's correspondent banking scheme has been very successful in increasing outreach. Its correspondent outposts increased from fewer than 6,000 in 2000 to 27,600 by the end of 2015. Moreover, in 2003 CEF became the first financial institution to offer its services in all of Brazil's municipalities. The number of Caixa Fácil accounts has grown exponentially. In 2003, there were 43,569 accounts, and by December 2015 this number had reached 9.7 million—although not all accounts remain active. The Caixa Aqui program exceeded CEF's initial expectations; CEF's projections contemplated breaking even after 36 months of operation, but this actually occurred after only 18 months.

Banco do Brasil

Banco do Brasil is the largest bank in the country, with assets representing 18 percent of total banking system assets at the end of 2014. This state-owned bank was created in 1808, when Brazil became a Portuguese colony. Until 1866, the bank was in charge of issuing Brazil's legal currency; but, when this power was revoked, it became a commercial bank and mortgage institution. At the end of the 19th century, the bank started to emerge as a development financial institution, providing credit to sectors considered of strategic relevance. Banco do Brasil currently provides retail banking services, underwrites and issues securities, and offers asset-management and leasing services. It is listed on the stock market, although the government still owns over 70 percent of its voting shares.

Banco do Brasil entered the correspondent banking market in 2003 through the creation of a subsidiary, Banco Popular do Brasil. Banco Popular was established as a universal bank, with a legal and brand identity and accounting framework separate from its parent and with the objective of providing financial services through local retailers, such as supermarkets, bakeries, and drugstores.

Banco do Brasil initially adopted a different approach than CEF to correspondent banking. First, as mentioned above, Banco Popular was established as a completely stand-alone subsidiary, not a division of Banco do Brasil. Customers of Banco do Brasil were allowed to use Banco Popular correspondents to make financial transactions on existing accounts, but Banco Popular customers could not use Banco do Brasil's network. Second, Banco Popular had a different operational approach than CEF. Whereas CEF is in charge of directly providing its correspondents with the necessary equipment and training, Banco Popular outsourced management and support of its correspondents, contracting with private firms to select banking correspondents, undertake initial investments, and train correspondents' staff members.[19] It also subcontracted most of its back-office operations to Banco do Brasil. This allowed it to maintain a lean structure, with only about 80 staff members. Finally, in contrast to CEF's focus on payments and banking transactions, lending was a large component of Banco Popular's intended core business.

Given its lack of experience in lending to low-income households, Banco Popular initially adopted an innovative (but risky) lending approach. Each new account holder was automatically eligible for a loan of 50 reals (about US$17 in 2004, when Banco Popular started its operations), without collateral requirements or proof of income. If the loan was repaid on time, then customers could access progressively larger loan amounts. If not, customers were recorded as poor borrowers. This lending strategy was expected to help Banco Popular develop credit histories for its customers, but actually resulted in significant credit losses. The fraction of loans overdue more than 30 days, a measure of portfolios at risk typically applied to microloans, reached 42 percent in 2007. This bad loan performance led to substantial losses, with accumulated financial losses between 2004 and 2007 exceeding US$61 million.

In 2008, Banco do Brasil went through an internal reorganization and increased its focus on lower-income consumers and the newly emerging middle class. It created a new lower-income segment department, which absorbed the operations of Banco Popular and centralized the administration of banking correspondents. The Banco Popular brand was retired, and correspondents started providing services under the MaisBB brand, with an increased focus on payments and banking transactions and the provision of current and savings accounts. In addition, Banco do Brasil struck an alliance with Banco Lemon, a bank that operated exclusively though correspondents, to absorb its correspondent network.[20] This meant the incorporation of more than 6,000 correspondent outlets. In 2011, Banco do Brasil further expanded it correspondent network when it won the exclusive right to distribute financial services through post offices.

Banco do Brasil had the third-largest correspondent network in the country by 2015, with 14,361 outlets—6,155 of which correspond to post offices. Over 355 million transactions were conducted through its correspondent outlets, including bill payments, account deposits and withdrawals, and applications for account openings, credit cards, and loans. About 12 percent of all personal loans granted by Banco do Brasil in 2015 were distributed through its correspondent outlets.

Policy Discussion and Conclusions

The experience with correspondent banking arrangements in Brazil suggests that these arrangements can play an important role in increasing financial services outreach and raises some interesting issues that deserve further discussion. We first analyze some open questions regarding the different roles the government has played in the expansion of correspondent banking in Brazil and then discuss some of the limitations of correspondent arrangements that emerge from this experience. We believe that a better understanding of these issues may yield significant insights for the debate on the state's role in increasing access to finance and may also help us understand to what extent this experience could be replicated.

The Brazilian government has been extensively involved in the development of correspondent banking, playing multiple roles. First, the growth in correspondent banking arrangements was, to a large extent, spurred by regulatory changes. The Brazilian Central Bank enacted regulations specifically targeting correspondent arrangements, clarifying the nature of the services provided, the institutions involved, and the resulting reporting obligations. Moreover, it also introduced regulatory changes in related areas, such as relaxing requirements for opening simplified accounts. All these changes created a favorable environment for banks to expand their outreach through correspondent outlets. Second, the government took a more active role in fostering correspondent arrangements, by auctioning off the rights to provide financial services through post offices. This enabled a significant expansion in the geographic outreach of financial services, without the public sector assuming credit or operational risks—its only role in this respect is the provision of physical infrastructure. The use of post offices to provide financial services also seems to have increased incentives for other banks to look for alternative correspondent networks. Third, the government (through state-owned banks) participated directly in the establishment of correspondent arrangements. As described in this chapter, two state-owned commercial banks (CEF and Banco do Brasil) operate some of the largest correspondent networks in the country. Arguably, this is partly a consequence of the large role that state-owned banks play in the Brazilian financial sector in general. Banco do Brasil and CEF jointly hold more than 30 percent of banking system assets. Finally, the decision to enter into a contract with CEF to make all payments of social benefits also contributed to the expansion of correspondent banking, because this bank needed to create a network to disburse payments in all municipalities throughout the country, which could then be leveraged for the provision of financial services.

The significant government involvement in the expansion of correspondent arrangements in Brazil raises some important issues. First, the growth in correspondent banking has been partly a consequence of regulatory arbitrage. In Brazil, strict labor laws, strong unions, and high regulatory requirements in terms of security and infrastructure exacerbate the high costs associated with opening and operating branches. Correspondent outlets do not face most of these restrictions.[21] Therefore, some may argue that, in the presence of regulatory barriers, correspondent banking constitutes a second-best solution to expanding branch networks, with the first-best being the relaxation of these restrictions. In this sense, Brazil's experience with correspondents may actually constitute a strong case for relaxing branching regulations. Nevertheless, there are large cost differentials between branches and correspondent outlets due purely to economic reasons, which may make correspondents an attractive tool for increasing outreach even in the absence of regulations constraining the expansion of branch networks.

Second, the use of state-owned infrastructure such as post offices for the distribution of financial services by private financial intermediaries could raise some concerns. In particular, the use of public infrastructure could be interpreted by customers as implying some type of state participation in the provision of financial services or an implicit guarantee. This problem could be ameliorated by physically separating financial services from other activities and using clear branding distinctions, as well as by introducing adequate regulations, although it may not be possible to completely eliminate it.

Third, the direct participation of state-owned banks in the establishment of correspondent arrangements raises some questions. It is not clear that state-owned banks have any intrinsic advantages relative to private banks in conducting correspondent arrangements or that there is any rationale for their direct intervention in this sector. In Brazil's case, as mentioned above, the significant participation of CEF and Banco do Brasil in correspondent arrangements may just reflect the large role they play in the financial sector in general. Also, CEF may have had a relative advantage in providing correspondent banking because it already had an agreement with lottery houses to distribute government benefits. However, this does not necessarily have to be the case. Some countries, like Colombia and South Africa, have conducted tender processes to enter into contracts with financial institutions to distribute social benefits. And, in Brazil, payments for pensions and official social security benefits are done through the entire banking system, according to the beneficiary indication. In principle, all banks could be allowed to offer basic deposit accounts to the beneficiaries of the Bolsa Família program. Although the law allows this, in practice the government has not made any arrangements to allow benefits to be deposited in banks other than CEF. Further research would be necessary to assess whether the large participation of state-owned banks in correspondent arrangements in Brazil has facilitated industry growth or has actually displaced activity by private financial intermediaries.

The Brazilian experience with correspondent banking suggests that the expansion of correspondent services beyond payments and simple banking transactions may be difficult. In particular, correspondents may not provide an adequate channel for improving access to credit. As the experience of Banco Popular illustrates, the lack of credit histories and accurate income information for many customers of correspondent outlets may expose banks to high credit risk. The fact that correspondent banking may not be an adequate channel for providing credit does not diminish its relevance because the provision of payment and savings services to poor households may yield significant benefits and may be as valuable as credit, if not more, in some cases.[22] Moreover, these services might allow banks to become acquainted with their customers over time, which might eventually result in more credit. Nevertheless, it is an important limitation that must be taken into account when analyzing alternative policies.

To conclude, we believe that correspondent banking constitutes an innovative alternative to traditional policies aimed at increasing financial services outreach. Those policies have usually relied on state-owned banks operating branches in remote areas or have mandated that private banks operate in these areas, typically at a loss. Brazil's experience suggests that the state may have an important role to play in facilitating correspondent banking arrangements by providing an adequate legal and regulatory framework. In many countries, banking regulations significantly restrict the types of activities that can be conducted outside branches. Relaxing these restrictions, introducing guidelines governing agency relations between financial institutions and correspondents, and establishing clear regulatory and reporting requirements for these types of arrangements may be necessary preconditions for the successful development of correspondent banking. The state might also have a more direct role to play by making available some types of public infrastructure for the distribution of financial services. However, it is not clear that it should play a more active role because correspondent arrangements can (and do) take place among private parties. Correspondent banking could be an important instrument for expanding the availability of financial services in remote areas in many developing countries, but its replication requires taking into account its particular operational risks and limitations, as well as tailoring arrangements and regulations to the local environment.

Notes

1. These cross-country differences in branch and ATM geographic penetration are explained by differences in financial development and economic activity, as well as population density and institutional factors. See Beck, Demirgüç-Kunt, and Martinez Peria (2007).

2. Within-country analyses of the geographic distribution of ATMs and bank branches show wide regional disparities, with urban areas having much higher densities of financial service outposts than rural areas. In the case of Mexico, for example, Deshpande (2006) reports that, whereas in some areas of Mexico City there are over 33 bank branches per 100,000 people, in certain districts of Chiapas (Mexico's poorest state) there is less than one branch per 100,000 people.

3. These types of arrangements are also referred to as "agent banking" in the literature.

4. See Scher (2001) for an overview of the postal provision of financial services and its evolution.

5. Anson et al. (2013) analyze the determinants of the use of postal savings accounts and find that post offices are more likely than traditional financial institutions to provide accounts to lower-income and less-educated individuals.

6. See Dias and McKee (2010), Lauer, Dias, and Tarazi (2011) and Dias, Staschen, and Noor (2015) for discussions of the risks of correspondent banking arrangements and the regulatory and supervisory responses.

7. Typically, in correspondent banking arrangements, all customer transactions through the POS terminal are done against an account that the agent has with the bank, to ensure that the customer always faces the bank's credit risk, and not the agent's. When a customer deposits cash through the correspondent, the bank automatically credits her account and withdraws the same amount from the agent's account, with the agent retaining the cash to compensate for the amount deducted from its account. In the case of a cash withdrawal, the opposite happens: the agent provides cash from the till to the customer, and its bank account is credited for a similar amount. The change in the agent's bank account balance, therefore, is given by the difference between the cash it receives and the cash it pays out for financial transactions. In practice, because most correspondent agents tend to take cash in on net, they need to periodically make deposits to ensure that they have enough funds in their bank accounts to continue processing transactions.

8. See Ivatury and Pickens (2006), Mas and Kumar (2008), *The Economist* (2009), IFC (2011), and GSMA (2016) for overviews of mobile money and its potential role in increasing access to financial services.

9. See Oxford Policy Management (2011) and AFI (2012) for cross-country comparisons of correspondent banking arrangements. See also Mas (2008b) and Faz and Garcia Arabehety (2015) for the case of Peru; Alarcon Lozano and Mandrile (2010) and CGAP (2016) for Colombia; and CGAP (2010a, 2012) and Kochar (2016) for India.

10. These countries are Bangladesh, Brazil, India, Kenya, Pakistan, and Tanzania.

11. See Nakane and Rocha (2012) for an overview of the recent evolution of the Brazilian financial system, with a focus on financial inclusion policies.

12. In Brazil, financial service provision through bank branches is complemented by service outposts, which offer a more limited range of services than branches.

13. The observed decline in the number of correspondent outlets in 2014 reflects revisions to the registry of correspondents by Central Bank authorities, not necessarily a reduction in the actual number of correspondents.

14. Since the mid-2000s there has been a significant expansion in credit promoters, companies considered banking correspondents that offer payroll-consigned loans on behalf of banks. These promoters, in turn, hire individual salespeople (informally referred to as *pastinhas*) to offer loans. The significant growth in the number of *pastinhas* (according to some estimates, there are currently almost half a million) has become a significant concern for the Central Bank, which has introduced regulations to increase bank control over them.

15. Banco Postal customers were formally customers of Bradesco, which owned the current and savings accounts opened through Banco Postal. To prepare for the loss of access to the postal network, Bradesco opened bank branches and expanded its nonpostal correspondent network in the most profitable municipalities where Banco Postal had opened accounts and attempted to move these clients to its new outlets (Bickerton and Steinhoff 2013).

16. Central bank regulations allowed the creation of simplified current and savings accounts in 2004, establishing limits regarding account balances, transactions, and fees. Offering these accounts is not mandatory, and in practice only state-owned banks offer these accounts because private banks have found them to be unprofitable (CGAP 2010b). As of December 2015, there were almost 14 million simplified current accounts, although less than 60 percent of them were active. Simplified savings accounts reached 5.6 million, more than three-quarters of which were active.

17. Although the law does not specify that benefits have to be deposited in a Caixa Fácil account, in practice the government has not allowed benefits to be deposited in other banks.

18. See Pickens, Porteous, and Rotman (2009) and Bold, Porteous, and Rotman (2012) for discussions of the use of government payments, such as social transfers and pension payments, to foster financial inclusion. CGAP (2011) analyzes the case of CEF and Bolsa Família.

19. In 2003, the Central Bank introduced new regulations allowing banks to outsource the management of agent networks to third parties, known as network managers. These firms provide a wide range of services, including the selection of agents, training, software development, cash handling, and the maintenance of POS devices. Most of the network managers have exclusive deals with a particular bank.

20. Under this agreement, Banco Lemon became an exclusive network manager for Banco do Brasil.

21. There have been several lawsuits in recent years demanding the equalization of wages and work conditions between workers of correspondent outlets and bank employees. This could have a significant impact on the functioning of correspondent arrangements.

22. The move in recent years away from microcredit, which consisted primarily in the provision of working-capital loans to microentrepreneurs, and toward microfinance, which encompasses all sorts of financial services, including credit, insurance, savings, and money transfer services, illustrates the increasing realization that low-income households may benefit from access to financial services in general, not only credit. Randomized evaluations of microsavings tend to find relatively large positive impacts on welfare from improvements in access to and usage of formal savings. See Karlan, Ratan, and Zinman (2014) for a review of these studies.

References

AFI (Alliance for Financial Inclusion). 2012. "Agent Banking in Latin America." Discussion Paper, AFI.

Alarcón Lozano, Daniel Mauricio, and Matteo Mandrile. 2010. "A New Agent Model for Branchless Banking in Colombia." Unpublished manuscript. International Development Law Organization (IDLO), Rome.

Allen, Franklin, Asli Demirgüç-Kunt, Leora Klapper, and Maria Soledad Martinez Peria. 2016. "The Foundations of Financial Inclusion: Understanding Ownership and Use of Formal Accounts." *Journal of Financial Intermediation* 27: 1–30.

Almandoz, Luis. 2006. Presentation given by the Manager of Agente BCP Channel, Bogota, November 30.

Anson, Jose, Alexandre Berthaud, Leora Klapper, and Dorothe Singer. 2013. "Financial Inclusion and the Role of the Post Office." Policy Research Working Paper 6630, World Bank, Washington, DC.

Banco Central do Brasil. 2015. Relatório de Inclusão Financeira No. 3 2015.

Beck, Thorsten, Asli Demirgüç-Kunt, and Maria Soledad Martinez Peria. 2007. "Reaching Out: Access to and Use of Banking Services across Countries." *Journal of Financial Economics* 85 (1): 234–66.

———. 2008. "Banking Services for Everyone? Barriers to Bank Access and Use around the World." *World Bank Economic Review* 22 (3): 397–430.

Berthaud, Alexandre, and Gisela Davico. 2013. "Global Panorama on Postal Financial Inclusion: Key Issues and Business Models." Universal Postal Union (UPU), Berne.

Bickerton, Geoff, and Katherine Steinhoff. 2013. "Banking on a Future for Posts?" Paper prepared for the 21st Rutgers University Conference on Postal and Delivery Economics.

Bold, Chris, David Porteous, and Sarah Rotman. 2012. "Social Cash Transfers and Financial Inclusion: Evidence from Four Countries." CGAP Focus Note 77, Consultative Group to Assist the Poor, Washington, DC, February.

Burgess, Robin, and Rohini Pande. 2005. "Can Rural Banks Reduce Poverty? Evidence from the Indian Social Banking Experiment." *American Economic Review* 95 (3): 780–95.

CGAP (Consultative Group to Assist the Poor). 2010a. "Technology Program Focus Country: India." CGAP, Washington, DC.

———. 2010b. "Technology Program Focus Country: Brazil." CGAP, Washington, DC.

———. 2011. "CGAP G2P Research Project: Brazil Country Report." CGAP, Washington, DC.

———. 2012. "National Survey of Banking Correspondents in India 2012." CGAP, Washington, DC.

———. 2016. "Banking Agents in Colombia: Rural Expansion and Its Frontier." CGAP, Washington, DC

CGAP (Consultative Group to Assist the Poor) and FGV (Fundação Getúlio Vargas). 2010. "Branchless Banking Agents in Brazil: Building Viable Networks."

Clotteau, Nils, and Bsrat Measho. 2016. "Global Panorama on Postal Financial Inclusion." Universal Postal Union (UPU), Berne.

Demirgüç-Kunt, Asli, Leora F. Klapper, Dorothe Singer, and Peter Van Oudheusden. 2015. "The Global Findex Database 2014: Measuring Financial Inclusion Around the World." Policy Research Working Paper 7255, World Bank, Washington, DC.

Deshpande, Rani. 2006. "Safe and Accessible: Bringing Poor Savers into the Formal Financial System." CGAP Focus Note 37, Consultative Group to Assist the Poor, Washington, DC, September.

Dias, Denise, and Katharine McKee. 2010. "Protecting Branchless Banking Consumers: Policy Objectives and Regulatory Options." CGAP Focus Note 64, Consultative Group to Assist the Poor, Washington, DC, September.

Dias, Denise, Stefan Staschen, and Wameek Noor. 2015. "Supervision of Banks and Nonbanks Operating through Agents: Practice in Nine Countries and Insights for Supervisors." Consultative Group to Assist the Poor, Washington, DC.

The Economist. 2009. "The Power of Mobile Money." September 24.

Faz, Xavier, and Pablo Garcia Arabehety. 2015. "Driving Scale and Density of Agent Networks in Peru." CGAP Brief, Consultative Group to Assist the Poor, Washington, DC.

GSMA. 2016. "2015 State of the Industry Report—Mobile Money." GSMA, London.

IFC (International Finance Corporation). 2011. "IFC Mobile Money Study 2011." IFC, Washington, DC.

Ivatury, Gautam, and Ignacio Mas. 2008. "The Early Experience with Branchless Banking." CGAP Focus Note 46, Consultative Group to Assist the Poor, Washington, DC, April.

Ivatury, Gautam, and Mark Pickens. 2006. "Mobile Phones for Microfinance." CGAP Brief, Consultative Group to Assist the Poor, Washington, DC.

Karlan, Dean, Aishwarya Lakshmi Ratan, and Jonathan Zinman. 2014. "Savings by and for the Poor: A Research Review and Agenda." *Review of Income and Wealth* 60 (1): 36–78.

Kochar, Anjini. 2016. "Branchless Banking: Evaluating the Doorstep Delivery of Financial Services in Rural India." Working Paper No. 566, Stanford Center for International Development, Stanford University.

Kumar, Anjali. 2005. *Access to Financial Services in Brazil: A Study.* Washington, DC: World Bank.

Kumar, Anjali, Thorsten Beck, Cristine Campos, and Soumya Chattopadhyaya. 2005. *Assessing Financial Access in Brazil.* Working Paper Series no. 50. Washington, DC: World Bank.

Lauer, Kate, Denise Dias, and Michael Tarazi. 2011. "Bank Agents: Risk Management, Mitigation, and Supervision." CGAP Focus Note 75, Consultative Group to Assist the Poor, Washington, DC, December.

Lyman, Timothy R., Gautam Ivatury, and Stefan Staschen. 2006. "Use of Agents in Branchless Banking for the Poor: Rewards, Risks, and Regulation." CGAP Focus Note 38, Consultative Group to Assist the Poor, Washington, DC, October.

Mas, Ignacio. 2008a. "Realizing the Potential of Branchless Banking: Challenges Ahead." CGAP Focus Note 50, Consultative Group to Assist the Poor, Washington, DC, October.

———. 2008b. "An Analysis of Peru's *Cajeros Corresponsales.*" Unpublished manuscript. Consultative Group to Assist the Poor, Washington, DC.

Mas, Ignacio, and Kabir Kumar. 2008. "Banking on Mobiles: Why, How, for Whom?" CGAP Focus Note 48, Consultative Group to Assist the Poor, Washington, DC, July.

Meyer, Richard L. 2015. "Financing Agriculture and Rural Areas in Sub-Saharan Africa: Progress, Challenges and the Way Forward." Working Paper, International Institute for Environment and Development (IIED), London.

Nakane, Marcio, and Bruno de Paula Rocha. 2012. "Policy Innovations to Improve Access to Financial Services: The Case of Brazil." Center For Global Development, Washington, DC.

Oxford Policy Management. 2011. "Evaluation of Agent Banking Models in Different Countries." Oxford Policy Management, Oxford, United Kingdom.

Pickens, Mark, David Porteous, and Sarah Rotman. 2009. "Banking the Poor via G2P Payments." CGAP Focus Note 58, Consultative Group to Assist the Poor, Washington, DC, December.

Prieto Ariza, Ana María. 2006. "Ampliación del Acceso a los Servicios Financieros mediante Corresponsales No Bancarios: La Experiencia de Brasil y Perú." Documentos Asobancaria 001971, Asobancaria.

Sanford, Caitlin, and Laura Cojocaru. 2013. "Do Banking Correspondents Improve Financial Inclusion? Evidence from a National Survey in Brazil." Bankable Frontier Associates, Somerville, MA.

Scher, Mark J. 2001. "Postal Savings and the Provision of Financial Services: Policy Issues and Asian Experiences in the Use of the Postal Infrastructure for Savings Mobilization." DESA Discussion Paper 22, United Nations, New York.

World Bank. 2014. *Global Financial Development Report 2014: Financial Inclusion.* Washington, DC: World Bank.

CHAPTER 7

Credit Guarantees: FOGAPE's Experience In Chile

Introduction

This chapter describes the experience of FOGAPE (Fondo de Garantía para Pequeños Empresarios, Small Enterprise Guarantee Fund) in Chile, a public credit guarantee scheme that provides partial guarantees for loans to micro and small firms.

Credit guarantee schemes are mechanisms whereby a third party—the guarantor—pledges to repay some or the entire loan amount to the lender in case of borrower default. The guarantor assumes part or all of the credit risk, reducing the risk faced by financial intermediaries and thus making it possible for borrowers that might otherwise face difficulties in accessing external finance to obtain credit or to improve the terms and conditions under which they can borrow.

Credit guarantee schemes are widespread, with more than 2,250 credit guarantee schemes of different types operating in over 70 countries by the early 2000s. In 2015, the total value of outstanding guarantees granted by credit guarantee schemes around the world reached about US$550 billion, with almost 9 million firms benefiting from these guarantees (REGAR 2016). Since the 1950s, governments have established public credit guarantee schemes, usually targeted at some sector, region, or type of firm—such as small and medium enterprises (SMEs), young firms, exporters, and innovators—considered to be underserved by private financial intermediaries and/or whose growth is thought to have positive externalities. Public credit guarantee schemes have become increasingly popular among governments during the past few decades and are now widespread in both developed and developing countries. Moreover, all multilateral development banks operate some form of credit guarantee scheme.

Public credit guarantee schemes significantly expanded in the aftermath of the 2008–09 global financial crisis because several countries (including Canada, Chile, Finland, France, Germany, Greece, Japan, the Republic of Korea, Malaysia, the Netherlands, and the United States) relied heavily on these schemes to compensate for the reduction in private bank lending.[1] In many countries, existing guarantee programs were ramped up, with increases in the total amount of funds available, the number of eligible firms, the percentage of the loan guaranteed, and/or the size of the guaranteed loans. In other countries, such as Ireland and the United Kingdom, new programs were introduced. The countercyclical use of credit guarantee schemes during the financial crisis led to a significant increase in their scale and scope. For instance, data for credit guarantee schemes in 18 European countries with available information show that the total value of outstanding guarantees grew by almost 38 percent between 2008 and 2010 (from about €56.1 billion to €77.1 billion), with the number of SMEs benefiting from these guarantees increasing from €1.5 million to more than €2.7 million over the same period (AECM 2013). Credit guarantee schemes in Latin America experienced an even larger expansion in terms of volume, with the total value of outstanding guarantees more than doubling between 2008 and 2010, from US$8.8 billion to US$19.3 billion (REGAR 2012).[2] The significant expansion of credit guarantee schemes during the crisis has implied a greater commitment of public finances and has increased their risk exposure, which could threaten the financial sustainability of some schemes over the medium to long term.[3]

Despite the increasing interest of policy makers in credit guarantee schemes, there is little theoretical analysis and empirical evidence to systematically inform their design, implementation, and assessment. Although these programs are usually justified on the basis of some social objectives, the rationale underlying the choice of credit guarantees instead of other instruments is usually left unexplained. Moreover, the precise goals of these schemes are often unclear, making cost-benefit analyses difficult.

This chapter describes the experience of FOGAPE, a public credit guarantee scheme that provides partial guarantees for loans to micro and small firms in Chile. This experience is closer to traditional state interventions in credit markets than some of the other experiences described throughout this book because FOGAPE's main role is to take counterparty risk. However, we think that FOGAPE's experience might yield useful insights regarding whether credit guarantees can be effective instruments for increasing access in a sustainable and market-friendly manner. In particularly, FOGAPE has managed to maintain low operating costs and has put in place an incentive structure for lenders that limits the amount of risk shifting to the public sector, avoiding some of the pitfalls that have affected most public credit guarantee schemes. This has allowed it to significantly scale up its operations, with the number of new loans guaranteed per year increasing from

200 in 1998 to almost 49,000 in 2014, while maintaining a good credit quality and remaining financially sustainable.

The remainder of this chapter is organized as follows. The next section provides a general overview of credit guarantee schemes, discussing how they may help overcome barriers to accessing finance. It also describes some of the main issues in the design of these schemes and briefly summarizes the evidence on the sustainability and economic impact of existing public guarantee schemes. We then describe the experience of FOGAPE in Chile. The final section concludes with a discussion of this experience and its implications for the debate on the role of the state in fostering access to finance, as well as the insights it provides regarding the design of credit guarantee schemes.

An Overview of Credit Guarantees

How Do Credit Guarantees Work?

As described above, credit guarantee schemes are mechanisms whereby a third party—the guarantor—pledges to repay some or all of the loan amount to the lender in case of borrower default. This reduces the lender's expected credit losses, even if the probability of default remains unchanged, acting as a form of insurance against default. The guarantor charges a fee for this service. A credit guarantee can lower the amount of collateral that the borrower needs to pledge to receive a loan because the guarantor effectively provides a substitute for collateral. Similarly, for a given amount of collateral, the credit guarantee can allow riskier borrowers to receive a loan and/or to obtain better lending conditions (for example, longer maturities, lower rates, higher loan amounts), because the guarantee lowers the risk faced by lenders.

Credit guarantee schemes can (and do) emerge privately. This typically happens for three reasons (Honohan 2010). First, guarantors might have some advantage in dealing with principal–agent problems. As discussed in chapter 2, asymmetric information and enforcement problems can lead to the exclusion of creditworthy borrowers from credit markets. In this situation, if guarantors have any informational or enforcement advantage over lenders, they can help overcome principal–agent problems and improve access to credit or reduce borrowing costs for certain borrowers. For instance, members of small business organizations might form a mutual guarantee association (MGA), in which firms deposit money into a fund that guarantees loans to members from financial institutions, to take advantage of the fact that they have better information about each other than lenders do. MGAs typically evaluate their members carefully and can thus act as a screening device, reducing asymmetric information problems. The fact that other firms are willing to accept joint responsibility for a loan to a given firm provides a positive signal to lenders regarding its credit quality. Moreover, MGAs have a group liability structure, because all borrowers backed by the scheme have a financial stake in the guarantee fund. This means that members face a cost in case of default by other members and therefore have incentives to monitor each other, ameliorating moral hazard problems.

Second, guarantors might have some advantages relative to lenders in spreading and diversifying risks. If lenders face some restrictions that prevent them from diversifying their loan portfolios (for example, because their portfolios are geographically concentrated or focused on certain types of borrowers), guarantors might be able to spread risks by providing guarantees to several lenders, thus improving risk diversification.

Third, credit guarantees can sometimes be used for regulatory arbitrage. This can occur, for instance, when guarantors face different regulations than lenders and can provide guarantees that allow an otherwise insufficiently secured loan to meet regulatory requirements.

None of these arguments implies a need for government participation in credit guarantee schemes. However, governments often get involved in these schemes, usually in two different ways. First, governments in many countries support private guarantee schemes, such as MGAs, by providing direct financial assistance and/or granting additional guarantees (for example, counterguarantees).[4] Second, governments can directly set up a public credit guarantee scheme. Beck, Klapper, and Mendoza (2010) conduct a survey of credit guarantee schemes around the world and find that the majority of credit guarantee schemes in developing countries are public schemes, whereas the majority of credit guarantee schemes in developed countries are MGAs. MGAs are particularly common in Europe. For example, Italy has about 950 MGAs; Germany, 24; Spain, 20; and France, 10 (ADB 2007). MGAs in most European countries are often coordinated through one or more guarantee federations.

There is significant debate regarding the role of public credit guarantee schemes in ameliorating problems of access to finance. Unlike MGAs, public credit guarantee schemes do not necessarily have better information about borrowers than lenders do, and thus do not directly reduce information asymmetries. Rodriguez-Mesa (2004) points out that credit guarantees can serve as a substitute for collateral, but they do not play any of the roles that collateral plays in reducing moral hazard and adverse selection because borrowers are not pledging their own assets and thus do not face an additional cost in case of default.[5] Vogel and Adams (1997) argue that public credit guarantee schemes can actually increase information problems by reducing lenders' incentives to carefully screen and monitor borrowers. On the other hand, public guarantee schemes might reduce information asymmetries, at least in the long run, by acting as a subsidy for lenders to learn about new groups of borrowers. We discuss these issues in more detail in this chapter's concluding section.

Public Credit Guarantee Schemes around the World

Credit guarantee schemes have existed in different forms at least since the 19th century. Some of the first credit guarantee schemes were mutual credit guarantee associations that developed out of guild or craft organizations in Europe. The first public credit guarantee scheme was founded in the Netherlands in 1915. Japan established a regional, government-run credit guarantee scheme in Tokyo in 1937, with schemes in other regions of Japan starting operations in the 1940s. A handful of other countries established public credit guarantee schemes in the 1950s. However, the majority of government-run credit guarantee schemes were established in the 1990s and 2000s (Pombo and Herrero 2003).[6]

The sizes of public credit guarantee schemes in terms of the volume of loans guaranteed vary widely across countries. Some of the largest public credit guarantee schemes are in Asia. The Japanese credit guarantee system is regarded as the largest in the world in terms of the volume of guarantees, with about 730,000 new loans guaranteed in 2013 and an outstanding stock of 3.1 million guarantees, totaling about US$305 billion. The second-largest scheme is in the Republic of Korea, with a stock of more than 400,000 outstanding guarantees in 2013, totaling about US$40 billion (almost 4 percent of Korean gross domestic product, GDP). In contrast, Beck, Klapper, and Mendoza (2010) find that most public credit guarantee schemes in their survey have a stock of less than 100,000 outstanding guarantees, with two-thirds of these schemes granting less than 1,000 new loan guarantees per year. Similarly, Calice (2016) surveys 62 public credit guarantee schemes around the world and finds that the median scheme in his sample served fewer than 1,400 SMEs in 2014. This small size typically results in high operating expenses, given the existence of economies of scale.

Design Issues

Public credit guarantee schemes around the world differ in their design—specifically in their management structure, operating rules, and the characteristics of their guarantees, such as the coverage ratio and pricing. These design choices can be critical for the success and financial sustainability of credit guarantee schemes because they influence the participation of financial institutions, administrative costs, and loan default rates. In this section, we briefly discuss these issues and review some international experiences.[7]

The first question that arises when designing a publicly funded credit guarantee scheme is whether the scheme should be solely publicly managed or whether all or part of its activities should be outsourced to the private sector. Running a credit guarantee scheme encompasses a number of tasks, including the management of the guarantee fund, assessing the loans to be guaranteed, and working to recover defaulted loans. Beck, Klapper, and Mendoza (2010) find that in most countries, the government is heavily involved in the management of the guarantee fund. However, loan assessment and recovery are typically undertaken by the lenders whose loans are being guaranteed. This approach appears to promote the financial sustainability of credit guarantee schemes. Schemes in which the government chooses borrowers and recovers loans typically have higher loan losses than schemes in which the lender performs these tasks, possibly because lenders have greater experience with credit appraisal and recovery than government agencies and might have more incentives to perform these activities.

The international experience suggests that it might be more cost-effective to have lenders assess the creditworthiness of the borrowers that are being guaranteed because lenders already have a credit appraisal infrastructure in place.[8] Moreover, loan appraisal by the guarantee scheme is likely to lead to a duplication of efforts between the scheme and financial intermediaries, because lenders are not likely to completely outsource screening of their borrowers to the scheme. The Korea Credit Guarantee Fund (KODIT), which appraises every loan by itself, had operating costs of 7.7 percent of its guaranteed loans by the end of the 1990s (Honohan 2010). Colombia's Fondo Nacional de Garantías (FNG) initially also appraised all loans in house and had operating costs of 4.2 percent of the value of outstanding guarantees. It then switched to a system in which lenders can appraise most loans themselves, lowering operating costs to less than 2 percent of the guaranteed amount.

On the other hand, having the lender decide which new loans will receive guarantees might lead to excessive risk shifting to the guarantee fund because lenders might not have incentives to adequately screen those loans that will be covered by the guarantee. There are at least two ways of mitigating this problem. First, lenders with high default rates can be charged higher fees for the guarantees. However, Beck, Klapper, and Mendoza (2010) find that only five (out of 39) credit guarantee schemes covered in their survey apply penalties in case of default. Calice (2016) finds that over 60 percent of schemes in his sample apply fixed fees without taking into account the riskiness of the loans or the performance of borrowers.

Second, credit guarantee schemes can influence lenders' incentives by adjusting the coverage ratio, that is, the fraction of the value of an individual loan that the scheme guarantees. When the scheme guarantees less than 100 percent of the value of a loan, part of the credit risk remains with the lender. This helps align the incentives of the guarantor and the lender because it encourages the lender to carefully screen and monitor the loans that are covered by the guarantee scheme. Levitsky (1997) argues that to ensure an appropriate alignment of incentives, lenders should assume at least 30 to 40 percent of the risk, and never less than 20 percent. On the other hand, there is a trade-off between lenders assuming a higher share of the risk and making the scheme attractive to them. Levitsky (1997) argues that guarantees with coverage ratios below 50 percent are not likely to be attractive for lenders. In practice, Beck, Klapper, and Mendoza (2010) find that 10 public credit guarantee schemes in their sample guarantee up to 100 percent of individual loans.

The remaining 29 schemes in their sample guarantee up to 75 percent of each loan on average, with coverage ratios ranging from 33 percent to 95 percent.

Another important consideration when designing a credit guarantee scheme is how claims are processed. Costly and time-consuming claims procedures can reduce the transparency and credibility of the scheme and might discourage lenders from participating. Therefore, setting clear rules regarding when and how to pay out guarantees as well as paying claims without a long and costly verification process are important considerations. Green (2003) points out that, in many developing countries, early guarantee schemes did not have clear conditions under which a guarantee could be claimed by lenders, leading to disputes between financial intermediaries and these schemes. He argues that introducing a time limit for the settlement of claims might increase transparency and also suggests making only larger claims subject to an extensive inspection before payment is made. Smaller claims can be processed without an ex ante inspection and can be randomly verified ex post, which speeds up the overall process.

Finally, another key design issue for public credit guarantee schemes is how to determine the fees charged for their guarantees. There are two separate considerations in this regard. The first is how to structure these fees. Some credit guarantee schemes charge a flat fee that is the same for all types of guarantees. Other schemes charge fees that vary with the characteristics of the guarantee or the guaranteed loan. For example, Brazil's SEBRAE (Serviço Brasileiro de Apoio às Micro e Pequenas Empresas, Brazilian service of assistance to micro and small enterprises) charges higher fees for longer maturity loans (Green 2003). Colombia's FNG charges fees that increase with the coverage ratio.

The second consideration regarding fees is determining their overall level. In principle, if the credit guarantee scheme has any informational or enforcement advantage relative to lenders and/or a better ability to diversify risks, it should be able to charge high enough fees to fully cover its administrative expenses and credit losses, plus its opportunity cost of capital, without requiring any government subsidies. On the other hand, if the public credit guarantee scheme addresses some market failures, this might justify some level of subsidization to lenders by charging fees that do not fully cover all its costs. In practice, most schemes charge annual fees of about 2 percent of the guarantee amount, which is usually insufficient to cover their operating costs (that is, administrative costs plus credit losses) (Gudger 1998; Green 2003; Calice 2016). This can affect the financial sustainability of public credit guarantee schemes, as discussed below.

Financial Sustainability and the Impact of Public Credit Guarantee Schemes

The performance of public credit guarantee schemes in terms of financial sustainability has been mixed, at best. As mentioned above, most of these schemes cannot cover their operating expenses with their fee income. For instance, Beck, Klapper, and Mendoza (2010) find that, of the 15 public credit guarantee schemes in their survey that report complete financial information, 11 have operating losses. The median public credit guarantee scheme in their survey charges 1.5 percent of the guarantee amount in fees, has administrative costs of 9 percent, and has credit losses of 5 percent. Even if fee income does not fully cover their total costs, public credit guarantee schemes can in principle be financially sustainable because they can make up for operating losses with the investment income from their guarantee funds. The provision of initial capital for these funds by the government constitutes an implicit subsidy, because this capital generates investment returns that can be used to finance their operations.

If the investment income is insufficient, the guarantee schemes might require additional government support. Gudger (1998) reviews the performance of a large number of credit guarantee schemes around the world and finds that this has been the case for most schemes. Beck, Demirgüç-Kunt, and Honohan (2008) estimate that the Mexican government subsidizes its credit guarantee scheme each year at a rate of about 2 percent of the guaranteed loan amount. In the United Kingdom, the same figure is about 15 percent. On the other hand, there are also examples of public credit guarantee schemes that are financially sustainable. For instance, the Small Business Administration (SBA) Section 7a program in the United States requires an annual subsidy of only about 0.1 percent of the value of outstanding guarantees (Beck, Demirgüç-Kunt, and Honohan 2008).

The overarching question related to the impact of public credit guarantee schemes is whether they lead to *financial additionality*, that is, whether they generate additional loans for the targeted firms and/or allow them to borrow at better terms (for example, longer maturities or lower rates), relative to what would have happened in the absence of the scheme. Given that the goal of credit guarantee schemes is to improve access to finance for certain groups of firms, their existence is difficult to justify if they do not lead to financial additionality. A further question is whether these schemes lead to *economic additionality*, that is, whether any increases in access to finance that they cause contribute to improving the performance of the supported firms (for example, higher growth, investment, employment, or innovation). An even more difficult question is whether these schemes generate positive spillovers and contribute to overall economic growth.

Accurately measuring financial additionality would require knowing whether the firms that participate in a given credit guarantee scheme would have been able to borrow (or under which conditions they would have been able to do so) in the absence of the scheme. This counterfactual is not observable. Most empirical studies attempt to overcome this identification challenge by comparing firms that have benefited from guaranteed loans with similar firms that have not received guaranteed loans. Most of the existing studies provide evidence of the financial additionality of credit guarantee schemes, typically in the form of better conditions in accessing credit, such as higher loan volumes, lower interest rates, and/or longer maturities. For instance, Zecchini and Ventura (2009) and de Blasio et al. (2014) find that Italy's Fondo di Garanzia increased lending to SMEs. Similar evidence of financial additionality has been found for the Small Business Financing Program in Canada (Riding, Madill, and Haines 2007), the National Guarantee Fund in Colombia (Castillo Bonilla and Giron 2014), SOFARIS (Société française de garantie des financements des petites et moyennes entreprises) in France (Lelarge, Sraer, and Thesmar 2010), the Special Credit Guarantee Program in Japan (Wilcox and Yasuda 2008; Uesugi, Sakai, and Yamashiro 2010), the Small Firms Loan Guarantee in the United Kingdom, and the U.S. Small Business Administration (Hancock, Peek, and Wilcox 2007), among others.

Despite this evidence of financial additionality, there is also evidence of sizable displacement effects and deadweight costs of public credit guarantee schemes. For instance, Zia (2008) finds that almost half of guaranteed loans in Pakistan went to financially unconstrained firms and estimates that this credit misallocation has an annual cost equivalent to 0.75 percent of GDP. Uesugi, Sakai, and Yamashiro (2010) find that the loosening of conditions for credit guarantees in Japan during the Asian financial crisis led to significant risk shifting because banks replaced nonguaranteed loans with guaranteed ones to minimize their exposure to risky assets. Moreover, there is also some evidence that public credit guarantees tend to be associated with lower firm creditworthiness and higher defaults (Ono, Uesugi, and Yasuda 2013; de Blasio et al. 2014; Saito and Tsuruta 2014), suggesting that these schemes might decrease lender incentives to adequately screen and monitor borrowers.

Evidence of economic additionality is scarcer; there are fewer studies on the topic, likely because of the difficulties in gathering the required data and accurately identifying any real effects. Craig, Jackson, and Thompson (2008) find that the employment rate is higher in U.S. districts that receive more guaranteed loans. Asdrubali and Signore (2015) find evidence that the European Union SME Guarantee Facility had a positive effect on firm employment in Central and Eastern European countries. Oh et al. (2009) find that participation in public credit guarantee schemes in Korea is associated with increased firm sales and employment growth, as well as higher wages and firm survival rates. In contrast, Kang and Heshmati (2008) also analyze the case of Korea and find only weak evidence of an effect on firm sales, productivity, and employment. Similarly, D'Ignazio and Menon (2013) and de Blasio et al. (2014) find little effect of credit guarantees on firm investment and sales in Italy.

Although a growing body of empirical work has analyzed the impact of credit guarantee schemes, this research faces significant limitations. The main challenge is the identification of an appropriate control group because firms that do not participate in a given credit guarantee scheme might be systematically different from participating firms. When measuring financial additionality, a further difficulty is that lenders might substitute guaranteed loans for other loans and borrowers might switch across lenders from unguaranteed to guaranteed loans, so that no additional lending might actually occur. Measuring economic additionality also raises some further difficulties. For instance, firms that receive credit guarantees and that grow because of the improved access to credit could displace firms that did not receive the guarantees, with little or no aggregate effects on growth and employment. Further work is required to address these challenges and accurately identify the impact of credit guarantee schemes.

We now turn to the description of FOGAPE's experience with credit guarantees in Chile. We then discuss in the final section the main insights regarding the design and functioning of credit guarantee schemes that emerge from this experience, as well as some of the arguments that might justify state intervention.

The Experience of FOGAPE

FOGAPE is a Chilean credit guarantee scheme funded by the national government and administered by BancoEstado, a large, state-owned commercial bank.[9] FOGAPE provides credit guarantees to financial institutions for loans to microenterprises (defined as those with less than US$100,000 in annual sales) and small firms (up to US$1 million in annual sales).[10] In 2009, in the wake of the global financial crisis, medium and large firms with annual sales of up to about US$20 million became temporarily eligible for FOGAPE's guarantees until 2010. In 2015 eligibility was temporarily extended for two years to medium firms with sales of up to US$4 million, as part of the government's measures to boost growth and productivity.

FOGAPE was originally established in 1980 with the goal of promoting access to credit for micro and small enterprises. However, for almost two decades only BancoEstado and two other banks used its credit guarantees, and the number of guaranteed loans was quite small, standing at only 200 in 1998 (DFID 2005). After discussions with financial institutions and representatives of the financial sector supervisory agency (Superintendencia de Bancos e Instituciones Financieras, SBIF) FOGAPE was reformed and relaunched in 1999. An important part of the reform consisted of simplifying and streamlining the claims procedure. FOGAPE's guarantees also became more liquid and are now paid out in full within 15 days of the claim being made.

When FOGAPE was established in 1980, the government granted it an initial capitalization of approximately US$13 million. This capital could be leveraged up to 10 times (that is, FOGAPE could provide guarantees for a maximum amount equal to 10 times the value of its capital). In 2000, FOGAPE merged with the Guarantee Fund for Exporting Firms, increasing its capital by US$15 million. In 2008 and 2009, FOGAPE received additional capital infusions of US$10 million and US$130 million, respectively, as part of the government's response to the financial crisis. Moreover, the maximum leverage ratio was increased to 11 times to allow FOGAPE to further expand its guarantee portfolio. In 2014, FOGAPE received an additional capital infusion of US$50 million, raising its total capital to about US$260 million at the end of 2015.

FOGAPE provides guarantees to new loans up to a maximum amount of US$200,000. Only firms that are up to date on all their financial obligations are eligible.[11] The maximum guarantee coverage ratio varies with the size of the loan, reaching 80 percent for loans below US$120,000 and 50 percent for loans above this threshold. FOGAPE's guarantees have a maximum maturity of 10 years, but there is no maturity limit for the guaranteed loans. Loans with maturity of one year or less accounted for more than 50 percent of the total amount guaranteed in 2014, whereas loans with maturities between one and three years accounted for about a third. Both working capital and investment loans are eligible for FOGAPE's guarantees. About 76 percent of all loans guaranteed between 2007 and 2014 were for working capital purposes, and this share has been increasing in recent years.

FOGAPE does not target its guarantees to any sector in particular. The only sector-related restriction is that no more than 50 percent of guarantees can go to a given sector. In 2014, most guarantees (34 percent) went to firms in the retail sector, followed by the service sector (19 percent). FOGAPE also does not have any explicit regional priorities or restrictions. The geographic distribution of its guarantees depends on the branch network of participating financial institutions, as well as on the presence of eligible firms. In 2014, almost 50 percent of FOGAPE's guarantees went to firms located in the Metropolitan Region of Santiago. This percentage corresponds approximately to the region's share of Chile's GDP (45 percent in 2014).

FOGAPE does not evaluate loans on a case-by-case basis. Instead, it allocates a total amount of guarantees to each participating financial institution, and these institutions then decide which particular loans to guarantee, subject to meeting FOGAPE's eligibility criteria. In fact, the borrower has no direct relationship with FOGAPE, and in many cases borrowers are unaware that their loan is subject to a guarantee (DFID 2005).

A rather unique feature of FOGAPE is that the allocation of its guarantee funds to financial institutions is done through auctions held four to six times a year. In each auction, FOGAPE offers a fixed volume of guarantees. Each financial institution submits secret bids requesting guarantees for a certain volume of loans with a given coverage ratio. FOGAPE allocates guarantees to those institutions requesting the lowest coverage ratio until the total amount of guarantees auctioned equals total bids. Thus, if the value of guarantees auctioned by FOGAPE exceeds the aggregate volume requested by participating financial institutions, then all institutions receive their desired amount of guarantees. On the other hand, if the amount requested by financial institutions exceeds the volume auctioned by FOGAPE, then guarantees are allocated to those institutions with the lowest requested coverage ratio, until guarantees are exhausted. In this way, the bidding process determines how risks are shared among FOGAPE and financial intermediaries. The maximum coverage ratio that bidders can submit is 80 percent for long-term loans and 70 percent for short-term loans. Each financial institution can be awarded no more than two-thirds of the value of guarantees auctioned each time. Following the bidding process, banks have three months to grant the corresponding loans. Financial institutions that use less than 80 percent of the guarantees awarded to them in an auction are excluded from the subsequent auction.

FOGAPE has managed to maintain low operating costs by letting financial institutions make all lending decisions. FOGAPE's administrative expenses amount to less than 0.1 percent of the value of the outstanding guarantees. As discussed in "Design Issues" above, letting lenders appraise loans for the credit guarantees may generate some incentive problems because lenders might not screen and monitor loans carefully, leading to higher default rates and credit losses. FOGAPE has several design features aimed at mitigating these incentive problems. First, as mentioned above, FOGAPE guarantees only up to 80 percent of the value of loans, so that part of the risk remains with the lender. The auctioning of guarantees fosters competition among financial institutions on the basis of the coverage ratio, providing additional incentives to screen and monitor borrowers and fostering risk discovery. Second, the fee that financial institutions pay for the credit guarantees depends on past default rates of guaranteed loans. This fee, however, is capped at 2 percent of the guaranteed amount per year. Finally, if claims from a given financial institution are too high, FOGAPE can (and does) exclude the institution from participating in future bidding processes until loan performance improves. This helps ameliorate incentive problems because lenders that reduce screening and monitoring today might lose profitable opportunities in the future.

Since FOGAPE was reformed in 1999, it has greatly expanded its outreach. The number of new loans guaranteed increased from 10,146 in 2000 to 24,077 in 2008 and then to 48,772 in 2014 (see figure 7.1, panel a). The value of new loans guaranteed shows a similar evolution, increasing from about US$135 million in 2000 to US$480 million in 2008 and then to US$1.2 billion in 2014 (figure 7.1, panel b). Although the number and value of new loans guaranteed increased steadily from 2000 to 2004, these figures then declined until 2008. This decline is explained by the fact that FOGAPE's leverage ratio was close to the legally allowed maximum during this period, constraining its expansion. As mentioned above, the maximum leverage ratio was increased from 10 to 11 times in 2008. This increase, combined with the capital infusions received in 2008 and 2009, allowed FOGAPE to significantly expand its operations during the financial crisis, playing a countercyclical role. The number of new loans guaranteed by FOGAPE more than tripled between 2008 and 2010,

FIGURE 7.1 Evolution of new loans guaranteed by FOGAPE

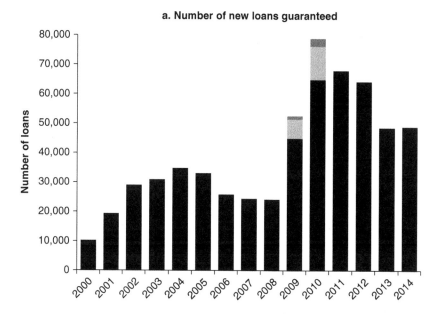

a. Number of new loans guaranteed

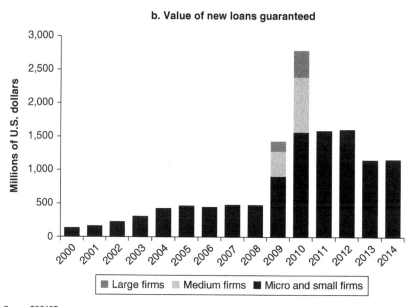

b. Value of new loans guaranteed

▨ Large firms   ▥ Medium firms   ■ Micro and small firms

Source: FOGAPE.
Note: Micro and small firms are those with annual sales below US$1 million. Medium firms are those with annual sales between US$1 million and US$4 million. Large firms are those with annual sales between US$4 million and US$20 million.

and the value of new loans guaranteed increased more than fivefold over this period. In addition, as mentioned above, medium and large firms were temporarily allowed to receive FOGAPE guarantees in 2009 and 2010. These firms represented only 16 percent of the new loans guaranteed in these two years but accounted for more than 40 percent of the total value of these loans. Two additional policy measures further contributed to FOGAPE's expansion during the crisis. First, the bank supervisor SBIF temporarily reduced capital requirements on loans guaranteed by FOGAPE, making its guarantees more attractive for financial intermediaries. Second, FOGAPE reduced its fees by half during 2009.

Since the global financial crisis, the number of new loans guaranteed by FOGAPE has steadily declined, from 64,841 in 2010 to 48,772 in 2014. The value of new loans guaranteed each year shows a similar evolution, decreasing from US$2.8 billion in 2010 to US$1.2 billion in 2014. This partly reflects the scaling down of the crisis response, as financial and macroeconomic conditions improved and the need for FOGAPE's guarantees to boost private lending decreased, as well as the fact that FOGAPE almost reached its maximum allowed leverage ratio in 2010. In addition, to a large extent motivated by FOGAPE's success, CORFO (Corporación de Fomento de la Producción de Chile, or Production Development Corporation, a government development agency) significantly ramped up its partial credit guarantee scheme, which focuses on micro, small, and medium firms, starting in 2011. As a result, financial institutions now have an additional source of government credit guarantees that, to some extent, competes with FOGAPE. The stock of outstanding credit guarantees granted by FOGAPE reached about US$1.1 billion at the end of 2014, with the stock of guaranteed loans reaching US$1.4 billion. Loans to micro and small firms guaranteed by FOGAPE accounted for more than 10 percent of all commercial loans to these firms in the Chilean banking system at the end of 2014.

FOGAPE has also supported the development of mutual guarantee societies (Instituciones de Garantia Reciproca), which are private financial institutions that provide partial credit guarantees to SMEs. These institutions, which started operating in 2009, issue certificates of guarantee that firms can in turn offer to banks as collateral to secure loans. FOGAPE provides counterguarantees to these institutions, increasing the certainty and value of the certificates for banks. Between 2010 and 2014, FOGAPE provided counterguarantees to mutual guarantee societies for about US$234 million, which represents about 4 percent of the total value of guarantees granted by FOGAPE over this period.

FOGAPE has historically shown a strong portfolio performance, but credit quality has deteriorated somewhat since its large expansion during the financial crisis. FOGAPE paid out claims, net of recoveries, of between 1.1 and 1.3 percent of outstanding guarantees from 2005 to 2007 (figure 7.2, panel a). In the crisis years 2008 and 2009, this ratio increased to 2 percent and 2.8 percent, respectively.

FIGURE 7.2 Evolution of FOGAPE's credit quality

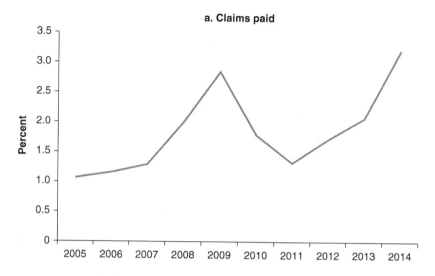

a. Claims paid

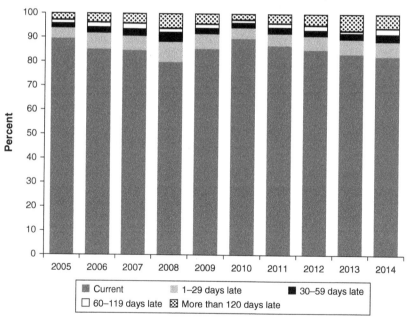

b. Outstanding loans guaranteed by delinquency status

Current   1–29 days late   30–59 days late
60–119 days late   More than 120 days late

Source: FOGAPE.
Note: Panel a shows the evolution of the ratio of paid out claims net of recoveries to the initial stock of outstanding guarantees. Panel b shows the evolution of the composition of outstanding loans guaranteed according to their delinquency status.

Portfolio quality improved in subsequent years, but has deteriorated recently, with claims paid, net of recoveries, reaching 3.2 percent in 2014. A similar pattern is visible when analyzing loan repayment performance. As shown in figure 7.2, panel b, the fraction of loans that are more than 30 days late increased from about 6 percent in 2005 to 12 percent in 2008. After improvement following the global financial crisis, this ratio increased again in recent years, reaching 11 percent in 2014. This ratio is higher than that for all commercial loans to micro and small firms in the Chilean banking system, which stood at about 7 percent at the end of 2014. Vintage analysis of guarantees shows that loans guaranteed in 2008 and 2009 display the highest default rates. It remains to be seen whether FOGAPE will be able to maintain its good portfolio performance going forward after its large expansion.

FOGAPE is designed to be financially sustainable. In principle, FOGAPE's management objective is for income from fees charged for the guarantees to be sufficient to cover credit losses and administrative expenses. The investment income on the fund's capital can then be used to increase the volume of guarantees provided. FOGAPE had net income of US$2.5 million and US$2.3 million in 2014 and 2015, respectively. These positive financial results are in part due to the fund's low administrative costs. However, as a result of the deterioration in credit quality described above, in recent years fee income has been insufficient to cover credit losses and administrative expenses, with the return on the fund's capital making up for the difference and helping finance FOGAPE's operations. If we exclude investment returns and other financial results, FOGAPE would have had operating losses of US$23.4 million and US$9.6 million in 2014 and 2015, respectively.

There is some empirical evidence suggesting that FOGAPE is associated with increased access to credit and other positive outcomes for participating firms. Larraín and Quiroz (2006) suggest that FOGAPE has generated additional loans for micro and small enterprises. As discussed previously, measuring financial additionality is complicated by a number of challenges, including the need to find an appropriate comparison group of borrowers and to account for possible substitution of unguaranteed for guaranteed loans from the same lender or across lenders. To find an appropriate comparison group for firms that receive loans guaranteed by FOGAPE, Larraín and Quiroz (2006) exploit the timing when different banks started participating in the scheme. In particular, they compare borrowers who received loans guaranteed by FOGAPE before 2004 to borrowers who received guaranteed loans after 2004. They find that borrowers that started participating in FOGAPE earlier are 14 percent more likely to receive a loan than those that started later. They also find some evidence of economic additionality because firms in the treatment group have higher sales and profits than firms in the comparison group. These findings, however, depend on the assumption that borrowers that received loans guaranteed by FOGAPE after 2004 are similar to those that received loans before 2004. This might not necessarily be the case; for instance, better-performing banks with better-performing borrowers might have started participating in FOGAPE earlier.

Alvarez, Belmar, and Opazo (2015) use propensity score matching to identify an appropriate comparison group for firms that receive loans guaranteed by FOGAPE. They find that FOGAPE's guarantees increase the probability that a firm receives a bank loan. They also find that guarantees are associated with increases in sales but not in other real firm outcomes, such as employment and investment. They argue that this is because FOGAPE's credit guarantees are mostly directed toward financing working capital.

Cowan, Drexler, and Yañez (2015) use a different strategy to examine the financial additionality of FOGAPE, focusing on banks' behavior. They argue that, although the amount of guarantees requested by a given bank in FOGAPE's auction is likely to depend on the amount that the bank is planning to lend, the actual amount allocated to the bank also depends on the bids of other banks as well as on other factors. The authors consider the difference between requested and allocated guarantees to be "unexpected," allowing them to identify the effects of receiving additional credit guarantees on bank lending. They find that banks that receive higher unexpected guarantee allocations make more loans to both new and existing borrowers.

In contrast to this evidence, some authors have questioned the extent of FOGAPE's additionality, as well as its effects on borrower incentives. Benavente, Galetovic, and Sanhueza (2006) find that approximately 80 percent of the firms that participate in FOGAPE had received loans from banks in the past and that many of the firms receiving guaranteed loans had already received guarantees before. This suggests that banks are not necessarily using FOGAPE as a temporary subsidy to learn about the creditworthiness of new borrowers, but rather just to reduce their credit risk exposure when lending to borrowers with which they are already familiar. Cowan, Drexler, and Yañez (2015) find that an additional $1 in guarantees is associated with an increase of 65 cents in new loans to SMEs, suggesting that part of the guarantee is being allocated to loans that would have been granted anyway. They also find evidence that firms with guaranteed loans are more likely to default than firms borrowing without guarantees and argue that this is due to adverse selection, with financial intermediaries selecting riskier borrowers to receive FOGAPE's guarantees.

Policy Discussion and Conclusions

FOGAPE's experience raises a number of interesting issues that deserve further discussion. We first briefly analyze some of FOGAPE's salient design features and then discuss some of the arguments that might support this type of state intervention. We end with a discussion of some open questions regarding this program.

We believe that a better understanding of these issues can yield significant insights for the debate on the role of the state in broadening access and can also help in understanding the value added of this type of intervention. We return to some of these issues in chapter 9.

FOGAPE has been able to provide partial credit guarantees on a relatively large scale while maintaining an adequate portfolio performance and achieving financial sustainability. As discussed above, these results seem to be rather uncommon among public credit guarantee schemes because most of these schemes operate on a small scale and are not financially sustainable. There are several factors that have contributed to FOGAPE's success. First, FOGAPE has a clearly market-oriented approach, focusing on the long-term goal of achieving a sustainable deepening of financial markets for micro and small firms, instead of just trying to increase the amount of credit that these firms receive, as has traditionally been the focus of state interventions in this area.

FOGAPE considers financial institutions as its primary clients and sees its role as providing products and services that assist these institutions in their commercial operations. It has developed close relationships with banks, interacting with them frequently through monthly meetings with all participating financial institutions and also through bilateral meetings with specific institutions. This close relationship has allowed FOGAPE to adapt the design of its guarantees to meet the needs of banks in serving micro and small firms. As a result, senior managers and those in charge of SME lending at participating banks consider FOGAPE a valuable partner. FOGAPE also provides training for frontline staff in financial institutions on how to use its products and has specialized support staff to address any issues or questions that may arise.

Moreover, FOGAPE's activities go beyond just providing partial credit guarantees. It has developed specialized knowledge of the market for micro and small firms and has close relationships with the different government agencies and support networks that serve these firms. As a result, it has become a key player in the design and implementation of public policies in this area and serves as a link between the private and public sectors. In addition, it provides banks with high-quality information about the specific sector covered by its guarantees, which is not available from any other sources. Detailed results on the performance of the portfolio of guaranteed loans are distributed to participating banks in monthly meetings.

A second factor contributing to FOGAPE's success is that it is perceived by market participants to be relatively free from political pressures. When FOGAPE was reformed and relaunched in 1999, it was necessary to build the confidence of private banks in the scheme because previous state interventions in credit markets had included instances in which financial intermediaries faced pressures to make loans at a loss to meet social and/or political objectives. The SBIF played a key role in this regard, by supporting FOGAPE's reform and encouraging banks to participate in the scheme. Moreover, the fact that FOGAPE is supervised by the SBIF and is also externally audited has increased transparency and confidence in the scheme.

Third, as described above, several design features have allowed FOGAPE to expand its outreach while remaining financially sustainable. A key factor behind FOGAPE's expansion following its relaunch in 1999 was setting clear rules for paying out guarantees and simplifying the claims procedure to make guarantees more transparent and liquid. FOGAPE's guarantees are now paid out in full within 15 days of the claim being made, making the scheme more attractive for financial institutions. This contrasts with the experience of many developing countries, where costly and time-consuming claims procedures, as well as the lack of clear rules, have led to disputes between financial intermediaries and public credit guarantees schemes, discouraging lenders from participating. FOGAPE manages to maintain low administrative costs by letting financial institutions decide which particular loans to guarantee. At the same time, as described above, FOGAPE has various mechanisms to encourage lenders to carefully screen and monitor guaranteed loans: (i) FOGAPE provides only partial guarantees, covering at most 80 percent of the value of individual loans, so that financial institutions bear part of the credit risk; (ii) the auctioning of guarantees on the basis of the coverage rate offered by financial institutions has fostered competition and has driven the average coverage ratio down, thereby providing stronger incentives for lenders to carefully screen and monitor borrowers; (iii) FOGAPE's fees are tied to past loan performance, again providing incentives for participating financial institutions to maintain good portfolio quality; and (iv) if claims from a financial institution are too high, FOGAPE can exclude it from future guarantee auctions until its performance improves.

An important open question regarding FOGAPE, as well as other public credit guarantee schemes, is to what extent state intervention through the direct provision of credit guarantees is warranted. Several theoretical arguments have been put forward by the literature in this regard. First, public credit guarantee schemes might address information problems in the longer run by acting as subsidies to financial institutions to cover the initial costs of learning how to lend to a particular group of borrowers. Private financial intermediaries may lack incentives to incur the upfront costs of learning about new sectors and devising the required lending techniques because, once their efforts prove successful, others can easily reproduce them (Besley 1994). In this situation, there might be a role for the state to promote innovation in financial markets by subsidizing the initial costs of lending to a new group of borrowers. According to this argument, public credit guarantee schemes may be operated at a loss while financial institutions develop new lending techniques and accumulate the required experience and information, including building borrower credit histories. This argument implies that credit guarantee schemes must be designed carefully to provide financial intermediaries with adequate incentives to set up the best technologies and to learn what really works, which requires some risk sharing between the scheme and lenders (Rodriguez-Mesa 2004). The idea behind this argument is that, once financial institutions have learned how to lend to the particular target segment, they will be able to continue providing financing without further subsidies. This implies that any subsidies should be temporary and that the guarantee scheme should end (or focus on a different group of borrowers) once financial institutions have acquired the required experience and information.

In practice, however, it may be challenging to determine when this is the case. Moreover, political incentives may make it quite difficult to eliminate a credit guarantee scheme once it is established and there is a group of firms and financial institutions that may benefit from it. As Vogel and Adams (1997) point out, no evidence exists of public programs that have been able to eliminate guarantees after a certain period. In addition, even if temporary subsidies to encourage lenders to venture into a new market are deemed necessary, it is not clear whether credit guarantees are the best tool for achieving this goal. Alternatively, governments could, for instance, provide direct subsidies to financial institutions for lending to firms in the target sector. In this case the public sector would face no credit risk. However, these direct subsidies would have to be designed carefully to ensure that they reach the desired targets.

A second line of reasoning often used to justify state intervention in credit guarantee schemes is that these schemes can help mitigate adverse selection and moral hazard problems. However, this argument can justify state intervention only if the government has an informational or enforcement advantage over private financial intermediaries, which is not typically the case. One exception might be state support for mutual credit guarantee associations, which have close knowledge of their members but might not have sufficient capital to set up a credit guarantee scheme on their own. In this case, the government could provide funding and/or reinsurance to the MGA. But, even in this case, state involvement should not go further than this because the government is unlikely to have any advantage in managing the credit guarantee scheme. Moreover, public funding might exacerbate principal–agent problems because it could reduce the incentives of MGA members to monitor each other, given that fewer of their own resources are at stake.

A third argument that might justify state intervention in credit guarantee schemes is that the state has a natural advantage in dealing with collective action frictions and, as a result, can spread risk more finely across space and time than atomistic agents (Anginer, de la Torre, and Ize 2014). Arrow and Lind (1970) show that, when risk is spread in small amounts over large numbers of agents, capital can be priced at risk-neutral prices. They argue that the state's intertemporal tax-and-borrowing capacity gives it a unique ability to spread risk.[12] Thus, the state has an advantage in terms of risk bearing relative to risk-averse private agents, and state credit guarantees (as opposed to subsidies or loans) are called for to encourage private investment or lending in the face of high risk or risk aversion.

Even if there are relevant (theoretical) arguments to justify the establishment of public credit guarantee schemes, some valid questions concerning FOGAPE's operations still remain. In the first place, some may question whether FOGAPE's continued involvement in the market for loans to micro and small firms is required. FOGAPE was established with the objective of fostering the development of credit markets for these firms. As discussed above, this argument can justify only a transitory intervention and implies that the scheme should end (or move on to another group of borrowers) once lenders have learned how to effectively serve the targeted group. However, in practice, it is difficult to determine when this point has been reached. Since the early 2000s, there has been a significant improvement in access to credit for micro and small firms in Chile. The number of micro and small firms with loans from financial institutions increased from about 500,000 in 2004 to 1.2 million at the end of 2015, accounting for more than 11 percent of the total corporate lending volume. According to firm-level surveys conducted by the World Bank, 72 percent of small firms in Chile had a line of credit or a loan from a financial institution in 2010, compared to only 42 percent of small firms in high-income countries. Moreover, only 10 percent of small firms in Chile considered access to finance to be a major constraint, compared to 18 percent of small firms in high-income countries. Interviews with banks conducted by Larraín and Quiroz (2006) suggest that FOGAPE was an important factor in the decision of many Chilean financial institutions to enter the micro and small firm market. This factor appears to have lost importance over time, however.

Second, another important question is whether FOGAPE has achieved the desired policy objectives of generating financial and economic additionality. The research by Larraín and Quiroz (2006); Alvarez, Belmar, and Opazo (2015); and Cowan, Drexler, and Yañez (2015) discussed above shows that FOGAPE's guarantees led to higher bank lending to micro and small firms. On the other hand, Benavente, Galetovic, and Sanhueza (2006) suggest that banks are not necessarily using FOGAPE as a temporary subsidy to learn about the creditworthiness of new borrowers but rather just to reduce their credit risk exposure when lending to borrowers with which they are already familiar. The fact that FOGAPE has experienced relatively low credit losses might also indicate that its guarantees are not necessarily reaching the riskier micro and small firms. In sum, although there is evidence that FOGAPE generated financial additionality, it is not clear whether the impact was as large as it could have been and whether FOGAPE is reaching those firms that would benefit the most from credit guarantees. Further research is necessary to examine these issues.

Finally, measuring FOGAPE's additionality alone is not enough to justify the use of public funds. The relevant question in this regard is whether FOGAPE has been a cost-effective way of achieving the observed results. Answering this question would require a rigorous cost–benefit analysis, as well as comparing FOGAPE to alternative state interventions. At a first glance, given the evidence of financial additionality and the fact that FOGAPE has been financially sustainable, it would seem to have been a cost-effective intervention to generate additional lending to micro and small firms. On the other hand, FOGAPE has received several capital infusions, which could have been used to fund other government programs. Moreover, credit guarantee schemes imply an implicit liability for the government, and it remains to be seen whether FOGAPE's good portfolio performance will continue in the future, particularly given the significant expansion of its operations during the financial crisis.

To conclude, FOGAPE's experience provides an interesting example of state intervention to foster access to finance, which is closer to more traditional interventions in credit markets than some of the other experiences described throughout this book. FOGAPE's experience suggests that public credit guarantee schemes can be financially sustainable and can reach a large number of firms. However, this success hinges on several design features that have allowed FOGAPE to keep its operating costs low and that prevent adverse selection and moral hazard among borrowers and lenders. The disappointing experience with many public credit guarantee schemes, especially in developing countries, suggests that getting the design right might be a significant challenge. Moreover, rigorous evidence on the impact of public credit guarantee schemes is still scarce. There is a need for more in-depth evaluations that jointly take into account financial sustainability and additionality and that assess these schemes against alternative policy instruments.

Notes

1. See OECD (2010, 2012, 2013) and World Bank (2013) for discussions on the use of public credit guarantee schemes as countercyclical tools during the financial crisis.

2. Note that these figures include data on both public and private credit guarantee schemes. In most countries the government gives significant support to private guarantee schemes, providing funding and offering counterguarantees. Data for European countries cover selected credit guarantee schemes in Austria, Belgium, the Czech Republic, Estonia, France, Germany, Greece, Hungary, Italy, Latvia, Lithuania, Poland, Portugal, Romania, Spain, Slovakia, Slovenia, and Turkey.

3. KPMG (2012) finds that public credit guarantee schemes used as countercyclical tools during the crisis reported increases in bad debts.

4. Counterguarantees are a reinsurance mechanism whereby a third party (the counterguarantor) assumes part of the risk from the guarantor. Public assistance for private credit guarantee schemes through counterguarantees provided by regional or national governments is commonly observed in Organisation for Economic Co-operation and Development countries, especially in the case of mutual guarantee schemes.

5. See chapter 2 for a discussion of the role of collateral in ameliorating problems of access to credit.

6. See Doran and Levitsky (1997); Gudger (1998); Green (2003); Beck, Klapper, and Mendoza (2010); and Calice (2016) for global surveys of credit guarantee schemes. Regional surveys of credit guarantee schemes are also available; see, for instance, Saadani, Arvai, and Rocha (2011) for the Middle East and North Africa; Samujh, Twiname, and Reutemann (2012) for Asia; Pombo, Molina, and Ramirez (2013) for Latin America; and Vienna Initiative (2014) for Central and Eastern Europe.

7. The World Bank Group and the FIRST (Financial Sector Reform and Strengthening) Initiative convened a global task force in 2015 to develop an internationally agreed-on set of good practices for establishing, operating, and evaluating public credit guarantee schemes (http://documents.worldbank.org/curated/en/576961468197998372/pdf /101769-REVISED-ENGLISH-Principles-CGS-for-SMEs.pdf). Calice (2016) analyzes the implementation of these principles around the world.

8. A similar argument could be applied to the case of loan recovery after a default.

9. See chapter 9 for a short description of BancoEstado.

10. FOGAPE also provides credit guarantees to exporting firms with up to US$16.7 million in annual sales.

11. This restriction is intended to avoid situations in which a financially distressed firm might use a newly issued loan guaranteed by FOGAPE to pay off other debts.

12. There is significant debate in the literature regarding the validity of the Arrow-Lind result that the social cost of risk tends to zero as the state spreads the risk associated with any investment project among a large population. Foldes and Rees (1977) argue that, under a more realistic formulation of fiscal policy, this result holds only under very stringent assumptions, and that therefore the practical circumstances in which the Arrow-Lind conclusions apply are extremely restricted. Gardner (1979) shows that the Arrow-Lind results hold only if the investment risk is arbitrarily small.

References

ADB (Asian Development Bank). 2007. "People's Republic of China: Development of Small and Medium-Sized Enterprise Credit Guarantee Companies." Technical Assistance Completion Reports, ADB, Manila, July.

AECM (European Association of Mutual Guarantee Societies). 2013. *Statistics AECM 2012*. Brussels: AECM.

Asdrubali, Pierfederico, and Simone Signore. 2015. "The Economic Impact of EU Guarantees on Credit to SMEs: Evidence from CESEE Countries." European Economy Discussion Papers 2, Directorate General Economic and Financial Affairs (DG ECFIN), European Commission, Brussels.

Alvarez, Roberto, Jose Belmar, and Luis Opazo. 2015. "Evaluating the Impact of Credit Guarantees in Chilean Firms." Proceedings of the 2015 World Finance Conference.

Anginer, Deniz, Augusto de la Torre, and Alain Ize. 2014. "Risk-Bearing by the State: When Is It Good Public Policy?" *Journal of Financial Stability* 10: 76–86.

Arrow, Kenneth J., and Robert C. Lind. 1970. "Uncertainty and the Evaluation of Public Investment Decisions." *American Economic Review* 60 (3): 364–78.

Beck, Thorsten, Asli Demirgüç-Kunt, and Patrick Honohan. 2008. *Finance for All? Policies and Pitfalls in Expanding Access*. Washington, DC: World Bank.

Beck, Thorsten, Leora Klapper, and Juan Carlos Mendoza. 2010. "The Typology of Partial Credit Guarantee Funds around the World." *Journal of Financial Stability* 6 (1): 10–25.

Benavente, J. M., A. Galetovic, and R. Sanhueza, 2006. "FOGAPE: An Economic Analysis." University of Chile, Department of Economics Working Paper wp222, Santiago.

Besley, Timothy. 1994. "How Do Market Failures Justify Interventions in Rural Credit Markets?" *World Bank Research Observer* 9: 27–47.

Calice, Pietro. 2016. "Assessing Implementation of the Principles for Public Credit Guarantees for SMEs: A Global Survey." Policy Research Working Paper 7753, World Bank, Washington, DC.

Castillo Bonilla, José Augusto, and Luis Eduardo Girón. 2014. "Cuantificación de la Importancia del Fondo Nacional de Garantías en la Movilización de Créditos a las Pymes." *Estudios Gerenciales* 30: 18–24.

Cowan, Kevin, Alejandro Drexler, and Álvaro Yañez. 2015. "The Effect of Credit Guarantees on Credit Availability and Delinquency Rates." *Journal of Banking and Finance* 59: 98–110.

Craig, Ben R., William E. Jackson, and James B. Thompson. 2008. "On Government Intervention in the Small-Firm Credit Market and Its Effect on Economic Performance." In *Entrepreneurship in Emerging Domestic Markets*, edited by Glen Yago, James R. Barth, and Betsy Zeidman, 47–67. New York: Springer.

de Blasio, Guido, Stefania De Mitri, Alessio D'Ignazio, Paolo Finaldi Russo, and Lavinia Stoppani. 2014. "Public Guarantees to SME Borrowing. An RDD Evaluation." Dipartimento di Scienze Economiche e Aziendali Marco Fanno, Università degli Studi di Padova.

DFID (Department for International Development). 2005. "Do Credit Guarantees Lead to Improved Access to Financial Services? Recent Evidence from Chile, Egypt, India and Poland." Policy Division Working Paper, UK Department for International Development, London.

D'Ignazio, Alessio, and Carlo Menon. 2013. "The Causal Effect of Credit Guarantees for SMEs: Evidence from Italy." Working Paper 900, Bank of Italy, Rome.

Doran, Alan, and Jacob Levitsky. 1997. *Credit Guarantee Schemes: A Global Perspective*. London: Graham Bannock and Partners.

Foldes, Lucien P., and Ray Rees. 1977. "A Note on the Arrow-Lind Theorem." *American Economic Review* 67 (2): 188–93.

Gardner, Roy. 1979. "The Arrow-Lind Theorem in a Continuum Economy." *American Economic Review* 69 (3): 420–22.

Green, Anke. 2003. "Credit Guarantee Schemes for Small Enterprises: An Effective Instrument to Promote Private Sector-Led Growth?" SME Technical Working Paper No. 10. United Nations Industrial Development Organization, Vienna.

Gudger, M. 1998. "Credit Guarantees: An Assessment of the State of Knowledge and New Avenues of Research." FAO Agricultural Services Bulletin 129, Food and Agriculture Organization, United Nations, Rome.

Hancock, Diana, Joe Peek, and James A. Wilcox. 2007. "The Repercussions on Small Banks and Small Businesses of Bank Capital and Loan Guarantees." Working Paper #07-22. Wharton Financial Institutions Center, Philadelphia.

Honohan, Patrick. 2010. "Partial Credit Guarantees: Principles and Practice." *Journal of Financial Stability* 6 (1): 1–9.

Kang, Jae Wong, and Almas Heshmati. 2008. "Effect of Credit Guarantee Policy on Survival and Performance of SMEs in Republic of Korea." *Small Business Economics* 31 (4): 445–62.

KPMG. 2012. *Credit Access Guarantees: A Public Asset between State and Market.* New York: KPMG International.

Larraín, Christian, and Jorge Quiroz. 2006. "Evaluación de la Adicionalidad del Fondo de Garantías de Pequeñas Empresas." BancoEstado, Santiago.

Lelarge, Claire, David Sraer, and David Thesmar. 2010. "Entrepreneurship and Credit Constraints: Evidence from a French Loan Guarantee Program." In *International Differences in Entrepreneurship*, edited by Josh Lerner and Antoinette Schoar. Chicago: University of Chicago Press.

Levitsky, Jacob. 1997. "Best Practice in Credit Guarantee Schemes." *The Financier—Analyses of Capital and Money Market Transaction* 4: 86–94.

OECD (Organisation for Economic Co-operation and Development). 2010. *Assessment of Government Support Programmes for SMEs' and Entrepreneurs' Access to Finance during the Crisis.* Paris: OECD.

———. 2012. *Financing SMEs and Entrepreneurs. An OECD Scoreboard 2012.* Paris: OECD.

———. 2013. *SME and Entrepreneurship Financing: The Role of Credit Guarantee Schemes and Mutual Guarantee Societies in Supporting Finance for Small and Medium-Sized Enterprises.* Paris: OECD.

Oh, Inha, Jeong-Dong Lee, Almas Heshmati, and Gyong-Gyu Choi. 2009. "Evaluation of Credit Guarantee Policy Using Propensity Score Matching." *Small Business Economics* 33 (3): 335–51.

Ono, Arito, Iichiro Uesugi, and Yukihiro Yasuda. 2013. "Are Lending Relationships Beneficial or Harmful for Public Credit Guarantees? Evidence from Japan's Emergency Credit Guarantee Program." *Journal of Financial Stability* 9 (2): 151–67.

Pombo, Pablo, and Alfredo Herrero. 2003. *Los Sistemas de Garantías para la Micro y la PyME en una Economía Globalizada.* Seville: DP Editorial.

Pombo, Pablo, Horacio Molina, and Jesús N. Ramirez. 2013. "Guarantee Systems Classification: The Latin American Experience." Inter-American Development Bank, Washington, DC.

REGAR (Red Iberoamericana de Garantias). 2012. *Situacion de los Sistemas de Garantia en Iberoamerica Año 2012: Tendencias y Perspectivas desde el Conocimiento de la Actividad.* Rio de Janeiro: REGAR.

———. 2016. *Situacion de los Sistemas de Garantia en Iberoamerica Año 2015: Tendencias y Perspectivas desde el Conocimiento de la Actividad.* Rio de Janeiro: REGAR.

Riding, Allan, Judith Madill, and George Haines Jr. 2007. "Incrementality of SME Loan Guarantees." *Small Business Economics* 29: 47–61.

Rodriguez-Mesa, J., 2004. "Debtor Enhancement Policies." Presentation at the Inter-American Development Bank Conference on Financial Products and Poverty

Reduction in Latin America and the Caribbean, Washington, DC, September 30 to October 1.

Saadani, Youssef, Zsofia Arvai, and Roberto Rocha. 2011. "A Review of Credit Guarantee Schemes in the Middle East and North Africa Region." Policy Research Working Paper 5612, World Bank, Washington, DC.

Saito, Kuniyoshi, and Daisuke Tsuruta. 2014. "Information Asymmetry in SME Credit Guarantee Schemes: Evidence from Japan." Discussion Paper 14-E-042, Research Institute of Economy, Trade and Industry (RIETI), Tokyo.

Samujh, Helen, Linda Twiname, and Jody Reutemann. 2012. "Credit Guarantee Schemes Supporting Small Enterprise Development: A Review." *Asian Journal of Business and Accounting* 5 (2): 21–40

Uesugi, Iichiro, Koji Sakai, and Guy M. Yamashiro. 2010. "The Effectiveness of the Public Credit Guarantees in the Japanese Loan Market." *Journal of the Japanese and International Economies* 24 (4): 457–80.

Vienna Initiative. 2014. *Credit Guarantee Schemes for SME Lending in Central, Eastern, and South-Eastern Europe: A Report by the Vienna Initiative Working Group on Credit Guarantee Schemes.* Luxembourg: European Investment Bank.

Vogel, Robert C., and Dale W. Adams. 1997. "Costs and Benefits of Loan Guarantee Programs." *The Financier—Analyses of Capital and Money Market Transactions* 4: 22–29.

Wilcox, James, and Yukihiro Yasuda. 2008. "Do Government Loan Guarantees Lower or Raise, Banks' Non-Guaranteed Lending? Evidence from Japanese Banks." World Bank Workshop on Partial Credit Guarantees, March 13–14, Washington, DC.

World Bank. 2013. *Global Financial Development Report 2013: Rethinking the Role of the State in Finance.* Washington, DC: World Bank.

Zecchini, Salvatore, and Marco Ventura. 2009. "The Impact of Public Guarantees on Credit to SMEs." *Small Business Economics* 32: 191–206.

Zia, Bilal H. 2008. "Export Incentives, Financial Constraints, and the (Mis)Allocation of Credit: Micro-Level Evidence from Subsidized Export Loans." *Journal of Financial Economics* 87 (2): 498–527.

CHAPTER 8

Microfinance: BancoEstado's Experience in Chile

Introduction

This chapter describes the experience of BancoEstado, a Chilean state-owned bank that launched a microfinance program in 1996.

Microfinance consists of the provision of financial services to low-income households and microenterprises. Access to credit by these groups is usually hindered by many difficulties, including a lack of viable collateral, no credit histories, and no reliable records. Also, low-income borrowers usually seek to borrow small amounts, making the transaction costs per unit lent very high. Microfinance institutions have developed a series of techniques that help ameliorate informational asymmetries and reduce transaction costs, such as group lending, frequent repayment schedules, and dynamic incentives. As microfinance has evolved, there has been an increasing flexibility in the use of these techniques, with business models and lending technologies now differing widely across microfinance providers. Moreover, microfinance institutions have increasingly expanded the range of financial services they offer, which now include credit, insurance, savings, payments, and money transfers.

Modern microfinance grew out of microenterprise lending experiences led mostly by nongovernmental organizations (NGOs) in a few developing countries, such as Bangladesh and Brazil, during the 1970s. These programs focused on providing credit to low-income entrepreneurs on the basis of group lending, in which borrowers group themselves to apply for loans and share responsibility for repayment. Some of these microcredit programs were quite successful, exhibiting low default rates and suggesting that credit could be provided to low-income

221

borrowers on a financially sustainable basis. This success revived interest in credit provision as a poverty reduction strategy, a strategy that to a large extent had been abandoned following the disappointing experiences with lending by state-owned financial institutions during the 1960s and 1970s. This led to a significant increase in donor funding for microfinance, especially from international development agencies, and a rapid expansion of microfinance institutions. At the end of 2013, there were over 3,000 microcredit institutions worldwide, serving 211 million clients. Microcredit generated considerable hope for poverty alleviation, culminating in the declaration of 2005 as "The International Year of Microcredit" by the United Nations and the awarding of the 2006 Nobel Peace Prize to the Grameen Bank—an early microfinance pioneer from Bangladesh—and its founder, Mohammed Yunus.

Microfinance presents itself as a market-based instrument for fostering access to financial services for low-income households, without the large subsidies and fiscal costs that have typically characterized state interventions in this area. Although microfinance was initially developed by nonprofit organizations, microfinance operations around the world have increasingly become financially sustainable and commercially viable. Over the last two decades, many microfinance NGOs transformed into formal financial intermediaries and commercial banks started offering microfinance services.

The increasing commercialization of microfinance has sparked a broad debate in the industry regarding the role of fully commercial, profit-seeking institutions. Moreover, concerns about predatory lending, borrower overindebtedness, and debt crises in some microfinance markets have somehow tarnished microfinance's public image.

This chapter describes the experience of BancoEstado, the only state-owned commercial bank in Chile, which established a subsidiary, called BancoEstado Microempresas, to provide loans to low-income entrepreneurs in 1996. This experience is closer to traditional state interventions in credit markets than the other experiences described throughout this book because BancoEstado directly lends to low-income households and microenterprises.

Many microfinance proponents argue that governments should not intervene directly in the provision of microcredit in most cases, given the negative past experiences with government lending to low-income households in developing countries.[1] Moreover, the presence of state-owned banks targeting low-income households can distort competition, discouraging the development of an active microfinance sector. On the other hand, state-owned banks might have some advantages in providing microfinance services in some cases. Many of these institutions have wide branch networks, institutional knowledge, and operational infrastructures than can be leveraged for the provision of microfinance. In fact, some state-owned financial institutions have developed successful microfinance programs. Two notable examples in this regard are Bank Rakyat Indonesia—considered a worldwide leader in micro-finance best practices—and Banco do Nordeste in Brazil.[2]

We think that BancoEstado's experience might yield useful insights regarding the functioning of microfinance operations in public banks and the potential for state-owned financial intermediaries to act in a market-friendly manner, avoiding the pitfalls that have affected past experiences with government lending. BancoEstado Microempresas is currently the leading microfinance provider in Chile and one of the largest in Latin America, with 522,000 customers and outstanding loan balances totaling almost US$1.2 billion at the end of 2015. Moreover, BancoEstado Microempresas has managed to maintain relatively high loan repayment rates and low operating costs by developing an institutional frame-work conducive to microfinance activities.

The remainder of this chapter is organized as follows. The next section pro-vides a general overview of microfinance, describing its evolution and discussing how it can help overcome barriers to access to finance. We then describe the expe-rience of BancoEstado in Chile. The final section concludes with a discussion of this experience and its implications for the debate on the role of the state in foster-ing access to finance, as well as the insights it provides regarding the functioning and design of microfinance programs in state-owned banks.

An Overview of Microfinance

Origins and Evolution of Microfinance

Microfinance consists of the provision of financial services to low-income house-holds and very small businesses. While microfinance originally focused on provid-ing working-capital loans to microentrepreneurs through the use of collateral substitutes, it has now expanded to encompass all sorts of financial services, including credit, insurance, savings, payments, and money transfers.

The concept of microfinance is not necessarily new. To a large extent, modern microfinance has emerged out of a number of different preexisting financial prac-tices. Small, informal savings and lending groups have existed in different forms in most countries for centuries.[3] Larger and more formal credit and savings institu-tions that provide financial services to the urban and rural poor started to emerge in Europe in the 19th century. The first cooperative credit associations were estab-lished in Germany in the 1840s, and the cooperative movement quickly spread throughout Europe. By the early 1900s, credit cooperatives were active in Canada, Japan, the United States, and parts of Latin America (Adams 1995). Many of today's financial cooperatives in developing countries have their roots in the European cooperative movement.

Modern microfinance grew out of microenterprise lending experiences, led mostly by NGOs in Bangladesh, Brazil, and a few other developing countries during the 1970s. These programs provided credit to low-income entrepreneurs on the basis of group lending, in which borrowers group themselves to apply for loans and share responsibility for repayment. Microcredit programs were exclusively focused on providing credit for income-generating activities; savings mobilization was largely seen only as a means to promote payment discipline. Early pioneers include the Grameen Bank in Bangladesh (arguably the best-known experience), the Self Employed Women's Association in India, and Accion International, which started its operations in Latin America and then spread to Africa and the United States.

By the late 1980s, microcredit programs had succeeded in showing that low-income entrepreneurs could be viable borrowers because many of these programs exhibited default rates similar to or even lower than those of commercial banks.[4] Moreover, the experience of the most successful programs suggested that low-income borrowers are willing to pay the high interest rates required to cover the costs of providing small loans. The relative success of these programs in providing financing to poor borrowers in a cost-effective manner stands in stark contrast to the disappointing experience with most state interventions to foster access to finance for low-income households in the 1960s and 1970s. As described in chapter 3, these interventions typically focused on providing credit at lower-than-market interest rates through state-owned financial institutions and resulted in high fiscal drains, as a consequence of low repayment rates and high operating costs. Furthermore, most directed credit programs failed to reach their intended clientele, typically by a wide margin.

The perceived success of microcredit programs in improving access to credit for low-income households and microentrepreneurs revived interest in credit provision as a poverty reduction strategy, a strategy that to a large extent had been abandoned following the aforementioned negative experiences with government lending. The 1990s saw a growing enthusiasm among governments and the international development community in fostering the development of microfinance, which resulted in the flow of large amounts of donor funding to microfinance activities in developing countries. Cross-border commitments for microfinance by public sector funders (including bilateral and multilateral development agencies and development finance institutions) reached about US$14.6 billion at the end of 2009, increasing to US$24.4 billion by the end of 2015 (Soursourian and Dashi 2016).[5] Development finance institutions—the private investment arms of bilateral and multilateral agencies (for example, the World Bank's International Finance Corporation, IFC; Germany's Reconstruction Credit Institute, KfW; and the Netherlands Development Finance Company, FMO)—started financing microfinance activities in the late 1990s, as part of their official missions to foster private sector development in developing countries. They have now become one of the main funding sources for the industry, accounting for more than 40 percent of total cross-border funds committed by international public and private sector donors and investors for microfinance in 2015 (Moretto and Scola 2017).[6]

In line with the increased government and international donor interest in the sector, microfinance institutions have experienced significant growth since the mid-1990s. According to the Microcredit Summit Campaign, the number of borrowers served by microcredit institutions increased from 13 million in 1997 to 113 million in 2005, reaching 211 million in 2013, including 114 million borrowers living in extreme poverty (figure 8.1).[7]

Starting in the early 1990s, many microcredit institutions expanded the range of financial products they offered as they increasingly realized that low-income households might benefit from access to financial services in general, not only credit. This resulted in the move away from "microcredit," which focused almost exclusively on lending, toward "microfinance," which encompasses a wide range of financial services, including credit, savings, payment and transfer services, and insurance.

FIGURE 8.1 Evolution of global microfinance

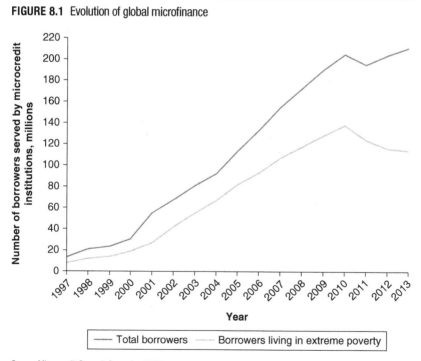

Source: Microcredit Summit Campaign 2015.
Note: Microcredit is defined as programs that provide credit for self-employment and other financial and business services (including savings and technical assistance) to very poor persons. Borrowers living in extreme poverty are defined as those living on less than US$1.90 per day at purchasing power parity.

As mentioned above, microfinance was initially developed by NGOs, with most of the funding being provided by international development agencies and, to a lesser extent, private foundations and individuals. In many cases, local governments also played a significant role. Donor support for microfinance institutions has usually taken the form of technical assistance, start-up grants, "soft" loans, and nonremunerated capital endowments.[8] Donor funding is typically used to cover the high initial fixed costs of microfinance operations or is invested in financial instruments to provide a stream of income to finance ongoing operations.[9] The expectation is that microfinance institutions will use this financial support in their early stages and, as they increase their outreach and capture economies of scale, will eventually be able to operate without subsidization.[10]

Since the mid-1990s, there has been an increasing trend toward microfinance institutions becoming commercially viable and self-sustainable, with many NGOs transforming into for-profit companies. The Bolivian NGO PRODEM was the first microfinance institution to transform into a commercial bank through the creation of BancoSol in 1992, to mobilize deposits and attract private investment.[11] Following this trend toward an increasing commercialization of microfinance, commercial banks have entered the microfinance market, either by providing financial services directly to low-income customers or by acting through existing microfinance institutions (for earlier discussions of this trend, see, for example, Littlefield and Rosenborg 2004; Isern and Porteous 2005; and *The Economist* 2005). According to data from Khamar (2016), commercial banks and other formal nonbank financial intermediaries operating in the microfinance sector had more than 78.4 million active borrowers in 2014, with their gross loan portfolios totaling US$70.6 billion.

As the microfinance sector has increasingly become commercially viable, it has also attracted growing interest from private sector investors. Investment funds focused on microfinance (usually referred to as microfinance investment vehicles) have experienced significant growth since the mid-2000s, with the number of funds increasing from 43 in 2004 to 113 in 2015 and their assets under management growing from about US$600 million to almost US$11 billion over the same period (Reille, Glisovic-Mezieres, and Berthouzoz 2009; CGAP and Symbiotics 2016).[12] Many of these investment vehicles were initially financed by development finance institutions, but they have increasingly attracted private capital, with institutional investors—such as commercial banks, pension funds, insurance companies, and foundations—becoming a major source of funding. Demand for microfinance investments from individual investors, including retail investors and high-net-worth individuals, has also increased significantly over the last decade.[13] In line with growing investor interest in the sector, microfinance institutions have been able to tap capital markets through bond issues, securitizations of microloan portfolios, and even equity issues.[14] Although this increased access to private capital by microfinance institutions constitutes a significant development, so far most of the private investment in the sector has come from socially motivated investors, not from purely commercial investors seeking to maximize risk-adjusted returns (Reille, Forster, and Rozas 2011; El-Zoghbi and Gonzalez 2013).[15]

The increasing commercialization of microfinance has sparked a broad debate in the industry regarding the role of fully commercial, profit-seeking institutions.[16] Opponents of commercialization argue that focusing on shareholder value maximization will lead institutions to deviate from the industry's original focus on poverty alleviation, which might ultimately hurt the poor (Bateman 2010; Yunus 2007, 2011). They stress concerns that profit-seeking microfinance institutions may be profiteering at the expense of poor borrowers by charging very high interest rates and exploiting their market power, and that commercialization may contribute to an unsustainable microcredit expansion, leading to borrower over-indebtedness and contributing to crises in some microfinance markets (Dichter and Harper 2007; MacFarquhar 2010; Polgreen and Bajaj 2010; Sinclair 2012).[17] In contrast, proponents of commercialization argue that the funding capacity of governments and international donors is limited, and that commercial funding is a much-needed source of capital to allow microfinance to reach the millions of households that are still excluded from the financial system (Von Stauffenberg 2007; Akula 2010; Rangan, Chu, and Petkoski 2011). They ague that profitability will help attract more capital and enable institutions to better meet the demand from low-income households for financial services.

Despite the trend toward increased commercialization and private investment, the reality is that a large fraction of microfinance institutions are still dependent on grants and subsidies from international donors and governments to finance their operations. Although many microfinance institutions have been able to achieve high loan repayment rates, this has not necessarily translated into economic profits, mainly because of the small scale of loans and the high operating costs of serving low-income borrowers. Cull, Demirgüç-Kunt, and Morduch (2016) analyze detailed accounting data for 1,335 microfinance institutions between 2005 and 2009 and find that two-thirds of these institutions had accounting profits (that is, were able to cover their costs with their revenues, without taking into account any implicit grants and subsidies). However, once they account fully for the opportunity costs of inputs, they find that that only a third of microfinance institutions had economic profits. Moreover, contrary to arguments that microfinance subsidies are temporary, Cull, Demirgüç-Kunt, and Morduch (2016) find that subsidies continue to be important for older institutions, with 76 percent of the subsidies going to microfinance institutions older than 10 years. Microfinance institutions that have become financially self-sustainable tend to be larger, which allows them to capture economies of scale, better diversify risk, and reduce operating costs per dollar lent. Many of these institutions also target households around or above the poverty line instead of the very poor who were the original focus of microfinance, allowing them to increase average loan sizes and reducing the incidence of operating expenses.[18] Microfinance institutions that strive for financial sustainability might have incentives to abandon their traditional very poor clientele and move up market, focusing on easier-to-reach richer clients who take out larger loans and make bigger deposits.[19]

In recent years, there has been a growing debate regarding the impact of microfinance on borrowers, and significant efforts have been devoted to rigorously assessing microfinance's effects. Microcredit proponents have traditionally argued that the provision of microloans to low-income borrowers contributes to poverty reduction (see, for instance, Daley-Harris 2003; Littlefield, Morduch, and Hashemi 2003; Yunus 2003; and Dunford 2006). On the other hand, some authors have questioned whether microcredit constitutes an adequate poverty reduction strategy, arguing that access to credit might not be the binding constraint for the poor (Adams and Von Pischke 1994; Dichter 2006; Karnani 2007; Roodman 2012).

Earlier empirical research suggested that microcredit leads to poverty reductions (Pitt and Khandker 1998). However, accurately identifying the impact of microcredit is quite challenging because borrowers are not selected at random from the population; borrowers are likely to be more proactive and to have better business opportunities than nonborrowers, and therefore they would have probably performed better even in the absence of any microloans. Several recent studies have tried to overcome this problem and identify the causal effect of microcredit by using randomized experiments. These studies tend to find little or no effect of microcredit on income and poverty, but find that microloans might help households deal better with shocks (see Banerjee 2013 and Banerjee, Karlan, and Zinman 2015 for reviews of these studies). For microcredit critics, these findings show that microfinance does not have a transformative effect in terms of lifting households out of poverty and that resources should be channeled to other instruments for fighting poverty. Microcredit proponents in turn have stressed the limitations of existing empirical research and argue against putting excessive weight on a small number of studies.[20]

An emerging view argues that the main benefit of microfinance for low-income households might not be fostering the growth of microbusiness, as traditionally argued by microcredit proponents, but rather helping households to cope with shocks and to better manage risks. Low-income households tend to have irregular income flows and face relatively large (unexpected) expenses (for health emergencies, weddings, funerals, and so forth) (Collins et al. 2009). Access to financial services can help households better manage their cash flows and deal with shocks. Thus, microfinance may contribute to poverty alleviation but not necessarily to poverty reduction. This argument is consistent with the evidence from the randomized experiments of the effects of microcredit described above. This view also supports the idea that microfinance institutions should expand the range of financial products they offer beyond credit. Consistent with this idea, randomized evaluations of microsavings tend to find relatively large positive impacts on welfare from improvements in access to and usage of formal savings (Dupas and Robinson 2013; Karlan, Ratan, and Zinman 2014).

How Microfinance Deals with Barriers to Access to Credit

Access to credit by low-income borrowers, especially in developing countries, is usually hindered by many difficulties, including a lack of viable collateral, no credit histories, and no reliable records. Also, providing loans to these groups tends to be very costly, given small loan amounts, relatively fixed overhead expenses and trans-action costs, and high screening, monitoring, and recovery costs. Microfinance institutions have developed a series of techniques to address these issues, which have attracted significant theoretical interest. Before turning to the description of these techniques, it is necessary to mention that, as microfinance has evolved, there has been an increasing diversity in the use of techniques, with business models and lending technologies now differing widely across countries and even across microfinance institutions within a given country. This is partly the result of the experimental nature of microfinance and also reflects the need to adapt to local conditions. Moreover, as the practices of microfinance institutions have evolved, their lending techniques have become increasingly similar to those of mainstream financial institutions (Honohan 2004).

The practice that has received more attention from theoreticians trying to understand how microfinance deals with information asymmetries and enforce-ment problems is group lending, according to which borrowers group themselves to apply for loans and share the responsibility for repayment.[21] Although loans are made to individual members of the group, the group as a whole is held liable for repaying the loan; and, if one member fails to pay, the entire group can be excluded from the program. This technique helps to ameliorate adverse selection problems because potential borrowers might have better information about their neighbors' creditworthiness than financial institutions (Ghatak 1999, 2000; Armendáriz de Aghion and Gollier 2000). As discussed in chapter 2, adverse selection arises because lenders cannot distinguish good credit prospects from bad ones, and as a result cannot charge different interest rates. In this situation, charging all borrow-ers a higher interest rate to compensate for potential credit losses can have a nega-tive effect on the credit quality of the pool of borrowers because a higher rate deters good borrowers from applying for loans. Therefore, lenders might choose to ration credit instead of increasing interest rates.

The use of group lending reduces the adverse selection problem by allowing financial intermediaries to effectively charge different interest rates to borrowers with different risk profiles. This happens because borrowers have information on the creditworthiness of other borrowers and therefore will choose to form groups with safe prospects, leading to an assortative matching: safe borrowers will form groups with safe borrowers, and risky borrowers will have no choice but to form groups with other risky prospects. Because projects undertaken by risky borrowers fail more often than those of safe borrowers, this assortative matching implies that risky borrowers have to repay for their defaulting group members more often than safe borrowers do; otherwise, they would be excluded from the program and would not get credit in the future. This means that, although all borrowers face exactly the same loan contract, with the same interest rate, safe borrowers in effect have lower borrowing costs than risky ones because they do not have to share the burden of default by risky prospects. This lower effective interest rate induces safe borrowers to enter the credit market and reduces adverse selection.

Group lending can also help to mitigate moral hazard. As described in chapter 2, a problem of ex ante moral hazard might arise if lenders cannot effectively monitor borrowers' actions after loan disbursement. Borrowers might have incentives to undertake riskier projects or exert less-than-optimal effort from the lender's perspective because they do not face the full costs of their actions in case of failure. Group lending can reduce this problem: group members have incentives to monitor each other and can impose social sanctions on members who undertake riskier projects or do not exert an adequate amount of effort (Stiglitz 1990). Group lending can also ameliorate ex post moral hazard (Besley and Coate 1995; Armendáriz de Aghion 1999), which arises when lenders cannot observe project returns. The joint responsibility within the group reduces the possibility of strategic default because group members can observe projects' returns and can impose social sanctions on those members who do not repay their loans when they would be able to do so.

Although group lending is the technique that has received most attention in the literature, microfinance institutions have also relied on a variety of additional lending techniques, typically used in combination, to mitigate the problems associated with providing credit to low-income borrowers. These techniques are playing an increasingly important role in microfinance as many institutions are moving away from group lending toward an individual-based approach (Beck et al. 2011; Giné and Karlan 2014; de Quidt, Fetzer, and Ghatak 2016).

One of these techniques is progressive lending, which involves increasing loan disbursements gradually over time, so that failure to repay an earlier loan causes borrowers to lose access to larger loans in the future. Progressive lending allows lenders to test borrowers with small loans, screening out those that are less likely to repay before taking on more credit risk (Ghosh and Ray 1999). It also increases the cost of default because failure to repay implies a cutoff from a growing stream of future loans (Armendáriz de Aghion and Morduch 2000; Egli 2004). However, progressive lending has some important limitations. First, with the existence of multiple lenders, the threat to curtail access to future loans might have little effect because borrowers can turn to another lender.[22] This highlights the need to develop adequate creditor information systems and to foster information sharing among microfinance institutions. Second, as loan size increases, the incentives for strategic default also grow, especially if the borrower has limited borrowing needs or envisions a final date in the relationship with the lender.

Another mechanism used by microfinance institutions is a schedule of frequent repayments, meaning that the repayment of the loan is made in several small installments, beginning almost immediately after disbursement. This allows lenders to notice with only a small delay if there are problems with repayment, acting as an early warning system and giving credit officers time to address the problem with borrowers to avoid complete default on the loan. Frequent repayment schedules also reduce the possibility of diverting funds to other uses. Moreover, this mechanism might be particularly useful for households that lack access to savings products and that have difficulty holding on to income, acting partly as a mandatory savings scheme.

We now turn to the description of BancoEstado's experience with microfinance in Chile. We then discuss the main insights regarding the design and functioning of microfinance operations in state-owned banks that emerge from this experience, as well as some of the arguments that might justify state intervention.

The Experience of BancoEstado Microempresas

BancoEstado is a Chilean state-owned bank created in 1953 to foster economic development through credit provision and to enhance access to financial services for the general population. BancoEstado also manages the Chilean government's treasury accounts. It cannot lend to the government or state-owned enterprises, although it can engage in leasing operations involving the public sector. BancoEstado is the only state-owned commercial bank in Chile and is currently the second-largest bank in the country, holding about 16 percent of total banking system assets as of the end of 2015. BancoEstado has one of the largest branch networks in Chile, with 380 branches as of the end of 2015. In 30 percent of the country's municipalities, namely the poorest and most remote ones, BancoEstado is the only financial institution with banking service outlets.

Traditionally, BancoEstado used the implicit subsidy of being the exclusive holder of treasury deposits, without having to pay any interest on the use of those balances, to finance its social goals. However, this strategy became increasingly difficult to sustain during the 1990s, as improved macroeconomic conditions resulted in a significant reduction in inflation rates. Also, the government reduced the idle balances held in its accounts, further eroding BancoEstado's traditional income source.[23] This led BancoEstado to start a modernization process to improve its operational efficiency and expand the range of financial services provided.

In 1996, BancoEstado created a stand-alone subsidiary called BancoEstado Microempresas (BEME, BancoEstado Micro Enterprises) to provide credit services to microfirms. BEME targets low-income entrepreneurs in both urban and rural areas. BancoEstado started its microfinance operations in 1995 with a pilot program involving only three bank branches in the city of Santiago in order to test and adjust its operational model. BEME initially focused on lending to microfirms to finance equipment purchases and working capital, but over time it has significantly widened its product range. The company first started expanding its credit products, which currently include not only business lending but also mortgages and student and consumer loans. Around 2002, it moved away from its focus on lending and started offering a wider range of financial products, including savings, payments, investment services, and insurance.

BEME is a stand-alone subsidiary owned by BancoEstado, with separate legal identity and accounting. The decision to create an independent subsidiary, instead of a microfinance unit within BancoEstado, was motivated by the larger flexibility that this organizational form usually offers.[24] Microfinance requires significant flexibility to create new products or adapt existing ones to better fit the needs of low-income customers. Also, the processes associated with the provision of microfinance tend to differ from those used in traditional bank operations. Even if banks explicitly recognize that microfinance is a very different product, bureaucratic barriers might restrict the autonomy of internal units. These units usually tend to have less freedom than stand-alone subsidiaries to introduce or modify products and processes and to follow different pricing strategies.[25]

BEME is not a financial intermediary but rather a service company. It provides microloan origination and collection services, but its parent bank actually funds and owns the loans. All the financial products offered by BEME (loans, savings, and so forth) are registered on BancoEstado's balance sheet. As a service company, BEME is paid a fee by its parent bank for providing promotion, origination, and collection services.[26] Similar organizational structures have been adopted by several commercial banks when entering the microfinance market, including SOGEBANK in Haiti, Banco del Pichincha in Ecuador, and Banco Real ABN-AMRO in Brazil (Isern and Porteous 2005).

An advantage of the service company structure, relative to the alternative of creating a separate financial firm to provide microfinance, is that the licensing and regulatory requirements for service companies are significantly lower than those for financial intermediaries. Service companies typically receive little or no separate regulation and supervision from banking authorities; the common practice is to consolidate them with their parent bank and impose all requirements on the consolidated entity. Another potential advantage of service companies is that they can focus exclusively on developing microfinance capabilities—like microloan origination, servicing, and collection—without diverting efforts to other tasks, such as liquidity management and obtaining funding.

Despite these advantages, the service company structure also has some drawbacks relative to the creation of a new financial intermediary to provide microfinance services. First, financial intermediaries can mobilize savings, developing a funding source independent of their parent banks. This might give them increased flexibility to pursue their expansion plans. In contrast, service companies cannot mobilize savings and therefore depend almost exclusively on their parent banks to fund their operations. In the case of BEME, this was not considered a significant issue, given that BancoEstado has a large deposit base that can be used to fund its microlending activities. Second, although service companies are legally separate entities from their parent banks, they derive all of their income from fees paid to them by their parents. As described above, because service companies are not financial firms, they do not own the loans they originate (these loans are registered on their parents' balance sheet) and their only income source are the fees that they charge to their parent banks for providing promotion, origination, and collection services. In contrast, financial intermediaries obtain interest income directly from their loan portfolios. Thus, service companies have less independence than financial intermediaries and may not be able to remain in existence if the parent decides to exit microfinance. Finally, there might be some concerns regarding agency problems between the service company and its parent. Because the service company does not own the loans it originates, it does not bear the credit risk and therefore might have fewer incentives to carefully screen and monitor borrowers and pursue collections. To address this problem, in the case of BancoEstado's microfinance operations, BEME is responsible for paying all the provisioning and write-off charges associated with the microloans that it originates. This implies that it bears all the credit risk and therefore should have adequate incentives to screen and monitor borrowers.

BEME has adopted a completely different commercial strategy than its parent, by tailoring its products to the needs of microentrepreneurs. A salient component of this strategy has been designing credit products that address the specific requirements of different sectors (for example, retail, fishing, and agriculture).[27] BEME executives have met with representatives of different industries to identify their needs and develop tailor-made products. For instance, when lending to entrepreneurs that operate school buses, repayment schedules do not include any installments during the school vacation period so that repayments match their cash flows. In another case, BEME started offering credit to fishermen to buy engines for their boats and negotiated price discounts with engine manufacturers. Another important aspect of BEME's commercial strategy has been designing products to meet the personal financial needs of microentrepreneurs and not only their business needs, recognizing that the financial condition of microfirms is closely related to their owners' personal financial situation.

As described above, BEME started its operations by providing loans to microentrepreneurs to finance equipment purchases and working capital. This type of loans still constitutes the bulk of its lending. These loans can be obtained by microfirms and self-employed workers with annual sales below UF 2,400 (approximately US$95,000 as of December 2016) that have been active for at least one year. Borrowers are not required to be customers of BancoEstado or to be formal firms. Loans maturities range from 90 days to 50 months, and interest rates vary with loan size, maturity, and borrower quality, from 17 to 34 percent per year.

Over time, BEME has significantly widened its product range. In 2000, it began offering special credit lines to finance the training of microentrepreneurs and their employees. In 2001, BEME launched a program to provide loans to facilitate access to technology, primarily computers and Internet service. BEME also introduced "quick" short-term loans for existing borrowers to take advantage of unforeseen business opportunities and developed several types of loans for rural producers. In terms of credit products to meet personal financial needs, BEME currently offers mortgages and consumer loans. The company complements its lending products with other financial services, including credit cards, savings and checking accounts, and payment services. It also offers life and health insurance and mutual funds.

BEME provides its services through BancoEstado's branches. This allows it to reach microentrepreneurs in remote and lower-income areas, giving it a significant advantage relative to other microfinance providers in Chile. Using BancoEstado branches also allows BEME to reduce its operating costs by sharing technological platforms, telecommunication networks, security systems, and other branch services and infrastructure. Furthermore, providing microcredit services in bank branches reduces transaction costs for borrowers who need to cash their loan disbursements or deposit their loan repayments. It also facilitates access to other financial products, such as checking or savings accounts, and increases cross-selling opportunities.

BEME has developed credit processes and tools specifically tailored for microfinance transactions. BEME's credit assessment process relies on visits by loan officers to the applicant's home or workplace to collect relevant information on income, expenses, and other financial obligations on a first-hand basis, given that most microentrepreneurs lack reliable written records. BEME's credit assessment takes into account all household income sources and expenses, not just those associated with the applicant's business activities. An important component of the credit assessment process is determining applicants' willingness to pay. To do this, loan officers typically consider applicants' reputation in the community, their willingness to provide the required information, and whether there are any inconsistencies in their verbal statements and/or application. The credit assessment process relies to a large extent on the ability of loan officers to collect adequate data on household and business cash flows and to evaluate the applicant's trustworthiness.

The credit assessment process described above can be very time-consuming and costly. This has typically constituted a significant barrier to providing credit to microentrepreneurs, especially given their small loan sizes, because it results in high transaction costs per dollar lent. BEME has developed several tools and mechanisms to reduce these transaction costs. First, it prescreens applicants in order to reduce the number of on-site visits that do not lead to lending. This screening is carried out by loan assistants on the basis of the borrower's application and includes a preliminary assessment of repayment capabilities. Second, BEME has developed a credit-scoring model that uses data on the demographic characteristics of the microentrepreneur, the features of the microenterprise, and payment history (when available) to assess borrowers' creditworthiness.[28] The use of this scoring system increases the efficiency of the credit process and allows loan officers to avoid on-site visits in some cases. Third, BEME makes intensive use of new technologies to increase the productivity of loan officers. A geo-referencing system that locates different customers and optimizes traveling routes was introduced to help loan officers organize their field visits. Officers use mobile technology to connect to BEME's network, check credit bureau information, and assess borrowers' creditworthiness in real time while visiting customers, resulting in significant cost and time savings. Finally, to serve remote areas, BEME introduced a system of *"plazas de trabajo,"* in which potential customers gather together in the same place on the same day. Grouping potential clients reduces the need for individual visits, decreasing transaction costs.

BEME has also developed mechanisms to ensure adequate repayment and collections. As in most microfinance programs, loan officers are responsible for the performance of the loans they originate. To increase their efficiency, BEME uses an online system that provides officers with up-to-date information on their loan portfolio, such as details on nonperforming borrowers, lists of borrowers whose repayments are coming due, and comparisons between their individual performance and that of the branch and the company as a whole. To make it easier for loan officers to manage their loan portfolio, there are only four predetermined dates for repayments each month, so officers do not need to monitor payments every day. Loan officers are responsible for pursuing collections for the first 15 days after loans become due; afterward, collections are transferred to a specialized firm. In order to deal with customers facing financial difficulties, BEME has developed a credit-restructuring process tailored to the microfinance sector. Moreover, BEME provides dynamic incentives to encourage repayment: borrowers that maintain a good credit record are automatically preapproved for further credit lines.

From the description given above of BEME's operations, it is clear that credit officers play a key role, actively participating in every step of the credit cycle. This has led BEME to focus significant efforts on its human resources management practices, including the selection and training of credit officers and their pay structures. Credit officers must undergo a three-month training program to become familiar with BEME's policies and procedures. This training includes an industry-specific component (for example, agriculture or retail) so that credit officers understand the needs of microentrepreneurs in a particular sector. BEME has also developed an employee incentive scheme that encourages loan recovery and profitability. The performance of loan officers is evaluated on the basis of a series of objective parameters, including not only the volume of loans granted but also the overall performance of their credit portfolio. This helps shift the incentives of loan officers away from simply disbursing credit toward focusing on the overall performance of the loans they grant. The pay structure of loan officers includes a quarterly bonus, which depends on meeting individual performance goals.

BEME has been very successful in expanding its outreach. The number of customers has increased, from about 56,000 in 2002 to 522,000 in 2015 (figure 8.2, panel a). About 70 percent of these customers had an outstanding loan or conducted transactions in the last three months of the year. BEME's lending volume has followed a similar trend, with total outstanding loans increasing from about US$62 million at the end of 2002 to about US$1.2 billion in 2015 (figure 8.2, panel b). BEME granted 111,000 new loans during 2015, for a total value of about US$675 million. BEME is the largest microfinance institution in Chile, with a market share of over 50 percent in terms of customers. It is also one of the microfinance institutions with the highest penetration rates (defined as the ratio of the number of microenterprise loans granted to the total employed population) in Latin America and the Caribbean (table 8.1).

Despite the significant growth in lending volume, BEME has historically shown a strong portfolio performance, although credit quality has deteriorated somewhat in recent years. As figure 8.3 shows, the share of nonperforming loans reached 3.1 percent as of June 2015, compared to about 2 percent for the Chilean banking system as a whole. Loans overdue more than 30 days, a measure of portfolio at risk typically applied to microloans, represented around 4.9 percent of BEME's outstanding loans as of June 2015.

BEME was designed to be a self-sustainable operation, without providing subsidized credit. BEME's high loan repayment rates and focus on cost control allowed it to become profitable after only three years of operation, exceeding initial projections that contemplated achieving profitability by the fifth year. In 2015, BEME had after-tax profits of about US$300,000, and accumulated profits between 2001 and 2015 totaled almost US$8 million.[29]

There is some empirical evidence suggesting that BancoEstado's microlending is associated with positive outcomes for borrowers, but more in-depth evaluations are necessary to accurately identify any causal effects. Benavente (2006) compares the performance of borrowers that received more than five loans from BEME with that of borrowers that received only two loans. He finds that higher loan use is associated with sales increases, with a large effect for microfirms operated by women. Although these results suggest that BEME's lending is associated with

FIGURE 8.2 Evolution of BancoEstado Microempresas

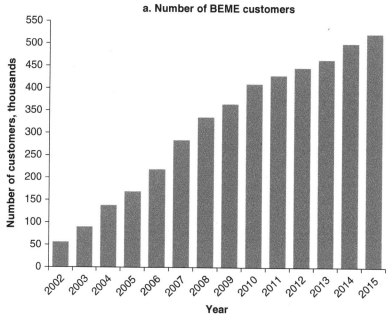

a. Number of BEME customers

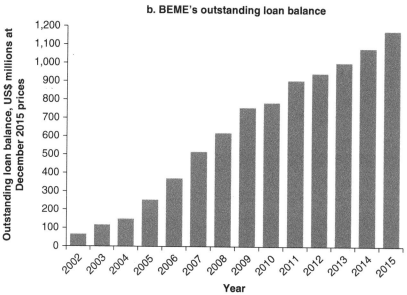

b. BEME's outstanding loan balance

Source: BancoEstado.

Note: This figure shows the evolution of the number of customers (panel a) and the outstanding loan balance (panel b) of BancoEstado Microempresas (BEME) for the period 2002–15. Data correspond to the end of each year.

TABLE 8.1 Microfinance institutions with the highest penetration in Latin America and the Caribbean, 2013

Name	Country	Penetration rate (%)
Compartamos Banco	Mexico	3.6
Pichincha Microfinanzas	Ecuador	2.7
BancoSol	Bolivia	2.6
Banco FIE	Bolivia	2.4
Banco ADOPEM	Dominican Republic	2.4
BancoEstado Microempresas	Chile	2.3
Banco ADEMI	Dominican Republic	2.3
Visión Banco	Paraguay	2.3
CRECER	Bolivia	2.2
Banco Solidario	Ecuador	1.9

Sources: Multilateral Investment Fund and Microfinance Information Exchange 2015.
Note: This table shows the 10 microfinance institutions with the highest penetration rate (defined as the ratio of the number of microenterprise loans granted to the employed population) in Latin America and the Caribbean in 2013.

FIGURE 8.3 Evolution of BancoEstado Microempresas' credit quality

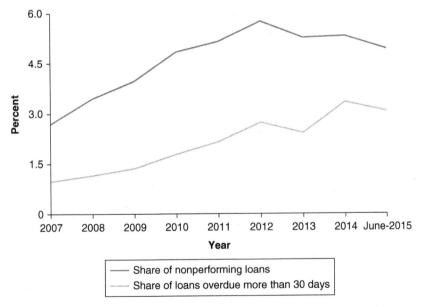

Source: BancoEstado.
Note: This figure shows the evolution of BEME's share of nonperforming loans and its share of loans overdue more than 30 days. Data correspond to the end of each year, except for 2015, for which data for June are reported.

positive outcomes, they should be interpreted with care because more frequent borrowers may differ systemically from less frequent ones, making it difficult to accurately identify the causal effect of BEME's lending.

Policy Discussion and Conclusions

The case of BEME raises a number of interesting issues that deserve further discussion. We first briefly analyze some of BEME's salient design features and then discuss some open questions regarding this experience. We believe that a better understanding of these issues can yield significant insights for the debate on the role of the state in broadening access and can also help in understanding the value added of this type of intervention. We return to some of these issues in chapter 9.

BEME seems to have been able to develop a financially sustainable microfinance operation, avoiding many of the pitfalls that have traditionally affected government lending programs. There are several factors that have played an important role in BEME's success.

First, BEME's approach to microfinance represents a significant cultural shift relative to traditional government lending programs aimed at low-income borrowers. These programs typically offer targeted credit at below-market rates and focus primarily on loan disbursements, rather than on loan recovery. In contrast, BEME was designed from the beginning as a profit-making operation. It does not use subsidized credit, but rather charges interest rates that allow it to cover the costs of lending to small, high-risk borrowers. It focuses on maintaining good portfolio quality and enforcing collections. To a large extent, the differences between BEME and traditional public lending programs arise from a different approach to borrowers. While state-owned banks typically view low-income borrowers as beneficiaries, BEME considers them customers who are willing to pay market prices for financial services and who repay their loans.

As described above, to achieve its objective of providing financial services to low-income borrowers on a sustainable basis, BancoEstado has developed an institutional framework conducive to microfinance activities through several mechanisms. First, there is no political intervention in the credit allocation process. This is a key precondition for developing successful government lending programs. The severe credit losses experienced by many state-owned banks can be attributed, to a large extent, to political interference in the banking business, not only through lending to politically connected sectors and firms but also through widespread debt forgiveness. In the case of BancoEstado, there is a strong commitment by political stakeholders to refrain from interfering in its operations. It is worth stressing that attempts to isolate banking decisions from political influence through the use of different institutional mechanisms cannot fully guarantee independence, and that success in this regard depends ultimately on the will of political stakeholders. This might constitute a significant constraint in replicating BEME's experience, especially in countries that lack an adequate institutional and political environment.

Second, commitment and leadership within BancoEstado have been very important for the development of its microfinance operations. The executive committee— integrated by BancoEstado's president, vice president, and general manager—has strongly supported the bank's microfinance program. Moreover, BEME's management team has shown strong commitment to the project and leadership capabilities to motivate its staff.

Third, BancoEstado has adopted an organizational structure that grants it significant flexibility for conducting microfinance operations. As described above, BEME is a stand-alone subsidiary owned by BancoEstado, with a separate legal identity and accounting. This gives it a high degree of autonomy in formulating operational policies, allowing it to tailor processes and products to the needs of low-income borrowers. In contrast, most government lending programs have typically focused on loan disbursement without adequately taking into account the specific needs of their target clientele. Moreover, BEME has a separate profit-and-loss statement, increasing transparency and facilitating the focus on profitability.

Finally, BEME has developed policies that increase staff accountability and provide incentives that are consistent with sound credit practices and financial sustainability. As described above, loan officers are evaluated on the basis of the overall performance of their credit portfolio, and their pay structure is designed to provide them with adequate incentives to focus on profitability. This represents a significant shift from the usual practices of state-owned banks, which tend to rely on public service–like pay scales that are mostly fixed.

An important open question regarding BEME's experience, as well as other experiences with microfinance programs operated by state-owned banks, is to what extent state intervention through the direct provision of financial services is warranted. On the one hand, state banks might have some intrinsic advantages in providing microfinance, relative to private intermediaries. Some of these banks might have specialized knowledge and human capital, because their staff might possess valuable information about local business conditions and individual borrowers, as well as the necessary skills to deal with low-income households. Some state-owned banks might also have repayment records on a large number of borrowers, which could help construct credit histories. Moreover, many public financial intermediaries have large branch networks that can be leveraged to provide microfinance services and reach low-income households in remote areas. The extent to which state-owned banks might have any advantages in providing microfinance is likely to depend on the overall institutional environment and on the specific institution being analyzed. In the case of BancoEstado, having one of the largest branch networks in Chile, with many branches located in middle- or low-income areas, gives it an advantage in reaching microentrepreneurs relative to other potential microfinance providers. Also, BancoEstado was already a trusted brand among low-income households before the creation of BEME, facilitating its expansion into microfinance.

On the other hand, many microfinance proponents argue that governments should stay away from direct microcredit provision in most cases and should focus instead on creating an adequate enabling environment. To a large extent, this argument is a result of the negative experiences with lending by state-owned banks and directed credit programs in the past. In addition, the presence of public banks targeting low-income households can distort competition in financial markets, discouraging the development of an active microfinance sector. The increasing commercialization of microfinance suggests that the industry can be commercially viable, reducing the need for public intervention. Moreover, most efforts to restructure public banks have been unsuccessful because they have failed to address the fundamental incentive and governance problems that characterize these institutions.[30] Without solving these problems, most restructured government banks sooner or later tend to go back to their previous practices, resulting in ongoing bad performance and the need for recurrent capitalizations. These experiences should temper enthusiasm regarding the potential for providing microfinance through state-owned banks on a sustainable basis.

BEME seems to have been able to avoid most of the problems that have characterized past experiences with government lending. However, even if BEME has been able to develop a sustainable microfinance program, some valid questions concerning its activities still remain. First, it is not clear to what extent BEME has strong relative advantages in providing microfinance, or if its customers could be served by private microfinance providers, and thus BEME might be actually displacing private financial intermediation. Chile's microfinance market is quite developed, with four private commercial banks (Banco de Chile, Banco del Desarrollo, Banco Santander-Banefe, and Banco de Crédito e Inversiones) providing microfinance services (either directly or through specialized divisions).

When BEME started its operations, microfinance had a relatively low penetration and was provided mostly by NGOs. The only commercial financial institution that participated in this market at the time was Banco del Desarrollo. Some argue that BEME played a catalytic role in the development of Chile's microfinance industry by showing that microfinance could be provided on a financially sustainable basis and generating a demonstration effect that prompted private financial intermediaries to enter the market (see, for example, Benavente 2006 and Larraín 2007).[31] However, even if BEME indeed played a catalytic role in Chile's microfinance sector, some may question whether its continued involvement in this market is required. In principle, if BEME is commercially viable and does not require any subsidies, BancoEstado could sell it to a private financial intermediary or to private investors and move on to other activities. Whether BancoEstado should continue its involvement in microfinance or not depends ultimately on its relative efficiency in providing microfinance services, compared to private providers. The fact that BEME's microfinance program is not separate from BancoEstado's operations (for instance, BEME uses BancoEstado's branches to distribute its services) and that it is a service company, and thus does not own the loans it originates and derives all of its income from fees paid by its parent, makes transferring BEME's operations to the private sector quite difficult.

Second, some might question to what extent BEME is addressing a specific market failure and actually solving a problem of access, or if it is just increasing the use of financial services per se. This is a difficult question to answer. Finally, it is not clear what the impact of BEME's lending is and whether it is an effective way of achieving the desired objectives of state intervention. As mentioned above, BEME's microcredit operations seem to be associated with positive outcomes for borrowers, but further research is needed to accurately identify the actual impact of its programs. Moreover, measuring benefits alone is not enough to justify the use of public funds. The relevant question in this regard is whether BEME has been a cost-effective way of achieving the observed results. Answering this question would require a rigorous cost–benefit analysis, as well as a comparison of BEME's microfinance program with alternative policy interventions.[32]

To conclude, BancoEstado's experience with microfinance provides an interesting example of state intervention to foster access to finance, which is closer to traditional public sector interventions in credit markets than the other experiences analyzed in this book. However, as highlighted in the above discussion, this intervention differs from traditional public lending programs in terms of its scope and design. BEME's experience suggests that the provision of microfinance services by state-owned banks might be an effective instrument for increasing access under some circumstances. However, the success of this type of intervention hinges on the development of an adequate institutional framework, including hard budget constraints, insulation from political interference in banking operations, strong leadership, staff accountability, and incentives to promote sound credit practices and financial sustainability. The disappointing experience with government lending programs in many developing countries suggests that creating such a framework can be a significant challenge.

Notes

1. For instance, the "Key Principles of Microfinance," adopted by the Consultative Group to Assist the Poor (CGAP, a consortium of over 30 public and private development agencies housed at the World Bank), which have been endorsed by the Group of Eight (G-8), explicitly state that "the government's role is as an enabler, not as a direct provider of financial services. ... The key things that a government can do for microfinance are to maintain macroeconomic stability, avoid interest-rate caps, and refrain from distorting the market with unsustainable subsidized, high-delinquency loan programs." See also Duflos and Imboden (2004).

2. See Yaron, Benjamin, and Charitonenko (1998); Patten, Rosengard, and Johnston (2001); Robinson (2002); and Seibel (2005) for analyses of the experience of Bank Rakyat Indonesia. Christen and Schonberger (2001); Sanchez, Sirtaine, and Valente (2002); Brusky (2003); and Fiori and Young (2005) describe the experience of Banco do Nordeste with microfinance.

3. One of the most common types of informal arrangements are rotating savings and credit associations (ROSCAs), which are found throughout the world under different names. These are collective associations, usually between friends and neighbors, where participants make contributions to a central pot that is then allocated to members, either following a preestablished order or through a lottery. See Armendáriz de Aghion and Morduch (2010) for an overview of ROSCAs.

4. Cull, Demirgüç-Kunt, and Morduch (2009) argue that "the greatest triumph of microfinance is the demonstration that poor households can be reliable bank customers."

5. Commitments include all funds set aside for active microfinance-related projects, irrespective of whether funds have been already disbursed or not.

6. The IFC had over US$4.5 billion in cumulative committed investments in more than 140 microfinance institutions across 61 countries as of June 2015 (IFC 2016).

7. Note that these figures should be interpreted with care. Adequately defining a microfinance institution is not straightforward because organizational forms and institutional arrangements differ across countries and there is some uncertainty regarding how the boundary of microfinance should be defined. For instance, there is no agreement on whether small-scale lending by commercial banks should be included or not. Microcredit Summit Campaign defines microcredit programs as "programs that provide credit for self-employment and other financial and business services (including savings and technical assistance) to very poor persons." Another potential problem with these data is that they are self-reported by microfinance institutions to the Microcredit Summit Campaign, and therefore part of the observed growth in the number of institutions and clients might be explained by improved data coverage (that is, already-existing institutions voluntarily reporting their activities for the first time), and not necessarily by an actual expansion of microcredit activities.

8. Loans accounted for the majority (52 percent) of cross-border commitments for microfinance in 2015, followed by grants (18 percent) and equity investments (13 percent). Multilateral development agencies typically channel their lending for microfinance through governments, whereas development finance institutions tend to lend to retail microfinance providers (directly, or through microfinance investment funds). Although debt accounts for the majority of funds committed for microfinance, grants remain the most common instrument by number of projects, with 40 percent of projects in 2015 having a grant component (Soursourian and Dashi 2016).

9. To a large extent, the arguments for this type of subsidies are similar to the infant industry arguments for tariff protection from trade. The expectation is that initial financial support will not reduce microfinance institutions' incentives to operate efficiently and innovate. However, as the lessons from trade show, this is not easily achieved because donors might face time-inconsistency problems. Even if donors claim that their support will be limited to providing financing only in early stages,

if a donor has invested significant funds in a microfinance institution and if many households are at risk of losing access to credit if this institution fails, it might be difficult to deny further financing.

10. Although there is wide acceptance of subsidies to cover initial start-up costs, there is much less agreement on whether microfinance institutions should be subsidized on an ongoing basis. To a large extent, this is a consequence of previous experiences with public sector interventions in credit markets and the potential negative incentive effects of permanent subsidies. See Armendáriz de Aghion and Morduch (2010) for further discussion on this issue.

11. See Mosley (1996), Gonzalez-Vega et al. (1997), and Schicks (2007) for analyses of the experience of BancoSol.

12. See Dominicé (2012) for an overview of microfinance investment vehicles.

13. According to CGAP and Symbiotics (2016), the majority (47 percent) of the funding for microfinance investment vehicles as of the end of 2015 was provided by institutional investors, followed by retail investors and high-net-worth individuals (28 percent). Public sector donors accounted for only 25 percent of the funding for these investment vehicles.

14. International donors and development agencies have played a key role in fostering security issues by microfinance institutions, arranging microloan securitizations, buying equity or junior tranches in structured finance transactions, and providing credit enhancements to these operations. Public donors have also facilitated access to bank lending for microfinance institutions by providing credit guarantees for commercial loans from private financial intermediaries. See Rahman and Shah Mohammed (2009), Swanson (2009), and CGAP and Grameen Foundation USA (2010) for analyses of structured finance transactions in microfinance. Lopez and de Angulo (2005) and Flaming (2007) analyze the use of credit guarantees in commercial loans for microfinance institutions.

15. According to data from GIIN (2016), worldwide investment funds focused on "impact investments" (defined as investments made "with the intention to generate measurable social and environmental impact alongside a financial return") held microfinance assets totaling about US$11 billion as of the end of 2015, representing about 14 percent of their total assets under management.

16. For overviews of this debate, see Armendáriz de Aghion and Morduch (2010) and Sabin (2016).

17. Increased competition and rapid credit growth, facilitated by the availability of external funding for microfinance institutions, have led to lower credit standards, overborrowing, and large-scale defaults in some microfinance markets, including Bosnia and Herzegovina, India, Morocco, Nicaragua, and Pakistan (CGAP 2010; Chen, Rasmussen, and Reille 2010; Viada and Gaul 2012).

18. Analyses of the operating costs of microfinance institutions suggest that economies of scale tend to become relatively unimportant after 2,000 borrowers, with average loan size being the main driver of operating expenses after achieving this threshold (Gonzalez 2007; Rosenberg, Gonzalez, and Narain 2009). Cull, Demirgüç-Kunt, and Morduch (2016) find that the median unit cost across microfinance lenders in

their sample is $14 in operating expenses for each $100 lent. They also find that commercial microfinance borrowers tend to make loans that are, on average, three times larger than those of microfinance NGOs, and that this allows them to reduce their unit costs to 11 percent (compared to 18 for the median NGO in their sample).

19. Significant debate remains in the microfinance community regarding whether microfinance institutions should focus on sustainability, even if this implies reducing their penetration among the very poor, or should focus on targeting the poorest of the poor and possibly remain dependent on subsidies. It is worth noting that it is not just the poorest who lack access to formal financial institutions and therefore can benefit from microfinance. Also, as Armendáriz and Szafarz (2011) point out, serving relatively richer clients can allow microfinance institutions to subsidize the very poor. See Christen (2001) and Christen and Drake (2002) for discussions of these issues.

20. As discussed by Banerjee, Karlan, and Zinman (2015), the failure to find significant effects in randomized experiments designed to identify the impact of microcredit may stem from the fact that microcredit take-up in these experiments was low and unpredictable, resulting in a lack of statistical power to detect potentially significant effects. Also, these studies measure the impact of microfinance only on marginal borrowers, and cannot say anything about the impact on inframarginal borrowers (that is, those already being served by microfinance lenders). In addition, microcredit randomized experiments tend to analyze outcomes over relatively short periods (for example, less than two years); and some outcomes, such as improvements in education and health, may take longer to materialize. Finally, as emphasized by Cull, Demirgüç-Kunt, and Morduch (2016), cost–benefit analyses are needed to complement impact studies, and even modest effects could imply large benefit–cost ratios if the subsidies required to provide microcredit are small, too, as suggested by some of their findings.

21. See Armendáriz de Aghion and Morduch (2010) for a review of the theoretical and empirical literature on group lending.

22. This type of problem has been associated with crises in microfinance sectors in several countries, including Bangladesh and Bolivia, two of the early microfinance pioneers (see Chaudhury and Matin 2002 for an overview of the case of Bangladesh; and see Rhyne 2001 for Bolivia).

23. Funds generated by government operations are now invested in liquid securities traded in capital markets. This has resulted in a significant reduction in the cash balances held in treasury accounts, from US$389 million December 1989 to only US$12 million by 2008.

24. See Westley (2006) for a discussion of the pros and cons of different organizational structures for commercial banks entering the microfinance market.

25. Another often-cited advantage of creating a stand-alone subsidiary is that this might limit the financial losses of the parent company to the initial capital provided. However, this is not always the case. For instance, when the subsidiary provides its services under the same brand name as the parent bank or consumers perceive a strong connection between the two, the parent bank might not be able to deny further financing because the subsidiary's failure could affect its reputation.

26. An important issue for the functioning of service companies is the determination of the fee structure. In principle, fees should be set so that, when the service company maximizes its own profits, it also maximizes those of its parent. This requires that the fees charged by the parent bank for its funding and for other services it provides, such as use of branch space and centralized services (accounting, telecommunications, information technology, marketing, and so forth), should match the actual cost to the parent of producing these services. Similarly, the fees that the parent pays to the service company for providing promotion, origination, and collection services should equal the revenue generated by the loan portfolio that the service company originates.

27. de la Torre, Martinez Peria, and Schmukler (2010) analyze lending to small and medium enterprises (SMEs) by commercial banks in 12 countries and report the use of lending practices similar to those of BEME, in which banks customize some of their products to the needs of particular groups of SMEs.

28. See Schreiner (2003) for an overview of how scoring works and its application to microfinance.

29. These figures should be interpreted with care. As described above, BEME's only revenue source is the fees it receives from BancoEstado for providing promotion, origination, and collection services. Moreover, BEME's loan portfolio is funded by its parent bank, and BEME also makes intensive use of BancoEstado's infrastructure and centralized services, paying a fee for all these services. Therefore, the extent to which these figures represent BEME's actual profitability depends on whether the fees charged by BancoEstado for its funding and services represent their real costs and whether the fees BancoEstado pays to BEME fully account for the revenues generated by the financial services that BEME originates.

30. See Hanson (2004) for a general discussion of attempts to restructure state-owned financial institutions.

31. Other authors have stressed the role of government lump-sum subsidies for microloans in fostering the development of commercial microfinance activities in Chile (see, for example, Christen 2001). In 1992, the Chilean Social Investment Fund introduced an auction system to subsidize the entry of commercial banks into microcredit. A lump-sum subsidy on a per-loan basis is auctioned off twice a year. Banks assume all credit risk and funding requirements. The winning banks are those that offer to provide the largest number of loans for the smallest subsidy.

32. In principle, cost–benefit analyses of microfinance should be compared to cost–benefit analyses of other possible interventions to make informed policy decisions. However, as emphasized by Armendáriz de Aghion and Morduch (2010), this has not actually happened in practice in most cases. See Khandker (1998) and Townsend and Yaron (2001) for two of the few existing rigorous cost–benefit analyses of microfinance programs.

References

Adams, Dale W. 1995. "Using Credit Unions as Conduits for Micro-Enterprise Lending: Latin-American Insights." Poverty-Oriented Banking Working Paper 12, International Labor Office, Enterprise and Cooperative Development Department.

Adams, Dale W., and J. D. Von Pischke. 1994. "Micro-Enterprise Credit Programs: Déjà vu." In *Financial Landscapes Reconstructed: The Fine Art of Mapping Development*, edited by J. F. A. Bouman and Otto Hospes. Boulder, CO: Westview Press.

Akula, Vikram. 2010. *A Fistful of Rice: My Unexpected Quest to End Poverty Through Profitability*. Cambridge, MA: Harvard Business Press.

Armendáriz, Beatriz, and Ariane Szafarz. 2011. "On Mission Drift in Microfinance Institutions." In *The Handbook Of Microfinance*. Singapore: World Scientific Publishing.

Armendáriz de Aghion, Beatriz. 1999. "Development Banking." *Journal of Development Economics* 58 (1): 83–100.

Armendáriz de Aghion, Beatriz, and Christian Gollier. 2000. "Peer Group Formation in an Adverse Selection Model." *Economic Journal* 110 (465): 632–43.

Armendáriz de Aghion, Beatriz, and Jonathan Morduch. 2000. "Microfinance Beyond Group Lending." *Economics of Transition* 8 (2): 401–20.

———. 2010. *The Economics of Microfinance, Second Edition*. Cambridge, MA: MIT Press.

Banerjee, Abhijit. 2013. "Microcredit under the Microscope: What Have We Learnt in the Last Two Decades, What Do We Need to Know?" *Annual Review of Economics* 5: 487–519.

Banerjee, Abhijit, Dean Karlan, and Jonathan Zinman. 2015. "Six Randomized Evaluations of Microcredit: Introduction and Further Steps." *American Economic Journal: Applied Economics* 7 (1): 1–21.

Bateman, Milford. 2010. *Why Doesn't Microfinance Work? The Destructive Rise of Local Neoliberalism*. London: Zed Books.

Beck, Thorsten, Samuel Munzele Maimbo, Issa Faye, and Thouraya Triki. 2011. *Financing Africa: Through the Crisis and Beyond*. Washington, DC: World Bank.

Benavente, Jose Miguel. 2006. "Programa de Crédito para la Microempresa BancoEstado." Unpublished manuscript. World Bank, Washington, DC.

Besley, Timothy, and Stephen Coate. 1995. "Group Lending, Repayment Incentives and Social Collateral." *Journal of Development Economics* 46 (1): 1–18.

Brusky, Bonnie. 2003. "From Skepticism to Success: The World Bank and Banco do Nordeste." CGAP Case Studies in Donor Good Practices No. 3, Consultative Group to Assist the Poor, Washington, DC.

CGAP (Consultative Group to Assist the Poor). 2010. "Andhra Pradesh 2010: Global Implications of the Crisis in Indian Microfinance." CGAP Focus Note 67, Consultative Group to Assist the Poor, Washington, DC, November.

CGAP (Consultative Group to Assist the Poor) and Grameen Foundation USA. 2010. *Securitization: A Technical Guide*. Washington, DC: CGAP and Grameen Foundation USA.

CGAP (Consultative Group to Assist the Poor) and Symbiotics. 2016. "Microfinance Funds: 10 Years of Research and Practice." White paper, Consultative Group to Assist the Poor and Symbiotics, Washington, DC.

Chaudhury, Iftekhar A., and Imran Matin. 2002. "Dimensions and Dynamics of Microfinance Membership Overlap: A Micro Study from Bangladesh." *Small Enterprise Development* 13 (2): 46–55.

Chen, Greg, Stephen Rasmussen, and Xavier Reille. 2010. "Growth and Vulnerabilities in Microfinance." CGAP Focus Note 61, Consultative Group to Assist the Poor, Washington, DC, February.

Christen, Robert P. 2001. "Commercialization and Mission Drift." Occasional Paper 5, Consultative Group to Assist the Poor, Washington, DC.

Christen, Robert P., and Deborah Drake. 2002. "Commercialization: The New Reality of Microfinance." In *The Commercialization of Microfinance: Balancing Business and Development*, edited by Deborah Drake and Elisabeth Rhyne. Bloomfield, CT: Kumarian Press.

Christen, Robert P. and Steven Schonberger. 2001. "A Multilateral Donor Triumphs over Disbursement Pressure: The Story of Microfinance at Banco do Nordeste in Brazil." CGAP Focus Note 23, Consultative Group to Assist the Poor, Washington, DC, December.

Collins, Daryl, Jonathan Morduch, Stuart Rutherford, and Orlanda Ruthven. 2009. *Portfolios of the Poor: How the World's Poor Live on $2 a Day*. Princeton, NJ: Princeton University Press.

Cull, Robert, Asli Demirgüç-Kunt, and Jonathan Morduch. 2009. "Microfinance Meets the Market." *Journal of Economic Perspectives* 23 (1): 167–92.

———. 2016. "The Microfinance Business Model: Enduring Subsidy and Modest Profit." Policy Research Working Paper 7786, World Bank, Washington, DC.

Daley-Harris, Sam. 2003. *State of the Microcredit Summit Campaign Report 2003*. Washington, DC: Microcredit Summit Campaign.

de la Torre, Augusto, Maria Soledad Martinez Peria, and Sergio L. Schmukler. 2010. "Bank Involvement with SMEs: Beyond Relationship Lending." *Journal of Banking and Finance* 34 (9): 2280–93.

de Quidt, Jonathan, Thiemo Fetzer, and Maitreesh Ghatak. 2016. "Commercialization and the Decline of Joint Liability Microcredit." Warwick Economics Research Paper Series 1119, University of Warwick, UK.

Dichter, Thomas. 2006. "Hype and Hope: The Worrisome State of the Microcredit Movement." Unpublished manuscript

Ditcher, Thomas, and Malcolm Harper. 2007. *What's Wrong with Microfinance?* Rugby, UK: Practical Action Publishing.

Dominicé, Roland. 2012. *Microfinance Investments: An Investor's Guide to Financing the Growth and Wealth Creation of Small Enterprises and Low Income Households in Emerging Economies*. Bellinzona, Switzerland: Symbiotics.

Duflos, Eric, and Katherine Imboden. 2004. "The Role of Governments in Microfinance." CGAP Donor Brief No. 19, Consultative Group to Assist the Poor, Washington, DC.

Dunford, Christopher. 2006. "Evidence of Microfinance's Contribution to Achieving the Millennium Development Goals." Paper prepared for Global Microcredit Summit, Canada, November.

Dupas, Pascaline, and Jonathan Robinson. 2013. "Why Don't the Poor Save More? Evidence from Health Savings Experiments." *American Economic Review* 103 (4): 1138–71.

The Economist. 2005. "Giants and Minnows." November 3.

Egli, Dominik. 2004. "Progressive Lending as an Enforcement Mechanism in Microfinance Programs." *Review of Development Economics* 8 (4): 505–20.

El-Zoghbi, Mayada, and Henry Gonzalez. 2013. "Where Do Impact Investing and Microfinance Meet?" CGAP Brief (June), Consultative Group to Assist the Poor, Washington, DC.

Fiori, Anita, and Robin Young. 2005. *Banco do Nordeste*. Washington, DC: US Agency for International Development.

Flaming, Mark. 2007. "Guaranteed Loans to Microfinance Institutions: How Do They Add Value?" CGAP Focus Note 67, Consultative Group to Assist the Poor, Washington, DC, January.

Ghatak, Maitreesh. 1999. "Group Lending, Local Information and Peer Selection." *Journal of Development Economics* 60 (1): 27–50.

———. 2000. "Screening by the Company You Keep: Joint Liability Lending and the Peer Selection Effect." *Economic Journal* 110 (465): 601–31.

Ghosh, Parikshit, and Debraj Ray. 1999. "Information and Repeated Interaction: Application to Informal Credit Markets." Unpublished manuscript. Boston University.

GIIN (Global Impact Investing Network). 2016. *Annual Impact Investor Survey—2016*. Global Impact Investing Network.

Giné, Xavier, and Dean Karlan. 2014. "Group versus Individual Liability: Short- and Long-Term Evidence from Philippine Microcredit Lending Groups." *Journal of Development Economics* 107: 65–83.

Gonzalez-Vega, Claudio, Mark Schreiner, Richard L. Meyer, Jorge Rodriguez, and Sergio Navajas. 1997. "BancoSol: The Challenge of Growth for Microfinance Organizations." In *Microfinance for the Poor?* Edited by Hartmut Schneider. Paris: Organisation for Economic Co-operation and Development.

Gonzalez, Adrian. 2007. "Efficiency Drivers of Microfinance Institutions (MFIs): The Case of Operating Costs." *MicroBanking Bulletin* 15: 37–42.

Hanson, James. 2004. "The Transformation of State-Owned Banks." In *The Future of State-Owned Financial Institutions*, edited by Gerard Caprio, Jonathan Fiechter, Robert Litan, and Michael Pomerleano. Washington, DC: Brookings Institution Press.

Honohan, Patrick. 2004. "Financial Sector Policy and the Poor: Selected Findings and Issues." Working Paper 43, World Bank, Washington, DC.

IFC (International Finance Corporation). 2016. "Issue Brief: Microfinance." IFC, Washington, DC, April.

Isern, Jennifer, and David Porteous. 2005. "Commercial Banks and Microfinance: Evolving Models of Success." CGAP Focus Note 28, Consultative Group to Assist the Poor, Washington, DC, June.

Karlan, Dean, Aishwarya Lakshmi Ratan, and Johnathan Zinman. 2014. "Savings by and for the Poor: A Research Review and Agenda." *Review of Income and Wealth* 60 (1): 36–78.

Karnani, Aneel. 2007. "Microfinance Misses Its Mark." *Stanford Social Innovation Review* 5 (3): 34–40.

Khamar, Mohita. 2016. "2014 Global Outreach and Financial Performance Benchmark Report." Microfinance Information Exchange, Inc. (MIX).

Khandker, Shahidur R. 1998. *Fighting Poverty with Microcredit*. Oxford: Oxford University Press.

Larraín, Christian. 2007. "BancoEstado Microcréditos: Lecciones de un Modelo Exitoso." División de Desarrollo Económico, Unidad de Estudios del Desarrollo, CEPAL, Naciones Unidas.

Littlefield, Elizabeth, and Richard Rosenberg. 2004. "Microfinance and the Poor." *Finance and Development* 41 (2): 38–40.

Littlefield, Elizabeth, Jonathan Morduch, and Syed Hashemi. 2003. "Is Microfinance an Effective Strategy to Reach the Millennium Development Goals?" CGAP Focus Note 24, Consultative Group to Assist the Poor, Washington, DC, January.

Lopez, Cesar, and Jorge de Angulo. 2005. "Bridging the Finance Gap: ACCION's Experience with Guarantee Funds for Microfinance Institutions." ACCION Insight Publication 15, September.

MacFarquhar, Neil. 2010. "Banks Making Big Profits From Tiny Loans." *New York Times*, April 13.

Microcredit Summit Campaign. 2015. "Mapping Pathways Out of Poverty: The State of the Microcredit Summit Campaign Report, 2015." Microcredit Summit Campaign, Washington, DC.

Moretto, Louise, and Barbara Scola. 2017. "Development Finance Institutions and Financial Inclusion: From Institution-Building to Market Development." CGAP Focus Note 105, Consultative Group to Assist the Poor, Washington, DC, March.

Mosley, Paul. 1996. "Metamorphosis from NGO to Commercial Bank: The Case of BancoSol in Bolivia." In *Finance Against Poverty*, edited by David Hulme and Paul Mosley. London: Routledge,

Multilateral Investment Fund and Microfinance Information Exchange. 2015. *Microfinance Americas: The Top 100*, 2014 edition. Washington, DC: Inter-American Development Bank.

Patten, Richard, Jay Rosengard, and Don Johnston. 2001. "Microfinance Success Amidst Macroeconomic Failure: The Experience of Bank Rakyat Indonesia during the East Asian Crisis." *World Development* 29 (6): 1057–69.

Pitt, M. and S. R. Khandker. 1998. "The Impact of Group-Based Credit Programs on Poor Households in Bangladesh: Does the Gender of Participants Matter?" *Journal of Political Economy* 106 (5): 958–96.

Polgreen, Lydia, and Vikas Bajaj. 2010. "India Microcredit Faces Collapse from Defaults." *New York Times*, November 17.

Rahman, Ray, and Saif Shah Mohammed. 2009. "Securitization and Micro-Credit Backed Securities (MCBS)." In *Microfinance: Emerging Trends and Challenges*, edited by Suresh Sundaresa. Northampton, MA: Edward Elgar Publishing.

Rangan, V. K., M. Chu, and D. Petkoski. 2011. "Segmenting the Base of the Pyramid." *Harvard Business Review* 89 (6): 113–17.

Reille, Xavier, Jasmina Glisovic-Mezieres, and Yannis Berthouzoz. 2009. "MIV Performance and Prospects: Highlights from the CGAP 2009 MIV Benchmark Survey." CGAP Brief, Consultative Group to Assist the Poor, Washington, DC.

Reille, Xavier, Sarah Forster, and Daniel Rozas. 2011. "Foreign Capital Investment in Microfinance: Reassessing Financial and Social Returns." CGAP Focus Note 71, Consultative Group to Assist the Poor, Washington, DC, May.

Rhyne, Elisabeth. 2001. *Mainstreaming Microfinance: How Lending to the Poor Began, Grew, and Came of Age in Bolivia*. Bloomfield, CT: Kumarian Press.

Robinson, Marguerite. 2002. "The Microfinance Revolution, vol. 2. Lessons from Indonesia." Washington D.C.: World Bank and Open Society Institute.

Roodman, David. 2012. *Due Diligence: An Impertinent Inquiry into Microfinance*. Washington, DC: Brookings Institution Press.

Rosenberg, Richard, Adrian Gonzalez, and Sushma Narain. 2009. "Are Microcredit Interest Rates Excessive?" CGAP Brief, Consultative Group to Assist the Poor, Washington, DC.

Sabin, Nicholas. 2016. "Microfinance: A Field in Flux." Research Paper 2016-10, Saïd Business School, University of Oxford.

Sanchez, Susana, Sophie Sirtaine, and Rita Valente. 2002. "Bringing Microfinance Services to the Poor: Crediamigo in Brazil." En breve No. 7, World Bank, Washington, DC, August.

Schicks, Jessica. 2007. "Developmental Impact and Coexistence of Sustainable and Charitable Microfinance Institutions: Analysing BancoSol and Grameen Bank." *European Journal of Development Research* 19 (4): 551–68.

Schreiner, Mark. 2003. "Scoring: The Next Breakthrough in Microcredit?" Occasional Paper 7, Consultative Group to Assist the Poor, Washington, DC.

Seibel, Hans Dieter. 2005. "The Microbanking Division of Bank Rakyat Indonesia: A Flagship of Rural Microfinance in Asia." Working Papers 2005/2, University of Cologne.

Sinclair, Hugh. 2012. *Confessions of a Microfinance Heretic: How Microlending Lost Its Way and Betrayed the Poor.* San Francisco: Berrett-Koehler Publishers.

Soursourian, Matthew, and Edlira Dashi. 2016. "Taking Stock: Recent Trends in International Funding for Financial Inclusion." CGAP Brief, Consultative Group to Assist the Poor, Washington, DC.

Stiglitz, Joseph E. 1990. "Peer Monitoring and Credit Markets." *World Bank Economic Review* 4 (3): 351–66.

Swanson, Brad. 2009. "The Role of International Capital Markets in Microfinance." In *Microfinance: Emerging Trends and Challenges,* edited by Suresh Sundaresan. Northampton, MA: Edward Elgar.

Townsend, Robert M., and Jacob Yaron. 2001. "The Credit Risk-Contingency System of an Asian Development Bank." *Economic Perspectives–Federal Reserve Bank of Chicago* 25 (3): 31–48.

Viada, Luis A., and Scott Gaul. 2012. "The Tipping Point: Over-Indebtedness and Investment in Microfinance." MicroBanking Bulletin.

Von Stauffenberg, Damian. 2007. "Remarks by Damian von Stauffenberg, Executive Director, MicroRate." *Microcredit Summit E-News* 5 (1), July.

Westley, Glenn D. 2006. *Strategies and Structures for Commercial Banks in Microfinance.* Sustainable Development Department Best Practices Series. Washington, DC: Inter-American Development Bank.

Yaron, Jacob, McDonald Benjamin, and Stephanie Charitonenko. 1998. "Promoting Efficient Rural Financial Intermediation." *World Bank Research Observer* 13 (2): 147–70.

Yunus, Muhammad. 2003. *Banker to the Poor: Micro-Lending and the Battle Against World Poverty.* New York: Public Affairs.

———. 2007. "Remarks by Muhammad Yunus, Managing Director, Grameen Bank." *Microcredit Summit E-News* 5 (1), July.

———. 2011. "Sacrificing Microcredit for Megaprofits." *New York Times,* January 15.

CHAPTER 9

Concluding Thoughts and Open Questions on the Role of the State in Fostering Finance

Introduction

The experiences described in this book illustrate problems of access to finance and highlight how innovative instruments and arrangements may help ameliorate these problems. All these experiences involve some form of direct intervention by the state, which raises two important questions. First, is there actually a need for direct state interventions to foster access to finance—that is, interventions that go beyond providing a good enabling environment? Second, if the state intervenes, how should interventions be designed—and what instruments should they use—so as to foster access in a sustainable manner, to minimize distortions, and to avoid the government failures that have accompanied many previous attempts at intervention?

In this concluding chapter we attempt to address these two broad questions, in light of the experiences described in the book. When thinking about these experiences, and more generally about the role of the state in broadening access to finance, many related questions emerge. For instance, how can we ensure that government interventions are complementary to, and crowd in, the private sector, instead of replacing it and crowding it out? Given limited resources, how should the state choose which interventions to undertake? Should direct public sector interventions be permanent? If not, what is the optimal exit strategy? If actual interventions respond to broader, noneconomic objectives, how can they be designed to minimize distortions? An important contribution of the analysis of the different experiences presented in this book lies precisely in triggering questions like these and in providing useful insights to try to address them.

The two broad questions posited above are difficult to answer and are the subject of much debate among academics and policy makers. The answer to the first question (is direct state intervention to broaden access warranted?) depends mainly on the extent and nature of market failures in the financial system and the state's advantage (relative to the private sector) in addressing them. As discussed in chapter 3, the presence of a market failure does not, in and of itself, imply that direct state intervention is warranted. To justify on economic terms the direct intervention of the state in financial markets, one must not just identify a relevant market failure but also argue convincingly that the state can actually improve on private outcomes. For instance, if the only sources of market failure in financial markets are information asymmetries and enforcement problems, direct intervention by the state (for example, through lending by state-owned banks) would improve on market outcomes only if the state has an advantage relative to the private sector in collecting and processing information about prospective borrowers, monitoring them, and enforcing contracts—something that cannot be claimed to hold in general. On the other hand, as we have argued elsewhere (Anginer, de la Torre, and Ize 2014), the state may have an advantage in addressing market failures in the presence of deep collective action problems (uninternalized externalities, coordination failures, or free-rider problems) or risk-spreading limitations, which tend to be prevalent in underdeveloped financial markets. State intervention in this case can improve on market outcomes not because the state has an advantage in dealing with asymmetric information and enforcement problems but because it can better resolve the collective action problems that undermine the market's ability to overcome agency frictions. And, even in this case, the benefits of direct state interventions would have to be weighed against any adverse effects, including issues of political inference and capture.

This said, when analyzing the experiences described in this book, it often appears that private market participants could, at least in principle, profitably carry out some of the activities undertaken by the state as part of these initiatives. However, that is not what we observe in reality; private parties are not the driving force behind these initiatives. Although it is hard to pinpoint exactly why market participants are not undertaking these activities, it seems that—because of coordination problems, limitations in risk-spreading capabilities, first-mover disadvantages, or simply a lack of knowledge or managerial capabilities—the private sector does not exploit all profitable opportunities to broaden access, thereby creating room for the public sector to play a useful role in ameliorating problems of access. In practice, it may be impossible to provide ex ante a definite answer to the question of which activities the public sector should undertake; the answer may only emerge ex post, once the state engages in a process of exploration and discovery to detect unexploited opportunities.

The second broad question (on the design of state interventions and choice of policy instruments to broaden access, once the state has decided to intervene) is also the subject of much discussion, but we believe it is somewhat easier to tackle conceptually. Once the state is set to intervene, discussing what policy instruments to use and how the intervention should be designed tends to raise fewer controversial issues. For instance, the literature has identified several generally accepted best practices to ensure that state-owned financial institutions are well run (Scott 2007; Rudolph 2009; Gutiérrez et al. 2011; IDB 2013). Even if it is easier to tackle conceptually, getting the institutional design of state interventions right tends to be challenging enough in practice. This is especially the case in countries with weak institutional environments, which are the ones where the benefits from interventions to broaden access are likely to be greater.

Even if one believes that direct state intervention to broaden access to finance is not warranted, the experiences described in this book yield valuable insights. First, they illustrate activities that might help to expand access to finance, regardless of whether the private sector or the public sector is the one taking the lead. Second, even if one disagrees with these policies, the state in many developed and developing countries continues to play a significant role in credit allocation through direct interventions in financial markets. This role has in fact expanded since the global financial crisis because central banks and governments around the world have acted as risk absorbers and have pursued a variety of strategies to prop up financing for the private sector, including via increased lending by state-owned banks and the expansion or creation of credit guarantee schemes.[1] Given this significant role, understanding the different forms that direct state interventions in financial markets may take—as well as their motivations, design, and potential impact—is important. Avoiding these issues because of ideological disagreement is unlikely to yield good policy analysis and advice.

As we discussed in chapter 3, there is a consensus that the state plays a fundamental role in the financial sector by providing an adequate enabling environment. In emerging markets, this consensus emerged after many years of widespread direct state intervention in the mobilization and allocation of funds, which had high costs and failed to achieve the desired expansion of access. Thus, since the 1990s, a view rooted in the laissez-faire spirit has gained ground. This view argues that policy failures tend to outweigh market failures and that, given a proper enabling environment, market-driven private finance will flourish and credit allocation will be socially efficient. Although the global financial crisis exposed many of the fault lines in this view—including the belief that financial markets self-regulate—it is fair to say that the laissez-faire view still seems to be the predominant view on the role of the state in financial development, at least among the economics profession (World Bank 2013, 2015). However, as stressed throughout this book, acknowledging the key role of the state in providing an adequate enabling environment does not imply that its role should end there.

The experiences analyzed in this book suggest that there is an emerging third view on the role of the state in financial sector development, even if this view has not yet been fully conceptually distilled. This third view is closer to the laissez-faire view, to the extent that it recognizes a limited role for the state in financial markets and acknowledges that institutional efficiency is the best way to promote healthy financial sector development over the long run. However, it contends that there might be room for well-designed, restricted state interventions to address specific problems of access. Fundamental to this view is that the state tries to complement and crowd in the private sector, and not to displace it. The experiences in this book show that interventions can take different forms that go beyond those traditionally used by the public sector, relying on new financial instruments or using traditional instruments in innovative ways to try to avoid some of the problems associated with past experiences. Moreover, although the state tends to play several roles in these experiences, a key one is its "catalytic" role—helping private parties overcome coordination problems to engage in financial contracting.

Our analysis provides some basic parameters to assess the types of interventions linked to the third view in a more systematic manner. It is worth stressing that these kinds of interventions tend to be more complex and difficult to evaluate than the direct loan provision by state-owned banks favored by the interventionist view. In most cases, these alternative interventions do not clearly displace private sector financial contracting, and they do not necessarily involve any subsidies. Also, the direct contribution of the state in increasing the availability of financing is less clear. The state usually takes multiple roles in these interventions, which makes it difficult to isolate the potential contribution of each role. Furthermore, the question of why the private sector does not undertake these interventions if they are profitable looms ubiquitously. In this chapter, we do not attempt to provide definite answers. In fact, we do not formally evaluate the specific experiences covered in the book or the pro-market activism view in general. Rather, we use these experiences as a starting point to discuss the role of the state in broadening access beyond the single focus on strengthening the enabling environment.

In the rest of this chapter, we tackle the two broad questions posited at the beginning in light of the experiences described throughout the book. We first discuss the second question, related to the design of direct government interventions to broaden access (assuming that the state has decided to intervene). In particular, we focus on the main institutional features of the experiences described in the book. We analyze the rationale for some of these features and discuss how they may help limit the potential costs of government interventions. We also discuss some challenges raised by the institutional mechanisms used in these types of intervention. Subsequently, we turn to the first question, namely, whether there is actually a role for direct state interventions to foster access to finance, beyond providing an adequate enabling environment. Given that the answer to this question depends on an assessment of the relative importance of market and government failures, we discuss some of the main elements to be taken into account when evaluating direct state interventions to promote access to finance. Even though these two questions are discussed separately, they are highly intertwined in practice. Moreover, these questions are part of a much larger debate on the general role of the state in the economy, which obviously we do not cover here in detail.

Before proceeding with the analysis, it is worth clarifying what we do and do not address in this chapter. In most of the experiences described in this book, the state performs several simultaneous functions; but we focus mainly on its "catalytic" role of coordinating private parties to overcome problems of access to finance. Although in these experiences this catalytic role tends to be lumped together with risk taking by the state (through credit provision and/ or credit guarantees), distinguishing between these two roles conceptually is important. There might be grounds for risk bearing by the state, based on its relative advantage in spreading risks (Arrow and Lind 1970), but this function is conceptually different from the catalytic role and should be assessed independently. We believe that the catalytic role of the state constitutes the most innovative element of most of the experiences described in the book and that risk taking by the state is not necessary for their success. It is worth stressing that this excludes the cases of FOGAPE (Fondos de Garantías para Pequeños Empresarios) and BancoEstado (analyzed in chapters 7 and 8, respectively), which are closer to traditional direct state interventions in financial markets and, by their very nature, imply risk bearing by the state.

The rest of the chapter is organized as follows. The next section analyzes the design features that seem common to the interventions described throughout the book. After that, we discuss which elements are important to consider when evaluating the role of the state in fostering access to finance. The fourth section concludes with some final remarks.

Main Features of Innovative Experiences to Broaden Access

The experiences described throughout this book tend to share several characteristics that seem to be rooted in important historical, political, and/or economic reasons. These characteristics include (i) outsourcing, (ii) hard budget constraints, (iii) market friendliness, and (iv) bundling. In the rest of this section, we describe these features and analyze how they may help limit the potential costs of government interventions. We also analyze some challenges raised by these features.

By *outsourcing* we mean that the interventions described throughout the book are implemented by government agencies outside the Ministry of Finance or the Treasury. In principle, any type of government agency could have implemented these interventions. In practice, this is not the case. What we observe is that they are typically implemented by development banks or state-owned commercial banks.

Most of these institutions had the legacy of the model of state interventions associated with the interventionist view, whereby the state provided direct financing to key sectors, but have undergone significant institutional changes. These include changes in management practices, funding and revenue sources, and even institutional mandates, as discussed below.

The interventions described in this book typically rely on a different type of public sector management, more focused on business practices. For instance, NAFIN (Nacional Financiera) and FIRA (Fideicomisos Instituidos en Relación con la Agricultura) underwent significant institutional and management changes and expanded the scope of their activities to develop new products to foster financial intermediation and generate higher revenues. In some cases, these interventions even involve the establishment of new, separate units with management and human resource practices that differ from those in public sector entities. For instance, as described in chapter 8, Chile's BancoEstado created a separate unit to conduct business with microenterprises, following different commercial and human resource procedures than those used for the bank's traditional lending operations.

The institutions implementing the interventions described throughout the book tend to face *hard budget constraints*. Although the specific mechanisms used to introduce and enforce these constraints vary across institutions, in general terms this has involved (i) the elimination of budgetary transfers and (ii) granting limited initial capitalization to these institutions, subject to the requirement that such capital has to be preserved. Examples of this are FOGAPE in Chile and NAFIN and FIRA in Mexico. Moreover, these institutions in some cases face legal constraints on their borrowing capability, in order to eliminate the possibility of potential bailouts ex post. In the case of BancoEstado, the state also eliminated the implicit subsidy derived from the deposit of public funds, forcing BancoEstado to look for profitable business opportunities to compensate for the shortfall in revenues.

The use of hard budget constraints seems to be driven by loss intolerance in the public sector, which is rooted in two main factors. First, past experiences with costly interventions have led governments to try to limit the cost of public policies, particularly in the financial sector, where losses can easily escalate. In particular, past experiences of direct government lending were marred by unduly high subsidies, high administrative expenses, high default rates, and political capture, resulting in the need for recurrent government recapitalization of state-owned financial institutions and high fiscal costs. Although some of state-owned banks' losses may have been inherent to their role in fostering economic development (as discussed below), a significant fraction were the result of mismanagement and political capture. From this perspective, the hard budget constraints can be viewed as a way of avoiding the mistakes of the past because they limit the scope for operational losses on a systematic basis.

However, one could reasonably question to what extent these institutional arrangements are time consistent and will continue to work as intended, given political economy considerations. For instance, if a state-owned bank that plays an important role in financing small and medium enterprises (SMEs) or another socially preferred sector faces large credit losses, the government may be compelled to ignore its prior commitment not to provide additional capital. These political economy constraints are likely to be more binding in countries with weaker institutions, which are precisely the ones where government intervention to foster access may be more beneficial.

Second, loss intolerance might also be motivated by the fact that it is difficult to disentangle losses due to the inherently nonprofitable nature of many of the activities of state-owned banks and losses due to mismanagement (arising from lack of managerial ability, political capture, or corruption). In other words, there is a signal-extraction problem at the core of the principal–agent problem between the managers of these institutions and the state. Imposing hard budget constraints by limiting transfers and granting limited initial capitalization to these institutions can be seen as a contractual arrangement to overcome this problem: if an institution shows the capacity to be self-sustaining, while at the same time fulfilling some type of development role, then the public sector could provide further capital infusions to help the institution expand its activities. If, on the other hand, the institution is not self-sustaining, the losses of the public sector are limited to the initial capital provided. Signal-extraction problems are, of course, not inherent to state-owned banks. The private sector is plagued with them, and they might heavily influence the behavior of agents such as bank managers and asset managers.

Although the imposition of hard budget constraints can be rationalized as a way to avoid the high costs of past government interventions in credit markets and/ or as an optimal response to the signal-extraction problem, it has come at a cost. In particular, hard budget constraints have created a tension within state-owned banks. There is an inherent tension between their mandate to contribute to economic development by fostering access to finance (which implies undertaking risky activities and, in many cases, assisting disadvantaged firms and households, potentially at a loss or with a lower profitability than other activities) and to operate at a financially sustainable level and avoid structural operating losses. We label this tension the "Sisyphus syndrome."

It is not obvious how or whether the Sisyphus syndrome can be resolved. One view is that this tension will cause state-owned banks to deviate from their mandates and behave more like private commercial banks. In their efforts to abide by the hard budget constraints, state-owned bank may compete for lower-risk lower-cost clients with private financial intermediaries, displacing rather than crowding in the private sector and deviating from their social mandates. Anginer, de la Torre, and Ize (2014) find that development banks actually tend to be more conservative than commercial banks, taking fewer risks than commercial banks with similar capital levels. They argue that this is because, given the signal-extraction problem described above, the more risk the manager of a development bank takes, the more exposed he or she becomes to the risk of occasional losses due to bad luck being interpreted as the outcome of bad management. This is compounded by the relatively short time horizons the political system uses to evaluate managers and by the fact that, in evaluating the performance of development banks, there is a bias in favor of penalizing mistakes over rewarding successes. Thus, the limited capacity of the political system to understand or handle accidental losses leads development bank managers to take less risk than might be socially optimal.

A possible way to fully resolve the Sisyphus syndrome would be to clearly identify the subsidy component incorporated in the mandate of state-owned banks and to explicitly finance it through the government budget. In line with this argument, in 2009 the Mexican government introduced a counterguarantee financed directly from the federal budget to support credit guarantees provided by development finance institutions to borrowers in riskier and socially preferred sectors, making subsidies more transparent. However, it is still an open question whether this approach can effectively resolve the tension that state-owned banks face between the need to maintain a sound financial performance and to fulfill specific policy objectives; estimating risks and calculating the value of the subsidy component is not straightforward, and allowing permanent budgetary transfers could potentially lead to a repetition of the high losses that have characterized past interventions in credit markets.

Alternatively, state-owned banks may find some ways to at least partly ameliorate this contradiction. For instance, these institutions could engage in both socially oriented activities (potentially with higher risk and/or lower profitability) and commercially viable activities, using the profits from the latter to subsidize the former. Another option could be for these institutions to take a middle-of-the-road approach, engaging in activities that (at least partially) fulfill some social mandate, but at the same time do not imply systematic losses or high risks. Under this modus operandi, this institutional arrangement could be sustainable over time.

Beyond the features common to the institutions behind the experiences described in this book, these interventions share two additional characteristics. They are *market friendly*; in other words, these interventions focus on complementing private financial contracting, not displacing it. These interventions are directed at addressing the underlying causes of problems of access, not at increasing the use of financial services per se. In many cases, they involve the state's acting in a catalytic role to overcome coordination failures and help private financiers develop solutions to ameliorate problems of access.

Finally, in most of the experiences described in this book, the state performs several simultaneous functions, *bundling* different financial products and services in the same operation. For example, FIRA coordinates with different stakeholders to arrange structured finance deals, provides credit guarantees, and grants financing.

NAFIN provides the platform for reverse-factoring transactions and grants loans to the financial institutions that participate in these transactions. As discussed in our analyses of the different experiences throughout this book, this bundling is likely the result of the institutional design of the state-owned banks that implement these interventions. First, these institutions are typically assessed on the basis of quantitative measures, such as the volume of loan disbursements or the amount of guarantees provided, giving them incentives to structure interventions around these products, even if the value added of these interventions lies mainly in services other than loans and guarantees. This suggests that, as institutions move toward more catalytic interventions, where the role of the state is to resolve coordination failures and foster contracting among private parties and not necessarily to take risks via loans or guarantees, new performance metrics and monitoring and evaluation procedures may be necessary.

Second, the Sisyphus syndrome described above may also play a role in bundling. Because hard budget constraints imply that they must be profitable, these institutions have incentives to combine more profitable products with less profitable ones in the same operation, even if the former are not needed. Bundling allows these institutions to generate revenues from some of their activities and subsidize others to meet their development mandate. This might lead to cross-subsidies across products for a single client and/or across multiple clients. Bundling also allows institutions to generate revenues without charging for some of their services, such as coordination, which may be harder to price.

Although bundling might be the result of institutional incentives, it also generates various problems. First, it may introduce distortions in financial markets if loans or guarantees are priced below their fair value, or if subsidies are excessive or misdirected. For instance, FIRA may solve a market failure by acting as an arranger of structured finance transactions; but at the same time, it may displace private financial intermediation by providing underpriced loans and guarantees in the same transaction. Second, bundling can generate problems with overall pricing, given that not all the products are priced independently. Third, bundling might obscure the contribution of the different elements of an intervention. Financial market participants cannot choose the most valuable component of the bundle. For example, financial intermediaries might be interested only in structured finance products from FIRA but not in its lending. This makes it more difficult to evaluate where the value added of an intervention comes from.

From Providing a Good Enabling Environment to Market-Friendly Activism: New Roles for the State?

We now turn to the more difficult question of whether direct state involvement to ameliorate problems of access to finance is warranted in the first place. We discuss first what it means for the state to provide a good enabling environment, as the laissez-faire view supports. Then, we analyze the catalytic role of the state in coordinating private parties to overcome problems of access, which is consistent with the third view. We believe that the catalytic role of the state constitutes the most innovative element of the experiences described in this book. When analyzing this catalytic role, we discuss which elements seem necessary for this role to add value and make state interventions meaningful. Whether there is a real need for the state to play a catalytic role will remain an open question, but we hope that our discussion will provide a general framework for analyzing this type of intervention.

Our view is that there is more room for the state to play a catalytic (coordinating) role to broaden access through targeted interventions than to act as a financier; however, risk taking by the state via loans or guarantees can also be justified in some cases, albeit under strict conditions (Anginer, de la Torre, and Ize 2014). The catalytic function of the state can be more valuable in promoting access to financial services, and less prone to error, than policies aimed at internalizing the social externalities of access. The state can indeed partner with the private sector in developing initiatives that are beneficial for all parties and help overcome problems of access to finance. Moreover, to the extent that it is difficult to identify ex ante where the socially suboptimal gaps in access to finance are and how to deal with them, having an active state somewhat engaged in the financial system, for instance through development banks or state-owned commercial banks, may facilitate the process of exploration and discovery needed to detect unexploited opportunities to complete markets.[2]

What Does Providing a Good Enabling Environment Actually Mean?

No one questions the key role of the state in providing a good environment for the financial system to flourish. This role is usually considered to entail at least two functions: (i) safeguarding the stability and soundness of the financial system through supervision and regulation, and (ii) providing an adequate contracting and informational environment.

The first function of the state in providing a good environment for financial contracting is the supervision and regulation of financial intermediaries and markets. There is a consensus on the need for such regulation and supervision, despite much disagreement on the overall role of the state in the financial system.[3] Debates in this regard focus on how best to design regulations and supervisory arrangements to ensure the safety and soundness of the financial system. For example, there are active academic and policy discussions on the benefits of deposit insurance, market discipline, bailouts, and macroprudential policies, to name a few. The global financial crisis highlighted major shortcomings in regulation and supervision and in national and international arrangements for crisis management and surveillance, reopening debates in all these areas.[4]

A discussion of all these issues is beyond the scope of this book. Although financial sector regulation and supervision are not directed toward fostering financial deepening or broadening access, by reducing the probability that the financial system will break down, they allow private parties to safely engage in financial contracting and contribute to financial development.

The second function of the state in relation to the enabling environment is to establish the general framework for contracts among private parties to be written, executed, and enforced in a timely and cost-effective manner. Of course, a good enabling environment is needed not only for financial contracting but also for all private agents to be able to engage in mutually beneficial transactions. Much of the literature on economic growth emphasizes the key role of transparency and well-defined property rights and contracting institutions to help market participants effectively overcome information asymmetries and contract enforcement problems.[5] As discussed in chapter 2, financial transactions typically involve a promise between two agents to exchange current resources for future resources; the temporal nature of these transactions introduces uncertainty and makes them very sensitive to information asymmetries and difficulties in monitoring borrower actions and enforcing contracts. Financial contracting depends on the availability of accurate and timely information on prospective borrowers, as well as on the certainty of the legal rights of creditors, stockholders, and borrowers and the predictability and speed with which these rights can be enforced. In fact, a large and growing literature provides evidence consistent with the idea that a better institutional environment fosters financial development and contributes to broadening access to finance.[6]

Although there seems to be general agreement on the key role of the state in providing an adequate contracting and informational environment, what this role actually entails is not as straightforward as usually assumed. The most restrictive view in this regard argues that the state should focus exclusively on setting clear rules and enforcing them through the judicial system so that private financial contracting flourishes and market discipline operates to the full extent. But translating general concepts into specific laws and regulations is not straightforward. Financial development is not amenable to a one-size-fits-all or a "template" approach. Moreover, the enabling environment, even in terms of rule setting, goes beyond general property rights and contractual institutions. In many cases, the required rules and enforcement institutions are sector or even product specific. This requires a much more direct relation between the government and market participants to understand exactly what is required in each case.[7]

The enabling environment for financial contracting includes a host of elements that go beyond general rules and the ability to enforce them through an independent and well-functioning judicial system. These include, for instance, credit-reporting institutions (credit registries and bureaus), collateral registries, and payment and settlement systems. Some of these could in principle be provided by the private sector, but there are several reasons why this may not be the case and why therefore a more active role for the state may be warranted. For instance, although the open and transparent exchange of credit information could potentially benefit both borrowers and lenders, coordination failures and monopoly rents can create important barriers to the development of a private credit-reporting infrastructure (Bruhn, Farazi, and Kanz 2013). In this situation, the state can play an important role by providing incentives for information sharing, mandating information sharing among private lenders, and/or establishing public credit registries. Similarly, the state can play an important role in establishing and operating payment systems and fostering the development of a robust infrastructure for securities and derivatives clearance and settlement (World Bank 2013). Although most proponents of the laissez-faire view would consider that state intervention would be warranted in these cases as part of its role in providing an adequate enabling environment for financial markets, it is worth highlighting that this implies much more direct involvement by the public sector than is usually acknowledged.

In line with these arguments, the experiences discussed in this book suggest that the state's role in "creating a proper enabling environment" spans a whole gradient of activities that go from rule setting and enforcement to the direct provision of certain financial infrastructures and services. This suggests that the contrast between the interventionist and the laissez-faire views that dominates most of the policy debate may be too simplistic because it ignores significant elements that make the extremes less discontinuous than would appear at first sight.

The State's Catalytic Role in Broadening Access to Finance

The experiences described in this book portray several instances of the state playing a "catalytic" role, helping resolve coordination failures among private parties to overcome problems of access to finance and complete markets. This role implies varying degrees of active state involvement—from writing specific regulations to providing access to infrastructure, creating platforms, and directly coordinating private intermediaries to engage in specific financial transactions. In some of the experiences described, the private sector would naturally engage in private contracting if certain conditions were met; the state intervention aims to make sure that these conditions are satisfied, by providing the required regulations and infrastructure. In some sense, the state just responds to what the private sector needs. These interventions seem to be closer to those proposed by the laissez-faire view. For instance, this is the case for correspondent banking in Brazil, where the state has engaged in writing the required regulations and auctioning off the use of the post office network to distribute financial services. An example of more active state involvement is the case of NAFIN, where the state provides an electronic platform for private intermediaries to conduct factoring transactions (overcoming coordination problems that might prevent the emergence of private market infrastructure); in principle, there is no need for the state to act as a lender or to be directly involved in these transactions.

Aside from providing platforms or infrastructures for financial contracting, the experiences described in this book also include instances in which the state plays a more active role in financial contracting but that are still far from direct risk-taking. In these cases, the state takes the lead and initiates activity among private parties that would otherwise not engage in contracting. The state promotes interactions among private participants that in principle are in their best interest but that private parties by themselves would not initiate. This is, for instance, the case with FIRA, as an arranger of the structured finance transactions (not as lender or guarantor). These interventions create mechanisms for private contracting to arise, without which it would not materialize. They are different from the role of the state as a direct provider of financial services because, in principle, the state does need to be part of the financial contract or take counterparty risk.

As stressed in the discussion above and in our analyses of the different experiences throughout this book, we observe that in practice the catalytic role tends to be lumped together with risk taking by the state (through credit provision and/or credit guarantees). However, a case can be made that risk taking by the state is not necessary for the success of the catalytic interventions described in this book (excluding the cases of FOGAPE and BancoEstado). When the state plays a catalytic role, its involvement is not related to financing. The fact that the state tends to bundle activities and provide finance as part of the package does not mean that private markets are unable to raise the required funds for those operations to take place. Therefore, even if in practice state institutions combine the catalytic and risk-taking roles because of institutional incentives, these roles are conceptually different. It is an open question, however, whether catalytic interventions would be as effective always and everywhere if they were to be unbundled from finance or risk taking by the state.

Even if purely catalytic interventions by the state do not involve risk taking, proponents of the laissez-faire view might still frown upon these interventions. They could argue that the market failures associated with collective action problems are not as extensive as proponents of catalytic interventions argue. Given well-defined property rights and good contractual institutions, private parties by themselves might be able to overcome coordination problems and create mechanisms to address problems of access to finance. Moreover, governments face specific problems that may make the cost of interventions higher than the benefits of solving market failures. Government interventions, even if purely catalytic, could lead to serious errors (policy failures), despite good intentions, or could be distorted by political interference and capture.

Final Remarks

The debate about the role of the state in the financial sector will likely continue. There are valid arguments on both sides. Many of those who believe in minimal state intervention, arguing that the state should limit its role to providing a good enabling environment, might acknowledge that financial markets do not always work as desired and that there might be untapped opportunities to overcome problems of access to finance. However, this does not imply support for direct state intervention (because the existence of market failure does not necessarily imply that it can be solved by the state in a cost-effective manner), but rather is an acknowledgment that financial markets are subject to imperfections and are far from being fully efficient and complete. On the other hand, those who support a more active role for the state in financial markets would probably acknowledge the risks and potential costs of public sector interventions, and are unlikely to support widespread direct government involvement in the allocation of credit, as in the past.

Despite the open nature of the debate, the experiences analyzed in this book deserve attention and provide food for thought regarding the role of the state in promoting access to finance. In particular, several conclusions about the role of the state can be drawn from our analysis.

First, the argument that the state should focus just on improving the enabling environment can be misleading. When performing this supposedly hands-off role, the state actually participates much more actively in financial markets than one would infer at first sight from the proponents of the laissez-fare view. Moreover, the ability of the state to identify gaps in access to finance and enact laws and regulations required to address them might be enhanced if it were involved as a more active participant in the financial sector. How active this role needs to be is a question for further debate.

Second, direct government involvement in the allocation of credit at subsidized interest rates, as proposed by the interventionist view, is hard to justify in most cases. This involvement does not address the underlying causes of problems of access to finance but rather simply treats the symptoms. In addition, even if the state would like to increase the supply of credit to firms in certain sectors (for instance, because they generate positive externalities), it is not obvious that the best way to do so would be direct lending by state-owned banks; the state does not necessarily have an advantage relative to private financial intermediaries in screening and monitoring specific borrowers. Finally, and more fundamentally, if the objective is to address uninternalized externalities, why resort to credit provision instead of using taxes and subsidies, which are better suited for this purpose?

Third, there seems to be room for the state to play a catalytic role to overcome problems of access to finance. This may be especially warranted if the constraints on broadening access to finance stem from deep collective action problems (uninternalized externalities, coordination failures, or free-rider problems), where the state tends to have advantages relative to decentralized private players. In practice, analyzing the experiences described in this book suggests that private market participants could profitably carry out some of the activities undertaken by the state as part of these initiatives. Although it is hard to pinpoint exactly why market participants are not undertaking these activities, it seems that coordination problems, limitations on risk-spreading capabilities, first-mover disadvantages, or simply a lack of knowledge or managerial capabilities may prevent the private sector from exploiting all profitable opportunities to broaden access. The fact that the private sector does not exploit these opportunities does not mean that they are not worth seizing or that the state should not seize them. Furthermore, the experiences described in this book suggest that risk taking by the state is not key for the success of purely catalytic interventions. Although there might be grounds for risk bearing by the state, this function is conceptually different from the catalytic role and should be assessed independently.

Evaluating state interventions in financial markets, including the experiences we describe in this book, is always hard. However, there are some elements that should be taken into account when thinking about them. In principle, it would be ideal to conduct rigorous ex ante and ex post analyses of the costs and benefits of these interventions in order to make informed policy decisions. Ex ante, the state needs to conduct cost–benefit analyses to decide which activities to undertake. Ex post analyses are necessary to determine whether interventions have met their objectives in a cost-effective manner and should be continued or not, and whether any changes are necessary.

In practice, not many of these analyses are conducted in a systematic and consistent manner to inform policy making, although more has been done in recent years. Indeed, over recent decades, there has been a rising emphasis on evidence-based policy making, including by means of rigorous impact evaluations of government programs. However, the number of rigorous evaluations of state interventions in financial markets is still quite small, and research in this area significantly lags behind work analyzing government interventions in other areas (for example, social assistance).

In an ideal world, the state would conduct rigorous cost–benefit analyses of the different potential interventions in financial markets, comparing their expected social costs and benefits, to decide which interventions to undertake. However, this is not how things work in practice. Interventions in financial markets are often initiated in a relatively decentralized manner by state-owned banks or other agencies. As a result, the decision to engage in different interventions is typically driven by idiosyncratic factors. Public institutions already involved in the provision of financial services might have incentives to find new projects and reinvent themselves over time. For example, some institutions may explore new activities as more traditional businesses become less profitable, or as government funding become scarcer.

For instance, this was the case with BancoEstado, which had to look for profitable business opportunities (while still trying to abide by its social policy mandate) after the government eliminated the implicit subsidy that was derived from the deposit of public funds. This is not too different from what happens in the private sector; for instance, private banks in Latin America have increasingly engaged with SMEs as large corporations have started obtaining financing in domestic and international capital markets.

Other interventions may respond to more specific demands, such as the low growth of credit to the private sector in Mexico following the 1994 financial crisis, which prompted both FIRA and NAFIN to look for innovative ways to foster access to finance. The decentralization of the decision-making process implies that state interventions are conducted without gaining a general perspective on the different problems of access to finance in the economy. For example, even when a specific intervention may help broaden access to finance for a particular sector, is this intervention better (in terms of increasing overall welfare) than alternative interventions to foster financing for a different set of borrowers? Also, interventions are mostly decided by taking a partial equilibrium view that does not consider their potential general equilibrium effects. How does broadening access for a particular set of borrowers affect other borrowers and the overall functioning of the financial system? Despite these drawbacks, the decentralization of the decision-making process for state interventions is not without its benefits. It may be impossible to identify ex ante where the holes in access to finance are and how to deal with them. Having state entities such as development banks and state-owned commercial banks actively engaged in the financial system may facilitate the process of exploration and discovery needed to detect unexploited opportunities to complete markets and broaden access.

The initiatives undertaken in a largely decentralized fashion by state-owned banks are also not typically preceded by rigorous cost–benefit analyses. This does not happen in practice for several reasons. First, it is often hard to perform rigorous ex ante evaluations when thinking about novel interventions like the ones described in this book. There is usually much uncertainty about their expected effects. And the interventions tend to have multiple objectives, which in many cases are not easily quantified, making it hard to evaluate them on a comparable basis. Of course, one could argue that all these issues render the need for rigorous analysis of the interventions more pressing, not less. State-owned banks could, for instance, conduct small-scale experiments or pilot projects before scaling up their interventions so as to better understand their potential costs and benefits and to identify any unintended consequences. However, this may be too costly and time consuming. In many cases, decisions must be made quickly. And small-scale experiments may not provide conclusive evidence on the potential effects of a given intervention once it is implemented at a larger scale.

Second, as emphasized throughout this book, it may be impossible to identify ex ante where the holes are in access to finance. Public banks may need to engage in a process of exploration to detect untapped opportunities to broaden access. Therefore, they may not be able to simply list all possible interventions ex ante and choose the best one. Rather, once a potential gap in access is detected, they may need to decide whether to intervene or not. Given the aforementioned difficulties in conducting detailed cost-benefit analyses, this decision may be based in some heuristic rule, such as whether the intervention meets some social mandate, its expected return is not below the institution's cost of capital, and its credit risk is not too high.

The fact that interventions may not be chosen following rigorous ex ante analyses makes the need for ex post evaluations more pressing.[8] In particular, it would be useful to consistently and rigorously evaluate both the additionality of interventions (for example, whether access to finance has actually broadened) and their impact on recipients. All interventions need to be monitored and evaluated, and corrected or terminated if necessary. The ability to modify or terminate interventions that fail to meet their objectives in a cost-effective manner is key in order to avoid the policy failures that have accompanied many previous attempts. However, in most cases there might be little institutional incentive to perform rigorous ex post analyses and to terminate unsuccessful experiences. State-owned banks tend to focus on the sustainability and profitability of their operations, not so much on the social rate of return. Moreover, these institutions are typically assessed on the basis of quantitative measures of output, such as the volume of loan disbursements or the number of guarantees provided, and not on their impact. This is partly a legacy of the interventionist view; the role of these institutions was seen as directly increasing the availability of financing. It also reflects the fact that objective quantitative measures may be easier to evaluate for the political system than concepts such as additionality, which are more difficult to identify. Moving toward more catalytic interventions, where the role of the state is to foster contracting among private parties without risk taking by the state, may therefore require new performance metrics and monitoring-and-evaluation procedures for government-owned banks. Of course, this is not a trivial task and would also likely require an improvement in these banks' analytical capabilities, as well as a shift in their board's focus toward the additionality and impact of their activities.[9] Other institutions, such as external evaluation units, and the academic community may also play an important role in contributing to and validating the assessment of the impact of interventions. Moreover, institutional mechanisms need to be put in place to reduce political capture and ensure that unsuccessful interventions will be downscaled or terminated.

To conclude, what we have done in this book is just a first step toward better understanding some innovative state interventions to broaden access to finance and, more generally, the emerging new view on the role of the state in the financial sector. To be sure, much more work needs to be done to fully grasp the potential value added of these interventions and better calibrate the adequate role of the state. The debate on the role of the state in financial markets tends to be driven by preconceived views on whether market failures or government failures are more important, without much rigorous analysis. Having an open mind about the pros and cons of state involvement, including more systematic and rigorous analysis of interventions, would be a significant step forward.

Even though skeptics might not be convinced by the interesting experiences discussed in this book, these initiatives deserve serious attention, not least because governments are conducting them and will likely continue to do so, in part because there are strong political incentives for governments to be seen as proactive. Ignoring these interventions because of ideological disagreements is unlikely to yield good policy analysis and advice, and would only make us less able to deal with the real complexities of financial development in a pragmatic, constructive manner.

Notes

1. See World Bank (2013) for an overview of the policy responses to the global financial crisis.

2. Rodrik (2004, 2008) and Rodrik and Hausmann (2006) discuss the need to design mechanisms that allow the state to collaborate with the private sector to facilitate the discovery process of uncovering where the binding constraints to growth may lie, and argue that development banks may be well suited to play this role. A similar argument has been made regarding the use of lending by state-owned banks as a countercyclical tool. In order to be able to rapidly expand credit to the private sector in response to economic downturns, state-owned banks need to be familiar beforehand with the market in which they operate and must already have experienced professional staff in place. Once a downturn hits, it is too late for the state to try to create the required institutional capacity to expand credit to the private sector.

3. See de la Torre and Ize (2013) for a discussion of the foundations of microeconomic and macroeconomic prudential regulation and an overview of the related literature.

4. See Claessens and Kodres (2014) for an overview of the regulatory responses to the global financial crisis.

5. See, among many others, Hall and Jones (1999); Acemoglu, Johnson, and Robinson (2001); Easterly and Levine (2003); and Rodrik, Subramanian, and Trebbi (2004).

6. Chapter 2 presents a brief overview of the empirical evidence on law and finance. See Beck and Levine (2005) and La Porta, Lopez-de-Silanes, and Shleifer (2008) for earlier reviews of this literature.

7. See IDB (2015) for a discussion of similar issues in relation to industrial policies (that is, policies whereby the government attempts to shape the sectorial allocation of the economy).

8. See IDB (2013) for an overview of conceptual issues related to the ex post evaluation of public development banks and their initiatives.

9. In line with this argument, in 2009 the Mexican government introduced several measures to strengthen the accountability of development financial institutions, including the requirement to publish indicators measuring their services to their target populations. In addition, the Ministry of Finance will conduct and publish independent evaluations on these institutions.

References

Acemoglu, Daron, Simon Johnson, and James A. Robinson. 2001. "The Colonial Origins of Comparative Development: An Empirical Investigation." *American Economic Review* 91: 1369–401.

Anginer, Deniz, Augusto de la Torre, and Alain Ize. 2014. "Risk-Bearing by the State: When Is It Good Public Policy?" *Journal of Financial Stability* 10: 76–86.

Arrow, Kenneth J., and Robert C. Lind. 1970. "Uncertainty and the Evaluation of Public Investment Decisions." *American Economic Review* 60 (3): 364–78.

Beck, Thorsten, and Ross Levine. 2005. "Legal Institutions and Financial Development." In *Handbook of New Institutional Economics*, edited by Claude Ménard and Mary M. Shirley. New York: Springer.

Bruhn, Miriam, Subika Farazi, and Martin Kanz. 2013. "Bank Competition, Concentration, and Credit Reporting." Policy Research Working Paper 6442, World Bank, Washington, DC.

Claessens, Stijn, and Laura Kodres. 2014. "The Regulatory Responses to the Global Financial Crisis: Some Uncomfortable Questions." IMF Working Paper 14/46, International Monetary Fund, Washington, DC.

de la Torre, Augusto, and Alain Ize. 2013. "The Foundations of Macroprudential Regulation: A Conceptual Roadmap." Policy Research Working Paper 6575, World Bank, Washington, DC.

Easterly, William, and Ross Levine. 2003. "Tropics, Germs, and Crops: How Endowments Influence Economic Development." *Journal of Monetary Economics* 50: 3–40.

Gutiérrez, Eva, Heinz P. Rudolph, Theodore Homa, and Enrique Blanco Beneit. 2011. "Development Banks: Role and Mechanisms to Increase Their Efficiency." Policy Research Working Paper 5729, World Bank, Washington, DC.

Hall, Robert E., and Charles I. Jones. 1999. "Why Do Some Countries Produce So Much More Output per Worker Than Others?" *Quarterly Journal of Economics* 114: 83–116.

IDB (Inter-American Development Bank). 2013. *Public Development Banks: Toward a New Paradigm?* Washington, DC: IDB.

———. 2015. *Rethinking Productive Development, Sound Policies and Institutions for Economic Transformation.* Washington, DC: IDB.

La Porta, Rafael, Florencio Lopez-de-Silanes, and Andrei Shleifer. 2008. "The Economic Consequences of Legal Origins." *Journal of Economic Literature* 46 (2): 285–332.

Rodrik, Dani. 2004. "Industrial Policy for the Twenty-First Century." CEPR Discussion Paper 4767, Centre for Economic Policy Research, London.

———. 2008. "Normalizing Industrial Policy." Commission on Growth and Development Working Paper No. 3, World Bank, Washington, DC.

Rodrik, Dani, and Ricardo Hausmann. 2006. "Doomed to Choose: Industrial Policy as Predicament." Discussion Paper, Harvard University, Cambridge, MA.

Rodrik, Dani, Arvind Subramanian, and Francesco Trebbi. 2004. "Institutions Rule: The Primacy of Institutions over Geography and Integration in Economic Development." *Journal of Economic Growth* 9 (2): 131–65.

Rudolph, Heinz P. 2009. "State Financial Institutions: Mandates, Governance, and Beyond." Policy Research Working Paper 5141, World Bank, Washington, DC.

Scott, David H. 2007. "Strengthening the Governance and Performance of State-Owned Financial Institutions." Policy Research Working Paper 4321, World Bank, Washington, DC.

World Bank. 2013. *Global Financial Development Report 2013: Rethinking the Role of the State in Finance.* Washington, DC: World Bank.

———. 2015. *Global Financial Development Report 2015/16: Long-Term Finance.* Washington, DC: World Bank.